IN THE SHADOW OF SAINT DEATH

*The Gulf Cartel and the Price of America's
Drug War in Mexico*

MICHAEL DEIBERT

LYONS PRESS
Guilford, Connecticut
An imprint of Globe Pequot Press

To buy books in quantity for corporate use
or incentives, call **(800) 962-0973**
or e-mail **premiums@GlobePequot.com.**

Lyons Press is an imprint of Globe Pequot Press.

Project Editor: Lauren Brancato
Layout Artist: Mary Ballachino
Map: Alena Joy Pearce © Morris Book Publishing, LLC

Library of Congress Cataloging-in-Publication Data is available on file.

ISBN 978-0-7627-9125-5

Printed in the United States of America

10 9 8 7 6 5 4 3 2 1

To the hundreds of thousands of people in Mexico, Guatemala, Colombia, and other countries who lost their lives as their governments, at the demand of the United States, prosecuted a war that should have never been fought

To all in those countries who have worked to give justice to the victims

To all in those countries who worked to give their nations functioning institutions of governance, an endeavor which, in the face of the violence, money, corruption, and impunity arrayed against them, represented nothing short of a revolutionary act

And in memory of Sebastian Montiel Quezada, the Mexican

The Mexican's indifference toward death is fostered by his indifference toward life. He views not only death but also life as non transcendent. . . . We kill because life—our own or another's—is of no value. Life and death are inseparable, and when the former lacks meaning, the latter becomes equally meaningless. Mexican death is the mirror of Mexican life. And the Mexican shuts himself away and ignores both of them.

—OCTAVIO PAZ, *El Laberinto de la Soledad*

You can have everything. But it has a price.

—FORMER HITMAN FOR LOS ZETAS DRUG CARTEL

Contents

ACKNOWLEDGMENTS

The story of the relationship between Mexico and the United States, and the history and policies that have contributed to it, is a long and complicated one, of which the book you hold in your hands is but one episode. Nevertheless, in exploring this aspect of Mexican history, a number of individuals proved to be of invaluable assistance.

In Mexico itself, Franc Contreras, Luis Oscar Hinojos Aguirre, Javier Esteban Hernández Valencia, Gustavo Pacheco, Michael Weissenstein, Katrin Mader, and Sonja Wolf all contributed to my ability to write this account, as did a great number of people who, because of concerns about their safety with the situation as it is in Mexico today, will have to remain nameless. To those people, never doubt, however, that I am forever in your debt for all that you were willing to show me and share with me.

On the US side of the Rio Grande, Guadalupe Correa-Cabrera of the University of Texas at Brownsville, Mark Clark of the Galeria 409, and Virginia Ramos, who first strolled with me across the bridge into Matamoros years ago, helped me decode the intricacies of life on both sides of the border. The journalists of the Rio Grande Valley, Marcia Caltabiano-Ponce, Lynn Brezosky, and Ildefonso Ortiz, who knows more about organized crime in the area than anyone I know and who I hope one day will write his own book, provided context and contacts that proved invaluable.

Thanks very much to both my agent, Adriann Ranta, and my editor, Jon Sternfeld, for believing in the value of this endeavor.

In Miami, where much of this book was written, I would like to thank Anna Edgerton, Anna Blash, Daniela Guzman Peña, Natasha Del Toro, Noelle Théard, and Kym Quidiello for their friendship, and further afield, Hilary Wallis, Anastasia Kitova, Justin Cappiello, Ben Fountain, Meghan Feeks, Sutton Stokes, Gerry Hadden, Philip Schnell, Erin Mobekk, and Pedro Rodriguez.

I thank my family, Benjamin Deibert, Christopher Deibert, Caleb Deibert, Elizabeth Deibert, and James Breon, for seeing me along this road.

And I remember, in recent years, *los que se fueron:* Jann Deibert, Joseph Deibert, Leah Breon, Sebastian Quezada, and Philippe Allouard.

Because this is a book about organized crime, drug trafficking, violence, and failed policies, it does not focus on the many wonderful aspects of Mexico and its culture. The warmth of Mexico's people, their unsurpassed work ethic, their devotion to family, their subtle, seductive cuisine, and their incredibly deep and diverse traditions of art, music, and literature are all touched upon, but there is a universe of those to be explored beyond the pages of this book, and I hope that readers will do so.

To the people who live in the affected communities in Mexico who can't just pack up and leave or walk back across the bridge to El Norte like I can, to those who dare still speak out, to the poor people who pile onto buses and on the tops of trains to get from places such as El Salvador, Honduras, Guatemala, and elsewhere, heading to Mexico's northern border and, once there (and en route), face killers with weapons in their hands and an idiotic wall (both real and metaphorical) constructed by my own country: You are braver than I could ever be.

Michael Deibert
Miami, Florida
June 2014

Note on Names

Following the Spanish custom, the surnames of most of the protagonists in this book are first presented containing both the paternal and maternal family names, thereafter using only the protagonist's first name and paternal surname.

Acronyms

AFI—Agencia Federal de Investigación (Federal Investigation Agency)

CCSPJP—Consejo Ciudadano para la Seguridad Pública y la Justicia Penal (Citizen Council for Public Safety and Criminal Justice)

CEDH—Comisión Estatal de los Derechos Humanos (State Commission for Human Rights)

CEM—Conferencia del Episcopado Mexicano (Mexican Episcopal Conference)

CISEN—Centro de Investigación y Seguridad Nacional (Center for Research and National Security)

CJNG—Cártel de Jalisco Nueva Generacían

CNDH—Comisión Nacional de los Derechos Humanos (National Human Rights Commission)

DFS—Dirección Federal de Seguridad (Federal Security Directorate)

FEVIMTRA—Fiscalía Especial para los Delitos de Violencia contra las Mujeres y Trata de Personas (Special Prosecutor for Crimes of Violence Against Women and Human Trafficking)

GAFE—Grupo Aeromóvil de Fuerzas Especiales (Special Forces Airmobile Group)

ICE—US Immigration and Customs Enforcement

INCD—Instituto Nacional para el Combate a las Drogas (National Institute to Combat Drugs)

INEGI—Instituto Nacional de Estadística y Geografía (National Institute of Statistics and Geography)

PAN—Partido Acción Nacional (National Action Party)

PF—Policía Federal (Federal Police)

PFM—Policía Federal Ministerial (Federal Ministerial Police)

PFP—Policía Federal Preventiva (Federal Preventive Police)

PJF—Policía Judicial Federal (Federal Judicial Police)

PRD—Partido de la Revolución Democrática (Party of the Democratic Revolution)

PRI—Partido Revolucionario Institucional (Institutional Revolutionary Party)

SAGARPA—Secretaría de Agricultura, Ganadería, Desarrollo Rural, Pesca y Alimentación (Secretariat of Agriculture, Livestock, Rural Development, Fisheries and Food)

SEDENA—Secretaría de la Defensa Nacional (Secretariat of National Defense)

SIEDO—Subprocuraduría de Investigación Especializada en Delincuencia Organizada (Assistant Attorney General's Office for Special Investigations on Organized Crime)

SSP—Secretaría de Seguridad Pública (Secretariat of Public Security)

UGOCP—Unión General Obrera, Campesina y Popular (General Popular Union of Workers and Farmers)

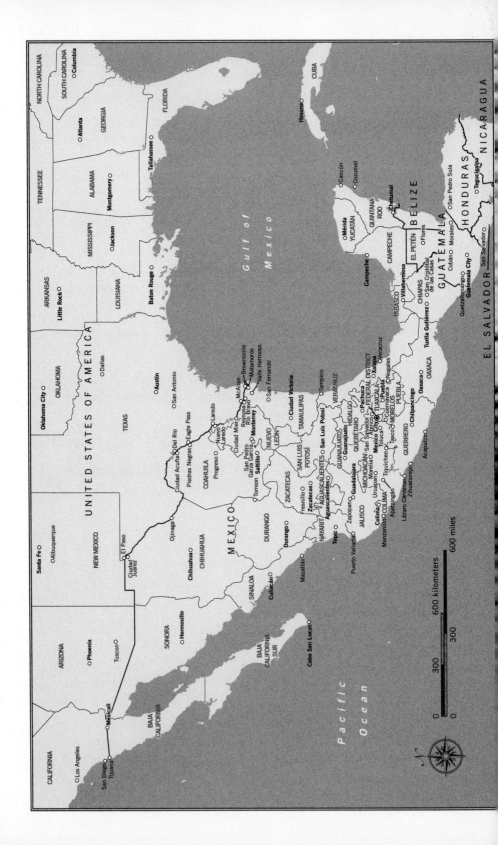

PROLOGUE

In the lingering chill of May you would see the faces staring back, haunting in their silence and mystery. Carlos Alberto Simental, seventeen years old. Fernando Tejeda Loya, thirty-nine years old. Kelvin Alvin Palomo Nava, twenty-two years old. Plastered to the front door of the morgue in Matamoros in the Mexican state of Tamaulipas, just across the Rio Grande (Río Bravo if you were Mexican) from Brownsville, Texas, the faces and names belonged to people who had disappeared in the state over the previous year. From inside the squat, gray structure of the morgue itself, a sickly whiff of human decay was unmistakable.

The road they had disappeared from was *Carretera Federal 101* (Mexican Federal Highway 101), which stretched from the state of San Luis Potosí through the Tamaulipas state capital of Ciudad Victoria to Matamoros, 198 miles to the north, hugging the Sierra Madre Oriental *cordillera* and passing through Mexico's San Fernando Valley. The road had earned the rather more descriptive name *la carretera de la muerte* (Highway of Death) from the residents of Tamaulipas. At the time of my visit in early May 2011, Mexican authorities had exhumed more than 190 bodies from forty separate pits over the previous month, and the families of hundreds of missing people had offered DNA samples to help try to identify the dead. By the time the authorities finished digging, they would have 193 bodies.

Along with the other neologisms entering the Mexican vocabulary to describe the scorched-earth war Mexican president Felipe Calderón had been waging against the drug cartels since 2006 (and that the cartels had been waging against one another)—from *narcocorridos* (narco songs) to *narcomantas* (narco banners) to *narcobloqueos* (narco blockades)—another had been added: *narcofosas* (narco graves). It was believed that those in the morgue had been the victims of *Los Zetas*, a drug cartel made up largely of deserters from Mexican (and, increasingly, Guatemalan) Special Forces army units who had acted for years as the armed enforcers of the Gulf Cartel, a criminal organization born and bred in Matamoros with an illicit lineage stretching back decades. The Gulf Cartel was a regional anomaly among Mexico's drug-trafficking organizations, almost all of which could trace their roots back to the Pacific Coast state of Sinaloa, its rugged landscape dotted with marijuana and poppy fields. It was the Gulf Cartel's leaders that would facilitate the entrance into the drug trade of this highly trained and ritualistic group of killers, whose excesses even the cartel's own brutal bosses could not have foreseen.

Since early 2010, the Gulf Cartel—so bold that they would wear flak jackets with the letters CDG (for *Cártel del Golfo*) emblazoned on the side—and Los Zetas had been fighting a bloody war of attrition for this slice of the border. To the west of Matamoros lay the Tamaulipas border city of Nuevo Laredo, and on the American side, Laredo, Texas. Laredo was the largest inland port along the US-Mexico border, boasting over $168 billion in legal imports and exports and, more to the point, approximately 3.5 million trucks crossing annually. From Laredo, one could drive all the way up to Minnesota on Interstate 35 and branch off into virtually any major highway in the United States, an appealing prospect for drug traffickers looking to supply America's ravenous maw in its hunger for cocaine, marijuana, methamphetamine, and other drugs.

When it came to explaining the bodies in the pits, though, some said Los Zetas believed they had been seizing members of *La Familia Michoacána,* a rival drug gang from the southwestern state of Michoacán that Los Zetas had once trained and who, some said, had been covertly coming into the region by bus to help the Gulf Cartel battle their former allies. Others said Los Zetas had kidnapped people to swell their ranks and killed those who refused to work for them. Still others said Los Zetas had killed some of the missing merely for sport. One Mexican newspaper, *El Informador,* based in Mexico's second largest city, Guadalajara, published a horrifying account from an alleged survivor of the killings. The survivor described how one of Los Zetas' leaders, a former smuggler and car thief named Miguel Ángel Treviño Morales—born in Mexico but raised largely in Laredo and Dallas—beat a victim's head with a wooden plank "until it was completely destroyed" before ordering kidnapped men to fight to the death, gladiator style, to determine who would join the group's ranks. The account was replete with other stomach-churning details of the murder of women and children who fell into the cartel's clutches.

It was hard to find anyone in Matamoros to ask about the graves, however, because, just before my taxi driver and I arrived at the morgue, a gun battle had erupted in the city when a group of Mexican marines had driven headlong into a convoy of startled cartel gunmen. Masked soldiers and police still raced up and down the street, their *Xiuhcoatl* (the word meant "turquoise-serpent" in the Nahuatl language) assault rifles poised menacingly at the ready. Near the morgue, black-clad policemen, their identities hidden under ski masks, set up checkpoints, while convoys of Mexican marines sped across the broad boulevards of Matamoros.

"They recruit boys from thirteen to seventeen years old," a university student from Matamoros, speaking in hushed tones about the cartels, had told me a day earlier as we had sat together outside on a low wall despite the breeze. "The police are also involved in this." It was more or less common knowledge, now that Los Zetas had spun off on their own, that the Gulf Cartel was largely made up of former and active-duty Tamaulipas state police officers.

Like Brownsville—a beautiful, atmospheric old town, by far the loveliest along the Texas border—Matamoros, though a more ramshackle place with a rather bloody title, has considerable charm. (Its official name—*Heroica Matamoros*—means the Heroic Moor Killer, but in fact it came from a revolutionary Mexican priest, Mariano Matamoros.) On peaceful days around the Plaza Hidalgo, named after Miguel Hidalgo y Costilla, a priest and key leader of Mexico's 1810 to 1821 War of Independence from Spain, one could sit in the Café Paris there and sip good coffee, served either *lechero* or *americano,* while watching families stroll through the plaza and the bootblacks and newspaper vendors—some, like the taxi drivers, *halcones* (literally "hawks," but in practice lookouts or spies) for the cartel—ply their trade. A simple church, the *Parroquia de Nuestra Senora del Refugio,* sat on the opposite corner. The city also boasted a first-rate museum, the *Museo de Arte Contemporáneo de Tamaulipas.* For decades, and indeed for centuries for some, the same families had lived dual lives, crossing back and forth across the border at will, to work, to shop, to fall in love, to dream.

But peaceful days were hard to come by in the Matamoros of today. The previous November, Antonio Ezequiel Cárdenas Guillén, better known by his nickname *Tony Tormenta* (Tony the Storm), had met his end in a gun battle with the Mexican military that raged throughout the city for many hours. Along with Jorge Eduardo "El Coss" Costilla Sánchez, a former Matamoros municipal police officer, Tony Tormenta had taken the reins of the Gulf Cartel after his brother, Osiel Cárdenas Guillén, was extradited to the United States in 2007. Though the Mexican government initially said that four gunmen, two marines, and a soldier had been killed in the assault that took down Tony Tormenta, Matamoros residents put the number of dead that day at closer to fifty.

As I was sitting in a Mexican restaurant in Brownsville chatting with a friend of mine, a Mexican political scientist, she told me matter-of-factly that "the current levels of violence are changing the entire culture of the border region. [They] have escalated to unprecedented levels, and the new practices by killers are extreme and have never been observed in the past. How can someone justify to himself assassinating dozens of men, women, and children? The economic explanation is definitely an important one, but there must be more elements in these new and extreme forms of violence. A new culture and new beliefs are taking hold."

Her observations were anything but distant and academic. The university campus where she worked in Brownsville, just across the Rio Grande from Matamoros, has been struck on three separate occasions by bullets fired during confrontations on the Mexican side.

"There is practically anarchy here," a businessman from the nearby Tamaulipas city of Reynosa had told me, talking about the Tamaulipas border region. We chatted in his modest dwelling having driven through streets where buildings would suddenly spring up pockmarked and shredded by bullet holes. "Many people have abandoned their homes."

Along with a new vocabulary, the violence was bringing with it an entirely new iconography. Strolling the streets of Brownsville at dusk that May, I found two images that I had seen often on both sides of the border gazing out at passersby from clothing shops and discount stores. The first was a visage of dapper, mustachioed solemnity: the face of Jesús Malverde. Often depicted today on T-shirts and baseball caps with marijuana leafs wreathing his face, Malverde was said to have been an outlaw from Sinaloa. The main shrine dedicated to Malverde—allegedly executed by authorities in about 1909 and revered as a quasi-saint by many in Mexico's criminal underworld—is in the Sinaloan city of Culiacán, birthplace of the eponymous *Cartel de Sinaloa* (Sinaloa Cartel), then headed by Joaquín "El Chapo" Guzmán Loera, perhaps Mexico's most famous drug trafficker. The other image was that of a hooded, scythe-wielding skeleton, *Santa Muerte* (Saint Death). Like Jesús Malverde, Santa Muerte had become an object of veneration among Mexico's criminals, and shrines were frequently found in drug stash houses on both sides of the border. Altars to *La Flaca* ("The Skinny Lady") adorned the roadsides of northern Mexico where the narcos proliferated.

A few months earlier, I had found myself in the Mexico City barrio of Tepito, a rough-hewn place with an evil reputation despite its importance in the history of both Mexico City and the country as a whole. In its present incarnation, Tepito serves as a clearinghouse with a seemingly endless open-air bazaar of contraband goods for sale. During Aztec times it had been an important area of the indigenous capital of Tenochtitlan, reselling beans and corn discarded by Aztec nobility to people of more humble means. It has been a place where outsiders often looked for Mexico at its rawest (the most iconic work of the American anthropologist Oscar Lewis, his book *The Children of Sanchez,* was written about a Tepito family and published in 1961).

It has also been a place where residents of Mexico City have sought to sate their desires, whether for a bit of stolen merchandise, a gun, or plentiful drugs (Natasha Fuentes Lemus, the daughter of the great Mexican novelist Carlos Fuentes, died in the neighborhood in August 2005 of a rumored drug overdose). Tepito also hosts the main shrine in Mexico to Santa Muerte, and I watched one afternoon as worshippers there prayed and offered candles to an actual skeleton in a wedding dress protected behind a thick pane of glass.

I had first become aware of the violence ripping Mexico apart during the summer of 2008 in Guatemala, a country immediately to Mexico's south where I had been reporting on and off since 2003, and which, along with Haiti and the Democratic Republic of Congo, had become one of my areas of focus. My girlfriend at the time and I were near the end of an isthmus-long trip from Panama to Belize when, upon passing through Guatemala, I decided to detour from sailing down the scenic Rio Dulce to visit Morales, a town of fifty thousand in the heartland of the country's cattle-raising and farming industries. More infamously, Morales had also become an epicenter of Guatemala's booming trade as a drug transshipment point, as a country boasting both Caribbean and Pacific coastline, vast swaths of little-patrolled jungle, and a 541-mile border with Mexico would inevitably become.

In March of that year, Juan "Juancho" José León Ardón, a local drug lord and would-be patron of the *Unidad Nacional de la Esperanza* (UNE) party of then-president of Guatemala Álvaro Colom, had met his bloody end along with ten other men in a wild shootout at the La Laguna spa in neighboring Zacapa State, cut down by a group of Zetas. Guatemalan police later recovered sixteen semiautomatic AR-15 assault rifles and an M-16. Along with the body of Juancho—who had fled a Mexican prison in 2001—and several of his bodyguards were found the bodies of two Mexican nationals. Among the Zetas blazing away in Guatemala that day was Daniel Pérez Rojas, alias *El Cachetes* (Cheeks), who had once been one of the bodyguards for Osiel Cárdenas.

It was said that Los Zetas had made their first appearance in the country a few years earlier, invited in as Gulf Cartel emissaries by another Guatemala drug lord, Juan Alberto "Chamalé" Ortíz López, who ran a narco empire on the other side of the country in the department of San Marcos, which boasted both a Pacific coast and a little-patrolled border with Mexico. Chamalé himself was believed to have had a close relationship with Obdulio Solórzano, a UNE deputy from the Pacific Coast department of Escuintla who had served in Guatemala's congress until that year and sat on the executive committee of the party.

Juancho had been a heavy cocaine user and drinker himself, and had gotten his start in cattle rustling in the early 1990s before moving on to drug trafficking and stealing drug shipments passing through the region. People told me that he had been attacked by at least thirty men that day, something virtually unheard of since Guatemala's long civil war officially ended in 1996.

Visiting Morales was a surreal experience. Men descending from pickup trucks and sport utility vehicles with blacked-out windows sported visible Glock pistols and Uzi submachine guns. Sprawling and curiously empty new luxury hotels dotted the dusty streets. A resident told me that the local body count there usually numbered well over a dozen a week.

"There has been a great increase in violence in the area in the last several months, which would suggest that a turf war was going on," a religious leader working in the region since the late 1980s told me. "Weekends here are dangerous."

When I met him in the capital Guatemala City during the same visit, I found Frank LaRue, a veteran Guatemalan human rights advocate and head of the Guatemalan civil society organization *Instituto Demos,* in a state of some agitation as he envisioned what Juancho's death signified for Guatemala.

"Guatemala is already a weak, almost nonexistent, state that does not guarantee security or justice or health or education," he told me as his staff shuffled boxes around the organization's new office, which was located in a house that had been LaRue's former boyhood home. "If the cartels from Mexico begin to move down and Guatemala completely collapses into their hands, then you will have a real problem."

LaRue, who had survived numerous military dictatorships in Guatemala and would go on to be appointed Special Rapporteur on freedom of opinion and expression by the United Nations, didn't know it at the time, but he was painting an exact picture of the future.

Mexico's future.

CHAPTER ONE

The Frontier

BIRTH (AND DEATH) OF A NATION

The state of Tamaulipas hugs the Rio Grande in a narrow line that includes two major industrial cities—Nuevo Laredo and Reynosa—as well as the smaller Matamoros, in some ways the aging dowager economically but, as noted, certainly the most charming of the three. As the western border of the state dips south, the Sierra Madre Oriental mountain range eventually rises along its border with the state of Nuevo León, while as one travels east the land eventually flattens out to pastureland dotted with various strains of cactus. Once the Rio Grande arrives at the ocean a few miles east of Matamoros, on its eastern fringes Tamaulipas then descends languidly south along the Gulf of Mexico. It encompasses the conjoined port cities of Tampico and Ciudad Madero (which many Mexicans regard as a single entity) before ending at the border with the state of Veracruz, its eponymous port the ·chief entry point for thousands of African slaves brought in to Mexico between the 1500s and early 1800s.

The exact meaning of the word *Tamaulipas* remains the subject of some debate even today. Many agree that "tam" comes from an Huastec indigenous word meaning "place where" while some suggest that "holipa" means "pray a lot," thus making Tamaulipas "the place where people pray a lot." The state was originally an area inhabited by the aforementioned Huastec people, who existed more or less independently until their defeat by the Aztec emperor Montezuma in the mid-1400s. To this day, the region where the present-day states of Tamaulipas, Veracruz, Puebla, Hidalgo, San Luis Potosí, Querétaro, and Guanajuato intersect is referred to as *La Huasteca,* and is well known throughout Mexico for its distinctive music and dance. Like most of Mexico's indigenous people, the Huastec fell under the dominion of the Spanish when the invading forces of Hernán Cortés captured the Aztec capital of Tenochtitlan (located in the heart of present-day Mexico City) in November 1519.

Spain would go on to rule Mexico for three hundred years as part of the sprawling *Virreinato de Nueva España* (Vice Royalty of New Spain), comprised of the European nation's far-flung colonies. In September 1810, in the town of Dolores near Guanajuato, the Roman Catholic priest Miguel Hidalgo y Costilla issued a rousing call that crystalized the Mexican desire for independence from the Spanish crown in what would become *El Grito de Dolores* (The Cry of Dolores) or simply *El Grito.* A revolutionary struggle was born (Hidalgo was executed by the Spanish a short time later) and war raged until September 1821, when the pro-independence forces emerged victorious and the Spanish withdrew.

The history of Mexico in the decades immediately after independence was one of nearly endless war and ceaseless intriguing both on the part of Mexico's own political class and its foreign rivals.

The military dictator Antonio López de Santa Anna would be Mexico's president on eleven separate occasions between 1823 and 1847. When Texas declared itself independent from Mexico in 1836, Santa Anna personally led forces to quell the rebellion, an expedition that ended in disaster. Though Santa Anna's forces triumphed at the famed Battle of the Alamo, they were eventually defeated and Santa Anna himself captured, resulting in the eventual loss of the entire territory of Texas to the United States.

In 1838 an even more useless war, comically named the *Guerra de los pasteles* (The Pastry War) broke out, so-called for the looting of a French-owned pastry shop near Mexico City that France used as a pretext to invade the country via the Gulf Coast. This resulted in the capture of most of the Mexican navy at Veracruz, while Santa Anna emerged from brief retirement, led the resistance to the French, and resumed the presidency shortly thereafter.

The Mexican-American War raged between 1846 and 1848. It ended with the Treaty of Guadalupe Hidalgo, which would eventually result in a radical definition of the border between Mexico and the victorious United States and Mexico losing roughly half its national territory. The 1853 Gadsden Purchase would extend the United States, gobbling up even more Mexican territory. Between 1857 and 1861, Mexico witnessed the *Guerra de Reforma* (Reform War) between Liberal and Conservative forces, the former favoring a federalist government and a limited role for the Catholic Church and the latter wanting a dominant central state, possibly even a monarchy. In the middle of the Guerra de Reforma, the Liberal Benito Juárez, an indigenous Zapotec attorney from Oaxaca, became president.

One of the most memorable figures from the period in Tamaulipas was a red-bearded hell-raiser named Juan Nepomuceno Cortina, and his life and career give a flavor for the convoluted, schizophrenic binational life along the border in the mid-1800s. Born the son of the town's mayor of Camargo, Tamaulipas in May 1824 into a ranch-owning family, Cortina was raised largely in Matamoros, experienced Comanche raids in his youth, and fought on the Mexican side with irregular troops during the Mexican-American War. The Cortinas lost a considerable amount of family land holdings after the border changed following the conflict and Texas joining the United States in February 1846. Like many on both sides of the border after the war, Cortina reportedly turned to cattle rustling and other forms of banditry. Brownsville and Matamoros—interlinked communities at the time—were rapidly expanding, attracting fortune seekers from far and wide. One of them was Connecticut transplant Charles Stillman, who scooped up disputed land and became fabulously wealthy through various smuggling endeavors. After the Mexican defeat, a large number of Mexicans traveled north, living on the outskirts of Brownsville in squalid conditions, and often enduring rough treatment by Anglo and European Texans. They also fell under the sway of local competing—and often quite violent—Texas political factions that would pay and organize immigrants to (illegally) cast ballots in local elections. It was a rough life, buffeted by epidemics of cholera and yellow fever, made even more challenging by unscrupulous local politicos who organized mini-pogroms against Mexicans.

In July 1859, Juan Cortina shot and wounded a Brownsville sheriff he had witnessed brutalizing an elderly Mexican man during an attempted arrest. The incident appeared to make Cortina throw caution to the wind and, in the early morning darkness of September 28, 1859, he attacked Brownsville with around seventy-five other gunmen, largely, some believe, to settle a score with a German immigrant named Adolphus Glavecke. Glavecke had married into the Cortina family, and Cortina blamed him for any number of transgressions, though both Cortina and Glavecke had been indicted by a Brownsville court for cattle rustling. At least five people, including an unarmed Mexican, were killed by Cortina's men in the attack.

After the pleading of Matamoros politicians and businessmen fearful of the US response, Cortina abandoned the town two days later, shortly thereafter to issue a proclamation in which he stated "there is no need to fear" but rather that the raid had been "to chastise the villainy of our enemies" who had "connived with each other and form, so to speak, an inquisitorial lodge to persecute and rob us, without any cause, and for no other crime on our part than that of being of Mexican origin."

Subsequently, residents of Brownsville "watched in awe as Mexican soldiers crossed the Rio Grande to Texas to protect United States citizens from an irregular army of Mexicans led by a man who considered himself a United States citizen and who had once been a member of the Matamoros militia that now came to protect his enemies." Paramilitary forces were raised in Brownsville in due course, soon joined by a detachment of Texas Rangers led by John Salmon "Rip" Ford, a future Brownsville mayor. Local papers openly proclaimed the possibility of a race war. Thus began the Cortina Wars along the border, as they became known, and by the end of December "the whole county from Brownsville to Rio Grande City. . . . Had been laid to waste." Cortina's men suffered a withering defeat at Rio Grande City and eventually no less a personage than Robert E. Lee was sent to command the US Army and restore order. Cortina would later also fight the Confederate army during the US Civil War before opportunistically aligning with both sides in Mexico's looming internal armed conflict.

As Cortina fought his war along the frontier, a "Second Mexican Empire" was sleazed into existence by France's Napoleon III and Mexico's own fabulously wealthy hacienda owners following an 1861 French-led invasion of the country. As its figurehead the French-allied forces chose Ferdinand Maximilian Joseph, an Austrian nobleman who became Maximilian I and who had previously taken as his bride Princess Charlotte of Belgium, who thus became Empress Carlota. Interestingly enough, Carlota was the sister of none other than Belgium's King Leopold, who would spend the end of the nineteenth century and beginning of the twentieth turning the Congo into a mass grave of slave labor and exploitation. This European "emperor," though, landed in Mexico, a country where Liberal forces and his Conservative supporters were already at one another's throats and soon descended into open civil war. Benito Juárez was forced to decamp with his forces to Chihuahua, but Maximilian's reign ended badly when he and two of his generals were executed by a firing squad in Querétaro in June 1867. Carlota had returned to Europe to ask for support for her husband before his execution and lived on for many years afterward, dying insane and never having been able to admit Maximilian's death. Juárez would return as president in 1867 and serve until 1872, dying in office at the age of sixty-six.

From 1876 to 1911 the preeminent political personality in the country was Porfirio Díaz, who ruled the nation either directly as president or via weak proxies. Díaz was a complex figure, the son of a full-blooded Mixtec Indian from the southern state of Oaxaca and the nephew of the Oaxaca state bishop. During his long reign he would grow from a dashing, intense young revolutionary into a bushy-mustachioed and bemedaled dictator whose style of governance has been described as "tolerant . . . in religious matters and openly progressive in economic affairs . . . [but] completely illiberal politically."

The influence of the Díaz dictatorship on Mexico's northern border led to an economy that was semifeudal, and always informed by its tense relations with its neighbor across the Rio Grande. Once a major point of cross-border trade, and an important export point for the Confederacy during the US Civil War, Matamoros gradually submerged under the shadow of Nuevo Laredo, some two hundred miles to the west. The Díaz-allied Tamaulipas Irrigation and Development Company controlled 4.6 million acres of Mexican land, the majority of it within Tamaulipas itself. Between 1900 and 1910, armed would-be American colonizers occupied large areas of Tamaulipas and several other states. By 1910, Tamaulipas was among the states (along with Chiapas and Guerrero far to the south) that the historian John Mason Hart characterized as an area where "conflicting forces of economic intrusion and traditional society were especially strong."

Jesús Malverde and Santa Muerte

In 1909, as the long Díaz era was drawing to a close, a legend began to emerge from the hills of the Pacific Coast state of Sinaloa about a generous bandit named Jesús Malverde, who helped the poor inhabitants of the state even as he preyed upon its corrupt wealthy classes. In a typical example of upside-down justice in the Mexican hinterlands, after being betrayed by the comrade he trusted most, Malverde was hanged from a tree by the government. Thereafter, pilgrims began making the journey to a pile of stones and pebbles outside of Culiacán that some believed to be his grave, asking for favors and leaving alms. It was said he provided.

Eventually, the state government bulldozed the site and put up the Sinaloa state government building on top of it. There is some symbolism in that. Although there is no evidence that Malverde actually existed, and many believe that he was in fact an amalgam of two distinct Sinaloa highwaymen active at the time, his faith continued to reverberate through the neglected, benighted Sinaloan countryside. Eventually, the site of his shrine was moved two blocks away from where it had originally stood.

The origins of Santa Muerte were even older, with precursors of the present-day figure appearing only a hundred or so years after the first recorded vision of the Nahuatl-speaking *Nuestra Señora de Guadalupe,* better known in English as the Virgin of Guadalupe—the most celebrated Catholic icon in Mexico.

Seeing her ghastly appearance and scythe, many non-Mexicans often make the mistake of associating Santa Muerte with the Grim Reaper, when in fact her origins are considerably more obscure. Some believe that Santa Muerte may be an adaptation of Mictecacihuatl, the Aztec goddess of the underworld; others contend that she comes from the belief system of the Purépecha, an indigenous people from northwestern Michoacán who were never conquered by the Aztecs. Still others draw a link between

La Flaca and medieval Europe. The figure of *El Rey San Pascual* (The King San Pascual also known as *San Pascualito* or *San Pascualito Muerte*), a crown-topped skeleton, is said to be based on a vision of the clergyman Paschal Baylon that appeared during a plague in Guatemala in the 1650s. By the 1790s, mentions of Santa Muerte were appearing from central Mexican states such as Guanajuato in connection with the syncretic indigenous-Christian rituals of the Nahua people, and also in Querétaro.

Historically, however, the veneration of Santa Muerte has met with strong condemnation from the traditional Catholic Church. It has been called "a cult of crisis," not exclusively the domain of criminals, but rather of those going through extremely difficult times. Santa Muerte was, though, all in all, a darker and more nihilistic take on the folk saint culture from which both it and Jesús Malverde emerged.

REVOLUTIONARY MEXICO

A miner's strike in Sonora in June 1906 at Cananea—a town thirty-seven miles south of the Arizona border—took place at a copper mine owned by the US-based Anaconda Company, which controlled a staggering 350,000 acres in the state. At the mine, the workers had existed for years in a virtual state-within-a-state, with almost all materials and supplies imported from the United States and sold at US prices, despite the eroding value of Mexican currency during the US and European banking crises of the early 1900s. Demanding a shorter workday, better pay, and other changes, the striking miners were met with gunfire by the mine's management. They responded in kind, battling security guards and local police for two days before Arizona Rangers raced across the border to the mining facility. The rebellion finally ended when some two thousand Mexican troops arrived. Estimates of those dead in the uprising ranged from thirty to a hundred Mexicans and four Americans. If Mexicans ever needed an illustration that their welfare was a mere afterthought to the political and economic machinations of their leader Porfirio Díaz in Mexico City, beholden as he was to foreign interests, Cananea provided a stark one, and it was recognized as such at the time.

In 1910, Díaz snatched a likely electoral victory from Francisco I. Madero, a wealthy Coahuila businessman and politician, providing the final spark for what would become the Mexican Revolution. It was called a revolution, but it was in fact a multifront civil war consisting of various armies with overlapping and occasionally colliding agendas across a wide swath of the country. The struggle would produce some of the most colorful characters in Mexico's dramatic history

In the central state of Morelos, Emiliano Zapata, a mestizo of Nahua and Spanish ancestry from the village of Anenecuilco, had served as president of the village council, a local son whose family had farmed and raised livestock in the area for generations. He had witnessed firsthand the humiliations of the hacienda system, and soon was leading an irregular army in revolt, not only to support Madero but to enact broad social changes and land reform. These moves were anathema to the post-Díaz government of the slippery Coahuila politician-turned-president Venustiano Carranza. Zapata would be killed in April 1919 in an ambush by Carranza's soldiers, preceding Farabundo Martí of El Salvador (1932) and Augusto César Sandino of Nicaragua (1934) into the pantheon of revolutionary leaders in the Americas snatched from their moment in history by scheming politicians.

To the north, a Durango bandit named Pancho Villa, who had also known the sorrows of the hacienda, became a Maderist guerrilla leader there and in the state of Chihuahua. He would play a complex role in the tapestry of shifting political alliances in northern Mexico for the remainder of the war. At the same time, Villa became a well-known figure in the United States thanks to the writings of Americans such as the journalist John Reed (who would later pen a book about Villa, *Insurgent Mexico*) and Ambrose Bierce, who disappeared in Mexico after traveling with Villa's forces in 1913. The United States actively supported Villa, despite his criminal past, until breaking with him in favor of Carranza in 1915, leading to a Villa-led attack on New Mexico and a US military expedition into Mexico against Villa commanded by John J. Pershing. Villa would later be killed under mysterious circumstances in Chihuahua in July 1923.

After Díaz's overthrow and exile (he would later die in Paris), Madero would serve as Mexico's president from 1911 to 1913 when he was overthrown and later killed by forces loyal to the military officer Victoriano

Huerta. Many Mexicans still look to this event as the theft of the promise that the revolution once held out. Revolution and usurpation continued for years after until General Álvaro Obregón assumed the presidency in December 1920.

The years in between Díaz's abdication and the Obregón presidency were marked by violent confrontation with the United States. In Tamaulipas, bands of *campesinos* (peasants) invaded the US-controlled San Antonio de la Rusias hacienda and the Blaylock and La Palma colonies. In April 1914, the so-called Tampico Affair erupted when Huerta's forces seized nine US sailors in the Tamaulipas port of the same name. This in turn led to the American occupation of Veracruz that same month, an operation in which several hundred people would die and which was conducted in large part because Mexican authorities refused to honor US admiral Henry T. Mayo with a twenty-one-gun salute and hoist the US flag on Mexican soil after the sailors' return. US president Woodrow Wilson charged before Congress that "a series of incidents" in Mexico necessitated the use of "the armed forces of the United States in such ways and to such an extent as may be necessary to obtain from General Huerta and adherents the fullest recognition of the rights and dignity of the United States, even amidst the distressing conditions that now unhappily obtaining in Mexico." The United States, whose invading forces would include in their ranks a then-young captain named Douglas MacArthur, would occupy Veracruz for six months.

The postrevolutionary peace was short-lived, as the fervently secular and anti-theocratic president Plutarco Elías Calles presided over the Cristero War (*La Cristiada*), a pro–Catholic Church and antigovernment rebellion that erupted in western Mexico in late 1926. The war would eventually engulf thirteen states until the last flames of insurrection were put out two and half years later. It was a savage conflict during which peasant Catholic zealots were hung from trees and alongside railroad tracks, then their villages burned for good measure (and some ninety priests were killed, as well). An estimated seventy thousand people would die in the conflict.

As Mexico experienced waves of violence, so did the United States, though for very different reasons. In December 1917, under pressure from such groups as the Anti-Saloon League and the Woman's Christian Temperance Union, the US Congress passed the Eighteenth Amendment to the Constitution, which declared the production, transport, and sale of alcoholic beverages illegal. The amendment was then sent to the states to be ratified, a ratification that was certified in January 1919, and which took effect a year later, in January 1920.

The separate National Prohibition Act, commonly known as the Volstead Act, was enacted to give both the federal and state governments the power to enforce the the Eighteenth Amendment, and it became law on October 28, 1919. These two pieces of legislation became Prohibition, an effective national ban on alcohol that would last until 1933. During the thirteen years of Prohibition, millions of ordinary Americans would be turned into criminals because of a substance they chose to put into their own bodies, and the power and reach of organized crime in the United States would grow exponentially.

Almost from the start, Prohibition was a disaster. Throughout the United States, regional organized crime syndicates swooped in to provide a thirsty public with the libations they craved, and in addition to illegal homemade stills, now-illegal liquor flooded into the country, south from Canada, north from Mexico, and aboard "rum-runners" plying the Straits of Florida from Cuba and west toward Florida, Georgia, and elsewhere from the Bahamas. In Chicago the so-called Chicago Outfit of Italian-American Johnny Torrio was assisted and later superseded by his deputy Al Capone. The Chicago Outfit warred against the North Side Gang of the Irish-American Dean O'Banion, culminating in 1928's Saint Valentine's Day Massacre, which left seven men dead inside of a Chicago garage, photos of their blood-soaked corpses splashed across the nation's newspaper pages.

In Detroit, Abe Bernstein ran The Purple Gang, a mostly Jewish organization, while in New York, Arnold "The Brain" Rothstein ran a large section of illegal liquor activity until his 1928 murder, when his acolytes Meyer Lansky, Charles "Lucky" Luciano, and others would come to the fore. On the payroll of these criminal organizations were thousands of policemen, customs agents, border personnel, and local, state, and federal officials, all of whom were either corrupted by the fantastic wealth that supplying an illegal, in-demand market created or intimidated into silence by the great violence and impunity with which the criminal organizations were able to operate in such an environment. The ban on alcohol was regularly flouted by government officials, including those in both houses of Congress, who kept on drinking right through it. Finally, in 1933, US president Franklin Delano Roosevelt oversaw the repeal of Prohibition, and the citizens of a thirsty nation legally blew the foam off a glass of suds—some for the first time ever.

THE RISE OF THE PRI

In Mexico City, meanwhile, the revolution's victory had resulted in a squabbling for the spoils in search of a uniting theme or figure. Plutarco Elías Calles served as president from December 1924 to November 1928, and it had fallen to him to violently prosecute the Cristero War. He also attempted to create such a unifying party with his *Partido Nacional Revolucionario* (PNR). In 1938, Lázaro Cárdenas del Río, president from 1934 to 1940, changed the name of the party to the *Partido de la Revolución Mexicana* (PRM). The same year, Cárdenas nationalized Mexico's petroleum reserves along with all the machinery that foreign oil companies had brought into Mexico, leading to the founding of the state oil company *Petróleos Mexicanos* (Pemex).

Under the presidency of Manuel Ávila Camacho (1940–1946), the PRM was dissolved and the *Partido Revolucionario Institucional* (Institutional Revolutionary Party or PRI) under its present name was born during his last year. Through populism, bribery, and political dark arts such as vote-rigging and intimidation, the party would govern the country without interruption for the next fifty-four years. A nationwide system whereby local political bosses, known as *caciques* or chieftains, ruled the states took hold. Though the country's political culture was seemingly frozen in time during this era, its artistic culture underwent an unprecedented flowering. Artists such as Diego Rivera and Frida Kahlo would gain worldwide recognition throughout the 1930s, while Mexican writers such as Octavio Paz and Juan Rulfo decoded the Mexican identity even as they mythologized it. They paved the way for what today remains one of the most vibrant and diverse intellectual milieus in the Americas. Gazing around at the Mexican political system put in place after the revolution, Paz would conclude that governance in Mexico had always been marked by "the thread of domination," and in this sense "the Spanish viceroys and the Mexican presidents are the successors of the Aztec rulers."

Into this firmament, in 1915, had been born Juan Nepomuceno Guerra. Sharing a name with the storied Juan Cortina, Guerra came of age as a farm boy on his father's Tamaulipas ranch during the Great Depression, and by his teens was believed to be involved in smuggling operations between the United States and Mexico.

By the time the PRI was solidifying its control over Mexico, Juan Guerra was solidifying his control over Tamaulipas. He ran a nightclub, The Matamoros Cafe, and was a familiar figure around Matamoros, dressed in a Stetson hat and holding court behind the darkened glass doors of the Piedras Negras Restaurant, the walls adorned with pictures of horses from his five-hundred-acre ranch, *El Tlahuachal*. He reportedly killed his first wife in a fit of jealous rage in the 1950s, and later married a woman from Tampico with whom he had three sons. His thuggery did not confine itself to his personal relationships. In April 1960, Pancho Villa's son, Colonel Octavio Villa Coss, was gunned down in Matamoros shortly after seizing a shipment of contraband coffee (and allegedly refusing a bribe to return it). Guerra's bodyguard and chauffeur confessed to the crime, claiming Villa was plotting to kill their boss.

Despite the oft-repeated observation of the Peruvian author Mario Vargas Llosa that the PRI represented the "perfect dictatorship," the party maintained power through the use of sometimes extreme violence. Though his thick-rimmed glasses gave him a rather bookish appearance, Gustavo Díaz Ordaz's term as president (1964–1970) was marked by often brutal authoritarianism even as Mexico saw its economy grow and diversify.

A disturbance that began when police beat a group of high school students in Mexico City in July 1968 snowballed into a major mass student uprising in the capital, culminating in the appalling Tlatelolco massacre that October in the capital's Plaza de las Tres Culturas. Soldiers gunned down unarmed civilian demonstrators in an attack that one journalist said was worse than anything he had witnessed in the Middle East or Vietnam. At least forty-two people were killed, though the full death toll may have been much higher. Outraged, Octavio Paz, then Mexico's ambassador to India, resigned in protest. One week later, Mexico City hosted the Olympics. During the presidency of Luis Echeverría that followed, in June 1971, Mexico witnessed *El Halconazo* (the Corpus Christi Massacre), where government provocateurs in the capital again attacked student demonstrators (a security official later said the intent had been to intimidate recently released student leaders from the 1968 protests). Some estimates concluded that over one hundred people were killed in the assault.

There were movements against the PRI's brutal hegemony, particularly in the mountainous state of Guerrero that skirted the Pacific Ocean. One schoolteacher, Genaro Vázquez Rojas, helped found the *Asociación Cívica Nacional Revolucionaria* (ACNR) before his death at the hands of the army in 1972. Starting in 1967, a Guerrero teacher named Lucio Cabañas Barrientos led the *Partido de los Pobres* (PdlP) in the state, losing his life at the hands of Mexican troops in 1974 after he kidnapped then-senator and future governor of Guerrero State Rubén Figueroa Figueroa. To stifle such rebellions from taking hold, the PRI employed the *Dirección Federal de Seguridad* (DFS) from 1978 until 1982 under the command of Miguel Nazar Haro, as well as the *Brigada Blanca*, a paramilitary force (death squad would be more accurate) made up "of military and selected elements from various state and federal police forces" that killed, tortured, and "disappeared" Mexican citizens under the name of stopping guerrilla movements. At least seven hundred Mexicans were the victims of enforced disappearances by state security agencies during this period. One army general alone, Mario Arturo Acosta Chaparro, was accused of involvement in at least 143 disappearances.

On a less violent note, the *Partido Acción Nacional* (National Action Party or PAN), had been founded in 1939 by Chihuahua native Manuel Gómez Morín, the Michoacán politician Luis Calderón Vega, and other conservatives in the wake of their defeat in the Cristero War. The PAN sent its first federal deputies to congress in 1946, but their role as opposition for many years was largely symbolic. For the good of the country, the PRI said it would never allow the opposition to win a national election. It was a practice that some PRI politicians, including José Francisco Ruiz Massieu, who would serve as the PRI's governor of Guerrero from 1987 to 1993, referred to as "patriotic fraud."

The PRI was aided in its quest to retain power by a company with its roots in Tamaulipas. Emilio Azcárraga Vidaurreta had built the acquisition of a few regional radio stations around the Monterrey area in the 1930s into Mexico's first national television station, Canal 2, in 1951, and then eventually into dozens of media concerns. Upon Azcárraga's death in 1973, this hive of information and industry was eventually passed to Azcárraga's Texas-born son, Emilio Azcárraga Milmo, who became known as *El Tigre* and dubbed the whole enterprise *Televisa*. As much as any other figure, the younger Azcárraga came to exemplify the incestuous relationship between the PRI and the media.

THE BIRTH OF THE DRUG WAR

Apparently unbothered by the PRI's fraud and brutality, the United States, much as it had with alcohol in the 1920s, developed a fixation on the problem of illegal drugs. This was a subject on which it would inevitably have to interact with the Mexican government.

In June 1971, US president Richard Nixon, whose Comprehensive Drug Abuse Prevention and Control Act of 1970 is still viewed as the foundation for modern US drug policy, delivered his Special Message to the Congress on Drug Abuse Prevention and Control. Not surprisingly for a man waging a merciless war in Vietnam, Cambodia, and Laos, he reached for military metaphors:

> *In our history we have faced great difficulties again and again. Wars and depressions and divisions among our people have tested our will as a people—and we have prevailed. We have fought together in war, we have worked together in hard times, and we have reached out to each other in division—to close the gaps between our people and keep America whole. The threat of narcotics among our people . . . comes*

quietly into homes and destroys children, it moves into neighborhoods and breaks the fiber of community. . . . The magnitude of the problem, the national and international implications of the problem, and the limited capacities of States and cities to deal with the problem all reinforce the conclusion that coordination of this effort must take place at the highest levels of the Federal Government.

Nixon announced the creation of the Special Action Office of Drug Abuse Prevention, and stated that a psychiatrist, Jerome Jaffe, would lead it. Jaffe thus became the first in a long line of what would become colloquially known as "drug czars" in the United States, responsible for overseeing the US government's battle against illegal drugs. In 1989, these tasks would fall under the aegis of the newly created Office of National Drug Control Policy, which remains in place to this day. The War on Drugs, as it became known in the United States, had begun.

It first arrived in Mexico in the area where the states of Sinaloa, Durango, and Chihuahua intersect. In this wild, mountainous part of Mexico dubbed the Golden Triangle, marijuana and opium had been cultivated in abundance for decades. During the mid-1970s, the Mexican government flooded the states with at least ten thousand soldiers under the command of General José Hernández Toledo during what was dubbed *Operación Cóndor*, ostensibly to destroy the region's drug-producing capacity. The fact that Hernández had been one of the officers in charge during the 1968 student massacre made him perhaps not the best choice for such an assignment, but such legal niceties appeared of little concern to PRI president José López Portillo. Despite the arrest and torture of hundreds of people and the destruction of tons of marijuana and other drugs, drug trafficking did not, as Hernández had predicted it would, end in six months.

Not a single major drug trafficker was arrested. In fact, many of them simply moved their operations to other states before resuming business. Thousands of campesinos were driven from their small plots of land into the cities, and even years later many once-thriving communities remain little more than hamlets. It was an early glimpse of the essential futility— and humanitarian cost—of the drug war. It was also during this era that the Sinaloan folk saint Jesús Malverde, to whom homage had been paid in the region since the early part of the century, became identified with the drug trade and, incorrectly, dubbed a "narcosaint." In fact, the drug traffickers had simply been continuing local religious traditions that had long predated their bloody business.

There were precursors during this era of the violence that would come later. Pedro Avilés Pérez, a Sinaloa narco, achieved some level of fame for his drug-trafficking exploits before being killed by Mexican police in 1978. Pablo Acosta Villarreal, a US citizen whose father was born in the Texas town of Terlingua, carved out a drug-trafficking fiefdom in the dusty Chihuahua town of Ojinaga, just across the border from Presidio, Texas, until he too was killed in April 1987. Miguel Ángel Félix Gallardo, born in the Sinaloa capital of Culiacán in 1946, would form what would become the Guadalajara Cartel (named after Mexico's second largest city in the neighboring state of Jalisco) with three other Sinaloa natives: Rafael Caro Quintero, Ernesto "Don Neto" Fonseca Carrillo, and Juan José "El Azul" Esparragoza Moreno. (One of Pablo Acosta's main partners had in fact been Amado Carrillo Fuentes, the nephew of Ernesto Fonseca Carrillo.) It is believed that the cartel formally started operating around 1982.

The cartels would sometimes step out of line—such as with the February 1985 abduction, torture, and murder of Mexican-American DEA agent Enrique "Kiki" Camarena—but in the main, the agreement between the narcos, the PRI, and the security services held more or less intact. (An October 2013 article in Mexico's *Proceso* magazine would later claim that Camarena was in fact killed on the orders of the CIA after stumbling on the agency's use of Mexican narcos to funnel drug profits to Nicaragua's Contra rebels, then working to oust the leftist Sandinista government.)

One important organ of PRI's internal control of Mexico was the aforementioned DFS, which from 1947 until 1985 exercised vast and little-regulated powers that bled across the divisions between law enforcement and political enforcers. During the presidency of the PRI's Miguel de la Madrid Hurtado (1982–1988), the links between the DFS and the drug-trafficking organizations deepened significantly.

It was a symbiotic relationship that the US government nevertheless seemed content to turn a blind eye to, no matter how much it pointed to the futility of its own mission to eradicate drugs.

Speaking at a ceremony in the Rose Garden at the White House in June 1982, US president Ronald Reagan reached far enough back into history to evoke the Battle of Verdun in World War I, saying that "we're taking down the surrender flag that has flown over so many drug efforts; we're running up a battle flag." One could wonder how such rhetoric sounded to the residents of such US cities as Miami, Florida, which, despite an ever increasing militarization of the antidrug effort over the previous decade, had the highest murder rate of any city in the world the previous year. In the wake of the cocaine overdose death of the young basketball star Len Bias, the Reagan administration would also pass the Anti-Drug Abuse Act of 1986, which enshrined in federal law mandatory minimum sentences for drug offenses that had been jettisoned over fifteen years previously. When applied to offenses for crack cocaine (as opposed to the more expensive powder cocaine), the act subjected "people who are low-level participants to the same or harsher sentences as major dealers." Over a two-decade period, African Americans, who made up 15 percent of America's drug users, accounted for a staggering 74 percent of those sentenced to prison for drug offenses.

By the early 1980s, Juan García Ábrego, Juan Guerra's burly, mercurial Texas-born nephew, had been smuggling large quantities of marijuana into the United States for a decade. Ábrego was becoming an ever more prominent force in his uncle's Matamoros criminal organization, just as Colombian drug traffickers were looking for new routes to the United States after violence in Miami brought a massive law enforcement presence upon their old home there.

García Ábrego himself was no stranger to violence, despite his incongruously cheery nickname of *El Muñeco* (The Doll). One of his chief lieutenants, Oscar "El Profe" López Olivares (so known because of his stint as a rural schoolteacher), shot and wounded a rival drug trafficker named Casimiro "El Cacho" Espinoza in 1984. Espinoza survived but, in a notorious incident, a dozen of Ábrego's gunmen raided the Clinica Raya in Matamoros where Espinoza was recovering, spraying the rooms with gunfire and killing five people. Espinoza survived that attack as well, only to die of his wounds in a Monterrey hospital a short time later. López Olivares would later flee to the United States where he would cooperate with US officials and declare that in Mexico "drug trafficking—and this must be understood—is a government-run issue."

In addition to his propensity for violence, García Ábrego's web of corruption was extensive. Guillermo González Calderóni, one of the main commanders of Policía Judicial Federal (PJF) during the 1980s, was reportedly on Juan García Ábrego's payroll and amassed a fortune estimated at $400 million. Calderóni would eventually flee Mexico, become a DEA informant, and be murdered in McAllen, Texas, in 1993. Government prosecutors Octavio Porte Petit and Miguel Aldana Ibarra, the director for the Mexican division of Interpol, were also reported to be on the cartel's payroll. García Ábrego's cousin Francisco Pérez would later tell of delivering $500,000 to Javier Coello Trejo, Mexico's deputy attorney general from 1988 to 1990. Coello Trejo was demoted in 1990, allegedly because of abuses committed by police under his command. No mention was made of drug trafficking.

Warning Signs

The July 1988 presidential election in Mexico represented perhaps the gravest challenge yet to the PRI's political hegemony. The PRI candidate was Carlos Salinas de Gortari, a nimble-minded public administrator who, like many Mexican politicians of his generation, had gone to university abroad, in his case to Harvard. Salinas's opponents were formidable: Cuauhtémoc Cárdenas, a PRI luminary turned dissident (and son of former president Lázaro Cárdenas) who ran at the head of the left-wing *Frente Democrático Nacional* coalition, and the Sinaloa PAN leader Manuel Clouthier. When initial election night returns from around the capital showed Cárdenas running well ahead, a mysterious "computer crash" of the machines tabulating the votes was announced by the government, after which Salinas was declared the victor. Years later, Miguel de la Madrid, who had been president at the time, would admit what many had suspected all along, that the computer crash was a lie cooked up by the PRI and that Salinas had been fraudulently elected. It was a testimony to just how deeply the PRI was distrusted that, when Manuel Clouthier died in a mysterious car accident a little over a year later, many saw the hand of the Salinas government in his death.

Their concerns were not without basis in fact. The bent PJF commander Guillermo González Calderóni would later claim that, four days before the vote, García Ábrego had ordered the murders of Cuauhtémoc Cárdenas's advisers Francisco Xavier Ovando and Román Gil Heraldez. The US government was happy to ignore all of this, given Salinas's lively personality and decidedly warm words toward the United States. The Americans did this even as, after years of propping him up, they ousted Panamanian dictator Manuel Noriega from power when his involvement in the drug trade allegedly became too obvious even for the dark hand of America's intelligence services to cover up any longer, though they had been content to tolerate such activity in the past.

To say that US policy toward drug trafficking during this period was schizophrenic—demanding scorched-earth eradication policies while actively collaborating with known traffickers to achieve political goals— would be an understatement.

In December 1988, a report by a US Senate subcommittee chaired by then–Massachusetts senator (and future Democratic Party presidential candidate and secretary of state) John Kerry concluded that senior officials in the Reagan administration, including National Security Council employee Oliver North, had turned a blind eye to drug trafficking by Contra rebels working to violently overthrow the leftist Sandinista government in Nicaragua. North and his colleagues even went so far as to leak information to traffickers about DEA operations that put agents' lives at risk.

As the PRI were anointing their new leader, however, the reputation of Matamoros as a louche respite for day-tripping and spring-breaking gringos came crashing to the ground. In March 1989, a college student from the University of Texas at Austin named Mark J. Kilroy disappeared near the bridge connecting Brownsville and Matamoros. A month later, officials discovered Kilroy's body, along with those of eleven other murder victims, at a ranch in the Tamaulipas countryside after having found "a bloodstained altar with clothing and pictures of small children in a vacant house" in Matamoros. Kilroy had been abducted and sacrificed by a drug-gang-turned-cult led by Miami-born Cuban-American Adolfo de Jesús Constanzo. The gang had killed Kilroy and others "for protection" one member said. De Jesús had been aided by a Matamoros native and former honor student at Texas Southmost College, Sara María Aldrete Villareal, described as the "witch" of the organization.

Police later concluded that the cult killed as many as forty people. De Jesús was eventually slain during a police standoff in Mexico City, while Aldrete Villareal was arrested, convicted of several of the crimes on the ranch, and imprisoned. Though one of the culprits was not even Mexican, the bizarre, bloody nature of the crime led many to avoid Matamoros, and stick to the less lethal delights of South Padre Island on the Texas side of the border.

It was a dark blot on the robust transformation the region had been undergoing since the mid-1980s, when the north of Mexico had begun asserting its independence from the vortex of power in the nation's capital. The northern city of Monterrey, in the state of Nuevo León, boasted a roaring manufacturing sector and one of the most important universities in the country, the *Instituto Tecnológico y de Estudios Superiores de Monterrey* commonly referred to simply as *Tec de Monterrey* or just Tec. Large-scale protests had broken out in Ciudad Juárez and other parts of the country against the PRI's rule, but were especially prevalent in the North. In Matamoros, Juan Guerra was aging. A 1984 stroke had left him mostly wheelchair-bound, partially paralyzed and without the full use of his left hand.

Mexico was changing, and organized crime in Mexico would change along with it.

CHAPTER TWO

The Rise of the Gulf Cartel

It is believed that Juan Guerra handed over daily running of the organization to Juan García Ábrego by 1987. In January of that year, Tomás Morlet Borquez, a former federal policeman turned drug trafficker, was killed along with Saúl Hernández at the Piedras Negras. Morlet had previously been arrested—and then released—in connection with the kidnapping and murder of DEA agent Enrique "Kiki" Camarena. To kill Morlet during a sit-down in Matamoros was indicative of García's confrontational business style going forward.

While García Ábrego was creating the Gulf Cartel in Mexico, Colombia—the location of the main partners of Mexico's burgeoning drug organizations—was convulsing with violence between traffickers and the state.

By the early 1980s, a loose confederation of drug traffickers in Colombia's second largest city, Medellín, had coalesced into what would eventually become known as the Medellín Cartel, including such traffickers as Pablo Escobar, Carlos Lehder, Gonzalo Rodríguez Gacha, and members of the Ochoa family. The traffickers' capacity for violence was seemingly limitless, none more so than Escobar, who married narco wealth with political pretensions and even managed to get himself elected as an alternate representative to Colombia's congress in 1982 (he was driven out when his drug connections became well known). Terrified of being extradited to the United States to face drug-trafficking charges, Escobar instead declared war on the Colombian state as the head of *Los Extraditables,* a group of drug traffickers whose slogan was "Better a grave in Colombia than a prison cell in the United States."

In April 1984, Escobar masterminded the murder of Colombia's minister of justice, Rodrigo Lara Bonilla. In November 1985, members of the M-19 guerrillas working in tandem with Escobar stormed Colombia's Palacio de Justicia in Bogotá, holding the nation's Supreme Court hostage in a raid that, along with the heavy-handed response of security forces, would leave at least 120 people dead, including half of the Supreme Court. The leading contender for the nation's presidency in 1989, the Liberal Party's Luis Carlos Galán, was gunned down in the southern Bogotá working-class district of Soacha—supposedly on Escobar's orders. Then, in November 1989, Escobar blew up Avianca Airlines Flight 203 as it took off from Bogotá en route to Cali, killing more than one hundred people.

With such a head-on assault on the very pillars of the Colombian state, Escobar could not hope to last. García Ábrego demonstrated great forethought in forming an alliance between his Matamoros criminal organization and the Cali Cartel, based in the tropical Colombian city of the same name. As Escobar engaged in a ruthless war of attrition with the Colombian government, the Cali Crtel assumed ever greater importance in facilitating the delivery of cocaine from South America to the United States. It is now widely assumed that the Cali Cartel was also among the chief funders of *Los Pepes,* a group whose name was derived from the phrase *Perseguidos por Pablo Escobar* (People persecuted by Pablo Escobar). The group was made up of former Escobar associates working in collusion with elements of the Colombian security forces, and their attacks against Escobar eventually resulted in the latter's death in a hail of bullets on a Medellín rooftop in December 1993. The Cali Cartel was run in a less spectacularly violent fashion by the brothers Gilberto Rodríguez Orejuela and Miguel Rodríguez Orejuela, and their partner José Santacruz Londoño.

It was the Cali Cartel that García Ábrego decided to do business with, and by 1989 his criminal enterprise was believed to be moving somewhere in the neighborhood of forty tons of cocaine into the United States annually. He had purchased large ranches south of Matamoros where planes from Colombia loaded with cocaine could land, and from where the cocaine could be smuggled across the border from Matamoros to Brownsville. From there it would go onward to Houston and then to distribution hubs in Los Angeles and New York. South of the border, meanwhile, the Gulf Cartel's domain stretched from the Tamaulipas border towns of Matamoros, Reynosa, and Nuevo Laredo down to the state capital of Ciudad Victoria and the port of Tampico.

Along with the rise of the power of Mexico's drug-trafficking organizations and the attendant spread of organized crime, the border, always a place where the hand of the law had settled lightly, was becoming more deadly. In 1988, Héctor Félix Miranda, a journalist with Tijuana's *Zeta* magazine who specialized in reporting corruption and drug trafficking, was murdered, allegedly by Victoriano Medina Moreno, a security guard employed by Jorge Hank Rhon, the son of a former mayor of Mexico City. The younger Rhon had grown fabulously wealthy through a chain of offtrack betting parlors and, some charged, links to the drug trade. Félix had frequently mocked him as "The Abominable Snowman" because of his supposed fondness for cocaine. The journalist had also once written that Rhon had laundered money at his Agua Caliente Racetrack. Despite the strenuous efforts of Félix's partner at *Zeta,* Jesús Blancornelas, Rhon was never charged in connection with the crime. In 1989, Mexico created the *Centro de Investigación y Seguridad Nacional* (CISEN) under the command of the Interior Ministry, folding into its ranks the notoriously brutal (and compromised by drug trafficking) DFS.

Despite his boldness, however, Juan García Ábrego was not alone in his ambition.

The majority of Mexico's drug cartels can trace their roots back to the rough-hewn countryside of the state of Sinaloa, its hills dotted with marijuana and poppy fields. The godfather of large-scale Mexican drug trafficking was arguably Miguel Ángel Félix Gallardo, himself a Sinaloa native who—along with three partners—ran the organization that would become known as the Guadalajara Cartel until the fallout from the murder of DEA agent Enrique "Kiki" Camarena resulted in the arrest and imprisonment of Rafael Caro Quintero (jailed in April 1985), Ernesto "Don Neto" Fonseca Carrillo (also jailed in April 1985), and Juan José "El Azul" Esparragoza Moreno (jailed in 1986). Gallardo himself was arrested in 1989, but continued coordinating drug trafficking until he was transferred to the *Centro Federal de Readaptación Social Número 1*, known as *Altiplano*, in Mexico State in the 1990s.

After Félix Gallardo's arrest in 1989, the Guadalajara Cartel split apart, with factions in his native state of Sinaloa, in Tijuana, and in Ciudad Juárez all forming their own criminal organizations. In Tijuana, Félix Gallardo's nephews, the Arellano Félix brothers Eduardo Arellano Félix (thought by law enforcement to be the savviest of the lot), Ramón Arellano Félix (a violent, hulking bodybuilder), and Francisco Rafael Arellano Félix (the oldest of the brothers) formed their own cartel, which became known as the Tijuana Cartel. They were aided by Armando Martinez-Duarte, a Baja California police official who leaked information about law enforcement moves to target the cartel and helped to place corrupt individuals in positions of power within the police force.

The faction based in Sinaloa would become known as the Sinaloa Cartel and would be led by former Gallardo deputy Joaquín Guzmán Loera, known as *El Chapo* or "Shorty" because of his diminutive stature, and Héctor Luis "El Güero" Palma Salazar, who had recently emerged after an eight-year stint in prison. To show their displeasure at what they believed to be an attempt to usurp their rightful place at the top of a family drug empire, the Arellano Félix gang colluded with a Venezuelan drug trafficker, Rafael Clavel, to seduce Palma's wife, who was then murdered in San Francisco and a cooler containing her head delivered to Palma's house. Clavel also hurled Mr. Palma's two small children off a bridge in Venezuela before himself being murdered in a Venezuela prison.

Meanwhile, in Ciudad Juárez, just across the Rio Grande from El Paso, Texas, a drug smuggling enterprise that had been largely created by a corrupt CISEN commander named Rafael Aguilar Guajardo was taken over by Ernesto Fonseca Carrillo's nephew, Amado Carrillo Fuentes, when the latter arranged Aguilar's 1993 murder (much as he had betrayed Pablo Acosta nearly a decade earlier). A native of the Sinaloan city of Guamúchil, Carrillo Fuentes was soon moving so much cocaine into Mexico in the hollowed-out bodies of cargo jets that he earned the nickname *El Señor de Los Cielos* (Lord of the Skies). Working with Carrillo Fuentes were his brother, Rodolfo Carrillo Fuentes, the Sinaloa-born trafficker Juan José "El Azul" Esparragoza Moreno (recently released from prison), and a mysterious, Durango-born trafficker named Ignacio Coronel Villarreal, aka Nacho Coronel. Mario Arturo Acosta Chaparro, the army general so lethal during Mexico's war against leftist rebels and others in the 1970s, would at one point be arrested for protecting the cartel (he would be released after seven years when his conviction was overturned).

After the murder of Héctor Palma's family, a full-scale war erupted between the Sinaloa and Tijuana cartels, a struggle that Juan García Ábrego no doubt watched with glee from Matamoros. To buttress their forces, the Arellano Félix brothers increasingly employed gang members from Logan Heights, a traditionally Mexican-American neighborhood southeast of downtown San Diego, California. The leader of this posse of guns-for-hire from north of the border was David "Popeye" Barron Corona, a few years older than the rest and with a viciousness honed by several stints in prison. It was a typical example of cross-border criminal cooperation that would give lie to the oft-repeated (and thoroughly meaningless) charge that the United States was being "invaded" by Mexican criminals. Crime, as any 1920s bootlegger could have told US politicians decades earlier, respected no borders.

In November 1992, Sinaloa Cartel gunmen—some said there were at least forty—tried to kill the Arellano Félix brothers at a Puerto Vallarta disco and failed, though six people perished in the ensuing shootout. To pay the favor back, Tijuana Cartel gunmen allegedly tried to ambush Chapo Guzmán at the Guadalajara airport, an attack that killed Guadalajara's Catholic cardinal, Juan Jesús Posadas Ocampo. No definitive explanation has ever been offered for how the Tijuana hitmen, Chapo, and the cardinal all ended up at the same airport, at the same time, on the same day. The cardinal bore not even the slightest resemblance to the drug lord, but had served as bishop in Tijuana and had close ties to the Arellano Félix family. The Logan Heights boys scattered, some captured and tortured by Mexican authorities, some arrested in the United States, others vanished in the wind. Their leader, David Barron, as it happened, would later die in the November 1997 crossfire of a failed attempt to kill the publisher of *Zeta* magazine, Jesús Blancornelas, in Tijuana. The picture of Barron's body slumped against a low wall, his gun still in his hand and a lake of blood issuing from his head, would become one of the iconic images of the Mexican drug war. Two months later, Chapo Guzmán would be arrested in Guatemala and deported back to Mexico. He would be convicted of drug trafficking and other offenses, and eventually held in *Puente Grande* maximum-security prison in Jalisco. Héctor Luis "El Güero" Palma Salazar would, for a time, elude capture.

In the United States, the late 1980s and early 1990s brought an explosion of violence largely due to the drug trade centered on crack cocaine, a cheap, smokable form of the powdered substance. In New York City alone in 1990, 2,245 people were killed, a terrifying escalation of 17.8 percent from 1989 that the city's police commissioner attributed directly to the combination of firearms and the drug trade. That same year in Philadelphia, there were 525 people slain, a record up to that time. For its part, Chicago, also an active drug distribution hub, saw a record 849 murders during 1990.

In Mexico, a reported May 1991 Gulf Cartel plot to kill imprisoned Colombian drug-trafficking rival Oliverio Chávez Araújo led to an eruption of violence at the Cereso prison in Matamoros that killed eighteen people and became a two-week siege. When the siege ended, it was revealed that both García Ábrego and Chávez Araújo had been showering prison officials with gifts and bribes for some time. It was rumored, however, that a García Ábrego deputy, Tomás "Gringo" Sanchez González, had overstepped his bounds by ordering the plot into action, and that when word reached García Ábrego, Sanchez González paid for his boldness with his life. The Americans had picked up on García Ábrego by now, after an FBI raid on a Gulf Cartel–linked farm in Harlingen, Texas, near Brownsville, turned up cocaine worth more than $100 million—the second largest drug seizure in US history at that time.

García Ábrego would be the subject of a Dallas grand jury's secret indictment in February 1990 that charged both him and his cousin Francisco Pérez with drug trafficking. Ignorant of the threat he faced and virtually under the noses of federal officials, García Ábrego passed most of 1990 in McAllen, Texas, and at a rented house in the Chicago suburbs, taking a break from the heat of running his drug empire in Mexico. Though the Matamoros criminal organization was now indisputably in the hands of García Ábrego, its leader had moved his base of operations to Monterrey in 1989; for the next five years he would change his location around the city every few weeks and sometimes every few days.

As García Ábrego was busy running the cartel, Juan Guerra was often living at a home he owned in Brownsville, or at his ranch, *El Tlahuachal*. The now-elderly Guerra even served a few weeks in jail on tax evasion charges. Around 1992, Hugo Baldomero Medina Garza, aka *El Señor de los Trailers* ("Lord of the Trailers"), known for his skill at moving contraband, began working with the cartel. By 1993, García Ábrego was the subject of an unsealed indictment in Houston for drug trafficking, money laundering, bribery of an undercover FBI agent named Claude de la O, and ordering "acts of violence including the murders of numerous individuals."

But the drug game was hardly the only game in town in northern Mexico. After several years of negotiations, President Salinas, US president George H. W. Bush, and Canadian prime minister Brian Mulroney met in San Antonio, Texas, to sign the North American Free Trade Agreement (NAFTA) in December 1992. A year later, the treaty was ratified by the US Congress. The pact made it more attractive for US firms to shift jobs to Mexico—not less—and that's just what they did. US corporate investment in manufacturing facilities in Mexico rose from $1 billion to $2.5 billion in NAFTA's first year. The United States also slashed tariffs on many Mexican manufactured goods, especially in the textiles and apparel industries, while Mexico cut tariffs on agricultural and livestock products and "virtually all manufactured goods" from the United States.

It was a moment of glory for Salinas who, around this time, attended an elegant dinner at the Mexico City home of former minister of finance Antonio Ortiz Mena for some of the richest men in Mexico, including Televisa boss Emilio "El Tigre" Azcárraga Milmo, telecommunications billionaire Carlos Slim, and the banking magnate Roberto Hernández Ramírez. At the dinner, the government demanded $25 million from each of those in attendance "to save the PRI." Azcárraga went so far as to suggest that it should be $50 million each. In the end, the men, living in a nation where more than half the citizens lived below the poverty line, agreed to raise $750 million, not for the country, but for the PRI.

But despite the intrigue in Mexico City, and despite the fact that, in 1993, the PRI's Manuel Cavazos Lerma became governor of Tamaulipas, stubbornly retaining the state for the party's apparatus, northern Mexico, it seemed, was the promised land that, along with the long-hoped-for opening in the political process, would help drag Mexico from a corrupt, feudal past into a pluralistic, bountiful present. There were problems along the border to be sure—drug trafficking and organized crime—but these had always been there. As politicians and columnists chimed in supporting NAFTA's supposed great benefits to the Mexican economy, what could go wrong?

After the passage of NAFTA, the Mexican *maquiladora*, as low-cost manufacturing plants were called, sector boomed, attracting to industrial centers such as Reynosa and Nuevo Laredo immigrants not only from elsewhere in Mexico's northern states such as Tamaulipas and Nuevo León but also from poverty-stricken southern states such as Oaxaca and Guerrero. Throughout much of the 1990s, the maquiladora industry accounted for more than half of the industrial activity in Tamaulipas. In 1993, the *Grupo Reforma*, a Monterrey-based media company that had been publishing the highly successful *El Norte* daily newspaper in their native city since 1972, launched Reforma, a Mexico City–based venture that, quite famously, chose to separate its editorial department from its commercial division, a unique move in Mexico at the time.

The year 1994, however, was an extraordinarily chaotic one for Mexico. On New Year's Day, a mostly indigenous rebel group, the *Ejército Zapatista de Liberación Nacional* (EZLN), seized several towns in the southern state of Chiapas, and their nonindigenous spokesman, Subcomandante Marcos, became something of a global media phenomenon. The government would later claim that Marcos was in fact a Tamaulipas native named Rafael Sebastián Guillén Vicente, the son of a furniture store owner from Tampico who had worked as a Mexico City philosophy professor before joining the revolutionary left. Stunningly, Marcos's sister, Mercedes del Carmen Guillén Vicente, was even a PRI activist who had held several high-ranking party positions in the state throughout the 1980s and at the time was a PRI deputy for the state congress there. A relatively new military body, less than a decade old, the *Grupo Aeromóvil de Fuerzas Especiales* (GAFE), some of whom had benefited from US training, was deployed against the Zapatistas, though the exact actions they undertook while in Chiapas remain something of a mystery.

Following the Zapatista uprising, the PRI's presidential candidate, Luis Donaldo Colosio, was gunned down at a campaign event in a poor neighborhood in Tijuana, allegedly by a lone, deranged gunmen, an explanation many Mexicans to this day don't believe. The credibility of the explanation eroded further when Eduardo Valle, a gadfly journalist known as *El Búho* (The Owl), then serving as an adviser to Attorney General Jorge Carpizo, resigned his position in May 1994 saying that the Gulf Cartel were in fact behind the killing and that they had so infiltrated the PRI and the government that justice for Colosio was impossible to achieve.

"I recognize that I am not capable of apprehending the *public* head of the Gulf Cartel," Valle stated pointedly in his resignation letter. "I did all I could with the instruments at my disposal. I failed."

Many analysts would later argue that, rather than with the Zapatista uprising, the "old" Mexico of the PRI's iron-clad control came to an end the way it was born, with blood, on the streets of Tijuana that day.

Only six months after Colosio's slaying, the PRI's secretary general and former brother-in-law of Carlos Salinas, José Francisco Ruiz Massieu—the former Guerrero governor who had spoken of the PRI's "patriotic fraud" but had recently become convinced that the old system must change—was gunned down in Mexico City on September 28. Ruiz Massieu's alleged assassin, Daniel Aguilar Treviño, was from a poor family in the small pueblo of Corralejo in Tamaulipas's San Fernando Valley. He had worked in California for a time, his mother said. In a seventeen-page letter he would later send to the *Multivision* television station, Aguilar would claim that Ruiz Massieu was killed by "the Salinas machine" because he "knew the order to assassinate Colosio was forged in [the presidential headquarters at] *Los Pinos*," and that the government had "delegated" the killing to their *éminence grise*, José María Córdoba Montoya.

Aguilar also claimed that government agents had kidnapped his family to ensure his silence. A PRI congressman from Tamaulipas, Manuel

Muñoz Rocha, who had been linked in the press with the fugitive police-man Guillermo González Calderóni, was implicated in the case and later went into hiding, but not before placing a phone call to the Chamber of Deputies and sending a letter to the attorney general in which he accused a jailed PRI official from Guerrero, Abraham Rubio Canales, of involve-ment in the crime. Shortly thereafter, public communication from Muñoz Rocha ceased and he was never seen again. It was believed that bones found at a ranch might have belonged to the fugitive legislator, but Mex-ico's attorney general later said DNA tests had been inconclusive because the remains had been "polluted."

Into the vacuum left by Colosio's death stepped (or was pushed) Salinas's former secretary of education and Colosio's campaign manager, Ernesto Zedillo. Shattered by Colosio's assassination and by no means a political natural, Zedillo nevertheless ran in the 1994 elections and won against Cuauhtémoc Cárdenas of the leftist *Partido de la Revolu-ción Democrática* (PRD) and Diego Fernández de Cevallos of the PAN. Zedillo took office in December of that year, helped greatly by Televisa coverage that virtually acted as one long pro-Zedillo campaign adver-tisement. A few months later, Carlos Salinas's brother, Raúl Salinas de Gortari, was convicted of masterminding the Ruiz Massieu assassination, a conviction that was later overturned. After launching a bizarre hunger strike to protest his brother's arrest, Salinas fled abroad into exile, where he remained for several years.

To make the situation in the country seem even more chaotic, between October and mid-December 1994, Mexico's foreign reserves had plum-meted from $17 billion to $6 billion, leading to a 50 percent collapse of the Mexican peso against the dollar.

Throughout the next year, hard times buffeted Mexico's narco oligarchy as well.

In June 1995, the Sinaloa Cartel's Héctor Luis "El Güero" Palma Salazar was arrested when his private plane crashed in Sonora, after which he was taken to a safe house where he was protected by federal police but was arrested when the army got word and stormed the build-ing a short time later. In Colombia, the Cali Cartel's Gilberto Rodríguez

Orejuela and Miguel Rodríguez Orejuela were both arrested. Both men were subsequently extradited to the United States where they were sentenced to decades-long prison sentences for conspiring to import cocaine. José Santacruz Londoño was also arrested that summer, but escaped six months later and was subsequently slain by police in Medellín in March 1996.

In Mexico itself, the PRI showed its old, sanguinary face when at least seventeen peasants were massacred in Guerrero by federal police officers in an atrocity that many human rights activists blamed on the state's PRI governor, Rubén Figueroa Alcocer. A government prosecutor later claimed the slaying had been "an accident." In the United States, having Democrat Bill Clinton in the White House did not lead to much change in America's draconian approach to drug policy. In 1980, before Ronald Reagan took office, drug convictions accounted for fifteen inmates per one hundred thousand adults. Roughly four years into Clinton's presidency, in 1996, that figure had grown nearly tenfold to 148 out of one hundred thousand. This despite the fact that Clinton had admitted smoking marijuana himself while a student at Oxford University in the United Kingdom.

The Ruiz Massieu assassination had thrown unwanted attention on the criminal monarchy ruling Tamaulipas. The FBI put García Ábrego on its list of ten most wanted fugitives, a first for a drug lord, and offered a $2 million reward for information leading to his capture. Only ten months later, on the night of January 4, 1996, at a ranch in the town of Villa Juárez in Nuevo León, García Ábrego was arrested by more than a dozen federal police officers, whose ranks he had once lavished such vast sums of money on. The following day, Juan García Ábrego, the once-mighty lord of Tamaulipas, was extradited to the United States, "stuffed into an airplane like a cat into a bag" in the words of the Mexican journalist Alma Guillermoprieto.

But some in Mexico had paused to wonder if, even out of the country, the don's reach had truly been extinguished. In August 1996, months after García Ábrego began enjoying the hospitality of US authorities, the Mexican journalist Yolanda Figueroa, a contributor to the magazine *Viva*, had published *El Capo Del Golfo: Vida Y Captura De Juan García Ábrego*, her account of the recently extradited drug lord's rise and fall. The book was launched with great fanfare in Mexico City's Coyoacán neighborhood, but Figueroa's somewhat complicated personal life made her position as a chronicler of one of Mexico's most powerful drug cartels even more fraught. Her husband, Fernando Balderas, was an adviser to the *Policía Judicial* in the capital and, depending on whom one spoke to, either a principled rebel or an enthusiastic participant in the basest sort of corruption. Nevertheless, the residents of the upscale Jardines del Pedregal neighborhood of Mexico City were shocked when, just before Christmas, both Figueroa and Balderas were found beaten to death in their home along with their three children, ages eighteen, nine, and eight.

Mexico City investigators later claimed that the murders were unrelated to either Figueroa's reporting or Balderas's time with the police, but were rather the result of a homicidal plot by the family's maids and drivers after Balderas had turned two female servants into "sexual slaves." As with many politically sensitive investigations in Mexico, there was a sense that the full truth was not being revealed and might in fact never be.

By the time one journalist caught up with Juan Guerra in the Piedras Negras Restaurant in 1996, after the arrest of Juan García Ábrego, he denied being involved in organized crime. Guerra acidly told the curious reporter that "I don't smoke, I don't drink and I don't sing," a declaration made while seated under a cage of chirping canaries. Later, however, the Mexican news magazine *Proceso* quoted him as saying that García Ábrego had been a "hard head . . . men like him end up in jail or in the cemetery." After García Ábrego's arrest and extradition to the United States, Guerra, who would die peacefully in 2001, had supposedly joked, with his typical acid humor, that it must have been one of the provisions of NAFTA.

CHAPTER THREE

Enter Los Zetas

THE FRIEND KILLER

As one family saw its fortunes turn sour, another family saw them rise to dizzying heights. Following García Ábrego's capture and extradition, the Gulf Cartel went through a process of reorganization common to many multinational businesses in crisis. First García Ábrego's brother, Humberto García Ábrego, tried to take the reins of the organization, and failed. Then a pair of drug traffickers, Óscar Malherbe De León and Raúl Valladares del Ángel, attempted to climb to the top but were soon arrested, as was another failed leader, Hugo Baldomero Medina Garza. The trafficker Sergio Gómez, alias *El Checo*, attempted to seize control, but was assassinated in Valle Hermoso, Tamaulipas in April 1996.

Finally, the running of the organization would fall to two friends, both sons of Tamaulipas with extensive connections to law enforcement: Salvador "El Chava" Gómez Herrera and Osiel Cárdenas Guillén. El Chava Gómez was a car thief and trafficker who had been active around Tamaulipas for a number of years. His partner, however, would prove himself to be a unique and ambitious figure in the history of Mexican organized crime.

Osiel Cárdenas had been born in Matamoros in 1967 to a somewhat complicated family life. The man listed as his father on his birth certificate, Enrique Cárdenas, was apparently not his biological father but rather an uncle, a source of great consternation to a young boy who turned into a highly rebellious youth in a poor family trying desperately to make its way out of poverty and into the middle class. Cárdenas was working as a waiter and an auto mechanic in Matamoros by his early twenties, and later had risen through the ranks of the PJF before leaving to head the organization Juan Guerra had founded. It is believed that, in his dotage, the former leader favored Cárdenas as the Gulf Cartel's head.

Cárdenas would not run his empire by himself. He would have help. There was his brother, Antonio Ezequiel Cárdenas Guillén, a man whose violent personality earned him the nickname Tony Tormenta (Tony the Storm), and whom one individual familiar with his quirks described to me as "quite a few bricks short of a load." Another brother, Homero "El Majadero" Cárdenas Guillén, worked to smuggle cocaine across the Rio Grande to Brownsville and from there to the hubs of Houston and Atlanta. Yet another Cárdenas brother, Mario, had been arrested in 1995 and would remain in prison for the next eleven years, but, until a stint in maximum security, would still help coordinate aspects of the family's criminal empire from behind bars.

Cárdenas's nephew, Rafael "El Junior" Cárdenas Vela, would also be taken into the fold. Jorge Eduardo Costilla Sánchez, a stocky, mustachioed Matamoros municipal police officer, better known as El Coss, who had been born in the city as the son of a local school principal, would defect to the cartel and rise rapidly within its ranks. Matamoros native Mario Armando "El Pelón" (Baldy) Ramírez Treviño, aka X-20, a former judicial police officer, was another deputy, as was Víctor Manuel "El Meme Loco" (Crazy Meme) Vázquez Mireles. Orders went out from Osiel Cárdenas to the press in Tamaulipas that reporters were "never to speak of me nor of the cartel." Those who ignored these instructions did so at their peril.

Around the same time as the ascent of Gómez and Cárdenas in the Gulf Cartel, other cartels were forming around Mexico to challenge the traditional order of things. La Familia Michoacána (The Michoacán Family, often referred to simply as La Familia) was formed by Nazario Moreno González aka El Más Loco (The Craziest One), who had been born in the poor, rural Tierra Caliente of Michoacán and had trafficked drugs in California and Texas while living illegally in the United States. Moreno was assisted in the formation of the cartel by Servando "La Tuta" Gómez Martínez, a former schoolteacher in Michoacán. Another Michoacán cartel, the *Cártel de los Valencia* (also known as *El Cártel del Milenio* or Milenio Cartel), was founded in the late 1990s by Armando

Valencia Cornelio and several of his cousins after splitting off from the Sinaloa Cartel.

Ernesto Zedillo appointed the PAN politician Francisco Molina Ruiz to head the *Instituto Nacional para el Combate a las Drogas* (INCD), a position at which the latter lasted for only eight months. To replace him, in late 1996, Zedillo announced that he was appointing José de Jesús Gutiérrez Rebollo, a Mexican army general—a selection that was praised by, among others, Clinton administration drug czar General Barry R. McCaffrey. Ignoring the rot at the heart of the state police forces around Mexico, Zedillo would create a new law enforcement body at the national level, the *Policía Federal Preventiva* (PFP), whose numbers would soon grow to around eleven thousand. They were tasked with overseeing security in federal areas such as highways, ports, and the like, with around 10 percent of the force being drawn from the CISEN. The administration would also fire over seven hundred of the PJF's roughly forty-four hundred officers, replacing them with more than one thousand military personnel.

The desire to tamp down on violence in Mexico had been helped somewhat two years earlier by the passage in the United States—a favorite one-stop gun shop for Mexican cartels—of the Violent Crime Control and Law Enforcement Act of 1994, and specifically a subsection known as the Assault Weapons Ban, which prohibited the manufacture for civilian use of certain semiautomatic firearms in the United States. The ban encompassed such weapons as variants of the AK-47 (popularly called a *cuerno de chivo*, "goat's horn," among the narcos), Uzi, Colt AR-15, and Street Sweeper, among others, and also banned large-capacity magazines capable of holding more than ten rounds. In the United States itself, the ban led to a 66 percent drop in traced assault weapons used in the commission of crimes.

The fanfare for Zedillo's new drug czar proved to be short-lived, however, and in February 1997, José de Jesús Gutiérrez Rebollo was arrested and charged with being on the payroll of Amado Carrillo Fuentes, the head of the Juárez Cartel. He was subsequently convicted and sentenced to a decades-long prison term. It had become obvious that Mexico's war on the cartels would require more than easy optics.

In Matamoros, Osiel Cárdenas was girding his organization for war against the Sinaloa Cartel, and in doing so he would make a fateful decision that would have an impact on organized crime and the lives of ordinary Mexicans for years to come.

In early 1997, Cárdenas reached out to Arturo Guzmán Decena, a GAFE soldier who had been trained in the use of explosives, counterespionage, and guerrilla warfare. He had a tempting offer for him: Leave the poorly paid military and come work for the Gulf Cartel, where the possibilities for power and enrichment were virtually limitless.

Along with Guzmán Decena would eventually come around thirty other military personnel, forming what would become known as Los Zetas (The Z's), after a Mexican military radio code for high-ranking officers. These included his two chief deputies, Rogelio González Pizaña, known as *El Kelín* or Z-2, and Heriberto Lazcano Lazcano, known as *El Verdugo* (The Executioner) or Z-3, who hailed from a poor family in the town of Apan in Hidalgo State. There was also Jesús Enrique Rejón Aguilar, known as *El Mamito* or Z-7, who would later be instrumental in recruiting members of *Los Kabiles*, the special operations force of Guatemala's army trained in jungle warfare and counterinsurgency tactics, into Los Zetas. Others included Galdino Mellado Cruz (El Mellado or Z-9), Gustavo González Castro (*El Erótico* or The Erotic One, a name whose bizarre provenance I have never been able to discern), Efraín Teodoro Torres (Z-14), Raúl Lucio Hernández Lechuga (*El Lucky* or Z-16), and Jaime González Durán (*El Hummer*), who would go on to become one of Osiel Cárdenas's bodyguards. There was also Daniel Pérez Rojas (*El Cachetes* or Cheeks) who would later help kill Juancho León in Guatemala, Miguel Ángel Soto Parra (*El Parra* or *El Chocotorro*), Mateo Díaz López (*Comandante Mateo*), and Flavio Méndez Santiago (*El Amarillo*).

Eventually a small-time smuggler and gang member named Miguel Ángel Treviño Morales (no relation to the Gulf Cartel's Mario Armando "El Pelón" Ramírez Treviño), who had been born in Nuevo Laredo but grew up largely in Laredo and Dallas, would also join the group, going first by the code name L-40 and then by Z-40. At 5'8" and with a resume that included stints as a gardener and a car washer, Treviño perhaps at first seemed like an odd choice to join a group of professional soldiers, but he had been moving marijuana into the United States since the early 1990s, and his contacts proved useful in helping Los Zetas dominate Nuevo Laredo. Something about his cindery near-black eyes also suggested a ferocity that lay just beneath the surface. One of Treviño's brothers, Omar Treviño Morales, would also join Los Zetas, becoming Z-42. Another brother, José Treviño Morales, remained in the United States and over time would launder tens of millions of dollars of the organization's drug profits through horse racing endeavors in Texas and Oklahoma. A friend of Z-40, another small-time criminal from Nuevo Laredo named Iván Velázquez Caballero (aka *El Talibán* or Z-50), would also come on board.

The Gulf Cartel enforcement cells would be refined even further with names linked to their locales, *Los Metros* for those in Matamoros, *Los Rojos* for those in Reynosa, *Los Lobos* for those in Nuevo Laredo, and so on. Over time, the geographic significance of the names would be lost but the names themselves would stick. Los Zetas would set up highly sophisticated training camps for new recruits such as the Treviño Morales brothers in several areas of Tamaulipas and, it is believed, at least one in Texas. Perhaps sensing a useful bludgeon against the Sinaloa Cartel right next door, Cárdenas also allowed Los Zetas to train La Familia during their early years as a cartel. As the Gulf Cartel was growing in size and ferocity and Los Zetas were making the first appearance on the scene, the governor of Tamaulipas was the PRI's Manuel Cavazos Lerma, an economist who had been in office since 1993 and would serve until 1999.

So Osiel Cárdenas would have his army in Los Zetas, but to intentionally misquote the character of Alfred the butler from the Batman movies, in his greed he turned to a group of men that he didn't fully understand. Despite what had seemed like years of intense violence preceding them, Los Zetas would turn out to be far more unpredictable, confrontational, and savage than what had come before them. Somewhere, years before, in the pages of *The Labyrinth of Solitude*, Octavio Paz had written that Mexicans are "a ritual people"; so it would prove to be with Los Zetas, a group that, far beyond being ruthless drug traffickers, would rapidly descend into something akin to a murder cult—their deeds, both among themselves and toward their enemies, carried a ritualistic element largely absent from the drug war before.

As Los Zetas entered the scene at the behest of Osiel Cárdenas, another major figure would exit it, to the Gulf Cartel's benefit. Amado Carrillo Fuentes, the once-dominant Lord of the Skies of the Juárez Cartel, is believed to have died during a plastic surgery procedure in July 1997 at Santa Mónica Hospital in Mexico City. Shortly afterward, Nacho Coronel defected to the Sinaloa Cartel and began to rise quickly in its ranks. Rule of the Juárez Cartel would eventually fall to Carrillo's brother, Vicente Carrillo Fuentes, known as The Viceroy, working with the Sinaloa-born trafficker El Azul. The Juárez Cartel would also eventually fold within its ranks a highly lethal group of *sicarios* (assassins) known as *La Línea* (The Line), who were affiliated with the El Paso–based Barrio Azteca gang.

In the world of politics, the PRI's Tomás Yarrington became governor of Tamaulipas in February 1999. At first blush Yarrington, forty-two years old at the time he took office, seemed very much of the new breed of PRI technocrat. He was a former federal deputy for Tamaulipas and a former mayor of Matamoros with degrees from both the Monterrey Institute of Technology and the University of Southern California. Rick Perry, who would become the longest-serving governor in Texas history after taking over for president-elect George W. Bush the following year, called Yarrington "a strong leader of the people of Tamaulipas, and a partner in our vision for building stronger trade relationships between Mexico and Texas." Yarrington would later give Perry an expensive wooden chest as a gift. However, Yarrington also had an extraordinarily close relationship with organized crime in the state, the full extent of which would become clear in succeeding years.

Despite the PRI's dominance in Tamaulipas, the party's iron grip was beginning to slacken elsewhere. Back in 1989 the PAN's Ernesto Ruffo Appel became the first opposition governor (of Baja California) in the country. PAN candidates soon ran up electoral victories for the northern states of Chihuahua (Francisco Barrio in 1992) and Nuevo León (Fernando de Jesús Canales Clariond in 1997) as well as in western Mexico (Alberto Cárdenas in the Pacific state of Jalisco in 1995) and central Mexico (former Coca-Cola executive and rancher Vicente

Fox in Guanajuato in 1995 and Ignacio Loyola Vera in Querétaro in 1997).

Following Yarrington's assumption of the governorship, in July 1999, El Chava Gómez was murdered, reportedly on the orders of Osiel Cárdenas, by Arturo Guzmán Decena as Cárdenas assumed full control of the Gulf Cartel. The betrayal and murder of his former partner would earn Cárdenas the sobriquet *El Mata Amigos* (The Friend Killer), a name he hated but which would follow him for the rest of his criminal career. With his growing power also came a growing family, as Cárdenas had married Celia Salinas Aguilar, with whom he had three young children. Exactly what the US plan was to deal with the Gulf Cartel was open to debate In October 1998, before FBI agents raided a home in Houston owned by Tony Tormenta, they sat outside and watched as the Gulf Cartel kingpin ambled away. A search of the house later turned up "cash, numerous vehicles, cocaine, marijuana, firearms" and an entire boat, a "1996 Sea Doo Bombardier with expired Florida registration." The FBI's explanation for letting the drug lord go—that they didn't have adequate resources and didn't know much about him or the organization he worked for—strained credulity.

Cárdenas was so sure of his power in Tamaulipas that, in a famous November 1999 incident, he personally confronted DEA agent Joe Du Bois and FBI agent Daniel Fuentes as they drove through Matamoros chatting with a confidential informant who also happened to be a reporter for a local newspaper. Blocking the agents' vehicle, Cárdenas alighted from his car brandishing a gold-plated AK-47 and strapped with a Colt pistol with a gold grip. Backed up by at least a dozen gunmen who included El Coss, Tony Tormenta, and El Meme Loco, Cárdenas demanded the agents hand over the informant. Du Bois later told the *Houston Chronicle* that "I knew what they'd do to me, I'd seen many pictures of the bodies they leave behind. . . . [We] decided if we are going to die, we are going to die here."

After an expletive-laden exchange during which Cárdenas told the agents he "didn't give a damn" who they were and Du Bois telling the drug lord that he was "fixing to make 300,000 enemies" (an exchange during which Fuentes also had a gun in his hand, ready to shoot Cárdenas in the head), the drug trafficker relented, waving the agents away with the warning "You fucking gringos, this is my town, so get the fuck out of here before I kill all of you. Don't ever come back."

The encounter with the agents didn't seem to unduly concern Cárdenas, and the following month, no doubt feeling his power at its apex, like any generous CEO, he threw a lavish New Year's party for his cartel associates, close friends, and family to ring in the new millennium at a posh disco in Cancún.

THE COWBOY

In 2000, Mexico experienced a political earthquake. Vicente Fox, a 6'4" former governor of Guanajuato fond of cowboy hats and boots, defeated the PRI's Francisco Labastida and the ever unlucky Cuauhtémoc Cárdenas of the PRD to assume Mexico's presidency. Fox declared that his government was "going to give the mother of all battles against organized crime in Mexico," a bizarre turn of phrase considering it was first uttered by Iraqi dictator Saddam Hussein before his resounding defeat during the first Gulf War.

Fox created the *Agencia Federal de Investigación* (AFI), a body intended to be modeled on the FBI, and into which was folded the duties of the old, drug-compromised PJF federal police force. Fox also created a *Secretaría de Seguridad Pública* (SSP) to ostensibly supervise the PFP created by the Zedillo government several years before. As always, the exact division of duties between the country's various law enforcement bodies was still murky. This, combined with the difficulty of vetting officers when so much of the law enforcement hierarchy (to say nothing of the body politic) remained corrupted, made the impact of such personnel shuffling negligible in the grand scheme of the country's eroding security situation.

The removal of the PRI as the sole hand on the levers of power in the country caught the narcos somewhat on the back foot. There was no longer a monolithic political force to do business with, and national power was fracturing into different interest groups, as state power had begun to do so long ago. The PAN and the PRD could now exert actual political influence. Though northeastern Mexico for the most part stubbornly remained PRI territory, this was a new and strange world that drug lords didn't entirely comprehend.

In January 2001 after eight years in prison—several of which were allegedly spent living a life of great luxury and privilege—El Chapo Guzmán escaped from the supposedly maximum security Puente Grande prison, allegedly by hiding under dirty clothes in a laundry cart. A number of individuals familiar with organized crime in Mexico, however, have expressed their doubts about such a scenario; some, including the journalist Anabel Hernández, went as far as to suggest that the Fox administration was somehow involved in Guzmán's escape. Suspiciously, the prison's camera surveillance tapes for the night Guzmán escaped were all "erased."

Tasting freedom once more and sliding with relative ease back into his former life as a drug lord, Guzmán oversaw the Sinaloa Cartel as it coalesced around himself and three other individuals: the older Ismael "El Mayo" Zambada García and the former Juárez Cartel members Ignacio "Nacho" Coronel Villarreal and Juan José "El Azul" Esparragoza Moreno, the latter known for his collaborative or "peace-making" approach to the drug business, often counseling conciliation over war.

It was during 2001, in the middle of the governorship of the PRI's Manuel Ángel Núñez Soto in Hidalgo, that Osiel Cárdenas allegedly ordered Heriberto Lazcano to expand and deepen the Gulf Cartel's presence in other states throughout Mexico, including, in particular, Hidalgo itself, of which Lazcano himself was a native. Protected witnesses would subsequently describe how Los Zetas expanded throughout each of the state's eighty-four municipalities while "under the protection of police, military and state and municipal authorities" to create a "criminal megastructure" that linked Zetas' operations there to those in Veracruz, Puebla, and Mexico State. That same year, Cárdenas sent Efraín "Z-14" Torres to take over "the plaza"—as drug-trafficking hubs were referred to—at Miguel Alemán, where the government had previously simply charged low-level traffickers fees to move loads across into Texas. Torres was eventually sent to take over Veracruz for the cartel as well.

By November 2001, in Tepito, just in time for Day of the Dead, a shrine was inaugurated by adherents of Santa Muerte, solidifying the identification of the neighborhood in many peoples' minds with Santa Muerte and, fairly or unfairly, with the drug trade. In truth, however, Santa Muerte's presence in the area was hardly new, and in his 1961 book about Tepito,

The Children of Sanchez, American anthropologist Oscar Lewis referred to a "Dark Saint" from whom inhabitants of the area solicited favors.

The year 2002 was one of realignment in the world of Mexico's drug cartels. On the government side, the old, corrupt PJF would be integrated into the new AFI. On the side of the narcos, Tijuana Cartel leader Ramón Arellano Félix was killed in a gun battle with police at a roadblock in Mazatlán, Sinaloa. His brother, Benjamín Arellano Félix, was captured only weeks later. (He would eventually be extradited to the United States to face drug-trafficking charges.) Control of the Tijuana Cartel thus fell to another brother, Francisco Javier Arellano Félix.

Los Zetas clearly disturbed and unnerved the Gulf Cartel's rivals, none more so than Chapo Guzmán and his allies. By this point, those allies included four brothers from Sinaloa related to Guzmán by marriage—Arturo Beltrán Leyva (*El Barbas* or The Beard, formerly associated with Amado Carrillo Fuentes), Alfredo Beltrán Leyva (*El Mochomo* or The Desert Ant), Héctor Beltrán Leyva (*El Ingeniero* or The Engineer, a fairly common nickname in narco circles), and Carlos Beltrán Leyva. Guzmán decided that he needed a similarly fearsome force to counteract Los Zetas and to further his own plans for expansion into new plazas, particularly the coveted area of Nuevo Laredo. He decided to unite with his erstwhile partners in the Beltrán-Leyva organization and form a band of assassins that would become known as *Los Negros.* Leading them was a very interesting fellow indeed.

Edgar Valdéz Villarreal grew up in Laredo, Texas, and went to United High School there, where he was a linebacker, and gained the nickname *La Barbie* due to his blond hair. After several scrapes with the law—the most serious of which involved a criminally negligent homicide charge (later dropped) connected to a traffic accident in 1992—Valdéz graduated from high school (a rare feat among the often barely literate narcos). Turning down his father's offer to pay for a college education, he delved more seriously into the marijuana smuggling business, which he had dabbled in before.

With local police closing in after an indictment against him had been handed down, he fled across the Rio Grande to Nuevo Laredo in 1998.

There he became affiliated with a local drug organization, *Los Chachos*, who, along with the rest of the local dealers, eventually lost the city to the Gulf Cartel and Los Zetas. La Barbie then joined with the Beltrán-Leyva organization, and by 2003, he was running Los Negros. Despite having a wife and children in the United States, he would marry the pretty daughter of another Beltrán-Leyva lieutenant, Carlos Montemayor González, known as *El Charro* (The Cowboy).

La Barbie proved himself a smooth operator in many situations. In March 2003, he and Arturo Beltrán Leyva are thought to have traveled to Mexico City carrying the offer of a $1.5 million bribe for AFI head Domingo González Díaz. In return, it is believed that González sent Adolfo Ruiz Ibarra, a close confidante, to Nuevo Laredo to assist the Sinaloa Cartel in its struggle against the Gulf Cartel. The Gulf Cartel sent their response to this arrangement two months later when both Ruiz and his brother were slain in a hail of gunfire.

On March 14, 2003, Osiel Cárdenas was arrested in a combined army and air force operation after a gun battle in Matamoros that left a number of people on both sides gravely wounded. He had been in the city to throw a party for his young daughter. Ironically, many of the officers who arrested him were from the GAFE, the same unit whose defectors had formed the original Zetas. A little less than two weeks later, El Meme Loco was arrested. Sensing weakness, the Sinaloa Cartel would soon begin its bloody lunge for Nuevo Laredo.

The PAN's Fernando Canales Clariond left the governorship of Nuevo León to become secretary of the economy in the Fox administration, resulting in the return of the PRI to the state governor's office in late 2003 in the person of José Natividad González Parás.

The Fox government did boast of some minor victories, including the August 2003 arrest of Cártel de los Valencia founder Armando Valencia Cornelio. However, around the same time, a nondescript house at 3633 Calle Parsioneros in Ciudad Juárez became the scene of a series of ghastly Juárez Cartel–organized executions of at least twelve people, whose remains were then disposed of beneath the structure. The killings, engineered by Juárez Cartel deputy Heriberto Santillán-Tabares, would have likely been just one more in the long line of crimes had one of Santillán's own lieutenants, a former Mexican police officer named Guillermo Eduardo Ramírez Peyro who went by the names "Jesús Contreras" and "Lalo," not also been moonlighting as Informant No. 913 for US Immigration and Customs Enforcement (ICE). A few months before the killings began, Ramírez had been stopped trying to drive into the United States with 102 pounds of marijuana hidden in the tires of his car. At the request of Texas assistant US attorney Juanita Fielden, lead attorney on a case against Santillán (whom Ramírez was informing on), drug charges were later dropped.

Ramírez had also been an informant for the DEA, who cut ties at this time. He even went so far as to record one of the murders he participated in and then play the recording for ICE agent Raul Bencomo. Nevertheless, Ramírez would be kept on ICE's payroll until February 2004, a period during which he was paid over $220,000 by the US government. Santillán was arrested a short time later and eventually sentenced to twenty-five years in prison. Ramírez himself would be arrested for being in the United States illegally and then, after an immigration board ruled against deporting him back to Mexico, let out onto the streets of the United States, a free man.

Interviewed about another great threat, Los Zetas, in October 2003, José Luis Santiago Vasconcelos, the top antidrug prosecutor with the *Subprocuraduría de Investigación Especializada en Delincuencia Organizada* (SIEDO), said of the group that "they are extremely violent, and they are very much feared in the region because of the bloodshed they unleash."

And they would unleash considerably more in the new year. In late January 2004, the discovery of the bodies of three men in Nuevo Laredo followed the shooting of three people including two police officers. Roberto Javier Mora García, the editorial director for Nuevo Laredo's *El Mañana* newspaper who had extensively covered the Gulf Cartel and harshly criticized Tamaulipas governor Tomás Yarrington, was stabbed twenty-six times near his home. Two men were eventually arrested, and though police advanced a crime of passion theory, it later was revealed that the men had been tortured before their confessions. Yarrington himself had been an honored guest in Austin when Rick Perry was sworn in to his first full term as Texas governor the previous year.

In May 2004, two dozen heavily armed, uniformed men believed to be Los Zetas set five Gulf Cartel members and over a dozen others free from the Apatzingán prison in far-off Michoacán. By that summer, what was left of the Arellano Félix organization in Tijuana was also thought to be contracting Los Zetas on a murder-for-hire basis. In a brazen show of force, heavily armed convoys of Gulf Cartel members and Los Zetas would drive around Nuevo Laredo, not always shooting but merely announcing their presence, terrifying people.

Also that summer, journalist Francisco Arratia Saldierna, whose column *Portavoz* (Spokesman) appeared in *El Imparcial* and *El Regional* in Matamoros, and *Mercurio* and *El Cinco* in Ciudad Victoria, died after Gulf Cartel enforcers in Matamoros broke his fingers with a hammer, poured acid on the wounds, and beat him until his heart stopped.

But the narcos showed they were not always adverse to the power of the media when a curious full-page ad appeared in the Nuevo Laredo daily *El Norte* one day in September 2004. The ad was actually a statement by La Barbie (under his real name, Edgar Valdéz Villarreal) declaring himself to be an innocent businessman who had been chased out of Tamaulipas by corrupt local police officers. He then asked President Fox "to resolve the insecurity, extortion and terror that exists in the state of Tamaulipas, and especially in the city of Nuevo Laredo."

Significantly, in September 2004, the Assault Weapons Ban, passed in the United States a decade earlier, expired, thanks in large part to political pressure and lobbying by the National Rifle Association (NRA), an absolutist, single-issue body reminiscent in its messianic evangelicalism of the Anti-Saloon League's temperance crusade decades earlier. The effect of the lapse of the ban on Mexico would be immediate and dramatic.

According to a witness who was present at the meeting, all the major leaders of the Sinaloa Cartel—Chapo Guzmán, El Mayo Zambada, Nacho Coronel, El Azul, and Arturo Beltrán Leyva—met in Monterrey in September 2004 to discuss strategy. Among the ideas floated was the murder of Rodolfo Carrillo Fuentes, who was helping to run the Juárez Cartel since his brother's death seven years earlier, and framing Los Zetas for the killing, as well as invading the plaza in Nuevo Laredo to wrest control from the Gulf Cartel, with La Barbie, given his long experience in the area, being tasked as leading the charge. Rodolfo Carrillo Fuentes would be shot to death later that month in Ciudad Juárez and, though suspicion fell on the Sinaloa Cartel, culpability was never conclusively proven.

It appeared that the time might be ripe for a move to Nuevo Laredo. Los Zetas' leader Rogelio "El Kelín" González Pizaña (Z-2), was arrested at the Covacha nightclub in Matamoros after a gun battle that left two suspected cartel gunmen and one law enforcement agent dead; González himself was shot through the chest as he hurled grenades at oncoming officers. Taking the reins of Los Zetas would be Heriberto Lazcano, the former soldier from a poor family in Hidalgo who had joined the army at seventeen and then deserted to go to work for the cartel. Lazcano would lead the organization for nearly a decade, and the violent reputation his nickname *El Verdugo* (The Executioner) suggested would be borne out as Los Zetas rapidly expanded to new levels of influence and brutality.

On the last day of 2004, Chapo Guzmán's brother, Arturo Guzmán Loera, known as *El Pollo*, was shot and killed as he sat in a booth talking to his lawyer in the supposedly high-security Altiplano prison. It was believed that Osiel Cárdenas, also in Altiplano at the time, had orchestrated the hit.

By the end of 2004, Mexican traffickers were supplying an astounding 92 percent of the cocaine that entered the United States, up from 77 percent the year before. Fox's deputy attorney general for organized crime at SEIDO, José Luis Santiago Vasconcelos, stated that the weakened Arellano Félix cartel of Tijuana had merged with the Gulf Cartel, which Osiel Cárdenas was still running from a Mexican prison. Still busy on their home turf, Los Zetas were believed to have been behind the murder of six prison employees near the federal maximum-security prison in Matamoros.

In 2005, Tomás Yarrington was succeeded as the governor of Tamaulipas by another PRI stalwart, Eugenio Hernández Flores, former mayor of Ciudad Victoria. The PRI's Miguel Ángel Osorio Chong took over the reins of the governorship of Hidalgo from Manuel Núñez and, according to several protected witnesses interviewed by the magazine *Proceso*, the influence of Los Zetas throughout the state, which had become so pervasive during the governorship of Núñez, deepened and expanded.

It was becoming ever more dangerous to be a journalist in Mexico. In April, Dolores Guadalupe García Escamilla, host of the *Punto Rojo* program on Stereo 91 XHNOE in Nuevo Laredo, was shot nine times outside the station half an hour after the station had aired her report on the slaying of narco defense lawyer Fernando Partida Castañeda. She died eleven days later. That same month, Raúl Gibb Guerrero, the editor and owner of the *La Opinión* newspaper in the city of Poza Rica in Veracruz, which had reported extensively on the Gulf Cartel, was ambushed and killed while driving in his car.

Nor was the lot of law enforcement an enviable one, either. Nine hours after being sworn in as Nuevo Laredo's new police chief, Alejandro Domínguez Coello was riddled with bullets by assailants alighting from three dark Chevy Suburbans. Domínguez Coello, who had once said that he didn't "owe anybody anything" and that "those who should be afraid are those who have been compromised" died at the scene. His successor was a cautious police officer named Omar Pimentel who had formerly directed the city's police academy. Pimentel had previously stated that "if I ever get a call, or a threat, I am leaving this job. . . . I am not going to hesitate for one minute." At one point, a journalist found Pimentel sitting at his desk reading a magazine article about himself with the headline *This man may be dead by the time you read this.*

Soon after the murder of police chief Domínguez Coello, Fox sent one thousand troops and federal agents to eight cities along the border, with the largest contingent going to Nuevo Laredo, in a campaign dubbed *México Seguro* (Safe Mexico). Simultaneously, Nuevo Laredo's entire police force—around 730 officers—was suspended pending drug and polygraph tests. Two weeks later, over forty people were rescued in Nuevo Laredo after apparently being kidnapped in collusion between local police and Los Zetas. During the course of 2005 the city—with a population of around 380,000—would officially see 180 murders. Many believe the toll was far higher.

But the lines between the criminals and the state supposedly committed to bringing them to heel were nothing if not blurry. Communication evidently flowed so freely between the Tamaulipas state government and the criminals that, after the carjacking of Hector Bolaños, a Mexican customs broker who worked on both sides of the border, the victim complained to Tamaulipas governor Eugenio Hernández Flores, and the car was returned, albeit slightly worse for wear. Between August 2004 and August 2005, at least forty-three Americans were abducted in Nuevo Laredo, with three turning up slain, seventeen released, and twenty-three missing.

In August 2005, twenty-eight-year-old Nuevo Laredo municipal police officer Adriana de León Martínez, a single mother of two, was gunned down on her way home, the fifteenth police officer to be killed in the city that year. Omar Pimentel, still police chief, did not attend her funeral. Pimentel would last eight months on the job before quitting, cheerily and unconvincingly stating that "everything is fine; everything turned out well," though, at the same time, he said that he was leaving "for mental health reasons." Shortly after he quit—perhaps finally receiving the unspecified "threats" that he had long feared—Pimentel vanished. At the time of this book's writing he has not been seen since.

By August 2005, Juan Reyes "R-1" Mejia Gonzalez, the Gulf Cartel's plaza boss in Guerrero, was also helping to coordinate the Cartel's distribution of marijuana and cocaine in the Dallas area, as well as distributing drugs to Houston, Chicago, and Atlanta.

The government of Guatemalan president Oscar Berger warned that Los Zetas were recruiting into their ranks members of Los Kabiles, the Guatemalan army's counterinsurgency unit, which boasted a horrific human rights record in Guatemala itself. Mexico's Ministry of Defense announced that Los Zetas had further trained Kabiles on a ranch in Tamaulipas. Seven former Kabiles members were captured by the Mexican army in possession of six machine guns and $100,000 in Mexican and Guatemalan currency. An explosives expert, a driver trained in defense tactics, and a squad leader were among those arrested. A US Homeland Security Department intelligence alert also mentioned the suspected presence of Kabiles within the Zetas.

In late November 2005, Nuevo Laredo police arrested twenty-year-old Gerardo "El Gera" Reyes Uresti, an alleged Sinaloa Cartel hitman suspected of involvement in at least eight killings including that of a Nuevo Laredo city councilman from the PRI. Before he was beheaded by a fellow inmate in La Loma prison, Reyes Uresti allegedly told police that he was paid $3,000 per killing. He claimed to have received orders from a Laredo, Texas, businessman named Alberto Briceño, aka *El Beto*. By late 2005, the town of Miguel Alemán was so in the grip of the traffickers that Gulf Cartel sicarios in ostrich-skin boots were walking openly armed throughout town. For at least two years the cartel, who at the time had Samuel "El Metro 3" Flores Borrego as its Miguel Alemán plaza boss, would pay Texas police officer Romeo Javier "Compadre Nacho" Ramirez at least $30,000 in bribes to help facilitate their movement of drugs into the United States.

A DVD postmarked from San Antonio arrived at the Mexico City offices of the *Dallas Morning News* in early December 2005. In the video four bound and beaten men—two of them shirtless—are seated atop black plastic garbage bags taped to the floors and the walls of a room, while an off-camera voice questions them. The men admit to working for Los Zetas, and confess to, among other crimes, the murder of Nuevo Laredo's police chief Alejandro Domínguez Coello six months earlier. They also charged that SIEDO's José Luis Santiago Vasconcelos had been passing information on to Los Zetas and the Gulf Cartel.

The video had been filmed in Acapulco the previous May. The off-camera voice doing the interrogating allegedly belonged to La Barbie. At one point, the voice says "You're it" and a pistol appears at the back of the head of one of the men. It fires, spraying blood, and the man topples forward, dead. Subsequently, Vasconcelos strongly denied all the allegations against him.

Fox's much-vaunted AFI had become thoroughly corrupted by organized crime by the end of 2005, with one-in-five officers in the seven-thousand-member force under investigation for committing crimes, and a number working on behalf of the Sinaloa Cartel in its battle against the Gulf Cartel. Around 780 agents from the old, corrupt PJF had been retained. The Mexican journalist Ricardo Ravelo characterized Fox's battle against the drug lords thus far as if he was fighting an unbeatable hydra-headed monster, whereby the moment one drug leader or organization was decapitated, another immediately grew in its place. A number of observers were prone to taking a less charitable, more conspiratorial analysis.

As 2006 began, near Neely's Crossing, Texas, some fifty miles east of El Paso, at least ten heavily armed men in Mexican army uniforms traveling north from the border in three SUVs ran headlong into a group of Texas sheriff's deputies and Texas state troopers. The armed men returned across the Rio Grande as both sides eyed each other warily with weapons drawn. Law enforcement officials later found about fourteen hundred pounds of marijuana in one of the SUVs that had gotten a flat tire and become stuck on the Texas side of the border.

Had the encounter happened only a few months later, one could fairly ask where the weapons the armed men were carrying had come from. Beginning in 2006, the Tucson office of the US Bureau of Alcohol, Tobacco, Firearms and Explosives (ATF), a law enforcement body under the jurisdiction of the US Department of Justice, would initiate a duo of destructive, poorly thought out projects that would cross administrations and political ideologies and flood Mexico with even more guns. Operation Wide Receiver would allow hundreds of firearms to be purchased in the United States and then watched as they were trafficked to Mexico in an effort to link them to big-time cartel operations.

Was Mexico's great vexing problem a lack of guns? In Acapulco in January 2006, at least three police officers and four suspected narcos were killed when the occupants of an SUV stopped by police opened fire. In March, Nuevo Laredo's Ramiro Téllez Contreras, a radio journalist for *Exa* 95.7 FM, who also served as the director of an emergency ambulance dispatch service, was shot and killed as he entered his pickup to drive to work. Six days later, four plainclothes PFP officers in the city were gunned down across the street from a grade school as it let out for the day. In mid April, two Acapulco policemen were decapitated and their heads dumped with a note telling police "So that you learn to respect."

In a breathtaking display of the Gulf Cartel leader's arrogance and omnipotence, Nuevo Laredo's *El Mañana* newspaper carried an advertisement purportedly paid for by Osiel Cárdenas Guillén praising the drug lord for making "thousands of children happy" by sending truckloads of gifts to a municipal *Día Del Niño* (Children's Day) party in nearby Reynosa. Reynosa's city council admitted that, at the end of the party, which they said had been sponsored by a beer company, two large trucks showed up with toys and a note saying they were from Cárdenas. During 2006, seven hundred small- and medium-size businesses would close in Nuevo Laredo, and at least forty of the city's business leaders decamped across the Rio Grande for Laredo.

The Gulf Cartel remained firmly in the sights of the United States. US authorities announced that they were offering $5 million for information leading to the arrest of El Coss, with US ambassador to Mexico Tony Garza calling him "the linchpin of a network of drug dealers and murderers." As the Gulf Cartel's Reynosa plaza boss Gregorio "El Goyo" Sauceda Gamboa's cocaine and alcohol addiction worsened, he was replaced by Los Zetas' Jaime "El Hummer" González Durán.

In a momentary bout of sanity, Mexican lawmakers passed a bill making it legal to possess twenty-five milligrams of heroin, a fifth of an ounce of marijuana, and a half a gram of cocaine in addition to small amounts of LSD, hallucinogenic mushrooms, amphetamines, and peyote. The law had been proposed by Vicente Fox himself in January 2004. Soon after the new bill was passed, the Bush administration began Operation Jump Start which, over the course of two years, would send six thousand US troops to the US-Mexico border at a cost of $1.2 billion, ostensibly to boost border security. The soldiers were mostly sent to work mending fences and building roads.

Despite the garish public violence that characterized the battles for Nuevo Laredo and Acapulco, and despite the tragic attacks against the press, between 1997 and 2006, Mexico's overall murder rate had actually fallen by 37 percent. All of that was about to change.

THE DARK HORSE

It is hard for many to remember now, but the victory of Felipe Calderón in the PAN's 2005 primary was something of a surprise to many observers. Calderón, who had served as Fox's secretary of energy until resigning after a falling out with his boss, had also served as the PAN's national leader, and as a national deputy from Michoacán on two different occasions. He was thought at first likely be outflanked by Santiago Creel, who had served as Fox's secretary of the interior.

Calderón had been born and raised in Morelia, the picturesque colonial capital of the state of Michoacán. His father, Luis Calderón Vega, had been one of the PAN's founders, but had quit in 1981, believing the party had been taken over by right-wing interests. The younger Calderón later moved to Mexico City, where he obtained a law degree from the *Escuela Libre de Derecho* and an MA in economics from the *Instituto Tecnológico Autónomo de México*. After serving as the PAN's director, he attended the John F. Kennedy School of Government at Harvard University, where he obtained an MA in public administration. In short, he was every bit the picture of the international, modernizing technocrat that the PAN liked to portray itself as nurturing. He was also extremely distrustful and suspicious of those around him, even of his closest political collaborators, and with good reason, it would turn out. Few aspects of his past, however, would prepare Mexicans for the style in which he would govern.

In the general election, Calderón would be helped immensely by the high-handed arrogance of his main opponent, Mexico City mayor Andrés Manuel López Obrador, who was running at the head of the PRD and decided to skip a scheduled debate, a move that Calderón's people used to label López Obrador (known in Mexico as AMLO) as a "coward." For its part, the PRI ran as its candidate Roberto Madrazo, the former governor of Tabasco. Calderón would also be helped by the fact that Mexico's business community spent more than $19 million on advertisements against López Obrador. In due time, some of the mayor's wilder claims would begin to seem not so far-fetched after all.

As Mexico prepared to vote, a dispute between government authorities and local flower vendors in the community of San Salvador Atenco in the Texcoco municipality of Mexico State erupted into a grotesque police riot. As the flower sellers—the majority of them women—arrived at San Salvador Atenco's market square, they were met by dozens of heavily armed state and municipal police dispatched by the state's young PRI governor, Enrique Peña Nieto. The security forces blocked the vendors' way, despite a previous agreement having been reached with municipal authorities allowing them to be there. Police responded brutally to the vendors' impromptu protest, killing two people (including a fourteen-year-old boy) and detaining hundreds. The following day, even more protests ensued and the police response was even more brutal. At least twenty-six women were tortured and abused by security forces, with a number raped and subjected to other sexual violence.

At the time of this book's writing, only one officer had been charged for the violence, with a misdemeanor "libidinous acts," and sentenced to time served and a small fine. A report by Mexico's *Fiscalía Especial para los Delitos de Violencia contra las Mujeres y Trata de Personas* (FEVIMTRA) concluded that at least thirty-four officers had been involved in criminal behavior. The event would come back to haunt the state's young governor, to say nothing of the women victimized, later on.

On July 2, 2006, both Calderón and López Obrador declared themselves winners of the electoral contest, with a preliminary tally by electoral officials giving Calderón 36.9 percent and López Obrador 35.7 percent. The wind was clearly at Calderón's back, however, with a number of governments, including that of US president George W. Bush (himself first elected in a disputed ballot), quick to give Calderón's victory the stamp of approval. Despite López Obrador's claims that the vote had been rigged, European Union observers who visited a third of the country's three hundred electoral districts "did not report incidents or irregularities that could cloud the transparency of the counting process or affect the results."

López Obrador was unmoved, demanding a vote by vote recount, leading a rally of at least 150,000 people in the capital's Zócalo and threatening that "there will be instability" if he was not made Mexico's president. Mexico's electoral tribunal rejected López Obrador's demand for a complete recount. A little over a week later, López Obrador supporters clashed with police outside of Mexico's Congress. By the end of August, the electoral tribunal unanimously rejected most of López Obrador's legal challenges to the electoral result, and the mayor vowed to create a "parallel government" in response. In the end, Calderón won by only 243,000 votes out of forty-one million cast. López Obrador's PRD became the second largest bloc in congress behind the PAN. The PRI, once preeminent, fell to third.

As Mexico's political crisis drew to a close, antidrug authorities north of the border scored a major victory when Francisco Javier Arellano Félix was captured by the US Coast Guard while incautiously fishing in international waters off the coast of Baja California. Leadership of the Tijuana Cartel then passed into the hands of Luis Fernando "El Ingeniero" Sánchez Arellano, a nephew of the Arellano Félix brothers, who then engaged in a war with Teodoro García Simental, aka *El Teo*, a onetime Arellano Félix lieutenant who decided the time was right to make a lunge for power. The upper echelons north of the border were hardly immune from corruption, either. Hardrick Crawford, the former special agent in charge of the FBI office in El Paso, was convicted of concealing and making false statements about his relationship with Ciudad Juárez racetrack owner José María Guardia, an alleged conduit for drug trafficking and money laundering.

In far away Washington, DC, that August, as if they wanted to wall themselves off from their responsibility for the deepening slaughter, the US House of Representatives for a second time passed a bill that would have great impact on border residents, even though it had been cosponsored by a man, Long Island Republican representative Peter King, whose congressional district lay two thousand miles from the nearest border crossing into Mexico.

The Secure Fence Act of 2006 mandated that the US government build seven hundred miles of double-layered fencing in addition to the seventy-five miles that already existed. It contained no provisions as to how the government was supposed to pay for it, despite the fact that Republicans estimated the cost would be more than $2 billion. Democrats charged the number would be closer to $7 billion. Another Republican member of Congress, California's Ed Royce, claimed that the wall was needed to prevent "infiltration by members of terrorist organizations like [the Lebanese Shiite militia] Hezbollah," a charge for which, at least regarding Mexico, no evidence at all existed.

A freshman Democratic senator from Illinois, Barack Obama, also voted in favor of the act. In a bit of soothsaying, a worried review of the law by the Congressional Research Service the previous year noted that it provided:

> *the Secretary of Homeland Security with authority to waive all laws*
> *he deems necessary for the expeditious construction of the barriers . . .*
> *and bars judicial review of such waiver decisions. . . . By including the*
> *language "no court," [the law] appears to preclude judicial review of*
> *a Secretary's decision to waive provisions of law by both federal and*
> *state courts.*

To oversee an endeavor of such questionable legality, President Bush selected Secretary for Homeland Security Michael Chertoff, a former US attorney who had coauthored the Patriot Act, a piece of controversial legislation in the wake of the September 11, 2001 terrorist attacks that, in the main, was openly scornful of the judicial process itself. Among other provisions, the Patriot Act allowed the government to tap phones and other communications while not identifying either the person or the facility under surveillance, conduct secret surveillance of non-US persons granted by secret courts, and allowed the government "to obtain the communication, financial and credit records of anyone deemed relevant to a terrorism investigation even if that person is not suspected of unlawful behavior." The authoritarian streak contained within the law would become ever more apparent in Chertoff's dealings with border communities in connection to the fence. Those more familiar with the region questioned the wisdom of trying to wall the United States off from its southern neighbor, with Arizona governor Janet Napolitano saying "show me a 50-foot wall and I'll show you a 51-foot ladder at the border."

Felipe Calderón was officially declared Mexico's president-elect by the Federal Electoral Tribunal on September 5. Though his balding pate and preternatural graveness made him seem far older, he was only forty-three years old. Manuel López Obrador held another rally in the Zócalo where he shrieked, as if at the Mexican state itself and to confirm the worst allegations about his temperament, "to hell with their institutions!" He later swore himself in—illegally—as president while his supporters vowed to block Calderón's inauguration.

In an unusual move, in the early morning hours of December 1, 2006, Calderón was sworn in at Los Pinos in a ceremony during which Vicente Fox handed him the ceremonial presidential sash. Speaking in a televised address to the nation, Calderón declared that "today should put an end to our disagreements and from there, start a new stage whose only aim would be to place the interests of our nation above our differences."

The PRD deputies in Mexico's congress had different ideas, however, and later that day, they seized the speaker's platform and blocked the doors to the building. Calderón was able to slip in, however, in the midst of a sea of supporters and took a rather-speedier-than-usual oath followed by a national anthem that almost drowned out the jeers coming from the PRD section of the house.

As if in ghastly welcome, a few weeks earlier, on September 6 at about 1:30 a.m., a group of gunmen firing their weapons in the air had barged into the Sol y Sombra nightclub in the city of Uruapan in Calderón's home state of Michoacán. After ordering all the patrons to lie down on the floor, the invaders tossed five human heads into their midst. They also unfurled a banner that read:

La Familia no mata por paga, no mata mujeres, no mata inocentes. Sólo muere quien debe morir. Sépanlo toda la gente: esto es justicia divina.

(The family does not kill for pay, it does not kill women or innocents. Only those who deserve to die will die. Everybody understands: this is divine justice.)

It was later believed that the dead men were low-level methamphetamine dealers who had become addicted to their own product. A bartender at the club interviewed later said "this is not something you see every day."

It would be.

Chapter Four

No Truce and No Quarter

In their book *Sacrifice: Its Nature and Functions,* the French sociologists Henry Hubert and Marcel Mauss wrote of the religious nature of sacrifice that the act establishes "a means of communication" through the mediation of a victim, "a thing that in the course of the ceremony is destroyed." And so it would become in Mexico's drug war. The bodies of victims without number would be a canvas on which the factions would, with bullets, blades, and other implements, carve out their messages to one another. None would prove more adept, or more enthusiastic, at mastering this bloody grammar than Los Zetas.

Former Gulf Cartel leader Osiel Cárdenas was transferred from Mexico to the United States on January 19, 2007, in a move the US officials hailed as "a monumental moment in our two nations' battle with the vicious drug traffickers and criminals who threaten our very way of life." After having "agreed to cooperate with the federal government"—a shocking admission for a Mexican drug lord—Cárdenas would eventually be sentenced to twenty-five years and forfeit $50 million in assets during a "highly secretive hearing" that was closed to the public. If he served his full sentence, Cárdenas would be sixty-seven once he was released.

After Cárdenas's extradition to the United States, the lines of command and control between the Gulf Cartel and Los Zetas became ever more blurred. Control of one wing of the Gulf Cartel fell to a co-ownership by Osiel's brothers, Tony Tormenta and Mario "El Gordo" Cárdenas Guillén, along with El Coss, who was thought to be the real power behind the group. They were aided by a wily financial operator by the name of César "El Gama" Dávila García, who proved himself expert at laundering the cartel's profits and diversifying its investments. By this time Tony Tormenta's exceedingly violent personality had more than earned his sobriquet, and El Coss had developed the garish, grandiose tastes that befit an up-and-coming drug lord, including buying two watches valued at $10,000 each made out of the actual metal of the ill-fated ship *Titanic,* perhaps curiously unfortunate symbolism.

But real power in fact fell to Los Zetas' Heriberto Lazcano. Within months of the Cárdenas extradition, Mexican military reports were concluding that Lazcano was in fact in charge of the cartel, and also predicted the emergence of Miguel "Z-40" Treviño as a possible major drug-trafficking kingpin. It was believed that Miguel Treviño oversaw control of the state of Nuevo León, El Coss ran Matamoros, Gregorio "El Goyo" Sauceda Gamboa ran Reynosa (with assistance from his brother Héctor Manuel "El Karis" Sauceda Gamboa), and Iván "El Talibán" Velásquez Caballero controlled Quintana Roo and Guerrero. In Michoacán the organization was based on the networks of what had been the *Cártel del Milenio.*

The reports also noted the expansion of the activities of Los Zetas beyond just drug trafficking and into widespread extortion and kidnapping, especially of migrants heading through Mexico on their way to the United States. Pushed into an ever tighter knot of potential routes into the United States by the militarization on the US side of the border, the migrants were driven into closer proximity to—and ever greater threat by—the narcos. Among the great ironies of the frequently twinned US drug and immigration policies was the fact that, by approaching immigration on military terms, the US government provided the drug cartels in general and Los Zetas in particular with an invaluable source of additional income—the immigrants—with which they could continue to flood the United States with drugs.

By 2007, Los Zetas had also begun recruiting a female unit of young women from poor backgrounds that they dubbed *Las Panteras* (The Panthers), who acted as bodyguards, spies, and assassins for the cartel. One such operative, Ashly Narro López, aka *Comandante Bombón,* would play a key role in a Zetas hit squad in Quintana Roo and participate in the murder of Mexican general Mauro Enrique Tello Quiñones. To facilitate the shipment of goods, local police chiefs were paid around $7,800 a month, while low-level officers got around $400 per week. Local reporters got anywhere from $1,550 to $3,876 monthly.

By this point, Los Zetas were well on their way to becoming a highly diversified criminal organization that only used drug trafficking as one of their many avenues of making money, with the others including the aforementioned kidnapping, extortion, mining, and theft and resale of Mexican state resources such as natural gas.

In a radio interview before his inauguration in 2006, Calderón said that "drug violence has overwhelmed the governments" in the states of Tamaulipas, Sinaloa, Guerrero, and Michoacán. There were twenty-one hundred drug-related murders in Mexico that year, a marked increase from thirteen hundred in 2005, and some six hundred of those killings had taken place in Michoacán. The value of heroin production in Mexico had increased 58 percent.

In Reynosa that November, the banda singer Valentín Elizalde, a man known as *El Gallo de Oro* (The Golden Rooster), played a concert during which he crooned "*A Mis Enemigos*" (To My Enemies). The song's video had depicted violent gunfights and heavily armed men driving around in pickup trucks, and its lyrics were taken by many as a paean to the Sinaloa Cartel—an association not lost on Los Zetas. Elizalde was gunned down along with his driver and assistant shortly after the concert under orders that had allegedly come from Los Zetas' El Hummer. The suspected triggerman, Raúl Hernández Barrón, another former soldier, would subsequently be arrested for the crime. For their part, the Gulf-Zetas alliance had been pumping out narcocorridos telling of their own exploits for some time, with one compilation, *Corridas del Golfo*, featuring such numbers as "*El corrido del Señor de la O*" (about Osiel Cárdenas) and "*La santisima muerte*" (about La Flaca herself).

Just after taking office in December 2006, Calderón sent over seven thousand members of the army and federal police to Michoacán. On January 3 he followed suit in Tijuana. The Pacific state of Guerrero, home to Acapulco, soon followed. In their first week in Michoacán, federal forces seized twenty tons of the methamphetamine precursor ephedrine. Though Calderón had recently visited Washington, DC, to discuss his planned antidrug offensive with Bush and US ambassador Tony Garza, American officials later claimed they were totally "blindsided" when the Mexican president sent soldiers to Michoacán without so much as a follow-up meeting. Hours after the announcement of the troop deployment, the body of Luis Felipe Zavala, the cousin of Calderón's wife, Margarita Zavala, was found in a car in the city of Naucalpan, just outside of Mexico City.

Mario "El Gordo" Cárdenas would soon be released from prison after serving an eleven-year sentence for drug trafficking, and began assisting Tony Tormenta and El Coss in running the Gulf Cartel. At a gathering of state governors, Calderón declared that his government was "fighting without pause" in order to "win the war on crime." Calderón knew the nature of the battle he faced, even going so far as to record a message to his children in case he lost his life in the struggle.

Calderón appointed thirty-eight-year-old Genaro García Luna, a career intelligence official and former head of the drug-riddled AFI, as the secretary for public security in his cabinet. Eduardo Medina Mora, the former head of CISEN, an intelligence service connected to the interior ministry, was selected as attorney general. Under Medina Mora, Noé Ramírez Mandujano, who under Fox had served as an official in the attorney general's office, would continue on as the head of the SIEDO, the division of the attorney general's office tasked with fighting organized crime. An army general, Guillermo Galván Galván, would head the *Secretaría de la Defensa Nacional* (SEDENA), the government department charged with managing the army and the air force. The navy—the *Secretaría de Marina* or SEMAR—would be under the command of Admiral Mariano Francisco Saynez Mendoza.

Were the institutions of Mexico—what there were—up to the task that Calderón was calling them to fulfill? Were local and state governments, the police, the judiciary, and, most of all, the viper's nest of competing interests and lobbies in the federal government and its labyrinthine bureaucracy, capable of responding to a war of this magnitude? Among analysts that I spoke with, there was a general consensus that the

PRI decided that they would not help in the clampdown and, indeed, in Tamaulipas, one resident told me "the state has not lifted a finger to do anything" to help Calderón prosecute his offensive.

An investigative reporter for *Tabasco Hoy*, Rodolfo Rincón Taracena, headquartered in the Gulf Coast state of the same name, disappeared in January 2007, after putting the finishing touches on an article examining how criminal gangs had been targeting ATM customers in the state capital of Villahermosa. The article came on the heels of one that Rincón had authored on *narcotiendas*—storefronts that sold drugs—complete with a map detailing drug distribution centers and a photo of a family allegedly selling drugs.

Following the slaying in Acapulco of seven law enforcement personnel connected to the state attorney general's office by attackers dressed in military uniforms—and a taunting note left saying the killers "could give a damn about the federal government"—Calderón, standing alongside the commanders of the army, navy, and air force, told military personnel at a base in Mexico City that there would be "no truce and no quarter" in his government's war against the cartels. In late February 2007, for the first time, Calderón sent around thirty-three hundred troops to Nuevo León and Tamaulipas. Hours later, the PRI politician Horacio Garza Garza, who had served two terms as Nuevo Laredo's mayor and also as a federal deputy, was shot and wounded and his driver killed as they headed to the city's airport.

Building on discussions that had taken place during Calderón's visit to Washington the previous November, at a bilateral presidential summit with President Bush in the colonial city of Mérida in March 2007, the pair agreed to develop a specific framework through which to address the problems of drug trafficking and organized crime, a plan that would eventually become known as the Mérida Initiative. The so-called "Four Pillars" of the initiative were to "disrupt organized criminal groups, strengthen institutions, build a 21st century border and build strong and resilient communities." During the first year of its operation, the US Congress approved $400 million in funding for Mexico and $65 million collectively for Central America, the Dominican Republic, and Haiti.

That Bush himself, a reformed heavy drinker, had been taped apparently admitting to having used marijuana in the past and elsewhere had refused to respond to direct questions about what had long been rumored to have been a youthful indulgence in cocaine seemed not to factor into this decision.

As Bush was being fêted at Mérida, the severed head of a small-time drug dealer and suspected police informant was hurled at the Villahermosa headquarters of the state police in Tabasco. Later that same month, a recording posted on the video-sharing site YouTube depicted the interrogation of a man in connection with the slayings of the seven security officials in Acapulco the month before. The man—clad in his underwear and with a "Z" written on his chest and "Lazcano" marked on one of his legs—is questioned and punched several times before being strangled and decapitated by a cord tied to metal rods cutting through his neck. The recording opened with the message "Do something for your country, kill a Zeta!" and ended with the message "Lazcano, you're next!" YouTube quickly removed the video and the Guerrero attorney general's office said they had no information about it. Though it seemed like a shocking crime at the time, it was merely a precursor of things to come.

That same month, during a shootout with the Mexican army in the Veracruz town of El Villarín, one of the founders of Los Zetas, Efraín "Z-14" Teodoro Torres, met his bloody end (though the government would not confirm his demise until months later). Hours after the body was buried, a group of armed commandos surrounded the cemetery, exhumed the corpse, and carted it away, a typical example of Los Zetas' ritualistic *esprit de corps*.

By mid April, there had already been more than seven hundred drug-related slayings in Mexico that year. Meanwhile, Mexico banned the importation of pseudoephedrine and ephedrine, essential ingredients in the concocting of methamphetamine or "meth," of which Mexico supplied 80 to 90 percent sold in the United States, according to the DEA. That same month, police found seventeen bodies dumped around the country, including five stuffed in an SUV in Cancún with their heads covered in tape and their hands bound, three more in an SUV parked in a middle-class Mexico City neighborhood, and yet three more burned in Culiacán.

Operators from the Gulf-Zetas alliance were falling like shell casings on a trigger-happy Saturday night. The government soon nabbed Juan Óscar Garza Azuara, alias *El Barbas,* one of the Gulf Cartel's principal lieutenants in Reynosa, at a nightspot called Club 57 in the city's colonial center. Less than a week later, it was the turn of Eleazar Medina Rojas, aka *El Chelelo,* snatched up by federal police in Nuevo Laredo along with an arsenal of weapons. The PFP referred to Medina as "one of the major killers and kidnappers in the service of the Gulf Cartel."

Nabor Vargas García, aka *El Débora,* one of the first soldiers to desert the army and help found Los Zetas, was seized after a wild shootout in Campeche that left two cartel suspects dead and two policemen wounded. By June, Calderón's security apparatus had also scooped up Luis "Z-12" Reyes Enríquez, alias *El Rex,* from the town of Atotonilco in Hidalgo, swooping in as Reyes, another army deserter and former federal police officer assigned to Matamoros, lay in bed hung over from partying the night before. Despite its casualties, however, the area under the alliance's control was expanding, with a takeover of Piedras Negras led by Omar "El 42" Treviño and Jesús Enrique "El Mamito" Rejón. A suspected Zetas attack on soldiers in the hamlet of Carácuaro in Michoacán left five troops and one cartel gunman dead.

In October 2007, Mexican authorities would make the largest seizure of cocaine ever reported in Mexico: 23.5 tonnes. During 2005 there had been sixteen hundred murders linked to organized crime in Mexico. During 2006 that number had grown to twenty-two hundred. By June of 2007, the number of dead was already at twelve hundred. Calderón's war against the narcos was certainly having an effect, though perhaps not the one most Mexicans had hoped for.

In June 2007, the US ATF formally initiated Project Gunrunner, which called for increased collaboration and coordination between the Mexican government and US law enforcement agencies, an increased use of tracing of firearms transactions, and closer collaboration between the ATF, the Organized Crime Drug Enforcement Task Forces (OCDETF), High

Intensity Drug Trafficking Area (HIDTA) task forces, and public outreach elements. Significantly, with regard to the firearms flooding south to Mexico, the project asserted that

> *straw purchasers should more frequently be viewed as persons whose conduct should be investigated as part of a larger conspiracy and as persons whose information, cooperation, and assistance should be exploited to the extent possible in furtherance of the ultimate goal of identifying key members of the trafficking enterprise and disrupting and/or dismantling of the trafficking operation.*

On another front, at a meeting in Brownsville to discuss the proposed border fence, local residents were startled to hear federal officials tell them that part of the University of Texas at Brownsville would be on the southern side—that is, the Mexican side—of the fence. The university's International Technology, Education and Commerce campus, its golf course, and a historic site were all to be cut off from the rest of the United States. Seemingly surprised when residents did not quietly acquiesce to such a plan, the officials promised to go off and study it some more. In an interview with the *Houston Chronicle*, Homeland Security secretary Michael Chertoff said that the United States would not rule out seizing privately owned land to further the construction of the border fence, snarlingly telling border communities that they wouldn't get veto power over whether or not the fence was built. He then went on to paint a dystopian picture of deserts and grasslands patrolled by a "virtual fence" of "drones, sensors, cameras, satellite technology and vehicle barriers."

Weeks later, however, Chertoff announced that the government was withholding further payments to Seattle's Boeing company because of software problems with nine ninety-eight-foot radar and camera towers that rendered them useless, though nearly three-fourths of the $20 million cost for the virtual fence had already been paid to the company. In an October 2007 interview with the Associated Press, Chertoff carried the administration's race-baiting ever further, asserting that the Bush administration's border fence had to be built because "illegal immigrants really degrade the environment" and that they brought with them "human waste, garbage, discarded bottles and other human artifacts." During a visit to Canada, Calderón had characterized calls in the United States for building a wall at the US-Mexico border as "a huge error" and compared the idea to the construction of the Berlin Wall.

Sometime during mid-2007—the exact date remains hazy—a group of Mexico's top drug kingpins gathered at the Cuernavaca mansion of Arturo Beltrán Leyva to discuss a possible truce. The meetings were not smooth as there was antipathy between some attendees, especially between La Barbie and Los Zetas' Miguel Treviño, whom the former blamed for the murder of his brother, Armando Valdez Villarreal. There is some evidence that elements of Calderón's administration—though not Calderón himself—knew about the meeting and, if not organized it, then at least actively encouraged it and sent representatives to act as semiofficial interlocutors. The result was a peace pact to decrease the level of violence connected with the drug trade around the country. It would hold for less than a year.

With Day of the Dead that November, thousands of Santa Muerte adherents flooded into Tepito to pay homage to the shrine that had been there for six years. Devotees brought the traditional *pan de muertos* pastry and *calaveras de azúcar* (sugar skulls) and feasted on five cakes and over a hundred kilos of chicken, mole, rice, chocolate, coffee, and atole the church provided.

Almost a month later, Zayda Peña, the lead singer of the band *Zayda y Los Culpables* (the Guilty Ones), whose mother worked for the public prosecutor's office, was shot in the back in a Matamoros hotel along with two others who died at the scene. Two days later, as Peña was wheeled out of surgery for her injuries, gunmen invaded the hospital and finished the job. Hours later, Sergio Gómez, the founder and lead singer of the duranguense band *K-Paz de la Sierra*—a band with no known links to the drug trade—was kidnapped along with several others after performing a concert in Michoacán. His body was later found outside of Morelia bearing signs of torture. The same week, Juan Antonio Guajardo Anzaldúa, a former mayor and congressman, was gunned down along with five others outside of a Río Bravo restaurant.

North of the border, by December 2007 Michael Chertoff had grown even more bellicose in his threats against residents on the US side of the border, saying that the Bush administration was "not open for endless talk" with landowners whose property the government wanted to seize to build its border fence, and that owners had a maximum of thirty days to respond to government demands to survey their land. If the land was needed to build the fence, Chertoff concluded, no doubt believing himself magnanimous, the government would pay for it but "we won't pay more than market price."

When a squad of federal agents encountered a group of assault rifle–wielding narcos in the Tamaulipas town of Río Bravo, across the border from Donna, Texas, in January 2008, the ensuing shootout raged for half an hour and left three suspected criminals dead and five soldiers and three federal police officers wounded. Among the ten men arrested by Mexican security forces were three US citizens, one resident of Texas, and two residents of Detroit. Police also recovered sixteen sniper rifles, seven machine guns, a grenade launcher, and two dozen automatic pistols. Deputy Minister for Public Security Patricio Patiño Arias would later say that the group was part of a Zetas cell that reported to Heriberto Lazcano.

A day later, two federal agents died and three more were injured when they were attacked by suspected Zetas in Reynosa. More than any of the cartel elements before them, Los Zetas seemed determined to make a show of actively defying the state, to have their default position as confrontation rather than coercion, and Tamaulipas was the center of their mayhem. PFP head Édgar Millán Gómez would confess to one reporter that "in Tamaulipas, you never know who is with you and who is against you." By this time, the Gulf-Zetas alliance had also developed deep contacts with the Italy's 'Ndrangheta criminal organization from the southern Italian region of Calabria, and a number of Gulf Cartel operatives would be arrested there during the coming year.

No doubt the Gulf-Zetas alliance watched with glee when, in January 2008, Alfredo Beltrán Leyva, aka El Mochomo (The Desert Ant), was captured in Culiacán along with three of his bodyguards, $900,000 in

US currency, and a cache of heavy weapons. The arrest was viewed as a particular triumph for Édgar Millán Gómez, a solidly built, clean-shaven career intelligence and law enforcement official who had been overseeing antidrug operations for the PFP. A day later, Millán supervised the arrest of eleven alleged Beltrán-Leyva hitmen and a massive cache of weapons at two Mexico City mansions. Millán's rumored favorite phrase—*ni un paso atrás* (not a step back)—seemed to be bearing fruit.

The arrest of Alfredo Beltrán Leyva would mark a fateful turning point in the relationship of the cartels both to the state and to one another. Arturo Beltrán Leyva, by this time himself a serious user of cocaine, believed that he knew who was responsible for his brother's betrayal. He would not forgive and he would not forget.

Speaking to the *Wall Street Journal,* Attorney General Eduardo Medina announced that west of Reynosa soldiers swooped down on the El Mezquito ranch to find eighty-nine assault rifles, over eighty-three thousand rounds of ammunition, and enough plastic explosives to bring down entire buildings.

The haul was perhaps not so surprising as, since 2006, the commander of the state police in Reynosa and Miguel Alemán, Gilberto Lerma Plata—a relative of the state's former governor, Manuel Cavazos Lerma—had been working closely with Gulf Cartel deputy Samuel "El Metro 3" Flores Borrego to smuggle bulk quantities of marijuana and cocaine into the United States. (Lerma Plata would be arrested in 2012 and plead guilty.)

At the beginning of March 2008, the Mexican army seized ninety-one assault rifles, grenades, bulletproof vests, and nearly a ton of marijuana during a raid in Tijuana. When Calderón's top law enforcement official, Genaro García Luna, had visited the city two months earlier, he had found a place still awash in violence.

In January 2008, a new joint US-Mexico program, dubbed eTrace, had been announced, designed to trace weapons seized in Mexico to their origins in the United States, acting to "terminate the illegal shipment of arms to Mexico and reduce the violence they cause on both sides of the border." It would be two years before the program became fully active. The downside of Calderón's militarized strategy was also becoming apparent, however. When Sergio Meza Varela and José Antonio Barbosa Ramírez happened upon a military checkpoint in Reynosa, at least three soldiers opened fire on their vehicle, killing Meza and gravely wounding Barbosa. No weapons were found in the cars and tests for gun residue found no evidence that either man had fired a gun.

In Guatemala that spring, Juancho León and ten others were slain during the course of a hit undertaken by the Zetas forces of Daniel "El Cachetes" Perez Rojas and at least partially coordinated by León's local rival, Horst Walter Overdick, known as *El Tigre*. A former cardamom and emerald trader from the Cobán area, El Tigre had become Los Zetas' most reliable partner in the country. The killings shook the nation awake to the presence of Los Zetas in Guatemala. The Mexican narcos had entered the country roughly at the same time as the beginning of the mandate of Álvaro Colom, who had just become president, and his tenure would forever be marked for their violence.

Guatemala's civil war had officially ended in 1996, but both before and after extensive criminal networks in the country, many with links to current and former members of Guatemala's military intelligence, had sought advantage over one another in the lucrative fields of the trafficking of narcotics, firearms, and people. According to a 2003 report by the Washington Office on Latin America, the two dominant groups at the beginning the millennium were *La Cofradía* (The Brotherhood), said to be led by former generals Manuel Callejas y Callejas and Luis Francisco Ortega Menaldo, and *El Sindicato* (The Syndicate), which the report said was led by former general Otto Pérez Molina, who had served as the Guatemalan military's representative during peace negotiations with rebel forces. Pérez Molina later left the military to form the *Partido Patriota* (PP) and serve as a deputy to Guatemala's congress.

The bitterness between Pérez Molina and Ortega Menaldo, in particular, was said to stem back to when each man backed different sides during the May 1993 "self coup" of President Jorge Serrano Elías, during which Serrano attempted to seize authoritarian powers. Ortega Menaldo supported the coup while Pérez Molina (successfully and to his credit) opposed it, leading to an enmity that endured. Pérez Molina had unsuccessfully run against Colom during the election the latter won. After the ballot there was a predictable arrangement, with one former Colom aide telling me frankly that "Colom's guys are Ortega Menaldo's guys."

Three months after the murder of Juancho León, the helicopter carrying Colom's minister of the interior, Vinicio Gómez, flying in a light rain over the department of Alta Verapaz, crashed. Gómez, the pilot, deputy minister Edgar Hernandez, and one other person were killed. Though there was no major storm in the area, the official cause of the crash was attributed to bad weather. According to an official with knowledge of the conversation who spoke to me, in the months before the crash, Gómez had quarreled violently with Carlos Quintanilla, an associate of Ortega Menaldo who was at the time the head of the *Secretaría de Asuntos Administrativos y de Seguridad* (SAAS), a body responsible for the president's personal security. The person familiar with the conversation said that Quintanilla was vexed at Gómez's plan to deploy hundreds of troops and antidrug agents along Guatemala's long border with Mexico. Quintanilla would subsequently be arrested, tried, and acquitted for placing listening devices in the offices and private chambers of both Colom and Colom's wife, Sandra Torres, presumably at the behest of organized crime.

At the end of March 2008, the Calderón government announced that it was launching *Operación Conjunta Chihuahua*, a joint effort by the federal police, the attorney general's office, and, initially, twenty-five hundred federal troops that Interior Secretary Juan Camilo Mouriño said would "return security to the citizens of Chihuahua that organized crime had torn" from them. Given the army's lack of training in domestic security operations, however, such a scenario was problematic from the start. It was made more so by the fact that, among the government forces deployed, one branch under the command of General Manuel de Jesús Moreno Aviña was based in Ojinaga, the dusty Chihuahua town that had served as the base for the drug lord Pablo Acosta until the latter's slaying in April 1987.

Over the next two years, Moreno would reportedly subject the residents of Ojinaga to a reign of terror, brazenly ordering the murder of innocent civilians and routinely using torture and disappearances against those who ran afoul of him. He was also, as it happened, a willing tool of the Juárez Cartel as they struggled for supremacy in the region. He would be removed from his post in September 2009 and, in late 2012, Mexico's Supreme Court ruled that Moreno and his subordinates were to be tried in a civilian court. As of the time of this book's writing, no trial has yet taken place.

The first months of 2008 would be brutal for Mexican law enforcement. In April 2008, Calderón appointed Édgar Millán Gómez as overall head of the PFP. A few days later, Roberto Velasco Martínez, the head of the AFI's organized crime division and PFP inspector, was slain. On May 8, Millán was ambushed at around 2:30 a.m. as he entered the Mexico City apartment where he was living. Riddled with bullets, he died at a hospital a few hours later. Speaking at an event in Guanajuato, Calderón called the killing "cowardly" and said that "the example of his life gives us strength to continue the struggle against those who attack the tranquillity and health of the Mexican people." An associate of the Beltrán-Leyva Cartel, Alejandro Ramírez Báez, was later convicted of the murder, believed to be violent retribution for the arrest of Alfredo Beltrán Leyva the previous January.

In further bitter score-settling by the cartel, the same day Millán was killed, a squad of at least fifteen men armed with machine guns and bazookas killed Chapo Guzmán's twenty-two-year-old son, Édgar Guzmán López, and at least three others in the parking lot of the City Club supermarket in Culiacán. At least twenty vehicles were damaged in the assault.

On June 26, the PFP commander in charge of monitoring trafficking and contraband, Igor Labastida Calderón (no relation to the president), was gunned down along with his bodyguard in a restaurant in the capital. The subject of rumors of links to Chapo Guzmán, Labastida had survived a previous assassination attempt five years earlier. He had been notably close to slain PFP director Édgar Millán Gómez and acting SSP head Genaro García Luna.

Tauntingly over the weekend of April 12–13, 2008, banners appeared in Nuevo Laredo bearing a phone number and reading:

Operative group "Los Zetas" wants you, soldier or ex-soldier. We offer a good salary, food and benefits for your family. Don't suffer any more mistreatment and don't go hungry.

In Tampico, similar banners bragged:

What else could you want?
The state of Tamaulipas, Mexico, the United States and the whole world: Territory of the Gulf Cartel.

Virtually at the same time, Reynosa police chief Juan Muñiz was arrested for being on the Gulf Cartel's payroll.

In the first months of 2008, Chapo Guzmán, a greedy, relentlessly ambitious man mad with grief after the death of his son, broke the peace pact that had been hammered out at Arturo Beltrán Leyva's Cuernavaca mansion the previous year and began a bloody struggle to wrest Ciudad Juárez from its eponymous cartel that would last for much of the next three years. The city, which had seen some of the first large-scale protests against the PRI's rule in the 1980s, and which became a laboratory for the neoliberal maquiladora version of Mexico's future, would become the murder capital of the world.

As Guzmán prepared his lunge into Ciudad Juárez, across the border Homeland Security secretary Michael Chertoff issued waivers suspending thirty laws that could interfere with the Bush administration's plans for its border fence, including many protecting the fragile environment in the Rio Grande Valley and other places, tut-tutting concerns of governmental overreach by saying "criminal activity at the border does not stop for endless debate or protracted litigation," a statement that the behavior of his own office and government illustrated quite well. Among the statutes Chertoff saw his department as being above was the Endangered Species Act of 1973, signed into law by Richard Nixon, father of the drug war.

By mid-May 2008, a coalition of Texas mayors and business leaders had filed a class-action lawsuit against Chertoff and other government officials to prevent construction of the border fence.

Nine men were killed in a single attack on a Culiacán auto repair shop on July 10, 2008, and, by mid-month, more than twelve hundred additional federal police were deployed to Sinaloa. In the midst of the anarchic violence, between early 2007 and mid-2008, the US government said, that the amount of cocaine seized in the country had dropped by 41 percent, that street prices had climbed by nearly a third and purity decreased by more than 15 percent. Many Mexicans would have no doubt asked if such number crunching was worth the price in destroyed lives their country was paying. As violence exploded around the country, Genaro García Luna told a reporter that Mexico was "obligated to confront crime" and that it would not consider "a pact" with the narcos. That summer, Noé Ramírez Mandujano, head of the attorney general's SIEDO anti–organized crime unit, left his position, and was reassigned as Mexico's representative to the Vienna-based United Nations Office on Drugs and Crime.

If anyone needed any further evidence of Los Zetas' desire to take on the Mexican state—and its utter disregard for civilian lives—it was provided during the September 15 Independence Day celebration in Morelia. As thousands of revelers packed the colonial streets of Calderón's hometown, two grenades were hurled into the thick of the crowd, killing eight people and wounding over one hundred. It was an attack designed to kill civilians, and not only against Calderón's heartland but also that of La Familia, who immediately sent out text messages to reporters and distributed flyers rejecting responsibility and promising to take revenge on the "coward" Zetas who "attack the country's peace and tranquillity."

The power of the cartels appeared to be ever ascendent. In mid-August 2008, the *Consejo Ciudadano para la Seguridad Pública y la Justicia Penal* (CCSPJP), an anticrime group led by an attorney named José Antonio Ortega Sánchez, called a press conference in Mexico City and played a recording that it said revealed former Tabasco state prosecutor (and PRI politician) Gustavo Rosario Torres and Tabasco's deputy attorney general Alex Álvarez discussing the arrival of a sum of money the group said was proceeds from a cocaine shipment. A second recording had Álvarez talking with what CCSPJP said was a Gulf Cartel–affiliated lawyer. Rosario vigorously denied the charges, and called the tape a "grotesque montage" spliced together from other things he had said.

In late August 2008, eleven decapitated bodies were found outside of Mérida in the Yucatan Peninsula, with police later saying that they found a Santa Muerte altar in the home of two men—known Zetas associates—arrested in connection with the slayings, leading them to speculate publicly that the missing heads may have been burned in a "ritual." A bloody hatchet was also found. A few weeks later, the bodies of twenty-four men were found in the La Marquesa park just west of the capital. Fifteen of the men had been decapitated. It was believed that the killings had been carried out by the Beltrán-Leyva Cartel.

Those looking toward officialdom for protection on either side of the border would also be proven unwise, Between January and October 2008, more than nine hundred policemen in Ciudad Juárez had left the police force, a number that included 334 who had been dismissed for failing psychological and background checks instituted to try to root out corruption. In Starr County, Texas, just west of McAllen and north of the border of Tamaulipas, the well-liked county sheriff, Reymundo "Rey" Guerra, was arrested along with nineteen others—including a member of the county hospital board and a grade school teacher—and charged with conspiracy to smuggle marijuana and cocaine from Mexico through the county. Guerra had an ongoing economic relationship with Miguel Alemán resident José Carlos Hinojosa, who, as it happened was also an accountant for the Gulf Cartel. In exchange for thousands of dollars in bribes, Guerra would tip the cartel off about potential busts and even try to find out the names of informants against them. Guerra was eventually—and curiously—sentenced to only five years for his part in the conspiracy, far less than the possible life sentence that he had faced.

Grotesqueries continued to abound. At the beginning of October 2008, police in the town of Ascensión in Chihuahua State opened an ice chest marked "vaccines" and discovered four human heads. The chest had been sitting unclaimed for a week. A few weeks later, a human head was found in an ice chest in the port city of Lázaro Cárdenas in Michoacán with a message reading "From the Gulf Cartel." Another head was found in a box in the parking lot of a police station outside of the capital bearing a message threatening La Familia. In the early morning hours of October 12, the US consulate in Monterrey was attacked by two men, one of whom fired several times at the facility and one of whom tossed a grenade, which did not explode. No one was hurt in the incident.

The night Barack Obama was elected president of the United States—November 4, 2008—Calderón's secretary of the interior, Juan Camilo Mouriño, was killed in a plane crash when the Learjet 45 he was traveling in crashed in Mexico City only blocks from Los Pinos, killing all eight people aboard. Among the passengers was organized crime prosecutor José Luis Santiago Vasconcelos, the official who had been accused of working with Los Zetas in the infamous La Barbie execution video. Camilo and Santiago had been returning to the capital from San Luis Potosí. Speaking to the nation, Calderón said that he instructed his staff to redouble their efforts "to work together and not give in, to work harder every day to achieve a Mexico in which we all believe."

The cause of the crash was ruled to be pilot error, with the pilot of Camilo's plane having followed too close to a Boeing 767 and thus experiencing severe turbulence in the much-larger plane's wake. Many Mexicans, however, continued to have their doubts.

On November 7, Los Zetas' Jaime "El Hummer" González Durán was seized by security forces in Reynosa. As the military sped to a waiting aircraft to spirit their prize off to a more secure location, three trucks of heavily armed men tried to spring their boss, but were successfully fought off. With El Hummer's arrest, the Mexican army also made the largest seizure of drug cartel weapons in the nation's history when they raided a Gulf Cartel safe house in Reynosa and found 540 rifles, 165 grenades, 500,000 rounds of ammunition, and fourteen sticks of dynamite. Héctor Manuel "El Karis" Sauceda Gamboa, the brother of Gregorio "El Goyo" Sauceda Gamboa, whom El Hummer had deposed in mid-2006, then took over as Reynosa plaza boss, a move that made Los Zetas suspicious that their comrade might have been betrayed. The other side of the country was hardly more peaceful. Over the weekend of November 28–30, thirty-seven people were killed in Tijuana, including a four-year-old, a thirteen-year-old, and nine adults whose headless corpses were dumped in a field.

The veteran crime reporter José Armando Rodríguez Carreón of *El Diario* in Ciudad Juárez, known as *El Choco* to his colleagues, was slain on November 13, shot and killed in front of his eight-year-old daughter. Some of Rodríguez Carreón's colleagues would later charge that "El Choco was killed by the state," by which many assumed they meant Chihuahua state attorney general Patricia González Rodríguez. In late November 2008, Noé Ramírez Mandujano, the former head of the attorney general's SIEDO anti–organized crime unit who had resigned in July, was arrested and charged with having accepted $450,000 in exchange for passing information about investigations and law enforcement actions to the Sinaloa and Beltrán-Leyva cartels.

In December 2008, Felix Batista, a Cuban-American kidnapping negotiator working for the Houston-based ASI Global security firm, was kidnapped outside of a restaurant in the Coahuila state capital of Saltillo, where he had been lecturing local businesses about how to avoid a similar fate. He has not been heard from since. In the Sinaloa town of El Rosario, a December gun battle in front of the police station killed ten people. As Christmas 2008 approached, teachers in Ciudad Juárez were told to turn over their year-end bonuses or their student charges would be kidnapped. In the Guerrero capital of Chilpancingo, twelve decapitated bodies, including at least seven soldiers, were found, including several arranged on a major boulevard with a sign bearing the warning *For every one of mine that you kill, I will kill 10*. A bag containing their heads was found nearby. Zulema Hernández, a sometimes mistress of Chapo Guzmán who had reportedly also gotten involved in the drug trade, was found dead in Mexico City, the letter "Z" carved into at least three different parts of her body. Though Hernández herself was believed to be an active participant in the drug trade, her murder, along with that of Chapo Guzmán's son, served to underline that, beyond the Mexican government's campaign, anyone connected with the narcos was not off limits in their war with one another.

As 2008 drew to a close, Attorney General Eduardo Medina Mora told the public that there had been a 117 percent spike in gangland killings in Mexico since the previous year. During the last three months of 2008 alone, there were 443 murders in Tijuana. By late 2008, the majority of betting parlors in Tamaulipas had closed because of narco demands for protection money. According to a report by the United Nations Office on Drugs and Crime, the United States, with a population of 310 million, consumed $37 billion of cocaine in 2008, while Europe as a whole, with a population of 830 million, consumed $34 billion.

When the United States Joint Forces Command published its Joint Operating Environment 2008 report, jarringly for the Mexicans, it contained the assessment that "two large and important states bear consideration for a rapid and sudden collapse: Pakistan and Mexico." The report went on to add that "the growing assault by the drug cartels and their thugs on the Mexican government over the past several years reminds one that an unstable Mexico could represent a homeland security problem of immense proportions to the United States."

Chapter Five

La Zona Libre

The relationship between Mexico and the United States has been nothing if not a fraught one for two ostensible allies. Felipe Calderón became the first foreign head of state to meet with President Barack Obama since the latter's election to the presidency when the pair lunched for two hours in Washington, DC. Calderón reportedly proposed the creation of a binational group of experts to explore security cooperation between the two countries. The new American president, the son of a black Kenyan father and a white mother from Kansas, had been elected on a wave of hope following the malaise of the Bush years (as typified by the blood-soaked adventure in Iraq). Obama did share one thing in common with his predecessor and with former US president Bill Clinton, though. As Clinton had and as Bush practically admitted he had, Obama had confessed to using illegal drugs—in his case both cocaine and marijuana—during his youth, though Obama, in his 1996 autobiography *Dreams from My Father: A Story of Race and Inheritance,* did so with a forthrightness that neither of the other men ever managed.

During the entire process of the debate about and construction of the border fence, the Bush administration treated the residents of the Rio Grande Valley as little more than subjects of an imperial dictatorship, and Michael Chertoff had played the role of the bootlicking court quisling and enforcer with relish. After Obama's inauguration, Chertoff was replaced by former Arizona governor Janet Napolitano, someone who, perhaps as a result of her long experience with the realities of life in the region, advocated for a somewhat different approach. A little over a year after Obama's inauguration, Napolitano announced that the administration was halting funding for the "virtual" border fence that would have further militarized the region saying that "the system of sensors and cameras along the Southwest border known as SBInet has been plagued with cost overruns and missed deadlines."

A stunning January 2009 assessment by the United States Government Accountability Office concluded that the so-called "pedestrian fencing" on the seven-hundred-mile border wall, that is, fencing designed to keep people from getting in and out of the United States on foot, had cost an average of $3.9 million per mile between 2007 and 2008. Nor had the money been spent with great care; it was revealed that at least a mile and a half of the border fence near Columbus, New Mexico, had been illegally built on Mexican territory.

It is, without dispute, a hideously ugly thing. As the ribbon of the Rio Grande meanders through the subtropical landscape of Tamaulipas and South Texas, the metal border fence rears up like a prison yard wall from the US banks of the river. As one drives west from Brownsville along the old Military Highway through Cameron County, past melancholy little cemeteries and mom-and-pop tortilla stands, one can see it, built well inland into the United States, pushing farmers' fields and even houses out back toward Mexico. Despite regular patrols by Border Patrol vehicles and the presence of cameras, at night the fence also helpfully throws vast swaths of the riverfront into deep shadow where once the land was fully exposed, thus aiding, as opposed to discouraging, drug trafficking and illegal crossings. At one stretch near Brownsville's Alice Wilson Hope Park, evening movements of drug loads over and through the fence became such a regular occurrence that locals began referring to the nocturnal assignations as "the Nine O'Clock Express." The very concept of the fence was greeted with derision by residents of the Rio Grande Valley.

Mark Clark had been traveling through Mexico for thirty years when he finally moved down to Brownsville in 2005 from Washington, DC. He bought a building only a couple blocks from the international bridge, a beautiful former customs house that he turned into a combination studio and living space. The first floor was a gallery that hosted an eclectic, rotating display of work by artists from both sides of the border while

Clark himself slept in a hammock on the second floor, surrounded by his paintings. One of them was a brilliant work called *Montezuma's Revenge*, which addressed and subverted many of the gringo stereotypes about Mexico, from masked wrestlers to bandidos with sombreros and skulls for heads and, of course, the usual assortment of narcos. Another had a comely bikini-clad Mexican babe floating down the Rio Grande away from infuriated border agents, laughing and waving beneath the words *Saludos desde el otro lado* (Welcome from the other side).

"Around 2009 it was open knowledge that border patrol changed shifts at five o'clock, and they would go to Los Fresnos to turn in their vehicles, which takes half an hour," Clark told me one day in his studio. "From five to six it was like King's X for everybody, you would see drug loads and armed men passing over from Mexico. Before, I used to know people who crossed loads on inner tubes, this border was just kind of open back then. Now, there's so much money these criminal syndicates have locked it all up and if you're not connected, forget about it."

After construction on the border wall had begun, Clark and other area artists decided to show their displeasure with the whole process the best way they knew how, through creative defiance in a series of protests that they dubbed Art Against the Wall. Around a dozen artists, some from as far away as McAllen and Houston, festooned the unsightly fence that blighted the bank of the Rio Grande in Brownsville's Hope Park with paintings and other artwork commenting on border issues. Among the most popular pieces were a pair of Border Patrol piñatas. The Border Patrol officers themselves watched uneasily from one hundred yards away.

NAFTA had proven to be, at best, a mixed blessing for the very poor Mexicans that it was theoretically designed to lift out of poverty.

The number of maquiladora jobs increased from 113,897 at the beginning of 1980 to 1,338,970 by October 2000. By the end of 2008, Mexico had overtaken Canada in its production of GM vehicles, with a total of 504,858 vehicles at four assembly plants in Mexico that year, 9 percent higher than the 463,869 vehicles produced by GM Canada. But the nature of the new economy, however, led to a terrible uncertainty for many along the border. After booming in the 1990s, the maquiladoras sector began declining sharply after October 2000 as the US economy began its long slide into recession. By the beginning of 2002, employment in the maquiladora sector had contracted by 21 percent while production had contracted by almost 30 percent. By mid-2010, the industry in Tamaulipas consisted of 200 maquiladoras employing fifty to four hundred employees per company, at an average salary of about 240 pesos (USD 18) per day. Around the same time, the highest level of Mexico's minimum wage was around 57.46 pesos a day, with wages in the second-highest category at 55.84 pesos. By mid-2010, Tamaulipas would represent 3.3 percent of Mexico's total GDP, and boast more than thirty petrochemical plants that accounted for 30 percent of the country's chemical and petrochemical production.

There were also local initiatives, such as the McAllen Economic Development Corporation (MEDC), which was founded in 1988 and helped to promote industrial development in Reynosa, "recognizing that if companies opened maquiladoras there, McAllen would benefit by providing inputs and offering management, engineering, warehousing, trucking, legal, and accounting services." By the mid-2000s, the MEDC had recruited 178 companies to the area in sectors including electronics, auto parts, and telecommunications. In the early part of the twenty-first century, relations between McAllen and Reynosa were so close that on the Spanish side of the border a new verb—*mcallenear*—had been coined meaning "to do McAllen."

On the road out toward Playa Baghdad in the industrial quarter of Matamoros, Spellman High Voltage, a company based in New York's Westchester County, has been operating in Mexico since 1996, and maintains two factories in close proximity to one another. Though the national minimum wage in Mexico is 58 pesos a day, at Spellman, which manufactures power supply devices and x-ray generators, the daily rate starts at 105 pesos.

"If we can create jobs here in Mexico, most people might not want to leave," Spellman general manager Ken Chandler, an American who grew up in Venezuela and speaks native Spanish, told me as we chatted in his Matamoros office. "If we can get people work, they'll find out they don't need to go to the States."

That certainly seemed to be the government's philosophy as, despite the roiling violence across the country, during Calderón's term in office Mexico would add more than 2.6 million new formal jobs to its already-existing 13.6 million, an improvement that nevertheless fell far short of the 1.2 million new people entering the workforce in Mexico each year. As economies around the world collapsed amid the 2008–2009 economic crisis, Mexico managed an average yearly growth of about 1.6 percent, well below its usual standards but by no means the wholesale collapse other countries faced.

But this all came at a price. According to a 2010 study by the Woodrow Wilson International Center for Scholars, between 2001 and 2008, Mexican spending on agriculture almost doubled, yet Mexico lost 20 percent of its farming jobs between 1991 and 2007, a loss of over two million jobs. The share of Mexico's workforce employed in the agricultural sector fell from 23 percent in 1990 to 13 percent in 2008. There were a number of reasons for this, including the old worry of corruption given the lack of transparency and accountability in doling out the farm subsidies. By the mid-2000s, Tamaulipas had the highest concentration of agricultural spending by Mexico's agricultural ministry, the *Secretaría de Agricultura, Ganadería, Desarrollo Rural, Pesca y Alimentación* (SAGARPA), 15 percent of that allotted to the whole country.

In the dairy industry, since the Agricultural Act of 1949, US dairy farmers had enjoyed advantageous price protection on many different crops and even many meats. When prices on certain products fell below certain levels, it was mandated that farmers were to be paid the difference. The agricultural sector, which had supported Mexicans for decades, was being decimated in favor of a more insecure future. By mid-2009, abutting the United States and its grinding, stubborn recession, Mexico's economy had shrunk by 9.7 percent from the previous year, with forty thousand manufacturing jobs lost in Nuevo León alone.

By the dawn of 2009, while the world's richest man, Carlos Slim, was a Mexican, with a fortune valued at $53.5 billion, half of Mexico's 107 million people lived in poverty, and some twenty million Mexicans had to get by on less than three dollars per day. Into that void arrived the drug trade. In an editorial the Catholic Archdiocese of Mexico would write, "we are a generous and hospitable people, without doubt, but now we are realizing with shock and shame that we have become a corrupt and murderous country."

And it was getting more so. Mexico's murder rate, which had been declining steadily in the years before Calderón's inauguration, had tripled during the course of 2008. In January 2009, Pemex workers found the bodies of four men on company property 93 miles northeast of Monterrey along the US-Mexico border.

María Santos Gorrostieta Salazar, who had been elected mayor of the Michoacán town of Tiquicheo, was attacked by gunmen along with her husband on January 16, 2009. Both survived with relatively minor injuries. After the attack, Santos Gorrostieta would be interviewed in the *El País* newspaper where she would say that "despite my own safety and that of my family, I have a responsibility to my people, with children, women, the elderly and men who are breaking their back every day tirelessly to procure a piece of bread. . . . It is not possible for me to cave into [threats] when I have three children whom I have to teach by example." In the Mexican political world where porcine opportunists and slit-eyed thugs were the norm, the young and photogenic Gorrostieta made a bracing change.

The beginning of 2009 marked a chaotic one for the Gulf-Zetas alliance. Mexico's attorney general's office went on record in saying that the Gulf-Zetas cartel had "the biggest presence and activity in crime and violence" in the country, and that they accounted for the majority of the 31,512 weapons seized since December 2005. A Mexican judge decided that there was enough evidence to order former PFP commander Javier Herrera to stand trial for charges that he had received money from the Gulf Cartel in exchange for protecting them from arrest. Meanwhile, the Gulf Cartel's Reynosa plaza boss, Héctor Manuel "El Karis" Sauceda Gamboa, was killed on February 17 when security forces attacked the home where he was staying in the southwestern part of the city.

Meanwhile, an underground rap duo made up of two Reynosa residents, Alejandro Coronado and Mauro Vasquez, had recorded a song called *"Reynosa La Maldosa"* (Evil Reynosa) in 2007 under the names Cano and Blunt, detailing their city's slide into drug war perdition. Eventually they would also record a song in tribute to the Gulf Cartel's Samuel "El Metro 3" Flores Borrego, saying how the narco "was from the government, now he's with the crew" and admiring how he "leads from the front" and that "with his cuerno (AK-47) he'll send you straight to hell."

One of Flores's main deputies by this time was Benicio López, a Houston native who had grown up in Roma, Texas, just across the border from Miguel Alemán, and went by the name *"Comandante Veneno"* (Commander Venom). Another former Roma resident who went to work with the cartel was Mario Peña, who graduated from small-time Texas criminality to becoming a Gulf Cartel enforcer under the name *"Comandante Popo."* Heavily tattooed and charismatic, Peña became somewhat legendary on both sides of the border in the Rio Grande Valley, working around Miguel Alemán before being murdered in the Comales area of Tamaulipas.

By this time, the Gulf-Zetas alliance also had deep links with street and prison gangs on the Texas side of the border, whom they sold drugs to. Texas gangs like *Hermandad de Pistoleros Latinos* and Tango Blast (referred to as *Los Vallucos* in the Rio Grande Valley) had "strong business connections with the Gulf Cartel and Los Zetas" and worked "to facilitate the transport of drugs into Texas." When a member of the Tri-City Bombers gang—so named for their axis of operating in the Texas cities of Pharr, San Juan, and Alamo—tossed a grenade through the window of a bar in Pharr, in January 2009, it was traced back to the same batch Los Zetas had used earlier to attack the US consulate in Monterrey.

For those sent back to Mexico from the United States through Matamoros and Reynosa, however, often hundreds of miles from their nearest families in Mexico, the reality was even grimmer. The new arrivals made easy prey for the cartels, both in terms of extortion and as a pool of desperate recruits.

Padre Francisco Gallardo López, a Catholic priest, runs the *Casa del Migrante* (Migrant House) in Matamoros, as well as a similar body in Reynosa and a satellite office at the main Matamoros bus station. He has been working with people deported from the United States to Mexico for nearly a decade. Speaking in his office, he tells me that sometimes two hundred people will be deported back across the bridge between Brownsville and Matamoros in a single day.

"The situation is very difficult for them," he says. "They arrive separated from their family, and this has a tremendous psychological impact. They are lost, they arrive without any official identity documents, without any money to get back to their place of family origin in Mexico. They are in a very delicate situation, and can be very susceptible to the pressure of armed groups, to whom the immigrants are viewed as products, not people."

At the *Central De Autobuses* bus terminal in Matamoros, a number of men ranging in age from their early twenties to their fifties gathered around the Casa's office there, trying to make sense of their new lives. They linger outside of the small bureau, or sit at a small desk there, logging onto their e-mail or Facebook accounts and trying to reconnect with the life they left behind in the United States. They weren't angels, nor did they claim to be.

One twenty-two-year-old, whom I will call Francisco, came to the United States when he was six years old and lived in Atlanta and Alabama. Dressed in a US baseball jersey from which tattooed arms protrude, he tells me about having committed an armed robbery when he was a juvenile, and subsequently being arrested for driving without a license as an adult. He was sent across the border in Matamoros. His nearest family members in Mexico are in far-off Mexico City.

"It's a whole different life here," he says, eyeing some of the hard-eyed *cholos* lingering at the bus station. "It's hard to adapt."

Another man, a thirty-one-year-old I will call Manuel, lived in Jackson, Mississippi, and worked on construction projects around the state including at the University of Mississippi in Oxford.

"If you look at those new buildings on the campus there," he says, with more than a trace of professional pride. "I helped build those."

To the west of Matamoros, in Reynosa, following the terminus of an often lethal highway, Pastor Hector Joaquin Silva de Luna runs the *Senda de Vida* (Way of Life) center in a dangerous, Gulf Cartel–controlled neighborhood. An Afro-Mexican man from the Pacific Coast city of Puerto Escondido in Oaxaca whose imposing frame is disarmed by a ready smile, Silva has run the center since being deported from Dallas after living illegally in the United States for nearly twenty years.

Visiting the Senda de Vida on a dusty back road, one immediately notices the *halcones,* the often nondescript young delinquents, street people, and others who act as the cartel's eyes and ears. They lurk across the street, walkie-talkies in their back pockets, reporting on the comings and goings there. Several times men, some armed, have forced their way into the center and tried to extract residents, usually women.

"The majority of people who arrive here have been exploited, mistreated, psychologically and otherwise," he says of the population of the spit-and-polish center he runs, with spotlessly clean residence halls and neatly tended flower beds. It is not an easy calling.

"I am living here between life and death," he says. "And it is only because of my devotion that I go on."

One resident, a woman whom I will not name, lived nearly her entire life in the United States before being deported to Mexico after being convicted on a drug charge, an event she sees as part of a divine plan.

"All my family members are on the other side; I had nowhere to go when I got here," she says. "When I was in prison I got close to God, and I asked Him to bring me to a place where I would walk with Him. God answered my prayer and brought me here."

The PRI governor of Nuevo León, José Natividad González Parás, charged that February 2009 protests against the army's presence in Monterrey—which saw roads blocked by masked men and burning piles of wood—were financed by "organized crime groups that are part of a national network." Among those arrested in connection with the protests was twenty-year-old Juan Antonio Beltrán Cruz, alias El Queco, rumored to be an affiliate of Los Zetas.

Later that month in an interview with the Associated Press, Calderón reacted strongly to suggestions that the relentless drumbeat of violence had made Mexico a failed or failing state, saying that, "I have not lost any part—any single part—of Mexican territory." He then called on the

United States to work harder to stem the flow of assault weapons across its southern border.

Also in late February 2009 in direct correlation to that violence, while announcing the arrest of fifty Sinaloa Cartel members in the United States, US attorney general Eric Holder alluded to the expiration of the assault weapons ban in the United States five years earlier by saying "there are just a few gun-related changes that we would like to make, and among them would be to reinstitute the ban on the sale of assault weapons. I think that will have a positive impact in Mexico, at a minimum." Obama had pledged to make the assault weapons ban permanent during his 2008 electoral campaign but once in office found that he lacked the votes in Congress to do so, a testament to how in thrall the US Congress was to the moneyed influence of the National Rifle Association, despite a broad majority of Americans—62 percent—supporting such a ban.

As the US Congress turned its back on any substantive gun control, the Calderón government sent five thousand additional troops to Ciudad Juárez in February 2009—bringing the total of troops in the city to seventy-five hundred. Gustavo de la Rosa Hickerson, the white-bearded attorney who headed up the Chihuahua's branch of Mexico's *Comisión Estatal de los Derechos Humanos* (CEDH) human rights body based in Juárez, told students at a conference at the University of Texas at El Paso that the Mexican army was seizing people illegally and subjecting them to torture. He added that the militarization of the fight against drug trafficking was "a public safety problem turned into a war" and that "the suspension of individual rights is a situation much more grave than the war among cartels."

At a press conference in Rio de Janeiro (and later at the Brookings Institute in Washington, DC) in February 2009, Calderón's predecessor Ernesto Zedillo, former Colombian president César Gaviria, and former Brazilian president Fernando Henrique Cardoso launched a report by a body the three men cochaired called the Latin American Commission on Drugs and Democracy. Titled "Drugs and Democracy: Toward a Paradigm Shift," the report stated that "prohibitionist policies based on the eradication of production and on the disruption of drug flows as well as on the criminalization of consumption have not yielded the expected results. We are farther than ever from the announced goal of eradicating drugs."

The report went on to note that, following Colombia a decade earlier,

Mexico has quickly become the other epicenter of the violent activities carried out by the criminal groups associated with the narcotics trade. This raises challenges for the Mexican government in its struggle against the drug cartels that have supplanted the Colombian traffickers as the main suppliers of illicit drugs to the United States market. . . . The traumatic Colombian experience is a useful reference for countries not to make the mistake of adopting the US prohibitionist policies and to move forward in the search for innovative alternatives.

The report advocated that nations "change the status of addicts from drug buyers in the illegal market to that of patients cared for in the public health system. . . . Evaluate from a public health standpoint and on the basis of the most advanced medical science the convenience of decriminalizing the possession of cannabis for personal use. . . . [And finally] redirect repressive strategies to the unrelenting fight against organized crime."

It was a welcome move coming from such an august assemblage (the commission also included among its members former Bogotá mayor Antanas Mockus, the Peruvian author Mario Vargas Llosa, and the Brazilian writer Paulo Coelho, among others), and showed that there was a growing effort to shift discussion on the drug issue from one which simply parroted US demands for a military solution. But the report passed with little attention in the United States, save for the chattering classes of Washington and New York. Nevertheless, coming from a group of Latin American leaders who had seen the front lines of the drug war the United States dictated that they fight on its behalf, the report was a significant sign that regional unity on the subject was beginning to crack.

But would Mexico crack first? By March 2009, according to the US State Department, 90 percent of the cocaine in the United States transited through Mexico. The profits from the traffic to Mexico's criminal gangs were believed to be somewhere in the neighborhood of $10 billion. That month, the Obama administration announced that it was sending 350 additional personnel from its Homeland Security Department to the US-Mexico border to reinforce security teams there, adding sixteen new DEA positions in the US Southwest and sending one hundred additional ATF agents as well. The White House also said that the FBI would boost intelligence work on Mexican cartels.

But in Mexico itself, things continued much as before. Bearing signs of torture, the body of Gonzalo Paz Torres, the city council chief of the blighted Michoacán town of Tancítaro, was found on March 6, 2009, a day after he had been kidnapped. Two weeks later, Gulf Cartel sicario Sigifrido Najera Talamantes, a suspect in the 2008 attack on the US consulate in Monterrey and the killing of soldiers, was captured in Saltillo, Coahuila. Authorities added charges of human trafficking and robbery of fuel from Pemex pipelines to homicide, drug-trafficking, and kidnapping indictments.

But the problem was no longer Mexico's alone, not that it ever was. In early 2009, security forces in Guatemala found a Zetas training camp a few miles south on the Mexican border near Ixcán in the heavily indigenous department of El Quiché. At least five hundred grenades and thousands of bullets were also seized. On April 9, a former Guatemalan soldier was killed along with two other men during a gun battle with federal police in Zacatecas. That same month, Guatemala security forces found a weapons cache near the nation's capital containing almost four thousand rounds of ammunition, 564 grenades, 11 M60 machine guns, eight antipersonnel mines, and two armored cars that they said had been destined for the Zetas. In the course of the previous year, Los Zetas' already-extant presence throughout Mexico's southern neighbor had now become pervasive.

In early April 2009 Mexican law enforcement personnel destroyed more than thirty Santa Muerte shrines along roadways in and around Nuevo Laredo, with some of the structures intended to be permanent enough that they were made out of marble. The shrine destructions were denounced by sect leader David Romo and prompted some two hundred people to march from Tepito to Mexico City's *Catedral Metropolitana* in protest charging that the belief system went far beyond its narco adherents. "I believe in Santa Muerte and I'm not a narco," one protester's banner read, while Romo himself declared that adherents were launching a "holy war" against what they charged was religious persecution. Romo also urged devotees to vote against "Catholic," i.e., PAN candidates, in the forthcoming elections.

In a mountainous region of Guerrero, fifteen suspected cartel gunmen and one Mexican soldier died after a military convoy allegedly came under fire from a group of gunmen it encountered near the town of San Nicolás del Oro on April 14. The lopsided casualty figures would come to be a more and more frequent facet of the government's direct encounters with cartel gunmen, and led many to question whether or not the military had been given an understanding—direct or tacit—to terminate the narcos when and where they could. The same day, four people were found slain in Michoacán. The following day, Barack Obama arrived in Mexico and met with Calderón in the capital.

Had they met a few days later, they could have perhaps discussed the case of John Philip Hernandez, a twenty-six-year-old Houston man, who had just been sentenced to eight years in prison for purchasing or helping to purchase more than one hundred military-style firearms, many of which ended up in the hands of Mexico's cartels, including a Bushmaster assault rifle recovered after a confrontation between the Mexican army and Los Zetas in Oaxaca and another recovered in connection with the kidnapping and murder of a Puebla businessman. Yet another was used during the February 2007 assault on the Guerrero state attorney general's office in Acapulco, an attack that left seven people dead.

The Hernandez arrest was merely a symptom of the wider disease. At gun shows in Texas, New Mexico, and Arizona, unlicensed dealers were not even obligated to record the buyer's name. Additionally, in Arizona, for example, no licensing or permit requirements whatsoever were imposed for purchasing firearms, including limiting the firearms a person could purchase by quantity or time period. Additionally, there was no federal statute specifically prohibiting firearms trafficking or straw purchasing, though there were a number of statutes prohibiting such things as individuals engaging in a firearms business without a license (the key word being "business") or knowingly making a false statement or presenting false identification in connection with a firearms purchase. The main driver in this unfettered access to lethal firepower was the American lobbying organization the National Rifle Association, a body that had originally served as something of a gun-safety and hunter's club but which during the presidency of Bill Clinton—who passed the assault weapons ban in 1994—had turned into an absolutist organization of wild-eyed antigovernment fanatics, led by their shrill vice president Wayne La Pierre and utterly in thrall to the gun industry rather than gun owners.

Displaying more courage than most politicians on either side of the border, the archbishop of Durango, Héctor González Martínez, stunned the Mexican press in mid-April 2009. When asked about the insecurity in the state, he said flatly that "*El Chapo* lives around (the Durango city of) Guanacevi. Everybody, including the authorities knows this." The archbishop also stated that drug trafficking and its violence had created "an almost chaotic psychosis" in the state. Following González's comments, Víctor Manuel Solís, spokesman for the Durango Archdiocese, told a local radio station that González's declarations were "reckless, dangerous and to a certain degree, irresponsible."

Adding a surreal twist to the drug war, Rafael Cedeño Hernández, the high-ranking capo of La Familia, was soon after arrested with forty-three other cartel members at a child's baptism at which, along with the child, were present such decidedly nonecclesiastical items as a number of assault rifles and hand grenades. Cedeño subsequently told authorities that, despite heading up one of the world's most violent drug-trafficking organizations, he advised La Familia members "to avoid drugs, hard drinking and maintain family unity."

The bodies of nine men, pockmarked with bullet holes, were found in and around Acapulco on April 24. A few days later, after months of relative calm, seven Tijuana police officers were slain within an hour of one another. In Reynosa, the former Gulf Cartel plaza boss Gregorio "El Goyo" Sauceda Gamboa, now greatly diminished through years of addiction, was arrested by Mexican authorities at the end of the month. In a daring mid May raid, twenty heavily armed men believed to be Los Zetas arrived in nearly a dozen vehicles and a helicopter at a prison in Zacatecas State and freed fifty-three prisoners with links to the Gulf Cartel. Around forty guards and administrators were subsequently arrested for being accomplices to the jailbreak.

A two-hour gun battle in the heart of Acapulco's hotel zone, sparked when police raided a house in the district, left fifteen suspected narcos, one soldier, and at least one civilian dead on June 7, and sent tourists and residents fleeing in terror. Police recovered dozens of guns, grenades, ammunition, and four Guerrero state police officers handcuffed in the garage. At least three civilians were wounded in the fighting. The gunmen were believed to be members of the Beltrán-Leyva Cartel. Two days later, gunmen shot and killed two police officers in the city.

By June 2009, an eerie calm had descended upon Nuevo Laredo as the Gulf Cartel and their Zetas allies had defeated the Sinaloa Cartel in their battle for control of the city. Now flooded with soldiers—some of whom observers charged had in fact sided with the Sinaloa Cartel— Nuevo Laredo also presented a somewhat more difficult target for a foreign cartel invasion than it had in previous years. The net winners in this struggle were Los Zetas, who emerged stronger and more independent than ever before.

Though Tamaulipas governor Eugenio Hernández Flores boasted about a June 2009 agreement, signed in Ciudad Victoria, whereby the FBI and DEA were to share intelligence and provide training to the Tamaulipas state police, given the fact that the Gulf Cartel largely *were* the state police in the state, many wondered how such an agreement would in fact work.

A June 26 encounter between police and cartel gunmen, allegedly Zetas, in the city of Apaseo el Alto in Guanajuato left twelve cartel gunmen dead and one police officer wounded. The state attorney general said the police had been checking a report of armed men in a building when they had been fired upon. The same day, gunmen in Sonora fired on a car carrying PAN congressional candidate Ernesto Cornejo Valenzuela, killing two people in the car but missing their intended target.

By that summer, La Familia was believed to have become the biggest maker of methamphetamine in Mexico, a status that was impacted little by the arrest of La Familia deputy Arnoldo Rueda Medina in Morelia. Later that day, gunmen believed to belong to La Familia attacked police and soldiers in the city and in five other cities around the states, killing five federal agents and two soldiers. Two days later, near the Michoacán municipality of La Huacana, a dozen bodies bearing signs of torture were found, and two more near the airport in Morelia. The same day as the discovery of the bodies, Rogelio Ramos, the police chief of the Coahuila border city of Piedras Negras near Eagle Pass, Texas, was dragged from his car and kidnapped, not to be heard from again. The twelve bodies found at La Huacana were later identified to be those of federal agents.

By mid-2009, Calderón had replaced both the AFI and the PFP, with, respectively, the *Policía Federal Ministerial* (PFM) and the *Policía Federal* (PF). Early July midterm elections saw a muscular return of the PRI, which became the most powerful force in Mexico's congress, besting both the PAN and the PRD, which came in third. The PAN also lost five high-profile gubernatorial races.

In an extraordinary bit of responsibility shirking, following the vote, Mexico State governor Enrique Peña Nieto blithely opined that "the PRI does not have a joint responsibility with the national government. . . . All we have is a majority in one house and our governorships. The executive has its agenda, and we have ours." Such an attitude was of a piece of that which had been in evidence among many PRI governors such as Peña Nieto in their resistance to making any moves of substance against the cartels in the states which they ruled.

That same month, Zetas gunmen and Mexican police fought for twenty minutes in the historic center of Veracruz in a battle that left two gunmen dead and several cars in flames. In late July, attackers believed to be Los Zetas attacked the home of the deputy commander of the Veracruz police, José Antonio Romero Vázquez, killing him along with his wife and four teenage children, two daughters and two sons, before setting the building on fire by exploding grenades inside it. Romero Vázquez had boasted an unblemished record as a police officer, and it was thought the attack might have been retaliation for the arrest of one of the Zetas' chief financial coordinators, Jorge Alberto Jiménez González, only days earlier.

By this time, in a cable from the DEA's Houston field office to DEA headquarters in Washington, the department was concluding that Los Zetas

> *are no longer solely operating as the enforcement arm of the Gulf Cartel. The strength of the Zeta force is their ability to corrupt, kill, and intimidate and these factors have given the Zetas the power to conduct activities throughout Mexico, and they have established a methodology to move into new territory and assert control over that geography. Zeta activities have evolved from drug trafficking to traditional organized crime as well. . . . While still closely allied with the Gulf Cartel, the Zetas have evolved into a separate drug trafficking organization that is independently transporting cocaine from Colombia to Mexico.*

Citing the murders of five people, including three innocent bystanders, in Birmingham, Alabama, in August 2008, the DEA and the US Department of State named the ten most-wanted members of the the the Gulf Cartel and Los Zetas and offered rewards up to $50 million for information leading to their capture. Those sought included Tony Tormenta, Juan Reyes Mejia Gonzalez, Samuel Flores-Borrego, Heriberto Lazcano, Miguel Treviño, and Alejandro Treviño.

On August 9, the Calderón government arrested Dimas Díaz Ramos, an alleged financial coordinator for the Sinaloa Cartel and associate of Ismael "El Mayo" Zambada García based in Culiacán who, the government said, had been planning to assassinate the president. The same day, at the Pulga Río market in downtown Monterrey, Raquenel Villanueva, a fifty-four-year-old attorney with a history of representing clients from the narco underworld, was walking with her teenage daughter. Several men approached Villanueva, who had survived four previous attempts against her life. One mowed her down with an AR-15 assault rifle and another administered a coup de grace with a bullet to the head. The next day, the government scooped up Juan Daniel "El Colosio" Carranco Salazar, the alleged leader of the Gulf Cartel's operations in Quintana Roo, including the resort city of Cancún, alleged instigator of the October 2008 attack on the US consulate in Monterrey, and the assassin of various military personnel.

On August 20, Mexico's *Comisión Nacional de los Derechos Humanos* (CNDH) announced that fifty-two journalists or media workers had been slain in the previous decade, with the vast majority of the killings remaining unsolved, and with seven other reporters having gone missing. As the Mexican media soldiered bravely on, some terrorized into silence but a substantial number continuing to do their jobs in what had become an increasingly lethal environment, individuals claiming to have found the key to decoding the complex and often overlapping criminal-political nexus in Mexico appeared. Unfortunately, their work sometimes served to only further obscure, rather than clarify. A good example of this trait is the widely quoted legal commentator and Columbia University professor Edgardo Buscaglia, who around the time of the CNDH report made the striking claim to *El Universal* that La Familia had infiltrated 85 percent of the economic sectors in Michoacán, Guanajuato, and Guerrero. Like a significant chunk of what Buscaglia would often claim, though, the charge was one made free of any sound methodology backing it up, though that did not prevent media outlets from repeating it as some sort of received gospel.

And the Mexican press was not alone in falling victim to violence. The body of Armando Chavarría Barrera, the PRD-affiliated president of the state legislature of Guerrero, was found early on the morning of August 20 in the passenger seat of a vehicle in the state capital of Chilpancingo. He had been shot to death. The same day, three human heads and three mutilated cadavers were found in the Guerrero municipality of Coyuca de Catalán. Human rights activists in Ciudad Juárez convened a *Foro Contra la Militarización y la Represión* (Forum Against Militarization and Repression) in the city, with the aim of highlighting military abuses there. Among the speakers were Josefina Reyes, a barbecue vendor from a largely agricultural community just south of the city who had been spurred to action by the detention of her son without charge by federal troops, and Cipriana Jurado, who ran the *Centro de Investigación y Solidaridad* (Center for Investigation and Solidarity) in the city. After her participation in the forum, Reyes's son was kidnapped from their home and later found dead, a crime that she blamed on the army.

Early September saw another wave of violence. In Ciudad Juárez, gunmen invaded a drug rehabilitation center, lined recovering addicts up against a wall, and gunned down seventeen people. In Michoacán, José Manuel Revueltas López, the deputy state director of public safety, was assassinated by gunmen in another vehicle as his car drove along one of Morelia's busiest thoroughfares. On September 6, José Francisco Fuentes Esperón, a university professor who had just launched his campaign as a PRI candidate for the state legislature in Tabasco, was murdered inside of his home in the state capital of Villahermosa along with his wife and two young sons. Three youths were later arrested for the crime, which officials said had been motivated by robbery and an "obsession" of one of the attackers with Fuentes's wife.

In early September, in a move that surprised almost everyone, Calderón nominated Arturo Chávez Chávez, who had served as attorney general of Chihuahua from 1996 to 1998, as his choice to replace Eduardo Medina Mora, the outgoing attorney general of Mexico. Chosen apparently for his loyalty to the oft-assailed Calderón, Chávez's nomination was met with outrage from human rights groups in Ciudad Juárez who accused him of, at the very least, essentially ignoring the murders of women that took place in that city during his tenure in office. A cable from the US Embassy in Mexico City to the State Department in the wake of the nomination said that the "choice was totally unexpected and politically inexplicable," noting that Chávez had "strong detractors within the Mexican human rights community because of his perceived failings in dealing with the murder of a large number of women in Ciudad Juárez."

As if to underline the failure of Chihuahua and the federal government to rein in the violence there, only days before the announcement the state's leading human rights advocate, the attorney Gustavo de la Rosa Hickerson of the CEDH, was told by a driver who cocked his finger like a gun at a traffic light in Ciudad Juárez, *Ya bájale porque te vamos a matar*

(Quiet down or we're going to kill you), and was forced to flee across the Rio Grande to El Paso. De la Rosa later said he believed his life was threatened for taking statements from victims of abuses by the Mexican army and police. De la Rosa would continue with his role at CEDH but would spend most of his off-hours living in El Paso from then on. Just to the east, General Manuel de Jesús Moreno Aviña, who had been terrorizing Ojinaga and allegedly working on behalf of the Juárez Cartel there, was removed from his post in September 2009.

For those who doubted that drug-related corruption respected no border, there was the case of former ICE agent Richard Padilla Cramer, who had retired from the force two years earlier and was arrested at his Arizona home after serving as paid consigliere for various drug traffickers while stationed in Guadalajara (where he worked closely with Mexican police), advising them about DEA investigative procedures and helping them track down snitches. Extraordinarily, Cramer was eventually allowed to plead guilty to a lesser charge of obstruction of justice and sentenced to a mere two years in jail by a federal judge in Miami.

And how would Mexico's bloody summer of 2009 settle into autumn? Five men were killed when a group of gunmen walked into Gabino's bar in Ciudad Juárez on October 5, six months after four other men had been killed in the same bar. The same day, police arrested Edward Vera Arias, a thirty-year-old Juárez Cartel sicario who admitted to personally killing at least thirty people, one for each year of his life. A few days later the tortured and bullet-riddled body of Estanislao García Santelis, the mayor of the border town of Palomas in Chihuahua, was found in a burned-out pickup. In an industrial zone of Tijuana the following day, factory workers arriving for their daily labor were greeted by the naked, mutilated body of Rogelio Sánchez Jiménez, a state official charged with distributing driver's licenses, hanging from a bridge.

CHAPTER SIX

By Fair Means or Foul

María Santos Gorrostieta, the independent-minded mayor of the Michoacán town of Tiquicheo, who had been the victim of an assassination attempt only the previous January, was again attacked by masked gunmen, as she was driving with her husband, José Sánchez Chávez, through the town of El Limón de Papatzindán on October 15, 2009. The mayor was left gravely wounded, but survived. Her husband was not so lucky, and died of his injuries. Santos would later post photos of her horrific injuries online and as part of a letter to the municipal officials in Tiquicheo in response to those who voiced doubts that she had even been attacked.

"I wanted to show you my wounds because I'm not ashamed that my body is mutilated like this," she told reporters, when asked why she posted the photos, which included that of a colostomy bag attached to her abdomen. "It is the result of shameful acts which have marked my life and the lives of my children. But I am not ashamed. I can't quit, not when I have three children whom I have to teach by example. Beside that I have the memories of my husband, the father of my children, who knew how to teach the value of things and fight for them."

That same month, a crackdown on the Michoacán-based La Familia operatives in the United States, dubbed Project Coronado, resulted in more than three hundred arrests in nineteen states. By this point it was believed that the cartel was operating so-called "superlabs" in Mexico that were capable of producing up to one hundred pounds of methamphetamine in eight hours. The leader of the *Unión General Obrera, Campesina y Popular* (UGOCP), Margarito Montes, was slain in Sonora, along with fourteen other people, when gunmen opened fire on his convoy from the roadside, ambushing the group as they left a commemoration for a 1937 land distribution measure.

The PAN politician Mauricio Fernández Garza, scion of an affluent Nuevo León family, could view his success in becoming mayor of San Pedro Garza García, an independent municipality within Monterrey's metropolitan area ranked as the nation's wealthiest, as personal vindication. Having been defeated by the PRI's José Natividad González Parás in a bruising 2003 campaign for the governorship of Nuevo León, when Fernández, who had campaigned on a security platform, was sworn in at the end of October, he was also able to announce to cheering supporters the death of Héctor "El Negro" Saldaña, a Beltrán-Leyva associate and kidnapper who had been threatening him. There was only one problem: Saldaña's corpse would not be found for another three hours and wouldn't be identified for two days. Next to the body were several notes, one quoting Job 38:15 ("The wicked are denied their light, and their upraised arm is broken") and another reading "for kidnapping," and signed by "*El jefe de jefes,*" a reference to Arturo Beltrán Leyva.

Fernández's statement during his inauguration that "by fair means or foul, we are not going to accept any kind of kidnapping . . . they will pay for it" began to take on an altogether different ring. Speaking to the publication *Milenio,* Fernández had said that he planned to put into action a "tough group" to take care of "complicated things." Mexico's *El Universal* newspaper asked if Fernández's approach evoked "white knights or death squads."

The picture was complicated still further by an audio recording that surfaced that quoted Fernández as saying that "the Beltrán-Leyva themselves are in agreement . . . they value living in peace, and we have to take advantage of that." At one point, Fernández displayed a large degree of misanthropy by telling a filmmaker that "the average human is mediocre, aggressive, destructive, envious and a lot of other things. . . . I don't think wars are won by nuns or something like that, wars are tough. And we haven't realized we are in a real war." He went on to say that his life's "vocation" was to "kill those bastards," presumably meaning those who did not meet his exacting standards.

In November 2009, four days after he assumed command of the police force in the industrial town of García near Monterrey, retired general Juan Arturo Esparza García was slain in a hail of two hundred bullets. State investigators would later arrest twenty people, the majority of them police officers, for involvement in the killing. It was an attack believed to be coordinated by the Zetas leader for Monterrey, Óscar Manuel Bernal Soriano, aka *El Araña* (The Spider).

The sorrows of law enforcement for the month didn't end there. On November 3, police had cornered and killed Braulio "Z-20" Arellano Domínguez, a close ally of Miguel Treviño, in the town of Soledad de Doblado in Veracruz. Four days later, the dismembered body of police commander Casto Acevedo Manzano, his torso and limbs in one pile and his head nearby, was found in the same town. On top of the torso was laid a message on which was scrawled *Esto es por faltarle a la letra Z* (This is for disappointing the letter Z).

And the US role in the violence in Mexico was about to get even more complicated. After four individuals conducted multiple purchases of assault rifles at a Phoenix gun store in October 2009, the ATF began a program, later dubbed Operation Fast and Furious, that "deferred taking overt enforcement action against the individual straw purchasers while seeking to build a case against the leaders" of criminal organizations in Mexico and the United States. The policy echoed the earlier "gun-walking" program that had been led out of the Phoenix office from 2006 to 2007 during the Bush administration dubbed Operation Wide Receiver. It was a strategy that would come back to haunt the Department of Justice and the Obama administration for years to come.

In the Sonora border town of Naco on November 20, Mexican security forces seized forty-one AK-47s and a Beowulf .50 caliber rifle en route to the Sinaloa Cartel. The weapons had been bought at a gun store in Arizona and, within twenty-four hours, crossed the border into Mexico. The weapons, it was later revealed, were linked to Operation Fast and Furious. Only three weeks later, forty-one AK-47 rifles as well as an AR-15 rifle and an FN 5.7 also believed to be bound for the Sinaloa Cartel were seized in the Baja California state capital of Mexicali, along with sizable amounts of cocaine and methamphetamine and $2 million in US currency. The recovered weapons were traced back to straw purchasers being monitored under Operation Fast and Furious.

In late November 2009, Calderón said that he had been left no alternative but to confront the cartels militarily, and that "the choice cannot be between combatting organized crime, as we are doing, or watching it take over Mexico, the way it was taking over Mexico before we acted."

Among those actions was the storming of a house in the Monterrey suburb of Juárez by Mexican navy troops on December 4, 2009, which succeeded in killing eight Zetas, including Ricardo "El Gori 1" Almanza Morales, an important Zetas leader in Nuevo León. It was believed that Almanza had been behind the November slaying of retired general and city of García police chief Juan Arturo Esparza García and his bodyguards. A shootout between Mexican security forces and a group of sicarios racing to free Almanza resulted in the deaths of five people. Only hours later, suspected Zetas gunmen assaulted a detention center in Escobedo, a Monterrey suburb, freeing twenty-three inmates and killing two federal police officers in the process. In a twenty-four-hour period on December 10 and 11, seven federal police officers and a civilian were killed in several different shootouts around Michoacán, and four mutilated bodies were dumped near a middle school in the Guerrero state capital of Chilpancingo with a note alluding to the Beltrán-Leyva Cartel. Four days later, gunmen speeding past in vehicles hurled fragmentary bombs at a police station in Morelia, severely injuring a pregnant woman and her three-year-old daughter.

As 2009 drew to a close, the picturesque city of Cuernavaca, long a refuge for the capital's wealthy and the memorable setting for the British author Malcolm Lowry's book *Under the Volcano,* was the scene of a ferocious gun battle on December 16. Over two hundred Mexican navy personnel raided a tony apartment complex only to be met with withering automatic weapons fire and hurled grenades. When the fighting was over, Arturo Beltrán Leyva and six of his gunmen lay dead. A member of the navy's Special Forces was also killed. The navy had narrowly missed

Beltrán Leyva at a party only six days before in the nearby town of Tepoztlán. There, police had arrested several people, including Mexican *norteño* singer Ramón Ayala, and engaged in a gun battle that killed three alleged cartel members. Beltrán Leyva was finally tracked down courtesy of US law enforcement agents who had been electronically spying on him for weeks if not months, and passed the information on to the special forces of the Mexican navy.

The government savoring of its victory over one of the country's most ruthless men was to be short-lived, however. During an emotional ceremony for Melquisedet Angulo Córdova, the member of the navy's Special Forces who had died in the assault on the Beltrán-Leyva compound, Mexico's secretary of the navy Mariano Francisco Saynez Mendoza presented the flag that covered the young soldier's casket to his mother, Irma Córdova Palma. The ceremony, in Angulo's home state of Tabasco, was broadcast live on Mexican television. Within hours, gunmen had stormed the family's home in the town of Paraíso, killing Angulo's mother, his sister, Yolidabey, his aunt Josefa Angulo Flores, and his brother Benito. Another sister was injured. Tabasco's attorney general Rafael González later said the killers were from Los Zetas. Another Beltrán Leyva brother, Carlos, would later be arrested in Culiacán.

As 2009 drew to a close, the violence in Ciudad Juárez defied belief. During December 14–15, at least eighteen people were killed in the city. On December 21, at least thirteen people died. By the end of the year, business groups in the city were calling for the United Nations to deploy a peacekeeping force there.

During 2009, the ATF's Office of Strategic Intelligence and Information Southwest Border Field Intelligence Support Team (FIST) and El Paso Intelligence Center (EPIC) identified over three hundred seizure events of firearms in Mexico, with the Gulf Cartel and Los Zetas making up 117 seizures, La Familia's involvement in fifty-three, the Sinaloa Cartel's involvement in forty-five, the Tijuana Cartel's involvement in thirty-four, the Beltrán-Leyva organization's involvement in thirty, and the Juárez Cartel and its subsets' (La Línea and Barrio Azteca) involvement in twenty-four.

Despite the battering it had taken from the narco violence and the drawdown prompted by the US recession, Mexico seemed more connected to the US than ever, and by the beginning of the century's second decade, more than $1 billion worth of imports and exports would cross the US-Mexico border, every day, while more than eighteen thousand US companies maintained operations in Mexico.

Cross-border trade cut to more illicit forms of exchange as well. Two of the largest banks in the United States, Bank of America and Wachovia (the latter became part of Wells Fargo in December 2008), laundered funds that enabled the Sinaloa Cartel to purchase a DC-9 that was seized by the Mexican military in Campeche with $100 million worth of cocaine on board.

Wachovia later admitted a total failure of oversight in its handling of $378.4 billion for Mexican currency exchange houses between 2004 and 2007, an amount equal to one-third of Mexico's GDP at the time, and the largest violation of the Bank Secrecy Act in US history. With criminal proceedings against the bank underway, Wachovia settled the case in a Miami court, paying the US government $110 million in forfeiture and a $50 million fine. US authorities thoughtfully allowed their "deferred prosecution" option to expire after a year.

José Treviño Morales, the brother of Zetas chieftain Miguel Treviño, used Bank of America accounts to launder Zetas drug money connected to a horse-buying and trading business he was overseeing in New Mexico and Oklahoma. Federal agents also observed known cartel members depositing drug-related funds in Bank of America accounts in Brownsville, Chicago, and Atlanta.

In the case of the global banking giant HSBC, due to its failure to monitor $670 billion in wire transfers and $9.4 billion in cash transactions from its Mexico bank operations between 2006 and 2009, HSBC would allow the Sinaloa Cartel, Colombia's Norte del Valle Cartel, and other narco traffickers to launder $881 million of drug money directly through its banking systems. HSBC was eventually ordered to pay a $1.9 billion penalty by the Department of Justice and US Treasury, a sum that also took into account violations of US sanctions the bank had committed with regards to transactions from Myanmar, Cuba, Iran, Libya, and

Sudan. A deferred prosecution agreement was once again reached and, once again, no charges were brought against the bank itself. The HSBC money laundering included such hard-to-detect gambits as drug dealers walking into HSBC's Mexican branches and depositing hundreds of thousands of dollars in cash at a single time.

As this all was going on, during the bailout of the US financial system that began in 2008, Bank of America received $45 billion, while Wells Fargo received $25 billion of US taxpayers' money, money that was also going, ostensibly, to fight the drug war.

At the time of writing, despite the United States having the highest rate of incarceration in the world (and despite more than half of America's federal inmates being in prison for drug-related offenses), no one ever went to jail for the banks' role in facilitating the cartels' bloody business. It was an irony not lost on the bankers themselves.

"The banks and the senior bankers feed off money. Money is the business of the banker and the drug dealer produces a lot of money," a former official with a US bank with extensive experience tracking and analyzing money laundering schemes told me.

"[But] the marriage is distorted and imbalanced in favor of the bankers," he continued. "Nowhere can this be seen more clearly than in the criminal justice system and the prisons, which are full of drug dealers and devoid of money-laundering bankers. One of the supreme ironies and twists in the US is the bankers using drug dealers' money to loan to security companies, to build yet more prisons, into which the drug dealers will be incarcerated for long periods of their lives. In the meantime, the bankers earn fees and net interest on the loans, which are used to buy upmarket properties, high end cars and luxury lifestyles. . . . The power of [the banks] is sufficient to influence policy."

The head of the UN Office on Drugs and Crime, Antonio Maria Costa, went even further, saying that he had personally reviewed evidence that during the global financial crisis organized crime groups possessed "the only liquid investment capital" available to a number of banks in desperate need of just that and, as a result, some $352 million in drug profits were absorbed—which is to say laundered—through the legitimate economic system. Costa said flatly that during the period "inter-bank loans were funded by money that originated from the drugs trade and other illegal activities."

The banking insider had a point.

Between 1989 and 2009, the private prison industry in the United States grew by an astonishing 1,600 percent. By the early part of the twenty-first century's second decade, private companies were imprisoning roughly 130,000 prisoners and around sixteen thousand civil immigration detainees in the United States at any given time. The two largest private prison companies, the Nashville, Tennessee–based Corrections Corporation of America (CCA) and the Boca Raton, Florida–based GEO Group (formerly known as Wackenhut Corrections Corporation) had a combined revenue of over $2.9 billion by 2010. Founded by Tom Beasley, a former chairman of the Tennessee Republican Party, along with an attorney, Doctor Crants, and Don Hutto, who at the time was the president of the American Correctional Association, CCA spends nearly $1 million a year on federal lobbying. Between 1999 and 2009, CCA's total spending lobbying the federal government was believed to have been in the neighborhood of $18 million.

Since 2000, CCA, GEO, and their nearest rival, Houston-based Cornell Company—have collectively contributed $835,514 to candidates for federal office, including senators and members of the House of Representatives, and at the state level have contributed well over $6 million. CCA also has long-standing links with the right-wing American Legislative Exchange Council (ALEC), an organization of state legislators, pushing for, among other measures, mandatory minimum sentencing statutes (many related to narcotics) designed to swell the prison population (and increase CCA's business), expansion of immigration enforcement, and promotion of prison privatization.

In a 2010 filing with the Securities and Exchange Commission in the United States, the CCA wrote that

the demand for our facilities and services could be adversely affected by the relaxation of enforcement efforts, leniency in conviction or parole standards and sentencing practices or through the decriminalization of certain activities that are currently proscribed by our criminal laws.

. . . Any changes with respect to drugs and controlled substances or illegal immigration could affect the number of persons arrested, convicted, and sentenced, thereby potentially reducing demand for correctional facilities to house them.

In a similar SEC filing, the GEO Group stated that

changes with respect to the decriminalization of drugs and controlled substances could affect the number of persons arrested, convicted, sentenced and incarcerated, thereby potentially reducing demand for correctional facilities to house them. . . . Reductions in crime rates could lead to reductions in arrests, convictions and sentences requiring incarceration at correctional facilities.

Immigration reform laws which are currently a focus for legislators and politicians at the federal, state and local level also could materially adversely impact us.

The lesson imparted from beyond Mexico's borders seemed to be thus: If you are Mexican and become involved in the drug trade, you should expect to die in the endeavor. If you are poor and become involved, you should expect to spend many years in prison. If you are wealthy and well connected, you can expect to continue on with your privileged life much as before.

As it happened, the banks were not the only ones implicated in the laundering of drug money. A *New York Times* article that quoted several current and former federal law enforcement officials outlined in startling detail how DEA agents "handled shipments of hundreds of thousands of dollars in illegal cash across borders . . . to identify how criminal organizations move their money, where they keep their assets and, most important, who their leaders are . . . [allowing] cartels to continue their operations over months or even years before making seizures or arrests."

The *Times* also later reported how American counternarcotics agents "conducted numerous wire transfers of tens of thousands of dollars at a time, smuggled millions of dollars in bulk cash—and escorted at least one large shipment of cocaine from Ecuador to Dallas to Madrid," all in an attempt to snare Harold Mauricio Poveda Ortega, aka *El Conejo* (The Rabbit), a Colombian drug trafficker with connections to that country's Norte del Valle Cartel who acted as one of the main suppliers for the Beltrán-Leyva Cartel. (Poveda Ortega was arrested in Mexico City in November 2010.) Given the destructiveness of Washington's other attempts at playing the cartels—Operation Wide Receiver and Operation Fast and Furious—the wisdom of such a program was far from certain.

CHAPTER SEVEN

Breaking Up

In January 2010, an event occurred in Reynosa that would have great significance for Mexico as a whole and the Gulf Cartel in particular. Following increasing tensions between the two groups since the 2007 extradition of Osiel Cárdenas, a group of Gulf Cartel loyalists led by Samuel "El Metro 3" Flores Borrego kidnapped and killed Víctor "Concord 3" Peña Mendoza, a Zetas lieutenant who was a close associate of Miguel Treviño. Supposedly the gunmen tried to convince Peña to switch sides before killing him, but the exact reason for the narco's death soon became less relevant than Treviño's volcanic reaction to it.

Despite being one of the few Zetas without a military background, Treviño had built up a reputation as someone not afraid to wade into the thick of battle with his men, gun in hand, and fight at their side. Heriberto Lazcano had detached himself from the daily battles of the crime syndicate to help run its ever more diverse criminal enterprise, often ensconcing himself in the sparsely populated brush-and-scrub desert vastness of Coahuila. Despite his bravery, however, Treviño, the former car washer with something to prove, also seemed to verge on the psychopathic. As the *Dallas Morning News* reporter Alfredo Corchado had noted, Treviño's philosophy of drug trafficking was reportedly as simple as it was chilling: If you're not killing somebody every day, you're not doing your job.

Upon hearing of Concord 3's fate, Treviño reportedly sent a message to El Coss demanding:

Hand over the assassin of my friend, you son of a bitch. . . . You have until the 25th, if you don't comply there will be war.

And war indeed there would be.

But, as if to underline that nowhere was safe, before the war began there would be news from the other side of the country. Over a twenty-four-hour period on January 10–11, 2010, sixty-nine people were killed around Mexico, bringing the year's total of violent deaths to 283, this barely a week into the new year. A third of those killed during the twenty-four-hour period died in and around Ciudad Juárez. Among the dead in Juárez in the first week of that year would be Josefina Reyes, the woman whose son's kidnapping and subsequent murder—crimes she blamed on the military—had spurred her into a flurry of human rights activity. She was gunned down at the barbecue stand she ran by a killer who then ambled casually away.

One early 2010 study by the University of San Diego's Trans-Border Institute concluded that drug-related violence in the preceding years was "driven by the splintering and competition among [cartels]. . . . As a result of Mexico's [pluralistic and decentralized] contemporary political situation," which had contributed to an environment of greater competition among the cartel and, thus, violence. In a revealing cable at the end of January, US ambassador Carlos Pascual, a Cuban-American former USAID official appointed by Barack Obama, wrote to Washington that Calderón's war against the narcos

> *has struggled with an unwieldy and uncoordinated interagency and spiraling rates of violence that have made him vulnerable to criticism that his anti-crime strategy has failed. . . . Mexican security institutions are often locked in a zero-sum competition in which one agency's success is viewed as another's failure, information is closely guarded, and joint operations are all but unheard of. Official corruption is widespread, leading to a compartmentalized siege mentality among "clean" law enforcement leaders and their lieutenants. Prosecution rates for organized crime-related offenses are dismal; two percent of those detained are brought to trial.*

The cable went on to outline tensions between the Mexican navy and the other branches of the armed forces, with the former considered to have gotten a far easier time of it publicly in its high-profile roles taking down drug kingpins like Arturo Beltrán Leyva. Nevertheless, Pascual concluded, "our ties with the military have never been closer in terms of not only equipment transfers and training, but also the kinds of intelligence exchanges that are essential to making inroads against organized crime."

On the last day of January, however, a slaughter took place in Ciudad Juárez that shook even violence-weary Mexico. Gunmen stormed a party for young university and high school students at a home in the working-class barrio of Villas de Salvárcar, opening fire and killing sixteen people. The dead ranged in age from fourteen to forty-two, including eleven teenagers. Among those killed were local high school football stars, would-be doctors, and others just beginning their lives.

On a state visit to Japan when he received news of the attack, Calderón badly misjudged the mood of both Juárez and Mexico when he said that the killings were committed "probably by another group, that is one of the hypotheses, there was some rivalry," the implication being that the victims were somehow involved in organized crime. This caused great anguish for the already-suffering families and, though the government sent an additional four hundred more federal police to Ciudad Juárez and though he quickly backtracked and apologized, when Calderón visited the city—the site of some of his earliest political activism on behalf of the PAN—he was jeered by an angry crowd.

It eventually was pieced together by investigators and others that the Juárez Cartel's gang of sicarios, La Línea, had carried out the killings, believing that the party had in fact been a fiesta by "Double A," that is, the hitmen for the Sinaloa Cartel, who called themselves *Artistas Asesinos* (Murder Artists). However, in fact, the party had been for a local "American-style" high school football team that had been celebrating winning the "AA" championship, combined with the celebration of a neighbor's birthday. The entire massacre appeared to have been a ghastly mix-up.

The whole story was related to me with a mixture of awe and disgust by the local Juárez journalist Luis Hinojos when we visited Villas de Salvárcar several months later. How could such a mistake have been made? How could so many children lose their lives for something so senseless? Earlier, someone in the city had told me "whatever sicario made that mistake paid for it with his life," but I wondered if that would indeed be the case. As we pulled down the street where the killings had happened, the burning morning sun of the desert city had turned to an overcast moody gloom, and the house where the massacre had occurred sat squat, locked up and silent. The street itself was empty, devoid of people. As we drove a little farther, we came upon two murals. The first was of a young man's face, long hair framing full lips and glasses. *En Memoria de Wicho*, it read, referring to one of the massacre victims. The other one quite different and almost certainly painted by drug traffickers, had the words *En la mira del Pueblo* (In the sight of the people) written above a target, in which were written the words "Felipe Calderón."

By the time of their split with the Gulf Cartel (a split during which at least one Zeta, Galdino "El Mellado" Cruz or Z-9, would side with his bosses against his former military comrades), Los Zetas had sunk their claws deeply into Guatemala. In January 2010, the Guatemalan newspaper *El Periódico*—the country's foremost investigative publication—was announcing on its front page *Los Zetas control the drug trade in Guatemala.* Los Zetas' hand was strengthened by the continued fracturing of its sometimes allies in the Tijuana Cartel as Mexican police on the Baja California peninsula nabbed Teodoro García Simental, aka El Teo, who had been battling against Luis Fernando Sánchez Arellano for control of the group since the arrest of the latter's uncle four years earlier. Less than a month later, five Tijuana police officers would be arrested for working with the gang.

Meanwhile, in Michoacán, on January 23, María Santos Gorrostieta, the mayor of Tiquicheo who had survived two attempts against her life the previous year (including one which had killed her husband), was again attacked, this time as she traveled with other PRI officials through the town of Ciudad Altamirano. Shot in the chest, leg, and abdomen, she was flown by helicopter to the state capital Morelia. She would survive, but would eventually migrate to the PRD, saying that the PRI had not supported her after the attempts against her life. Indeed, some accounts said the PRI had pressured her to resign after the attack and were actively seeking a replacement as she lay in a hospital bed fighting for her life. She would later run for congress on the PRD's ticket, and lose. Santos Gorrostieta would eventually remarry, to Nereo Patiño Delgado, one of the bodyguards that Leonel Godoy Rangel, the PRI governor of Michoacán, had assigned to her. As the couple left the chapel, they did so to the strains of "beautiful mariachi notes," a local paper commented. When her term as mayor of Tiquicheo came to an end in 2011—and with it her police protection—she would return, she hoped, to focus on raising her three children.

At the start of 2010, there was immense exhaustion with the ceaseless violence. In a barely veiled swipe at the militarization of the war against Mexico's cartels, in mid February, the *Conferencia del Episcopado Mexicano* (CEM), the official leadership body of the Catholic Church in Mexico, stated in a report that "the participation of the armed forces in the fight against organized crime has created uncertainty in the population. . . . The armed forces have the obligation to respect human rights." A survey by the Buendía & Laredo consulting firm found that 50 percent of those questioned believed the government offensive against drug traffickers made the country more dangerous, not less, and that half had felt personally threatened by criminal violence.

In Sonora that February, police arrested José Vázquez Villagrana, aka *El Jabalí* (The Boar), a US army veteran whom Mexican authorities said was a key facilitator for the Sinaloa Cartel in that state. As the month drew to a close, dozens of banners around Mexico, purportedly from Los Zetas, accused the government of protecting the Sinaloa Cartel. At the same time, as a direct result of the Gulf-Zetas rupture, nineteen people were slain throughout Tamaulipas, many in firefights between security forces and cartel gunmen. In the city of Miguel Alemán, across the Rio Grande from Roma, Texas, gunmen attacked the police headquarters and kidnapped six officers. The Gulf Cartel sent one of its top lieutenants,

Gilberto Barragán Balderas, aka *El Tocayo* (The Namesake), to try to ward off Los Zetas in the pivotal town.

A military patrol responding to reports of a shootout in the Tamaulipas town of Camargo, just across from Rio Grande City, Texas, found twenty-two abandoned vehicles pockmarked with bullet holes, half a dozen rifles, ninety-six ammunition magazines, twenty-three hundred bullets, and more than two dozen grenades. On February 23, 2010, up to forty attackers traveling in a convoy of SUVs bearing Veracruz license plates attacked a house where Oaxaca rancher Alfonso Maciel was staying, killing him and five other people, before moving on to kill four more at Maciel's own ranch. During the same period, hooded gunmen also kidnapped several of the state's policemen.

During three weeks over late February and early March 2010, some reports concluded that at least two hundred people were killed throughout Tamaulipas amid the fracturing of the Gulf-Zetas alliance. As he watched from afar as the criminal empire he had once lorded over crumbled, one wonders what went through the mind of Osiel Cárdenas when he was sentenced by a court in Houston to twenty-five years in prison and ordered to forfeit $50 million. As the cartels warred, all was not harmonious within the Mexican government either. A rift between Calderón and Secretary of the Interior Fernando Gómez Mont over the wisdom of the PAN forming electoral alliances with the PRD led Gómez to quit the party to which both he and the president belonged.

At the outset of March 2010, the Tabasco state prosecutor's office delivered the grim news that Rodolfo Rincón Taracena, the *Tabasco Hoy* investigative reporter who had disappeared after writing a series of articles on the narco business, had been killed and his body dissolved in acid by Los Zetas, according to an alleged Zetas hitman who had been arrested. *Tabasco Hoy* reporters who voiced skepticism about the probe—DNA tests proved inconclusive—were threatened. The same month, three reporters for Reynosa's *El Mañana*—Miguel Angel Domínguez Zamora, Pedro Argüello, and David Silva—went missing.

Between late February 2010 and mid March, eight journalists were kidnapped in Reynosa, with one found dead bearing signs of torture, two released alive, and five still missing. A banner strung in Reynosa's main plaza demanded the withdrawal of the military and was signed by a *Fusion of Mexican cartels united against the "Z."*

It had also become clear that a succession war was going on following the death of Arturo Beltrán Leyva between Arturo's brother Héctor Beltrán Leyva and La Barbie, the cartel's US-reared enforcer. Beltrán Leyva was backed up by his lieutenant, Sergio Enrique Villarreal Barragán, aka *El Grande,* a 6'7" former federal police officer from Coahuila who had opportunistically drifted between Mexico's cartels for years, while La Barbie was supported by Gerardo "El Indio" Alvarez-Vazquez (so named for his distinctly indigenous-looking facial features).

On March 12, eight youths were killed when gunmen assailed a party in the Sinaloan coastal city of Navolato, less than forty-eight hours after sicarios killed six young men and a woman at a wake in Ciudad Juárez. The same day as the Sinaloa killings, police in Nuevo León raided an apparent clandestine hospital for cartel gunmen, arresting medical personnel and at least three men with bullet wounds. Along the Sinaloa highway connecting Culiacán and the beach resort of Mazatlán, state authorities found the bodies of seven men shot to death in two cars, with the body of an eighth man—this one dressed in a counterfeit federal police uniform and holding a grenade—lying on the ground nearby.

In the course of a single Saturday—March 13, 2010—extreme violence erupted throughout the country. In the town of Ajuchitlán del Progreso in Guerrero in the middle of the afternoon, soldiers engaged in a firefight that killed eleven gunmen and one of their own. In Tuncingo, near Acapulco, five police officers were slain and five bullet-riddled bodies were found, two of which had been decapitated. Three other corpses—two of which had also been decapitated—were found in Acapulco itself. In Chiapas, a grenade exploded in the hand of a man—believed to be a Zeta—who was preparing to throw it at a group of police officers, killing him.

In Ciudad Juárez, US consulate employee Leslie Ann Enriquez Catton and her husband, Arthur Redelfs, who was employed as a prison guard in El Paso, and Jorge Alberto Salcido Ceniceros, the husband of another US consulate employee, died in a hail of bullets as gunmen fired on their cars leaving a child's birthday party in separate incidents. The baby of the first couple was left unharmed in the backseat of their white SUV. Salcido's two children, ages four and seven, were wounded but survived. Two days after the consulate killings, running gun battles in the picturesque Chihuahua town of Creel, a gateway to the Copper Canyon, left seven people dead, while in the southern reaches of the state, five bodies were found along a roadside. Also in Creel, as more than a dozen gunmen blocked a road into town, openly snorted cocaine, and brandished firearms before storming a house in an attack that killed nine members of a single family, security cameras from the Mexican police recorded the entire thing. The video was later broadcast on Televisa several weeks later. The US government would later finger the shooters in the consulate killings as belonging to the Juárez Cartel–affiliated Barrio Azteca criminal gang, which had its roots in US prisons.

Over a twenty-four-hour period on March 18 and 19, gunmen blockaded thirty roads in and around Monterrey, hijacking vehicles and driving them into the middle of the street to block traffic. As the army sent patrols into the streets to remove the roadblocks, gunmen opened fire just outside the gates of the Instituto Tecnológico y de Estudios Superiores de Monterrey, sparking a firefight in which two assailants died and a soldier was wounded. The same day, in the hamlet of Fresnillo near Monterrey, the army said that gunmen shot at a navy helicopter passing over the area, resulting in an exchange of fire that killed one of the assailants on the ground. Alberto "El Chico Malo" (Bad Boy) Mendoza, the leader of a Beltrán-Leyva faction in San Pedro Garza García, was arrested in the company of a companion, five assault rifles, and MEX 322,000 (USD 26,000).

On the same day that an assassination attempt on regional police chief René Castillo Sánchez killed a bodyguard and wounded three others in the state, Nuevo León governor Rodrigo Medina de la Cruz—who had succeeded José Natividad González Parás in that role in October of the previous year—announced that he was firing eighty-one state police officers that he suspected of corruption. The next day police in Guerrero discovered the mutilated bodies of a regional commander and a state police officer stuffed into plastic bags in Chilpancingo, while in Acapulco, outside the home of the city's former deputy traffic police chief, two more mutilated bodies were found belonging to the former deputy chief's nephews and a message threatening supporters of the Beltrán-Leyva Cartel. The question mark hanging over San Pedro Garza García mayor Mauricio Fernández Garza had grown larger after the recent arrest of Beltrán-Leyva lieutenant Chico Malo Mendoza, and Fernández Garza's subsequent admission that the narco had been a paid informant for his own intelligence operation, apparently conducted without the knowledge of the federal or state governments. In a separate raid on a Beltrán-Levya–linked complex, the Mexican military had discovered weapons and a Ford Explorer bearing the insignia of San Pedro Garza García's security forces.

By March 2010, the Gulf Cartel had managed to drive Los Zetas out of the colonial hamlet of Ciudad Mier in northern Tamaulipas, just south of Falcon Lake near the Texas border. Fighting between the two groups would continue there for months, though, as they vied for control of the territory. In a March 25 memo with the subject heading "Continuing Violence in Northern Mexico Between the Gulf Cartel and Los Zetas," the US Department of Homeland Security wrote that "the Gulf Cartel has been attacking small plazas in Tamaulipas even if they are not involved with Los Zetas. The attacks occur simply because the area belongs to the Zetas."

That same day Mexican marines killed six gunmen in the Nuevo León municipality of Cerralvo and, a day later, the head of Heriberto Omar Cerda Cadena, police chief of the municipality of Agualeguas, was found in his lap in the bed of a pickup truck along a dirt road. His brother was also found dead inside the vehicle. Both the windshield and the driver's side door bore the letters "C.D.G." scrawled in blood. March ended as violently as it had begun in Tamaulipas, with a clash between cartel gunmen and soldiers killing three in Río Bravo and narcobloqueos being erected around Reynosa, leading to a clash between soldiers and gunmen near the airport.

By this point Los Zetas activity in Tamaulipas was commanded by a diminutive psychopath named Salvador Alfonso Martínez Escobedo, aka *La Ardilla* (The Squirrel). To the south, on the Cuernavaca-Acapulco road, four decapitated bodies were found with a note threatening La Barbie. In a cable sent to Washington, the US Embassy in Mexico City estimated that there had been nine hundred killings nationwide during the month, murders which in Tamaulipas and neighboring states were abetted by the ability of cartels to operate "with near total impunity in the face of compromised local security forces."

In a significant development for narcos who sought to terrorize one another (and the public and the authorities) through use of violent images—while at the same time demanding silence or compliance from the media—March 2010 also marked the beginning of publication for the website Blog del Narco, produced, it was believed, by "a student in northern Mexico majoring in computer security." The site's first posting was about an unreported shootout in Tamaulipas, and cartels would soon begin using the site to send messages—and to terrorize—one another, as they would with another blog, Borderland Beat, that had been started the previous year. It was not enough to encourage them to stop, though, and five gunmen died in a battle with soldiers in Reynosa on April 2, the same day three bodies of men who had been shot to death turned up in Tijuana and in Morelia police found a pile of bodies onto which the letter "Z" had been carved.

In an extraordinary April 2010 interview published in *Proceso* magazine, the septuagenarian journalist and founder of the publication, Julio Scherer García—who once famously said "If the devil offers me an interview, I'm going to hell"—spoke with Sinaloa Cartel grandee Ismael "El Mayo" Zambada García. Zambada was sixty years old at the time of the interview and confessed to have been involved in the drug business since he was sixteen, a total of forty-four years. He said that even if the government succeeded in killing him or any of the capos, despite the temporary "euphoria" authorities might feel, it would change "nothing" because "as for the bosses, locked up, dead or extradited, their replacements are already out there." Perhaps the drug lord had reason to be generous with his time as, by spring 2010, it had become increasingly obvious that the Sinaloa Cartel was on their way to vanquishing their rivals in Ciudad Juárez and taking over the coveted drug-trafficking routes there after the group's bloody two-year war of attrition.

On April 8, the Mexican army handed law enforcement duties over to five thousand federal and three thousand municipal police in Ciudad Juárez for the first time in over a year. Those hoping that peace would follow them to the town were disappointed, however, when only days later gunmen firing on a police patrol killed six officers and a seventeen-year-old girl who happened to be passing by.

One Juárez resident was Rubí Marisol Frayre Escobedo, a beautiful girl with a newly born daughter who was sixteen years old when she had disappeared from the city in August 2008. To her great misfortune, her choice of partners was one Sergio Rafael Barraza Bocanegra, a young hoodlum with links to various criminal organizations in the city. After months of rigorous lobbying by Rubí's mother, Marisela Escobedo Ortiz, police arrested Barraza, who then directed them to the site of Rubí's body, which had been dismembered on a hog farm outside the city. Unbelievably, in April 2010, despite Barraza's directions to the body and the fact that he had boasted to several people of the killing, a three-judge panel in Juárez set the killer free, as the murdered girl's mother wailed "No!" in the courtroom. Though the judges were subsequently suspended—many believed they had been bribed though Barraza claimed he had been tortured by the police into confessing—Marisela Escobedo Ortiz swore that she would obtain justice for her slain daughter.

In mid-April 2010, the man in charge of the Guatemalan government's antidrug operations in the jungle-covered department of Petén—which boasted a long, little-patrolled border with Mexico—was arrested for providing intelligence to Los Zetas. A US State Department report at the time concluded that drug-trafficking organizations such as Los Zetas operated in a "prevailing environment of impunity" in "the northern and eastern rural areas" of Guatemala. By the end of the summer, the Mexican army in Veracruz would have arrested six former Guatemalan soldiers they said were linked to Los Zetas, and Guatemala's *Prense Libre* newspaper was concluding that Los Zetas were "everywhere" along the country's border with Mexico. They were everywhere along Mexico's border with the United States as well, as that same month, two brothers, ages five and eight, were killed during a shootout between narcos and soldiers in Nuevo

Laredo. Meanwhile, outside the town of Xalisco in the Pacific Coast state of Nayarit on April 7, police found twelve bodies in nearby fields, eight of them partially burned.

Also in Nayarit, Alejandro Coronel, the sixteen-year-old son of Sinaloa Cartel boss Nacho Coronel, was kidnapped from the El Tigre golf club in Las Varas, allegedly by Los Zetas, who then handed the boy over to operators of the Beltrán-Leyva Cartel, who killed him a short time later. In response, Coronel is believed to have dispatched a hundred gunmen who killed at least fourteen people around the state.

A day after the Coronel kidnapping, Sonora state attorney general Abel Murrieta said that at least eighty gunmen traveling in fifteen pick-ups invaded the town of Maycoba, killing at least four people. The same day, in Cuernavaca, police found the bodies of two men hanging from a bridge.

By this point, it had become apparent that the Gulf Cartel, La Familia Michoacána, and the Sinaloa Cartel had formed some sort of alliance to take on Los Zetas. At one point, banners hung around Tamaulipas, reading *The Gulf Cartel separates itself from the Z in our ranks. We don't want kidnappers, terrorists, bank robbers, rapists, child killers and traitors.* On April 12, five people were slain in a bar in the Tamaulipas town of Los Guerra while three more were shot as they jumped in a car to try to escape the attackers. The same day, the tortured bodies of six men were found along a roadside in Cuernavaca.

An attack on the convoy of Michoacán secretary of public security Minerva Bautista Gomez in Morelia on April 24 killed two bodyguards and two civilians and wounded Bautista Gomez herself. The convoy withstood a withering assault for fifteen minutes during which twenty-seven thousand rounds were fired while waiting for rescuers to arrive. It was believed that compromised law enforcement elements tipped off La Familia as to Bautista Gomez's movements, allowing them to attack at an area where cell phone and radio signals are tenuous and embankments rise on either side, making the convoy an easy target.

US intelligence sources were already concluding that the Sinaloa Cartel had wrested control of Ciudad Juárez from the Juárez Cartel, but events over the next several months would prove that assessment to be somewhat premature. Over a twenty-four-hour period in late April, sixteen people were killed in different shootings around the city, including eight people forced out of a bar and gunned down in the parking lot and another three slain in a shootout in front of an elementary school that sent students, teachers, and parents fleeing.

Across the country back in the Gulf-Zetas territory of Nuevo León, federal troops freed sixteen people held hostage at a house in the town of Sabinas Hidalgo and seized two tons of marijuana. The gunfight during the liberation claimed two lives. A day earlier troops had killed three suspected kidnappers and freed seven people in a raid on a rural ranch in the state. In the Tamaulipas town of Altamira, four inmates were slain as an armed gang attempted to storm the prison there. By the end of the month, it was estimated that at least 22,700 people had been killed in Mexico since December 2006.

Gerardo "El Indio" Alvarez-Vazquez, La Barbie's cohort from his faction of the Beltrán-Leyva Cartel, was captured on April 21 following a gun battle in an upscale Mexico City suburb. The arrest seemed to do little to quell the war of succession within the organization, though, as the Héctor Beltrán Leyva and La Barbie factions in and around Cuernavaca had brought the economy of the tourist town to its knees, with grotesquely mutilated bodies suspended from bridges in full view of passing motorists or dumped by the roadside. The internecine Beltrán-Leyva war was also thought to be behind the slaying of five men on a soccer pitch near Acapulco in May.

And the disappearances continued. In May 2010, five Pemex workers on their way to a gas compression plant near Reynosa disappeared. A relative of one of the victims said the workers had been threatened at gunpoint before by narcos who wanted the area around the plant empty so they could move drug shipments through it. The same month, the families of dozens of men who had disappeared in Coahuila over the previous year protested in front of Los Pinos, carrying banners reading *You took them alive, alive we want them.* By this point, Los Zetas' domination of Coahuila was so complete and the reputed collusion of the PRI governor there, Humberto Moreira Valdés, in office since 2005, was perceived as being so close that he was referred to disparagingly by his opponents as *El gobernador Zeta* (Governor Zeta).

After having arrested a truckload of gunmen there the previous month, by late June 2010, Mexican authorities in the tourist town of Taxco, famous for its jewelry, had hauled fifty-five bodies from the shaft of a disused silver mine. Forensic analysts said they believed that many of the victims had been thrown alive into the pit, which "was like quick-sand," and only died from injuries sustained on the way down or at the bottom of the fifty-story-deep grave.

As July 4 elections loomed around the PRI bastion of Tamaulipas, PAN leaders had expressed their concern that they had been unable to recruit candidates for three mayorships and two other local posts because of the pervasive climate of fear and threats from the cartels operating in the area. José Mario Guajardo, the PAN's candidate for mayorship of the Tamaulipas town of Valle Hermoso (about thirty miles southwest of Mat-amoros) was slain along with his son and an aide in a May 2010 attack at his agricultural supplies company after which the PAN's national director, César Nava, said that "all indications are that this is a crime committed by one of the cartels in Tamaulipas." Shortly after Mario Guajardo's slaying, Diego Fernández de Cevallos—the PAN's 1994 presidential candidate—was kidnapped from his ranch in Querétaro by criminals who demanded $100 million for his release. After eight months in captivity, he was freed for $30 million.

The PAN were hardly alone in enduring attacks, however, as the home of PRD politician Martha Porras, who had been seeking the may-orship in Nuevo Laredo, was set aflame, after which Porras and several of her relatives disappeared. The PRD's national leader, Jesús Ortega Mar-tínez, told journalists that "in Tamaulipas . . . it seems the only ones who are acceptable [to the narcos] are from the PRI." As if to reinforce such an image beyond the country's north, a twenty-year-old photo had sur-faced of the PRI's candidate for governor in Sinaloa (and former Culiacán mayor) Jesús Vizcarra Calderón celebrating the festival of the Virgen de Guadalupe with none other than the Sinaloa Cartel's El Mayo Zambada. Around the same time, Gregorio Sánchez Martínez, the PRD-affiliated mayor of Cancún who was running for the governorship of Quintana Roo, was indicted on charges of organized crime and money laundering by a judge who accused him of links to the Beltrán-Leyva Cartel and Los Zetas. The state's former governor, the PRI's Mario Villanueva, would eventually plead guilty in US court to laundering millions of dollars of cocaine trafficking proceeds.

In the beautiful Veracruz state capital of Xalapa, a city famed for its universities and cultural ambience and situated where mist-covered mountains begin to slouch through deep valleys toward the meandering coastline, a young businessman, Fouad Hakim Santiesteban, and his wife, Irene Méndez, were assaulted by gunmen on a busy street corner in June 2010. As sicarios forced Hakim into a car, his wife attempted to defend him and was gunned down. Hakim's body was found, his throat slit, a short time later. It was a crime that rocked the heretofore largely sedate Xalapa to its core. Hakim was the son of well-known local businessman Alfredo Hakim Aburto, a close friend of Veracruz governor Fidel Herrera Beltrán, while Irene Méndez was the daughter of Esther Hernandez-Palacios, a Université de Toulouse–educated poet and essayist who had served as the director of the Instituto Veracruzano de Cultura during the administration of PRI governor Miguel Alemán Velasco (1998–2004) and who was the granddaughter of former Veracruz chief justice Aureliano Hernández Palacios. According to locals, since the coming to office of Fidel Herrera Beltrán in December 2004, the state had fallen ever more under control of Los Zetas.

The grieving mother, Esther Hernandez-Palacios, would go on to write a book, *Diario de una madre mutilada* (Diary of a Mutilated Mother), based on her experiences and her struggle to obtain justice for her daughter. Veracruz governor Fidel Herrera Beltrán, highly allergic to criticism, seemed to take such action as a direct threat to his power.

When I visited the state where the rebel leader Gaspar Yanga had led a slave rebellion in the 1570s, I met with a longtime observer of state politics who told me bluntly that there was "a total agreement" between the governor and the cartels and that they were "totally protected." Not surprisingly, Herrera Beltrán had always vehemently denied such charges.

Later, José Carlos Hinojosa, an accountant for the Gulf Cartel, would—without directly naming the governor—tell a federal court in the United States about how he funneled $12 million in cartel money to Herrera's electoral campaign between 2004 and 2005. In exchange, the Gulf Cartel/Zetas alliance was able to move narcotics freely throughout the state. Herrera denied that, too.

Nearly three dozen gunmen assaulted the *Fe y Vida* (Faith and Life) drug rehabilitation clinic in Chihuahua City on June 10, 2010, killing at least nineteen people. As with the murder of sixteen teenagers in the city that had occurred the previous January, the attack was also believed to be the work of the Juárez Cartel. The masked assailants had first posed as police officers, but they then killed some of the men—addicts "seeking a way forward" in the words of the center's pastor—in the rooms before forcing the rest out into the street and gunning them down. The assault overshadowed the discovery of the bodies of eighteen men and two women dumped around the southern Tamaulipas municipality of Ciudad Madero. Four days later, gunmen in Michoacán ambushed a police convoy in Zitácuaro, killing ten. Several assailants were also killed. Hours after Mexican troops killed fifteen gunmen suspected of being allied to La Barbie in the Guerrero silver mining town of Taxco, Calderón gave a televised address in which he told the country that "this is a battle that is worth fighting because our future is at stake. . . . My government can't and won't let its guard down." In Sinaloa, meanwhile, the mustachioed, cowboy-hatted Sergio Vega, a banda singer known as *El Shaka* who often sang narco-ballads, was slain only hours after denying to reporters news circulating that he had been murdered.

But cartel violence continued to make good fodder for ambitious politicians north of the border. Arizona's erratic Republican governor Jan Brewer explained her state's harsh new immigration law by saying that Arizona "cannot afford all this illegal immigration and everything that comes with it, everything from the crime and to the drugs and the kidnappings and the extortion and the beheadings and the fact that people can't feel safe in their community. It's wrong! It's wrong!"

A few days later, Brewer upped the ante even further, telling a Phoenix television station that Arizona's "law enforcement agencies have found bodies in the desert, either buried or just lying out there, that have been beheaded." The statement was totally false; medical examiners for such border districts as Pima County and Pinal County said no beheadings at all had occurred. Questioned by journalists after a debate later, Brewer literally ran away from the assembled press and out into a parking lot.

On June 28, in an attack that was shocking even by the cartels' bloody standards over the previous four years, the PRI's candidate for governor of Tamaulipas, Rodolfo Torre Cantú, scion of a prominent Tamaulipas family, was slain along with four members of his convoy as they drove to the airport outside of Ciudad Victoria. Some saw the murder of the forty-six-year-old politician (who had enjoyed a 30 percent poll lead over his rival), as an attempt by Los Zetas to remove a politician that could be more sympathetic to the Gulf Cartel, as PRI politicians were often seen as being. Others believed that Torre had been removed by the Gulf Cartel themselves, specifically by El Coss, for being not sufficiently sympathetic to their interests. The bodies of Torre and his aides lying on a roadside sent shock waves through the country and marked the highest-profile killing of a political candidate since the killing of the PRI's presidential candidate, Luis Donaldo Colosio, in March 1994. A Torre supporter asked on the slain candidate's Facebook page, "How long are these things going to happen?"

CHAPTER EIGHT

Enemies Everywhere

Election Day, July 2010, saw the PRI losing the governorships in Oaxaca, Puebla, and Sinaloa, but winning in eight other states, including Tamaulipas, where Egidio Torre Cantú, the burly, mustachioed brother of slain gubernatorial candidate Rodolfo Torre Cantú, easily beat his opponent and went on to succeed Eugenio Hernández Flores. In the capital of the state of Chihuahua, narcos hung four bodies from bridges, and in Tamaulipas itself voter participation was thought to be around only 40 percent. Whether the results represented a resurgence by the PRI or a beating back to the old guard by the PAN/PRD alliance remained the subject of much debate.

July had started with a furious gun battle between unidentified criminal gangs near the US border in Sonora that left twenty-one people dead. The same day, Jorge Mario Moreno León, the son of Nepomuceno Moreno Nuñez, a Sonora street vendor, was traveling from Hermosillo to Ciudad Obregón with three friends. He never made it, and when it became clear that the police may have been involved with the younger Moreno's disappearance, the father began holding regular vigils in downtown Hermosillo demanding justice for his son.

As Mexico voted, a little-noticed killing in Guatemala that July would make knowledgeable observers try to decipher exactly what the tea leaves predicted for Mexico's southern neighbor. Obdulio Solórzano, the former Escuintla deputy and member of the executive committee of President Álvaro Colom's UNE party, perished in a storm of automatic weapons fire along with a bodyguard as he drove through Guatemala City's Zona 13 district. After his stint in Guatemala's congress, Solórzano had gone on to head the Fondo Nacional para la Paz (Fonapaz), a government organization set up in 1991 with the stated aim of funding programs to eliminate poverty. During his tenure it was discovered that some 1.4 billion quetzales (the Guatemalan currency) could not be accounted for, and that some thirty-two NGO projects had been overvalued to the tune of Q93.7 million. He was dismissed in June 2009.

According to an official I spoke with from an international body familiar with organized crime in Guatemala, Solórzano had long been the link between the San Marcos drug lord Juan "Chamalé" Ortíz—credited with first bringing Los Zetas to Guatemala—and several other drug traffickers and certain elements of the UNE. During Solórzano's time at Fonapaz, there was speculation that some of the inconsistencies in accounting may have been attempts to launder illicit drug profits.

Jose Rubén Zamora, the crusading editor of Guatemala's *El Periódico* newspaper, would later say that Guatemalan army general Mauro "Gerónimo" Jacinto (who was himself later murdered) described to him how Solórzano had funneled millions of dollars from drug traffickers such as Juancho León and from Los Zetas themselves into UNE campaign coffers to help Colom triumph in the second round of the contest over former general Otto Pérez Molina, who himself was frequently accused of having links to organized crime.

Back in Mexico in July, Calderón accepted the resignation of his secretary of the interior, Fernando Gómez Mont, who had served since the death of Juan Camilo Mouriño. His replacement would be José Francisco Blake Mora, a PAN politician with experience fighting drug-trafficking organizations in his native state of Baja California. In an escalation of the drug war that struck fear into the hearts of Mexicans across the country, a car bomb exploded in Ciudad Juárez on July 15, killing three people, after federal police and paramedics responded to a call reporting shots fired at a major intersection. The police later said the call was a trap. The bomb was thought to be in response to the arrest of a member of La Línea. The same day, shootouts in Nuevo Laredo wounded at least twenty-one people.

And the violence was spreading. That summer, Los Zetas were attempting to make serious incursions into the state of Jalisco, where they were met with ferocity by *La Resistencia*, an amalgam of sicarios drawn from the Gulf Cartel and the Sinaloa Cartel. Narcomantas signed by Cárteles de México Unidos asked that the Calderón government allow the group to end "this cancer" of the Zetas presence in Jalisco. By the end of July, nearly 230 people had been killed in cartel-related violence in the state, including thirteen policemen.

And as Los Zetas grew like a disease throughout the body of Mexico, where was the Gulf Cartel? By mid-2010 a serious split had developed between Gulf Cartel factions, with one side—Los Metros—aligned with El Coss, Samuel "El Metro 3" Flores Borrego, Mario "El Pelón" Ramírez, and Héctor "El Metro 4" Delgado Santiago, and another—Los Rojos— on the side of the Cárdenas family, specifically Mario "El Gordo" Cárdenas and Rafael "El Junior" Cárdenas, and Juan "El R1" Mejía González, among others. El Junior Cárdenas was also working as the plaza boss of Río Bravo at the time.

In Torreón, Coahuila that summer, in an attack reminiscent of the killings in Ciudad Juárez the previous February, gunmen attacked a party and killed seventeen people. At the scene, police found more than 120 bullet casings. The attack was believed to be a Sinaloa Cartel move against suspected Zetas collaborators. In response, the Zetas dumped four human heads in the town with a note saying the perpetrators would be punished. Subsequently, Los Zetas uploaded a video that showed them interrogating and shooting to death a policeman who was forced to "admit" that Sinaloa Cartel members had been let out of nearby Gómez Palacio prison in Durango to commit the killings.

To the east, gunmen in Nuevo Laredo forced drivers and passengers from buses and private cars and engaged in battles that reportedly left several gunmen dead. On the same day, the Mexican army said that it had seized two extended pickup trucks painted with army insignia in Ciudad Mier in Tamaulipas. Police had also discovered a clandestine grave outside of Monterrey that would eventually yield thirty-eight bodies. It was just a shadow of what was to come.

When army Special Forces stormed a house in a tony suburb of Guadalajara and killed the Sinaloa Cartel's Nacho Coronel, in many ways, it represented the government's biggest triumph since the killing of Arturo Beltrán Leyva eight months before. The same day as Coronel's killing, the bodies of thirteen men and two women were found along a Tamaulipas highway, all wearing white T-shirts with the letter "Z" painted on them. Following Coronel's death, a group of traffickers formerly under his command would form the *Cártel de Jalisco Nueva Generación* (CJNG), named after the state of which Guadalajara was the capital.

On August 4, Calderón's government announced that, by its calculations, more than twenty-eight thousand people had been killed in drug-related violence since the start of the government's crackdown in 2006. Speaking at an anticrime conference the same day, Calderón denounced the cartels for seeking "to replace the government . . . trying to impose a monopoly by force of arms, and are even trying to impose their own laws. . . . Their main business is not anymore even drug trafficking. Their business is dominating other people." The Mexican government said it had seized more than thirty-two thousand illegal weapons in the country in the past twelve months alone.

But there was by no means unity within the law enforcement bodies themselves. In early August 2010, two different groups of federal police officers brawled in Ciudad Juárez, with one group charging that officer Rodolfo Salomón Alarcón Romero, known as *El Chamán* (The Shaman), had falsely been accused of working on behalf of the Sinaloa Cartel—conducting kidnappings, executions, and the like—and another group attacking and punching Alarcón on live television, with one masked officer almost pleading with reporters that "We're not all thieves, we're not all corrupt." After fleeing Ciudad Juárez, Salomón would be captured a year later in Cuernavaca and charged with running a kidnapping and extortion ring.

At a meeting of Mexico's governors, Tamaulipas governor Eugenio Hernández Flores told Calderón that the "climate of lack of safety has reduced the flow of foreign investment, and it is urgent that a promotional campaign be designed to improve the country's image." The statement was particularly ironic given Hernández's choice of associates. Only a month before, Ismael Marino Ortega Galicia, one of Hernández's main bodyguards, had been arrested by the Mexican attorney general's office for being a Gulf Cartel sicario. At the same meeting, US Ambassador Carlos Pascual said that a "northeastern triangle of violence" had formed around Matamoros, Nuevo Laredo, and Monterrey. After having publicly waged the drug war during his own term (albeit with a conviction observers were by no means unanimous on), former president Fox, writing on his own blog, opined that Mexico "should consider legalizing the production, distribution and sale of drugs. . . . We should look at it as a strategy to strike at and break the economic structure that allows gangs to generate huge profits in their trade, which feeds corruption and increases their areas of power." He also called for an end to using the military for law enforcement duties.

Edelmiro Cavazos Leal, the youthful thirty-eight-year-old mayor of the town of Santiago near Monterrey, was kidnapped on August 15 and found days later, his hands bound and his head wrapped in tape. He had been shot to death. Seven police officers were later arrested for involvement in the killing. Authorities concluded that Los Zetas had ordered the hit when Cavazos began moving against officers secretly working for the cartel. It was believed that Ángel Virgilio Ávila Sánchez, alias El Vampiro (the Vampire), a Zetas leader in Nuevo León, had been the intellectual author of the crime. On August 19, Carlos Alberto Elorza, the judge tasked with investigating organized crime and money laundering charges against former Cancún mayor Gregorio Sánchez Martínez, narrowly survived an assassination attempt that killed one of his bodyguards. In what was believed to be the work of Héctor Beltrán Leyva, four decapitated bodies were hung from a bridge in Cuernavaca three days later—a Sunday—with a message reading "this is what will happen to all those who support the traitor Edgar Valdéz Villarreal."

CHAPTER NINE

The Ghosts of San Fernando

A severely wounded Ecuadorian migrant staggered to a military check-point in the San Fernando Valley—an area roughly the size of Dela-ware—in Tamaulipas about one hundred miles south of Matamoros on August 23, 2010. He told the soldiers who met him there that he had just fled Los Zetas, who had kidnapped and killed dozens of migrants at a nearby ranch. When the military raided the property the following day, media reported that after helicopters engaged in gun battles with cartel snipers, the soldiers found fifty-eight men and fourteen women had been slain. Three narcos and a marine died in the gunfight that followed the soldiers' arrival.

The victims the military found were people who had been heading north from places like Brazil, El Salvador, and Honduras to seek a better life in the United States. They ran the gamut from older men to pregnant women and young girls. It was Mexico's drug violence literally reaching out and touching the entire hemisphere. The Ecuadorian immigrant, later identified as eighteen-year-old Luis Freddy Lala Pomavilla, was taken to a hospital in Matamoros. It eventually became known that a second cap-tive, a Honduran, had also survived the massacre.

The Central and South American migrants, utterly vulnerable as they traversed Mexico to a hoped-for illegal sprint across the Rio Grande, had made irresistible targets for Los Zetas, whose attention to detail in these matters was well known. The journalist Oscar Martínez, a reporter for El Salvador's *El Faro* website, reported extensively on the experience of Central American migrants passing through Mexico, and estimated that there were at least six hundred migrants being kidnapped per year on the long route through the country, much of which passed right through Zetas territory.

Sensing a publicity coup, the Gulf Cartel allowed the Mexican and foreign press access to report extensively on the massacre, but it was a crime whose details Los Zetas were determined to keep from coming to light. Within days, two car bombs exploded in Ciudad Victoria, one outside of the office of the Televisa network, which had been reporting on the case. Remarkably, there were no casualties. Tamaulipas prosecutor Roberto Jaime Suárez Vázquez, assigned to look into the killings, was not so lucky. His body was found dumped along a roadside in the state shortly after he was kidnapped.

Marco Antonio Leal García, the mayor of the Tamaulipas town of Hidalgo, was slain in an attack that also wounded his young daughter on August 29. The day before, grenade explosions had rocked Reynosa. At least twelve people were reported seriously wounded.

By early September, of the seven men identified as suspects in the San Fernando massacre, only one had been captured alive. In addition to the three who had been slain in the initial shootout with the military, the bodies of three more had been found along a Tamaulipas roadside.

On the back of the San Fernando outrage, the Mexican government scooped up a big fish when it captured Edgar Valdéz Villarreal, the Texas-born narco known as La Barbie, in Mexico State, just outside the capital. At the same time as Valdéz's arrest, a twelve-hour gunfight between troops and gunmen in the city of Pánuco in Veracruz left one soldier and six gunmen dead. The government also announced that 10 percent of its federal police force had been fired during the previous year for failing to pass anticorruption tests. The day after his arrest, Valdéz, clad in a green Ralph Lauren polo shirt, was paraded, grinning, before the cameras, guarded by an escort of hooded Mexican soldiers.

The Mexican government subsequently released a series of videos containing edited excerpts of interrogations of La Barbie, who is questioned by an off-camera female voice as he fidgets nervously, eyes darting from side to side, and wiping the sweat from his brow with his manacled hands. Describing himself as a "friend of Arturo Beltrán," Valdéz states, rather dishonestly, that he "always worked alone" while trafficking marijuana and cocaine, even as he describes El Indio as "my compadre." He says that he was introduced to the upper echelons of Mexico's drug-trafficking world by El Chapo Guzmán deputy Jaime "El Güero" Valdez Martínez. One of his first tasks had been "to go and visit Osiel in Matamoros." There was a peace pact once, he says, hammered out at the now-famous meeting of cartel grandees in Cuernavaca in 2007, but El Chapo Guzmán broke it by invading Ciudad Juárez the following year. He paints a not-surprising portrait of Arturo Beltrán Leyva as a wild-eyed cocaine addict, saying "when he was high, he wanted to kill me. but when he wasn't high, we got along ok." On the tape, La Barbie also alleges that Beltrán Leyva called him to send in reinforcements after Mexican authorities surrounded the Cuernavaca residence where he was eventually killed, though he never did this. He saves special scorn for the "filth" Zetas, at one point stating that "even their mothers don't love them."

On September 2, Calderón delivered his annual state of the nation address to Mexico's people, saying that though he was "well aware that over the past year, violence has worsened" the country "must battle on . . . if we want a safe Mexico for the Mexicans of the future, we must take on the cost of achieving it today." At least thirty-two hundred federal police would be fired in early September, and a raid by soldiers against narcos believed to be Los Zetas at a ranch outside the Tamaulipas border town of Ciudad Mier in early September left twenty-five dead and freed three people believed to have been kidnapped. After the raid, police said they had recovered twenty-five rifles, four grenades, and forty-two hundred rounds of ammunition.

By this point at least 191 Mexican military personnel had been killed fighting drug gangs since December 2006. By the end of the summer of 2010, though, a joint US-Mexican report by two solidarity organizations concluded that

> *the military's role as the predominant force in counter-drug opera-*
> *tions has led to increased abuses due to the historic impunity enjoyed*
> *by the Mexican armed forces. Military forces are trained for combat*

situations, in which force is used to vanquish an enemy without regard for the enemy's well being. In contrast, domestic law enforcement authorities are trained to interact with civilians within at least a minimal framework of Constitutional rights. The difference in roles and tactics means that conflict and abuses are virtually inevitable.

At the same time, the US State Department announced that it was withholding $26 million of aid to Mexico out of the three-year-old, $1.4 billion Mérida Initiative due to concerns of abuses committed by Mexico's security forces. Though State Department spokesman Harry Edwards said that "no society can enjoy domestic peace and security without a functioning justice system supported by appropriately trained and equipped law enforcement and justice personnel who are respectful of human rights and rule of law," the United States also perplexingly announced that it would be releasing $36 million from earlier budgets, making the stated US concern about human rights abuses rather hard to take seriously.

Speaking before an audience in Washington, DC, in early September, US secretary of state Hillary Clinton raised eyebrows on both sides of the border when she stated that Mexico was "looking more and more like Colombia looked twenty years ago, where the narco-traffickers control certain parts of the country," and that "these drug cartels are now showing more and more indices of insurgency." The comments sparked angry denials from the Calderón government, with Calderón himself acerbically responding that "the main thing we have in common with Colombia is that both of our countries suffer from US drug consumption."

Not a week later, Alexander López García, the mayor of El Naranjo, a San Luis Potosí town just across the border from Tamaulipas, died in a hail of bullets when gunmen stormed his office during a meeting. López was the third Mexican mayor slain in less than a month. On a single day—September 9—twenty-five people were slain in Ciudad Juárez, while in Reynosa eighty-five inmates scaled a prison's twenty-foot walls and alighted to the outside world, evidently assisted in their task by prison guards. On September 11, police detonated a car bomb that had been found in a shopping center parking lot in Ciudad Juárez, while in Morelos, police found nine bodies in clandestine graves, believed to have been killed on the orders of La Barbie before his arrest.

With every arrest of an important cartel figure, the drug trade and the violence surrounding it continued on as if nothing had happened. Sergio Enrique Villarreal Barragán, the towering Héctor Beltrán Leyva deputy known as El Grande, was seized by the military in a luxury home in the city of Puebla, some eighty miles from the capital. Paraded before the media in now familiar fashion, Villarreal scowled in his jeans and black San Antonio Spurs T-shirt.

Luis Carlos Santiago, a twenty-one-year-old photographer for the Ciudad Juárez paper *El Diario*, was shot and killed in a September 16 attack that also wounded an eighteen-year-old intern, Carlos Sánchez Colunga. The two had been driving in a car belonging to Gustavo de la Rosa Hickerson, the attorney who headed up Chihuahua's CEDH human rights body, and whose son was an editor at the paper. The slain young photographer had become an orphan while still quite young and, "looking for the warmth of home," had grown close to the De la Rosa family. A subsequent narcomanta claimed that the killing was the work of La Línea on behalf of the Juárez Cartel and threatened to kill three police officers. *El Diario* would eventually run a front-page editorial pleading of the killers "we ask you to explain what you want from us, what you want us to publish or stop publishing."

As if refusing to acknowledge the ongoing slaughter consuming Juárez, Calderón's spokesman on security issues Alejandro Poiré reacted to the newspaper's plea by stating "in no way should anyone promote a truce or negotiate with criminals who are precisely the ones causing anxiety for the public, kidnapping, extorting and killing." Back in Tamaulipas, twenty-two suspected cartel members were slain and one soldier injured when soldiers raided a ranch near Ciudad Mier. Also seized in the raid were eighteen rifles, four handguns, 1,540 rounds of ammunition, fifty-five grenades, and military uniforms.

The two hundredth anniversary of Mexico's independence and the centennial of its revolution—September 15, 2010—was greeted with deep depression in the country. Writing in the *New York Times*, the historian Enrique Krauze lamented that

a handful of powerful criminal groups have unleashed a blood-soaked and utterly illegitimate wave of violence against the Mexican government and Mexican society. . . . We are dealing with a situation generated . . . by the market for drugs and weapons in the United States and by the refusal of many Americans to recognize their own portion of responsibility in these tragic events.

Just in time for the bicentennial, the Mexican director Luis Estrada released his film *El Infierno*—partially made with government funding—with the tagline *Mexico 2010: Nada que celebrar* (Nothing to Celebrate). The film traced the bloody progress of Benny García, played with great depth by the veteran Mexican actor Damián Alcázar. Deported from the United States to his hometown in northern Mexico with barely a penny, he finds the place under the thumb of a drug lord, Don José Reyes, whom his best friend, El Cochiloco, is now working for. Lacking other opportunities, Benny also takes up the narco life, with predictably disastrous results. The movie follows his exploits with a cast of narcos, simpering bishops, corrupt politicians, law enforcement officials, and other assorted predators. The film's tone of black comedy made it even more searing. As if to underline the film's motto, in Ciudad Juárez, independence festivals were canceled for the first time in the city's history.

Whereas Mexico's independence had been greeted by a cry of freedom, the month of September this time around would be marked by other things. September 17 was another blighted day for Mexico. An attack on a Ciudad Juárez bar killed seven people, the second such attack at the same bar in two months. In Guerrero, gunmen kidnapped nine state policemen, the bodies of two of whom were found shortly thereafter, with the rest found later dismembered in a ravine. Also in Guerrero, a passing vehicle hurled two human heads into a refreshment stand in Coyuca de Catalán. In the town of Mina, near Monterrey, troops killed three suspected cartel gunmen who had been traveling in an SUV with Texas license plates. The Zetas boss in Quintana Roo, José Ángel Fernández, was arrested by the army a week later. Among other crimes, Fernández was accused of ordering the firebombing of the Castillo del Mar casino in Cancún the previous month that killed eight people.

In Tancítaro, the town in Michoacán that had seen its city council chief kidnapped and murdered the year before, the bodies of Mayor Gustavo Sánchez Cervantes and city agricultural adviser Rafael Equihua Cervantes were found in the back of an abandoned pickup near Uruapan. They had apparently been stoned to death. Earlier in the year, Sánchez had fired sixty employees of the local Department of Public Safety for unspecified reasons. The same day in Coahuayana, also in Michoacán, five gunmen and a marine died. To the north in Reynosa, in yet another firefight, eight gunmen and a marine died. Prisciliano Rodríguez Salinas, the mayor of the small town of Doctor González in Nuevo León, was slain along with his driver as he drove away from his ranch near the town.

On September 29, Mexican marines conducting raids in Matamoros and Reynosa arrested thirty suspected Gulf Cartel members, also seizing fifty guns, including two shoulder-fired rocket launchers as well as twenty-one grenades and a cache of ammunition. The same day, an explosive device thrown at the city hall in Matamoros injured three people.

It is believed that it was around this time that Tony Tormenta was injured in a gun battle and sought refuge not in Matamoros, but across the Rio Grande in a house between Brownsville and South Padre Island in Texas, where he planned to recuperate from his wounds. The Mexican government had other plans, however, and on September 26 a military convoy—allegedly from the navy—stormed the Cárdenas family home in Matamoros, dragging both Tony Tormenta's wife, Hermelinda Rivera Alcantara, and his son, Jorge Cárdenas Rivera, from the building and into custody. Tony Tormenta allegedly responded to this affront by having several members of the armed forces kidnapped, at least two of whom were killed as, in his twisted logic, he believed this would be an impetus for negotiation. The military commander in Matamoros reportedly let it be known that, as far as he was concerned, following the deaths of members of the military, Tormenta was already a dead man.

By the end of fiscal year 2010, it was estimated that drug smuggling flights by ultralight aircraft across the US-Mexico border stood at 228, almost double from the year before. The civilian toll was also growing. As September ended, twenty mechanics on vacation from Michoacán were kidnapped in Acapulco. None of the men had criminal records, and it was speculated that they might have been seized by a cadre of gunmen by mistake. The cars the men were dragged from were later found abandoned. Over a month later, in a coconut grove outside the city, police found eighteen bodies in a mass grave after a video was posted depicting the execution of two men said to be from the Beltrán-Leyva Cartel who allegedly killed the mechanics on the orders of La Barbie's father-in-law, Carlos Montemayor González. The bodies of the alleged assassins were flung atop a grave with the sign *The people they killed are buried here.*

The same day the mechanics disappeared, marines arrested seventeen suspected Gulf Cartel members around Tamaulipas, also seizing forty-nine assault rifles, six grenades, and two handguns.

On Falcon Lake, a dammed section of the Rio Grande, which traverses the Texas-Tamaulipas border that had become a known narco smuggling hot spot, two Americans from McAllen, Texas, David and Tiffany Hartley, were attacked by gunmen while on their Jet Skis, Tiffany Hartley later said, as they were trying to take photos of a sunken church. David Hartley was shot, fell into the water, and his wife fled. Speaking with several individuals familiar with the case in the Rio Grande Valley, one could surmise that the circumstances of the shooting may have been more complex than they might have at first appeared. The severed head of Rolando Flores, the Mexican police commander tasked with investigating Hartley's disappearance, was subsequently discovered near Miguel Alemán.

And the violence was continuing to spread, beyond Mexico's border as well as within it. In October, it was the turn of the citizens of the town of Grano de Oro in Guatemala's El Petén region along the Mexican border, when the Guatemalan military confronted a ten-car convoy of armed men believed to be Los Zetas in a series of encounters that left five dead. Back in Mexico, Calderón sent a bill to Mexico's senate calling for the dissolution of Mexico's local police forces, citing their corruption and inefficiency. That month, two years after it was first announced, US and

Mexican officials finally began implementing a program designed to trace weapons seized in Mexico to their origins in the United States. Dubbed "eTrace," the system had been delayed because not enough investigators in Mexico had been trained or given access to the electronic database at the center of the program.

In Tijuana that October, Calderón feted former US vice president Al Gore, Twitter cofounder Biz Stone, and Wikipedia cofounder Jimmy Wales at the opening of a two-week festival designed to show off the city's economic and cultural potential, saying that Tijuana had "decided to show its true side." In the midst of the festival, however, sixteen people were killed, with victims of decapitation slayings discovered in the city's streets and others hung from bridges. That same week, in an interview with the Associated Press, Calderón drew a distinction between Tijuana and cities like Nuevo Laredo, Matamoros, and Reynosa where "the moment that the Gulf Cartel and its [former] associates, the Zetas, start fighting, there's a tremendous bloodbath."

And yet, in the Oaxaca town of Mártires de Tacubaya, the mayor-elect, PRI-member Antonio Jiménez Baños, was killed on October 8 while returning from his farm. Less than a month later, four days after he assumed command of the police force in the industrial town of García near Monterrey, retired general Juan Arturo Esparza García was slain in a hail of two hundred bullets. State investigators would later arrest twenty people, the majority of them police officers, for involvement in the killing.

In mid-October 2010, Mexico's W Radio broadcast a tape of a telephone conversation between the Michoacán PRD politician Julio César Godoy Toscano and La Familia chieftain Servando Gómez during which the narco told the politician "you can count on full support, you are going to win" and the two went on to discuss bribing an unnamed reporter. At the time, Godoy, along with thirty-five other people, was already under indictment for allegedly protecting the cartel. It was an indictment that his immunity as a legislator—he had literally snuck into congress under threat of arrest to take his oath the month before—protected him from. The tape was believed to date from the previous year. Godoy would subsequently be stripped of his immunity and disappear into the life of a fugitive.

On October 14, as narcobloqueos went up around the city and the PRI's Rodrigo Medina de la Cruz was giving a speech marking his first year as governor of Nuevo León, three gunmen and a marine were killed in a gun battle in the western reaches of Monterrey. The gunmen were believed to be from Los Zetas. A few days later, gun battles between cartel members and soldiers erupted amid narcobloqueos in Nuevo Laredo and Reynosa, sending parents racing to collect their children from school and leading factory owners to lock their gates, as one resident of Nuevo Laredo said "they are fighting with everything they have." In Matamoros, four were reported injured when gunmen tossed a grenade at a military barracks there. On October 21, soldiers arrested Óscar Manuel "La Araña" Bernal Soriano, the Zetas leader in Monterrey believed to have organized the killing of retired general Juan Arturo Esparza García earlier in the month after he assumed command of the police force in the Monterrey suburb of García.

In an illustration of just how undesirable a job in law enforcement had become, in the Chihuahua municipality of Práxedis Gilberto Guerrero, Marisol Valles García, a diminutive twenty-year-old college student, became the head of a police force of thirteen in an area where the Juárez and Sinaloa cartels were still continuing their scorched-earth war against one another. One of her predecessors in the job, Martín Castro, had been abducted in January 2009 and his severed head later deposited in front of the police station. As if to give Valles food for thought, a pair of videos posted online around the same time depicted Mario González, the brother of former Chihuahua attorney general Patricia González, handcuffed and seated in a chair as five armed men menaced him. Answering questions from an off-camera interrogator, González said that his sister had worked for La Línea, the gang of enforcers in the service of the Juárez Cartel, and had ordered several killings in Ciudad Juárez. A subsequent video depicted the beating and electrocution of a man believed to be González as the song "La piñata" played in the background. The male González was subsequently slain, his body dumped in a half-finished house in what federal officials later said was a Sinaloa Cartel hit conducted in collusion with Chihuahua state police.

CHAPTER TEN

States of Siege

I visited Ciudad Juárez that fall. I stayed at the Camino Real in El Paso, a hotel within walking distance of the international bridge that takes one into Juárez, and which possesses a hotel bar with an extraordinary ornate domed ceiling and excellent margaritas. At night, I could gaze from the hotel's upper floors across the fence—and the trickle of the Rio Grande beyond it—and see Juárez glowing infernally deep into the night. During the day, the Mexican journalist Luis Hinojos and I would drive through Juárez, interviewing people and taking in the very tense lay of the land.

At a ceremony for a local football (soccer) team at the Estadio Olímpico Benito Juárez, I chatted with the city's outgoing mayor, the Notre Dame University–educated PRI politician José Reyes Ferriz who, despite their difference in party affiliations, repeated many of Calderón's major themes.

"Most of the dead have to do with the war between organized crime and not with the civilian population," he said, disarmingly cheerful and slightly plump in a gray suit as we stood under the warm morning light. "One of the main problems we've had is that for many years corruption has grown within the police forces, and one of the major problems we had in the city was a very corrupt police department. They were working for the criminals, they weren't working for the citizens. You couldn't solve security issues if you didn't have police to solve those issues. We did a huge cleanup, and we have a much cleaner police force. Our next step needs to be judicial reform. We are having a lot of problems getting people in jail and keeping them there."

Others told a different story.

As I entered the offices of *El Diario*, the image of journalist José Armando "El Choco" Rodríguez Carreón, slain in November 2008, gazed down on me from a banner. *Justicia para El Choco*, it read, *sin periodistas no hay democracia.* Justice for Choco, without journalists there is no democracy. Only two weeks before, *El Diario*'s young photographer Luis Carlos Santiago had joined El Choco on the paper's roll of fallen reporters, having apparently made the mistake of driving a car belonging to human rights activist Gustavo de la Rosa Hickerson and getting gunned down by La Línea in the killing that had made the paper plead with the cartels to tell them what they had to do to avoid having any more employees slain.

"On one hand there are the threats, and then on the other hand there is pressure to 'do publicity'," *El Diario*'s editor, Pedro Torres Estrada, told me as we sat in the newspaper's offices. "It's a hostile environment to work in. There is constant pressure."

Later, as I chatted with Alfredo Quijano Hernánde, the editor of the paper *El Norte de Ciudad Juárez*, he told me much the same thing.

"You have a federal government that is a thousand kilometers away from here, and a state government that is more than 300 kilometers away," he told me. "And we have a municipal police department that practically doesn't exist, they have abandoned their function of protecting the community. We're in the hands of God and luck here in Mexico."

Luis and I drove around the outskirts of the city. Outside of the center, one found the grindingly poor slums of the world's new maquiladora-based economic order, which finally petered out into the stark desert. There were intense swirls of dust kicked up by the wind through weed-choked lots, and an eerie, deserted feeling away from the main boulevards. Such an environment must be fertile recruiting ground for the cartels, I thought. At stoplights, women and children in indigenous attire begged for money. Masked soldiers cruising through the streets with their machine guns mounted in the back of army-green pickups drove right past them without a second look. At one intersection, a billboard advertised good rates for property purchased in Dubai.

When we went to speak with the army's spokesman in Juárez, an attorney named Enrique Torres Valdez who had been the military's public face for the last two years, we found a surprisingly lightly guarded residence. We were greeted by an incongruously pretty secretary in a rather jarringly low-cut top and jeans who then ushered us to a dining room table where Torres sat. Heavy-set and slightly effeminate in manner, he told us that "relations between the police and the army are good." When I asked if the police were implicated in the violence, he gave me a look that said "Do you think I'm a fool?" and changed the subject.

My final interview in Juárez was with Gustavo de la Rosa Hickerson, the head of the state's branch of the CEDH human rights body, whose car the young *El Diario* photographer had been driving when he was killed. De la Rosa had been forced into a kind of quasi-exile in El Paso since September 2009, returning to Juárez to work but going back to Texas at night. We spoke at his office in a building disconcertingly made of sheer glass facing a busy street. Looking at De la Rosa, with his white beard and glasses, the image of Santa Claus was not only apt but unavoidable.

"The government says that 75 percent or something of these homicides are linked to organized crime, but there has never been a study of how many of these victims were in fact linked to criminal activity," De la Rosa told me. "There is an atmosphere of total impunity, that here in Juárez a person can kill another person for any reason. And the justice system has collapsed, in Juárez it is practically nonfunctional. The structure doesn't exist to have a basic application of justice here."

Later that same night, I ran into De la Rosa again at an atmospheric bar a few blocks from my hotel, surrounded by a slightly bohemian crowd and looking visibly more relaxed than when we had met in the glass-structured target earlier in the day.

Across the river, in the desert night, the killing in Juárez churned on.

A caravan of Zetas—consisting of at least eighty drug traffickers in an estimated twenty vehicles—clashed with Guatemalan army and police in a battle in the rural Petén in early October 2010 that left two security officers wounded by gunfire and a trail of terrified inhabitants in its wake. Hours later, another clash near the Petén village of Grano de Oro left five dead. Before the shooting had started, the Zetas convoy broadcast from a loudspeaker to "let us through, this has nothing to do with you, or there will be blood."

Though by that fall, the US Immigration and Customs Enforcement Academy was training Mexican customs agents in antinarcotic strategies at its headquarters in South Carolina, the last days of October 2010 were among the grimmest Mexico had seen of drug-related violence. One Friday night at a party for teenagers in the Ciudad Juárez neighborhood of Horizontes del Sur, gunmen demanding the whereabouts of an individual they referred to as *El Ratón* killed fourteen partygoers, the youngest of whom was a thirteen-year-old girl. The bodies of two men, one of them decapitated, were subsequently found in an SUV in the city with a note that accused them of killing women and children, believed to be in reference to the Horizontes del Sur killings. Then, on Sunday, thirteen people were slain during an attack on a drug rehabilitation facility in Tijuana, belying the Calderón government's message of the city's resurgence. The same day, three civilians—including a fourteen-year-old boy—were killed in a gun battle between soldiers and narcos in the Coahuila capital of Saltillo.

The following Wednesday saw fifteen people, a number of them recovering drug addicts, slain at a carwash in Tepic, the capital of the state of Nayarit, just south of Sinaloa. The entire police force of Los Ramones, a rural municipality some forty miles to the east of Monterrey, quit after their headquarters came under sustained attack by grenades and automatic weapons fire. In the Mexico City neighborhood of Tepito—the site of the main Santa Muerte shrine—six men hanging out near a convenience score were gunned down just after midnight by assailants in a white SUV. Residents said the men could frequently be seen in the neighborhood under the influence of alcohol and drugs. Over the last weekend in October, four US citizens were slain in Ciudad Juárez in various parts of the city. Two more US citizens, a pair of university students from El Paso, were killed in the city the following Tuesday.

In an indication of how pervasive the influence of the traffickers had become, in the town of Tezontle in Hidalgo, priests celebrated mass in a church that bore a plaque, on which was carved the legend *Donated by Heriberto Lazcano Lazcano, Lord, hear my prayer.* The Catholic hierarchy claimed to be unaware of the drug lord's connection to the building, saying that the chapel had been built as a community project. The Arch-diocese of Mexico would later publish an editorial on its website stating that "there are suspicions that donors connected to drug trafficking have helped with money from the dirtiest and bloodiest business, in the con-struction of some chapels. . . . This is immoral and doubly offensive, and nothing justifies it."

On Friday, November 5, 2010, the day of reckoning for the Gulf Car-tel's Tony Tormenta arrived. Following the arrest of his wife and son and repeated attacks on his Gulf Cartel faction, the Mexican military succeeded in luring Tormenta back across the border into Mexico from his hiding place in Texas. The gun battle started that Friday morning in Matamoros and lasted for much of the afternoon in various quarters of the city before security forces finally cornered Tormenta and his men in a house on Calle Abasolo. A final assault lasted over two hours, calling in nearly seven hundred troops, three helicopters, and seventeen vehicles. The gunfire was so loud that the University of Texas at Brownsville closed for the afternoon, afraid of being hit by stray bullets as it had been in the past. The government initially said that three gunmen, two marines, and a soldier were killed, in addition to the Gulf Cartel chieftain. Matamoros residents put the number of dead that day at closer to fifty.

"Someone who lives on the street told me that three military trucks pulled up and opened fire with .50 caliber machine guns," said one resi-dent. "There was blood and brains all over the place."

Even months later, as I stood in front of the building while a nervous taxi driver waited in the car, the bullet-pockmarked house—shredded is perhaps a better word—looked like it had been through a major battle in a war. Which, of course, it had.

Killed along with Tony Tormenta that day was Carlos Guajardo Romero, a portly, gregarious thirty-seven-year-old reporter for *Expreso*, who, according to several colleagues, had served as the Gulf Cartel's com-munications liaison with the press in Tamaulipas and whose car was in the boss's convoy when it came under attack by soldiers. At a cartel bar days later, journalists were summoned and informed of who would be Guajardo's replacement.

The day after Tony Tormenta's death, several poorly written banners appeared in several cities in Tamaulipas, Veracruz, and Quintana Roo crowing that *Once again the destiny of the traitors has been demonstrated, crushing the Gulf traitors*. The banners were signed *Sincerely, Los Zetas Unit*. Leadership of much of the cartel fell to El Coss, now assisted by a heretofore little-known narco, an American-born trafficker named Miguel Villarreal but better known as *El Gringo* or Gringo Mike, who would be controlling Reynosa.

Not to be left behind, twenty people were killed in Ciudad Juárez, while on a cliff outside of Oaxaca a severed head was found in a gift-wrapped box with a threatening message signed by Los Zetas.

By November 2010, the government of Guatemalan president Álvaro Colom declared a state of siege in the northern department of Alta Verapaz, a stronghold of Los Zetas. In response, men claiming to be from the cartel took to the airwaves of three radio stations and threatened to attack shopping centers, schools, and police stations if government pressure did not cease.

But despite the state of siege, Los Zetas were expanding still further. In late 2010, I met with an acquaintance with intimate knowledge of the drug syndicates' operations in Guatemala at a coffee shop in Guatemala City. As bow-tied waiters bused tables and easy-listening tunes played in the cafe only a few blocks from the city's posh Camino Real hotel, I listened as the contact told me a tale. The contact described how one of the wealthiest families from the eastern region of Guatemala that empties into the Gulf of Honduras, whose interests ran to transportation and construction endeavors but also to more illicit forms of entrepreneurship, received an offer that they couldn't refuse.

Called to a meeting in the town of Poptún in El Petén, the family's emissary found himself face-to-face with members of Los Zetas, whose message to their erstwhile Guatemalan competitors was clear and chilling: Join forces with the Mexican cartel or make a $1.5 million down payment and deliver monthly payments in the sum of $700,000. There would be no negotiation. The family, my contact said, was now in a panic and looking to leave the country, possibly for Costa Rica. Later, though, the family returned, and it appeared that some sort of deal had been hammered out.

In mid-November 2010, copies of a one-page letter signed by La Familia littered the streets of several towns in the state, in which the cartel promised to dissolve itself "if the federal and local authorities . . . promise to take control of the state with force and decision." The letter seemed to reinforce the perception that the cartel, still Mexico's major trafficker of meth, was falling on hard times. Subsequent narcomantas attributed to La Familia bemoaned the government's lack of interest in the offer.

Silverio Cavazos Ceballos, the former governor of Colima, was gunned down in that state's eponymous capital city in a November 21 attack the government attributed to La Familia, a characterization the victim's widow disputed.

Following the killing of Tony Tormenta, Los Zetas made a strong push to take Ciudad Mier, the city near Falcon Lake that the Gulf Cartel had seized earlier in the year. The roads around the town were littered with the shells of burned-out cars and roving convoys of gunmen engaged in furious gun battles lasting for hours. Dismembered corpses were strung up in the town square and a steel-plated ten-wheel gravel truck dubbed "The Monster"—complete with gun ports in its sides—served as a Zetas war wagon during their lunges toward the town. Extraordinarily, the Gulf Cartel brought it down, and eventually the vehicle sat, rusting and useless, by the roadside. By the middle of the month, the town was virtually deserted. Many residents sought shelter in the event hall of the Lions Club in Ciudad Miguel Alemán, creating the drug war's first displaced person's camp. The Calderón government's response was to send additional soldiers to Tamaulipas and Nuevo León in *Operación Coordinada Noreste* (Operation Coordinated Northeast), which it later claimed reduced crime in Tamaulipas by 48 percent. The citizens of Ciudad Mier, however, would not begin returning home until more than a month later.

Soon thereafter, police seized La Barbie's father-in-law, Carlos Montemayor González, known as El Charro (The Cowboy), who allegedly confessed the role of his faction of the Beltrán-Leyva Cartel in kidnapping and killing the mechanics in Acapulco two months previously. Montemayor had been living on a lavish ranch within the municipality of Naucalpan, northwest of Mexico City. There, among fabulously expensive horses and other vestiges of the equestrian life, he mixed with high-ranking government officials, including those close to the governor of Mexico State, PRI's Enrique Peña Nieto. As the month drew to a close, the government also nabbed another cartel grandee when it arrested José Alfredo Landa Torres, aka *El Flaco*, who police said was responsible for La Familia's operations in the Michoacán capital of Morelia. The cartel in the president's home state suffered another blow.

In late November, gunmen killed Hermila García Quiñones, the thirty-six-year-old female police chief of the Chihuahua town of Meoqui, who had taken her office less than two months before. Hours later, police in Chihuahua found eighteen bodies buried at a ranch outside Palomas, near the Texas border. In a small ray of hope for the battered city, police in Ciudad Juárez arrested Arturo "Benny" Gallegos Castrellón, one of the leaders of the Barrio Azteca gang, who then allegedly and improbably confessed to ordering "80 percent of the killings in the last 15 months" on behalf of the Juárez Cartel, including the shooting of the US consulate official and her husband earlier that year. Gallegos would later be extradited to the United States to face trial for the consulate slayings.

A video posted around this time showed a woman, Veronica Treviño Molina, interrogated by an off-camera interlocutor about her alleged "work" on behalf of Los Zetas in Tampico. Treviño claimed that work included "killing taxi drivers, police officers, innocent people and children." Several days after the video was shot, Treviño's head was found in an icebox. Her fate was thought to reinforce data collected by Mexico's Instituto Nacional de las Mujeres that the number of women imprisoned for federal crimes, many of which were drug-related, had quadrupled in three years and that women were playing an ever more prominent role in the drug business.

In early December, weary Mexico was again shocked with the revelations surrounding fourteen-year-old Édgar Jiménez Lugo, aka *El Ponchis*, arrested as he and two sisters tried to board a flight bound for Tijuana, from where he intended to cross into the United States, where his mother lived and where he had been born in San Diego. El Ponchis confessed to having participated in at least four decapitations while he was high on drugs in the service of the Héctor Beltrán Leyva faction of the cartel of the same name. He was subsequently sentenced to three years in prison, the maximum sentence allowed for a minor. (El Ponchis would eventually be released and return to the United States.) At a ranch outside the Tamaulipas municipality of Gustavo Díaz Ordaz, meanwhile, soldiers killed six gunmen when they allegedly opened fire on an army patrol on December 7.

Shortly after La Familia lieutenant Servando Gómez was revealed to be on the payroll of the Mexican government as part of the staff of an elementary school in his hometown of Arteaga, the cartel was dealt what appeared to be a mortal blow when leader Nazario "El Más Loco" Moreno González was killed on December 9, 2010, by police in the state (his body was never recovered). Moreno's alleged death came at the culmination of two days of gun battles that began when narco gunmen attacked police in Moreno's hometown of Apatzingán and went on to spread throughout the state and claim the lives of five police officers and three civilians, including an eight-month-old baby. Several days later, a "peace march" called by the local government in Apatzingán turned into something of a Moreno memorial service, with marchers holding up signs that read *Nazario will always live in our hearts* and *Long live La Familia Michoacána*. (On March 9, 2014, Mexican security forces announced that they had —again—killed Moreno in Michoacán, where he was said to be living in retirement since his "death.")

Hundreds of miles away from the violence in Michoacán, on Mexico's northern border, just west of Rio Rico, Arizona, near Nogales, US Border Patrol agent Brian A. Terry was shot to death in a December 14 gun battle after he and fellow agents confronted a heavily armed group of gunmen. The agents believed that the men had been robbing undocumented immigrants passing into the United States from Mexico. A pair of rifles that the ATF had been aware were purchased by a straw purchaser—but which they had made no attempt to seize as per the protocol of Operation Fast and Furious—were recovered at the scene of the killing. A suspect in Terry's murder, Iván Soto Barraza, would later be arrested in Sinaloa.

In the middle of December, Marisela Escobedo Ortiz, the mother of the murdered Juárez teenager Rubí Marisol Frayre Escobedo, planted herself in front of the offices of Chihuahua governor César Duarte Jáquez. Though she had said she had been receiving death threats from the family of Sergio Barraza, her daughter's boyfriend who had confessed to the killing, as well as from Los Zetas, she swore she would not stop agitating until Barraza was back behind bars.

However, on December 16, as she maintained her vigil, a car pulled up in front of the governor's offices, masked men leapt out, and, in full view of passersby, shot Marisela Escobedo Ortiz in the head and killed her.

By late December 2010, the epidemic of Zetas-linked violence in the Guatemalan department of Alta Verapaz had grown so severe that President Álvaro Colom declared a state of siege, a move that allowed the federal government, among other measures, to conduct searches without warrants, prohibit the possession of firearms, and place curbs on the press. In the first few days of the measures, security forces arrested ten alleged Zetas members. That number would soon double. A raid on a single farmhouse netted 220 assault rifles, and at least 335 police officers were transferred out of the department. At the same time, in the department of San Marcos, security forces arrested another ten men, including two from Tamaulipas, believed to be Zetas. Shortly after the state of siege was declared, men claiming to be Zetas arrived at radio stations in the departmental capital of Cobán and gave broadcasters an ultimatum: Read a message the group presented on the air or the stations would be burned down and the employees and their families killed.

"We are Los Zetas," the document began, before going on to threaten "to start a war in this country, in shopping malls, schools and police stations" and charging that "President Álvaro Colom received $11.5 million" from the criminal organization during his successful campaign for president. By the end of January, Colom announced he was extending the state of siege for another thirty days.

Just before Christmas 2010, attorney general Arturo Chávez Chávez announced that more than thirty thousand people had been killed in drug-related violence in Mexico since 2006. Before the end of the year the death toll had reached 3,111 in Ciudad Juárez alone. As the bloody year of 2010 drew to a close, Erika Gándara, the last remaining police officer in the Juárez Valley town of Guadalupe Distrito Bravo in Chihuahua, was kidnapped by armed men. She was twenty-eight years old at the time and was not seen again. The same day, in Nuevo León, the severed head of a federal police officer whose bullet-riddled abandoned car had been located the previous day was also found.

In Monterrey, four policeman and a doctor were killed in coordinated attacks, and the body of Gabriela Elizabeth Muñiz Tamez, aka *La Pelirroja* (The Redhead), who had recently been snatched by armed commandos from police custody after being arrested as part of a kidnapping ring in 2009, was found hanging from an underpass, partially clothed. Despite her disappearance initially being portrayed by authorities as an escape, messages appearing on various narco-related Internet message boards claimed that she had in fact been dispatched by *La Nueva Federación,* a supposed alliance of the Gulf Cartel, the Sinaloa Cartel, and La Familia, stating *pronto daremos la ubicación de su cuerpesito* (soon we'll let you know the location of her corpse). The message went on to threaten Los Zetas and their allies "who don't have balls to grab" and giving informants an e-mail address where they could send tips about the former soldiers before proclaiming "Merry Christmas! And a prosperous New Year!"

CHAPTER ELEVEN

The Highway of Death

The year 2011 began in customary sanguinary fashion. In the Gulf state of Tabasco, there was the garish slaying of two men dressed in clown costumes with a note left with their bodies accusing them of being informers. The body of Saul Vara Rivera, the mayor of the town of Zaragoza in Coahuila, was found across state lines in Nuevo León hours after he had disappeared while driving home from Saltillo. In Ciudad Juárez, a gang of teenagers speeding through the city with a ten-pound bale of marijuana shot it out with police. In Tijuana, the head—but not the body—of a local man was found dangling from a bridge. In the Casa Blanca neighborhood of the Veracruz capital of Xalapa, fourteen people were slain during the first few days of the year.

David Romo Guillén, the self-proclaimed head of the Santa Muerte church in Tepito, was arrested in early January 2011 on charges of kidnapping two elderly people and attempting to pass himself off as a member of Los Zetas, which, if true, was a potentially lethal transgression when one considers the Zetas treatment of impostors. Romo said he was the victim of political persecution and that he had been tortured while in police custody. He was subsequently convicted and sentenced to sixty-six years in prison, a bit of numerology that led to many mordant jokes in Mexico.

Though the drug trade had great durability, not all of the organizations involved in it could match such stamina. La Familia, greatly weakened and with a significant faction now under command of José de Jesús Méndez Vargas, aka *El Chango* (The Monkey), announced a one-month truce at the beginning of January 2011. However, there was no such truce in Acapulco where, in the space of four days that month, thirty-one people were slain, including two police officers and fourteen men who were decapitated and left with a note saying they had been killed by the Sinaloa Cartel. Across the country, in the Veracruz state capital of Xalapa, twelve suspected narcos and two soldiers died when a combination of marines, soldiers, and police stormed a cartel safe house.

During the month of January, Los Zetas' fortunes seemed to soar or wane depending almost on the day. Flavio "El Amarillo" Méndez Santiago, the Zetas boss in charge of operations in Chiapas, Oaxaca, and Veracruz and one of the original members of the organization, was arrested near Oaxaca City along with a bodyguard on the evening of January 17. Two days later, in a shootout involving the army and Mexican federal police, Zetas capo Leonardo "El Pachis" Vázquez, who was responsible for the cartel's operations in parts of Veracruz and Oaxaca, was killed in a running gun battle in the city of Poza Rica, which culminated in the parking lot of the El Gran Patio shopping mall. The same day, two police officers were slain in the Monterrey suburb of Guadalupe. At this point it was believed that control of Los Zetas' operations in Veracruz, as well as Puebla and Oaxaca, fell into the hands of Raúl Lucio "El Lucky" Hernández Lechuga, alias Z-16, one of the group's original founders.

That same month, Coahuila governor Humberto Moreira, whose connections to Los Zetas had long been the subject of rumors and innuendo, left the office to become the PRI's national president, a post he would formally take up in March. After a short interim administration headed by Jorge Torres López, Moreira's brother Rubén Moreira Valdez, also a PRI member and with whom Moreira's relations were said to be chilly, was elected to succeed him. Rubén Moreira would subsequently tell reporters that he found organized crime had seized "a monopoly on authority" in the state when he took office, that public officials had been active in protecting Los Zetas, and that drug traffickers had in turn funneled money to the PRI for its election campaigns. Jorge Torres López would eventually be indicted in a Texas court along with the state of Coahuila's former financial chief and charged with money laundering, bank fraud, and wire fraud.

In the Tamaulipas town of Valle Hermoso, a military patrol killed ten cartel gunmen on January 22, as a car bomb exploded in the state of Hidalgo, killing a police commander and wounding three officers, an attack that authorities believed was linked to Los Zetas. Shortly after seven men were killed at a soccer match in Ciudad Juárez, banners appeared throughout western Michoacán, purporting to be from La Familia and stating that the cartel had been "completely dissolved," though government officials dismissed the messages as a ploy.

All thirty-eight police officers for the Nuevo León town of General Terán quit at the end of January after the discovery of the beheaded bodies of two of their colleagues. In a cable directed to Washington, the US consul general in Monterrey dismissed the idea that the attacks were a response to "state government enforcement efforts" and wrote that "given the thorough penetration by the Zetas of the police forces in those municipalities that were hit, a much more likely explanation is that the attacks were a signal from the Gulf Cartel to the police to cease/desist their support of the Zetas and switch sides."

Next door in Tamaulipas, on January 26, American missionaries Sam and Nancy Davis were driving their 2008 Chevrolet 2500 pickup near San Fernando when three trucks tried to overtake them. The couple had been working in Tamaulipas for three decades. Sam decided not to stop, and gunmen opened fire, shooting Nancy in the head. Speeding to the international bridge at Pharr, Sam eventually got Nancy to the hospital at McAllen, where she died. On the morning of January 30, six bodies were found on the outskirts of Monterrey so badly burned that police could not even determine their gender.

As Mexico's security environment continued to deteriorate, its political culture remained as poisonous as ever. In Guerrero, a bitter gubernatorial contest pitted the PRI's Manuel Añorve Baños against his second cousin, the PRD's Ángel Heladio Aguirre Rivero, who had bolted from the PRI to run a successful insurgent campaign for governor in 2005. The PAN's candidate had dropped out late in the race and supported Aguirre in the latest example of the strange PAN/PRD bedfellows attempting to keep the reanimated PRI from resurrecting itself. Aguirre won after newspapers published allegations that Añorve had received millions of dollars from the Beltrán-Leyva Cartel.

In the midst of the new year's violence, five years after the Bush administration began its attempt to foist it on border communities in the United States, US president Barack Obama's Homeland Security secretary, Janet Napolitano, announced that the administration was canceling the virtual border fence with Mexico, which up to that point had cost US taxpayers nearly $1 billion to cover fifty-three miles of the border in Arizona alone. Her new plan however, sounded rather like the original, incorporating stationary radar, infrared and optical sensor towers, drones, and thermal imaging devices. The US Border Patrol itself boasted a staff of some 20,500 personnel, more than double its staff in 2004.

Assaults throughout Guadalajara on February 1 saw cartel gunmen hurling grenades at a police station and burning buses and commuter trains in seven separate incidents throughout Mexico's second largest city. The same day, a federal police officer and three suspected cartel gunmen were killed in Monterrey. A day later, in San Pedro Garza García, four suspected narco gunmen were killed by marines.

Narcomantas addressed to Heriberto Lazcano appeared in the states of Tamaulipas, Zacatecas, Morelos, and Guerrero around this time. In Reynosa, one banner read *You have already witnessed the killing and massacre of innocent people by Los Zetas. The war is against us Lazcano, not against families. Fight like MEN.* It was signed *Cárteles Unidos* (United Cartels).

In the Morelos cities of Temixco and Yecapixtla, identical banners read:

Lazcano, we are here. The war is between us. No more civilian deaths.

They were signed *CDG R1*, a reference to Gulf Cartel chieftain and Los Rojos leader Juan "El R1" Mejía González.

In Acapulco, another banner, also signed by R1, read:

Lazcano: The war is with us. Stop killing civilians and innocent families. Tell Miguel Treviño to quit hiding and come out and fight.

A month after becoming Nuevo Laredo's police chief, former general Manuel Farfán Carriola was murdered in a nighttime attack as he drove through the violence-ravaged city, an assault that also killed retired infantry lieutenant Guillermo Álvarez Hernández, who served as Farfán's secretary, and local official Raul Rivera Molina. It was assumed the attack was the work of Los Zetas. Speaking to a local television station after the killing, one woman said "if that happens to those who are in power, then imagine us." By early February, at least twenty-five children ranging in age from a few months old to ten had been found in Nuevo Laredo after their parents were apparently kidnapped.

On February 8, soldiers rescued forty-four Guatemalan migrants and three Mexicans who had been held captive in Reynosa. The next day, in the small town of Tabasco in Zacatecas, nine suspected cartel gunmen were killed when troops went investigating the inevitable "tip about the presence of armed men." Three days later, soldiers killed seven suspected cartel gunmen in the Monterrey suburb of San Nicolás de los Garza in a shootout that also saw a civilian motorist die when narcos attempting to flee crashed into his car. Hours later, another attack in Guadalajara saw six killed and thirty-seven wounded when gunmen opened fire and hurled grenades into a bar there.

In the small Tamaulipas town of Padilla, twenty-four hours of roiling violence believed to be between Gulf Cartel and Zetas elements over the night of February 13 claimed the lives of at least eighteen people, including seven dumped in the town's main square and five sprayed with bullets inside a car. At the same time, Nuevo León's director for public safety, Homero Guillermo Salcido Treviño, was kidnapped and his bullet-riddled body found in a burning truck in the middle of Monterrey. Two state police officers were subsequently arrested for involvement in the killing.

Mexican law enforcement was not the only authority under threat. Driving from Mexico City to Monterrey on February 15, a pair of US Immigration and Customs Enforcement (ICE) agents was attacked by a Zetas hit squad outside of San Luis Potosí. Some reports suggested that the pair was run off the road, at which point they were shot at point-blank range with an assault rifle through an accidently rolled-down open window, though an estimated ninety rounds failed to penetrate their vehicle's armor plating. Other reports said they were attacked at a fake roadblock.

Brownsville native Jaime J. Zapata, who had joined the agency in 2006 and served in Laredo before being posted to Mexico City, died in the attack, while his partner, Victor Avila, was gravely wounded. Zapata was the first ICE employee to be wounded or killed in the line of duty in Mexico. It was his ninth day on the job in the country, and his slaying was the highest-profile attack on US law enforcement personnel in the country since the torture and killing of Enrique "Kiki" Camarena in 1985. The car the men had been traveling in had diplomatic plates.

By the end of the month, the Ministry of Defense announced that they had "detained one of the likely perpetrators" in the attack. The man arrested, Julian Zapata Espinosa, known as *El Piolín* or "Tweety Bird" because of his diminutive stature, told soldiers that he believed Zapata's Chevrolet Suburban belonged to a rival cartel. The sicario had allegedly been working for a cell under the command of original Zetas member Jesús Enrique "El Mamito" Rejón Aguilar or Z-7, who was also believed to be involved in the killing. Eventually, yet another Zetas grandee, Luis Jesús Sarabia Ramón, aka *Pepito Sarabia*, who had been in command of a number of operations in Coahuila, Aguascalientes, and San Luis Potosí at the time, was also arrested.

Days after the Zapata killing, soldiers killed five assault rifle– and grenade launcher–toting gunmen in the Monterrey suburb of Guadalupe, while another five people died after clashing with the soldiers in Acapulco. The same day, four men, their hands and feet bound, were hurled from a six-hundred-foot-high bridge near the Guerrero state capital of Chilpancingo. A subsequent spate of attacks on taxi drivers in Acapulco—just as the Mexican Open tennis tournament was about to start—left twelve drivers and customers dead.

On February 25, the convoy of Jaime Rodríguez Calderón, the mayor of the Nuevo León town of García, north of Monterrey, was attacked by gunmen as it approached the latter city. Rodríguez's bodyguards returned fire, managing to kill three of the attackers. The attack occurred, the mayor said, after he fired the local police department and moved against narco-affiliated businesses. The fact that he survived the attack, and his brusque, take-charge manner, led Rodríguez to garner the nickname *El Bronco*, after an unbroken horse, and a corrido extolling his bravery was soon written. The mayor would be the victim of other attacks in the coming months, including one that would kill a young bodyguard. Meanwhile, three young girls aged twelve, fourteen, and fifteen were killed when gunmen opened fire on the home they were playing in front of in Ciudad Juárez. Three other children were killed the same day in an attack on a car in the city. Also slain in Juárez that month were the sister, brother, and sister-in-law of Josefina Reyes, the human rights activist who had been killed over a year before. All were seized from a car by armed men, and a little over two weeks later their bodies were discovered south of the city. Reyes's brother, Ruben, had been killed by unknown assailants the previous August.

In late February 2011, in an extraordinary interview with the Texas-based reporter Ildefonso Ortiz, a former Zetas operative who admitted to killing thirty-two people described the narco life he had recently abandoned as "a fantasy that one has in the head, but once you live it, you can only cry." The gunman, "Antonio," said that he had been employed by the Mexican attorney general's office at the same time as he was working for the Zetas before quitting to become a full-time sicario. Thus followed a dolorous life, fueled by cocaine and Buchanan's whiskey, of kidnapping, torture, murder, and gun battles with Mexican military and rival cartels, with safe houses full of kidnapping victims, uniforms of various military and police units, and weapons. After overdosing on cocaine three times, Antonio left Los Zetas, but only after completing a number of tasks that he refused to discuss and turning over all his properties, his cars, his money, and his weapons to the gang. He concluded that "it's better to live poor, like my old man would say, eating eggs and beans, than to live like this" and in an accompanying video of the interview advised "you can have everything. But it has a price."

A high price.

As March 2011 began, soldiers discovered seventeen bodies in a pair of clandestine cemeteries in the Guerrero town of San Miguel Totolapan, the third time since the beginning of the year that mass graves had been discovered in the state. In Culiacán, a police convoy transporting two prisoners was ambushed by gunmen traveling in at least twenty vehicles. Seven policemen and one of the prisoners were slain in what Sinaloa state attorney general Marco Antonio Higuera called "practically a massacre" that left twelve hundred shell casings at the scene. A day later, three severed heads were found in plastic bags in Acapulco, with a note saying the killings were in revenge for an attempted kidnapping.

After surviving for five months in her job as chief of police of the Chihuahua municipality of Práxedis Gilberto Guerrero—longer than anyone could have reasonably expected—twenty-year-old Marisol Valles García fled with her baby across the border from Ciudad Juárez to El Paso in early March 2011 after receiving threats against her life. Given the fact that one of her predecessors had been abducted and beheaded, few blamed her. The city of Práxedis Gilberto Guerrero later announced that it was firing her for failing to return to her job.

Over the night of March 9–10, banners hung in the Michoacán capital of Morelia, as well as in the cities of Apatzingán and Zitácuaro, announced the formation of a new cartel, *Los Caballeros Templarios* (Knights Templar), saying it was the successor to the greatly weakened La Familia.

The new cartel's name was a reference to a Christian military organization formed in Jerusalem that existed in Europe for two centuries during the Middle Ages, and the signs declared that, apparently in addition to trafficking drugs, the new group would combat extortion, kidnapping, and other crimes and prohibit other gangs from operating in the state. It was believed that former La Familia boss Servando "La Tuta" Gómez was at the head of the new group, while Jesús "El Chango" Méndez had largely taken over La Familia. Under Méndez's leadership, La Familia was believed to be heavily extorting miners and ranchers, forcing the former to pay $1.50 per ton of metal they sold and the latter to pay $1 per kilogram of meat.

Under Gómez's leadership, the Knights Templar—which, in its upper echelons, would also include the veteran drug trafficker Dionicio "El Tío" Loya Plancarte and Loya's nephew, Enrique Plancarte Solís—would continue the quasi-religious aspect of drug trafficking that Nazario Moreno González had brought to La Familia, distributing a pocket-sized twenty-two-page code of conduct to members that urged a "fight against materialism," respect for women and children, and ordered, startlingly, drug testing for all members. The cover of the booklet depicted lance-and-shield–bearing medieval horsemen.

By early March 2009, the US outlet CBS News and the nonprofit Center for Public Integrity reported that ATF agents had "allowed hundreds of guns purchased in the US to go into Mexico" as part of the gun-walking operations that had been underway since the Bush years. As the Mexican senate voted to summon the US ambassador to explain the nature of the program, PAN senator Luis Alberto Villarreal García stated that "carrying out this type of operation in our country is unacceptable. It violates trust and also undermines national sovereignty."

As if to underline how deeply the Mexican cartels depended on weapons from the United States, on March 10, the mayor, police chief, and a community trustee of the city of Columbus, New Mexico, just north of Chihuahua, were arrested for their part in a conspiracy that smuggled at least two hundred weapons across the border. The mayor, Eddie Espinoza, was subsequently convicted and sentenced to serve fifty-one months in federal prison. Columbus's police chief Angelo Vega and village trustee Blas "Woody" Gutierrez both pleaded guilty. Meanwhile on the outskirts of San Fernando in Tamaulipas, an army raid on a drug camp left eight suspected narcos dead. A day later, soldiers killed four presumed kidnappers during a gun battle in the town of China, near Texas.

Two days later, an inmate stabbed a prison warden to death in Nuevo Laredo.

As with so much of its foreign policy, the approach of the Obama administration to the violence ripping Mexico and elsewhere in Central America apart was distant and distracted. Even as hundreds of guns had been walked into Mexico by the ATF, by mid-March 2011, the Obama administration had begun sending unarmed Global Hawk drones at high altitude deep into Mexico to try to track the movements of traffickers, a move that Calderón was reported to have signed off on at a White House meeting with Obama in March 2011. By this point, it was also believed that several hundred US agents were operating in Mexico in tandem with the Calderón government in the drug war. These included at least sixty DEA agents, forty ICE agents, twenty marshals, and eighteen ATF agents. The State Department's Narcotics Affairs Section staff at the US Embassy in Mexico City alone numbered sixty-nine people. Relations hit a serious bump, however, when the organization WikiLeaks published cables in which US Ambassador to Mexico Carlos Pascual leveled scathing criticism at the Mexican political establishment and questioned the effectiveness of the armed forces. Pascual would quickly resign and be replaced by former US ambassador to Argentina and Afghanistan Earl Anthony Wayne.

Between March 15 and March 17, five children were killed in violence in Acapulco, including two boys, ages two and six, killed along with an elderly woman when gunmen attacked their home, and a four-year-old girl found shot in the chest in a car next to a dead woman, who had also been shot. Signed messages found in Michoacán along with two bodies during the same time period claimed the men had been killed by the Knights Templar. A few days later, masked gunmen stormed a bar in Acapulco and killed ten men. The same month, the CEDH in Michoacán in cooperation with a local university published a book of drawings by children between the ages of seven and twelve that depicted scene after scene of bloody carnage, which a member of the committee that selected the drawings said showed "explicit images of a society devoted to drug trafficking, violence, and of abuses against minors."

In late March, the Calderón government announced that Víctor Manuel Félix, the godfather of one of El Chapo Guzmán's sons and one of the Sinaloa Cartel's chief money launderers, was among eighteen people arrested in operations in Mexico and Ecuador that lasted several weeks.

In a reminder of what perhaps awaited Mexico's fallen drug lords, in late March 2011 the family of former Guadalajara Cartel leader Miguel Ángel Félix Gallardo wrote an open letter to Genaro García Luna that appeared in several Mexico City newspapers complaining:

For more than three years, without any justification, prison authorities have kept him segregated, isolated and without contact with other inmates, and have prevented him from participating in any physical, sports or educational activities.

The letter also denounced "unhealthy conditions, humidity, a lack of ventilation, bad odors and darkness" in Félix Gallardo's captivity.

On March 25, a group of sicarios working for the Gulf Cartel in Monterrey kidnapped and killed Televisa Monterrey program host José Luis "La Gata" Cerda Meléndez, reporter Luis Emmanuel Ruiz Carrillo from the Coahuila-based *La Prensa* (who was in Monterrey to write an article on Cerda), and Ruiz's cousin, Juan Roberto Gómez. Cerda's body was found on a Monterrey street with a message accusing him of working for Los Zetas. The bodies of the other two men were found next to a freeway. Several days later, the body of Noel López Olguín, a columnist for the newspaper *La Verdad de Jáltipan*, based in the Veracruz city of the same name, was found in a clandestine grave in the town of Chinameca in that state in an area dominated by Los Zetas. López had been kidnapped earlier that month. His column, *Con pluma de plomo* (With a Lead Pen), had frequently discussed drug traffickers by name. A local drug trafficker, Alejandro "El Dragón" Castro Chirinos, was subsequently arrested for the killing, as well as that of five police officers.

Along the cartels' second front, by March 2011, Guatemalan authorities were finding an average of twenty abandoned airplanes a year along the country's little-patrolled Caribbean coast. A Sinaloa Cartel–linked cocaine processing lab had also been discovered in the country's northeastern mountains. As the month drew to an end, Juan "Chamalé" Ortíz, the Guatemalan drug trafficker who was credited with first facilitating the entrance of the Zetas into Guatemala and who had been charged in a US federal arrest warrant issued in Tampa, Florida, with two counts of conspiracy to distribute cocaine, was captured by US and Guatemalan agents in the city of Quetzaltenango. He would eventually be extradited to the United States.

As March drew to a close, police found seven bodies showing signs of torture in a car abandoned at an upper-class gated community near Cuernavaca, while in Nuevo Laredo the army killed four alleged narcos and in

Monterrey a shootout killed two and injured three, including a two-year-old. During the twenty-four-hour period between March 31 and April 1, 2011, in Ciudad Juárez, twenty people were slain in incidents ranging from an attack on the La Barritas and El Castillo bars that included automatic weapons and Molotov cocktails to an assault on a food stand that killed four men and a ten-year-old boy.

One of those found dead in Cuernavaca was Juan Francisco Sicilia Ortega, the son of Javier Sicilia, a well-known poet and contributor to *La Jornada* and *Proceso*. At the funeral for his son, known as Juanelo, Sicilia read a poem:

> *El mundo ya no es digno de la palabra*
> *Nos la ahogaron adentro*
> *Como te (asfixiaron),*
> *Como te*
> *desgarraron a ti los pulmones*
> *Y el dolor no se me aparta*
> *sólo queda un mundo*
> *Por el silencio de los justos*
> *Sólo por tu silencio y por mi silencio, Juanelo.*

> *(The world is no longer worthy of words*
> *We have been suffocated inside*
> *As they suffocate you*
> *As they*
> *Tore out your lungs*
> *And the pain does not leave me*
> *All that remains in the world*
> *From the silence of the righteous*
> *Only for your silence and my silence, Juanelo.)*

He told those attending the funeral that it would be the last poem that he would ever write. The killing prompted Sicilia, a cerebral figure not known for his political pronouncements, into a frenzy of activity, confessing that while "poetry does not exist in me anymore," Mexico had "to rebuild the tissue of this nation—if we do not, we are going to enter hell." He added that "Mexico doesn't want to labor under this stupid war any more." Perhaps even Sicilia himself could not imagine quite how far his anguish would take him.

Two months later, police arrested Julio de Jesús "El Negro" Radilla Hernández of the *Cártel del Pacífico Sur,* a micro-cartel made up of remnants of the Beltrán-Leyva Cartel and based in Morelos, where Cuernavaca is located, for the killing. Three others were also arrested. The killing, it was said, occurred because one of the dead had the nerve to report an extortion attempt to law enforcement officials. The Cártel del Pacífico Sur was one of several smaller criminal groups made up of the once-powerful Beltrán-Leyva gang, with another mini-cartel, *La Mano con Ojos* (The Hand with Eyes), setting up shop in the gritty industrial city of Toluca, the capital of Mexico State, which surrounds but does not include the nation's capital. The latter group was led by Oswaldo "El Compayito" García Montoya, a former policeman and marine from Sinaloa and Beltrán-Leyva sicario who had bragged that he had killed three hundred people and ordered the killing of another three hundred. García Montoya had trained with Los Kabiles in Guatemala and admitted a role in the kidnapping of the twenty-four people killed in the September 2008 La Marquesa massacre but said he did not give the order to have the men killed.

Another of the Beltrán-Leyva Cartel's murderous progeny, the *Cártel Independiente de Acapulco* (CIDA), was made up largely of former La Barbie foot soldiers and operated in that Pacific Coast resort city, but further split apart when a group decided to strike out on their own and form a gang called *La Barredora* (The Street Sweeper). The latter gang was led by Christian Arturo Hernández Tarin, the son of a narco named Arturo Hernández González who had been close with the Juárez Cartel during the time of Amado Carrillo Fuentes. Yet another group, the *Cártel del Centro,* was led by Adrián Ramírez Soria, alías *El Hongo* (The Mushroom) and also operated in the area surrounding Mexico City, chiefly in the cities of Tlalnepantla and Tultitlán. Ramírez's odd nickname came from his short hairstyle, which some of his fellow narcos likened to a fungus.

A report from the Internal Displacement Monitoring Center released around the same time concluded that around 230,000 people had been displaced because of drug violence with "an estimated half of those displaced [crossing] the border into the United States, which would leave about 115,000 people internally displaced, most likely in the States of Chihuahua, Durango, Coahuila and Veracruz." By early April, the UN Working Group on Enforced or Involuntary Disappearances was expressing its concern over Calderón's military offensive against the cartels, noting that "the military is not trained to do public security tasks but to confront armed forces" and recommending that Calderón consider removing them from their visible role in the drug war. The request was met with skepticism not only by the government, but also by Mexican security analysts such as Jorge Chabat. The UN Working Group also noted that between April and September 2010, at least 11,333 Central and South American migrants had been kidnapped in the country.

In the town of El Higo near the Tamaulipas border in Veracruz, cartel gunmen and police blazed away at one another in an April 3 confrontation that left six policemen dead. Their weapons were then seized by their killers. The same day, a convoy of police and soldiers engaged in a gun battle with narcos after-hours at a shopping mall in Acapulco during which a soldier and two gunmen died. Shortly afterward, two severed heads were found on one of the city's main boulevards.

And, just as it seemed that the people of Mexico and the residents of Tamaulipas could endure no more, this:

Soldiers investigating reports that passengers had been kidnapped from buses along the *Carretera Federal* 101—*la carretera de la muerte* (the highway of death)—began to find a series of pits around the farming community of La Joya in the San Fernando Valley, where dozens of Central American immigrants had been slain a year before. Initially, eight separate pits were found, containing the bodies of fifty-nine people, including men and women. Police said that their first reports had come in late March when a Matamoros woman said that her husband had failed to arrive as scheduled from San Luis Potosí. A local priest told the *Washington Post* that "people began to disappear, first it was people with money, then it was anyone," and then related the story of a farmer's son sent back dismembered to his family after they could only raise half the ransom.

As the authorities began hauling the corpses to the morgue in Matamoros, Tamaulipas interior minister Morelos Jaime Carlos Canseco Gómez told reporters that many of the victims had apparently died from ten to fifteen days before their bodies were found. For their part, the Tamaulipas prosecutors said that eleven people had been arrested as suspects connected to the killings and five kidnapping victims located in raids had been released. The victims had apparently been hauled off the buses in the middle of a stretch of lonely desert between two army roadblocks. As the body count continued to climb, Mexico's minister of the interior José Francisco Blake Mora announced that even more federal troops were being sent to Tamaulipas, while Attorney General Marisela Morales announced that the government had linked the crime to Los Zetas.

Los Zetas, it seemed, believed that the Gulf Cartel had summoned reinforcements from the remnants of La Familia and other cartels elsewhere in Mexico, reinforcements that were slated to arrive, low-profile, in Matamoros, Reynosa, and elsewhere aboard public buses from the south. Though most of the victims appeared to have been simple laborers heading to the United States from elsewhere in Mexico to try their hand at making a go of it in *El Norte*, an acquaintance of mine in Reynosa swore that "God would not let that happen to innocent people." I didn't believe him, but I didn't blame him, either, for trying to make sense of such horror.

An alleged survivor of the abductions described Miguel "Z-40" Treviño as having been physically present and taken part in many of the executions. He also recounted bodies dissolved in vats of acid, the gang rape of women, and how, after one kidnapped passenger begged to be set free, offering money in exchange for his release, Treviño appeared to relent, contemptuously saying "Ok, faggot, go." As the man began to walk away Treviño attacked him with a mallet until his head was "completely destroyed."

Another report told the story of an *Autobuses de Oriente* bus that left a San Fernando town only to be waylaid on the highway by Zetas gunmen—again led by Treviño himself—with men separated from women and children as Treviño demanded "Who wants to live?" and circled the passengers, shooting those whose answers or actions displeased him. Most of those uncovered in the San Fernando pits were found to have died of blunt force trauma, and an alleged cartel operative later claimed that the heartiest victims were forced into gladiator-style competitions, with one beaten to death and the survivor sent on "suicide missions" against rival cartels. Soon the number of bodies topped one hundred, then 115, overwhelming the Matamoros morgue to such an extent that corpses had to be held in a refrigerated meat truck parked outside. One woman waiting outside for news of a vanished loved one told a radio station that "the people in this country should understand that life is not worth anything here." When all was said and done, the corpses of more than 190 souls were extracted from the narcofosas.

At a press conference held after the discovery of the pits, Isabel Miranda de Wallace, the head of the *Alto al Secuestro* (Stop the Kidnappings) organization—whose own son had been kidnapped and killed years earlier—said that she believed that mass graves in Tamaulipas could contain as many as five hundred additional corpses. When the government scooped up former soldier and Zetas member Édgar "El Wache" Huerta Montiel, he confirmed the theory that Los Zetas had been trying to exterminate what they believed were rivals sent north, and said that he thought the number of bodies buried in Tamaulipas was "more than six hundred." As was almost inevitable, in the face of such an outrage the political score settling began. Minister of the Interior Francisco Blake Mora blamed "fragile local institutions" and "the involvement of local security agents in crime" for the high body count.

In an April 2011 cable to US secretary of state Hillary Clinton, the US consulate in Matamoros concluded that the state government in Tamaulipas "avoided publicly drawing attention to the level of violence" there. Extraordinarily, as another cable noted, "none of Tamaulipas bus companies has filed an official complaint about [Zetas] attacks on buses or passengers, despite the fact that the kidnapping of bus passengers had been a widespread and [now] widely publicized phenomenon."

Shortly after the pits were found, the navy arrested Martín Omar Estrada Luna, alias *El Kilo,* who had been in command of the Los

Zetas cell in San Fernando. Like many Zetas, Estrada had deep links with the United States, having been born in Mexico but having grown up largely in central Washington State in the apple-growing farm town of Tieton, twenty miles from Yakima. A petty criminal, Estrada, whose stepfather was a US citizen, was deported from the United States twice before finally being expelled in January 2009 and dumped in Tijuana. Presciently, during one of his court appearances for immigration violations, felonies, and misdemeanors, an assistant US attorney wrote that Estrada "has not learned how to live in society without preying on others."

Once in Mexico, Estrada eventually headed east to Tamaulipas, where he had family, and rose rapidly through Los Zetas' ranks as their forces were battered by the killings and arrests of their members. Soon he was running an operation out of Ciudad Victoria's La Peregrina slum. During his time with Los Zetas, Estrada had also been—rather incautiously—keeping a photographic record of his hard-partying days, which police later recovered and which included photos of the gangster holding voluminous amounts of marijuana and a picture of a pistol with a gold cartridge and an engraving of Santa Muerte on it. One article in the Mexican press after his arrest described him as "narcissistic, cold, calculating . . . highly psychotic and violent."

By mid April, seventeen suspected Zetas and sixteen municipal police had been arrested for involvement in the killings. Kilo's girlfriend, a member of the Zetas' *Las Panteras* hit squad named Saraí Fabiola Díaz Arroyo but known as *La Muñeca* (Doll), was turned in by her own mother when the woman heard her daughter had been linked to the case. Another Zetas sicario—also an enthusiastic Santa Muerte devotee and former bricklayer from Nuevo Laredo named Enrique Aurelio Elizondo Flores, aka *El Arabe* (the Arab) and *El Cervo* (The Raven)—would be arrested some months later. By June, the number of those arrested would climb to seventy-three. Between Los Zetas' mass killing of immigrants in August 2010 and the slaying uncovered in April 2011, in the space of less than eight months a tiny corner of Tamaulipas had witnessed two massacres that had claimed 265 lives.

At the end of April 2011, Marco Antonio Gómez Rodríguez, a lawyer who was believed to formalize property deeds that would be handed over to Los Zetas as a form of ransom for those they had kidnapped, was arrested by federal police in the Quintana Roo city of Benito Juárez. Ten more suspected Zetas were killed at the same time by marines during an assault in Veracruz. In Miguel Alemán, a furious battle erupted between the Gulf Cartel and Los Zetas early on the morning of April 21. Soldiers were deployed to rein in the fighting, resulting in the death of one gunmen and one soldier. Eleven people were arrested and some twenty assault rifles seized. During the fighting, narcos threw grenades through the city streets with abandon and burned down three car dealerships and several other businesses. In formerly sedate Mexico City, a woman's torso, legs, and fingers were found scattered along a three-block radius of the tony, tree-lined San Miguel Chapultepec district. No one seemed to know who she was, or if they knew, they weren't telling. The same day, police in Acapulco found the bodies of four women and a fourteen-year-old girl, and a severed head was discovered in the beach town of Zihuatanejo near the city's bus terminal. A few days later, five decapitated bodies were found near the capital.

Before the month was out, the military rescued fifty-two more hostages—including twelve Guatemalans, five Salvadorans, thirty-four Hondurans, and one Nicaraguan—held by kidnappers in Reynosa. A group of Central American migrants freed by security forces in Tamaulipas later fingered agents from the government's *Instituto Nacional de Migración* (INM) as having pulled them off a bus and handed them over to the Gulf Cartel, a more or less routine occurrence in a body that had become thoroughly penetrated by organized crime. At least half a dozen INM employees were subsequently arrested. In Ciudad Juárez, meanwhile, police raided a home in an upscale section of the city and found three antiaircraft guns, several dozen grenades, a grenade launcher, several AK-47s, and other armaments hidden behind the mirrors of a home gym.

It was the chaos brought to the drug war by groups like Los Zetas that led to the appointment of military men like ex-general Carlos Bibiano Villa to head civilian law enforcement agencies. Bibiano was a descendent of Pancho Villa and bore a striking resemblance to his more-famous relative, with his bushy mustache and intense gaze. He had been appointed to head the police in the city of Torreón in Coahuila in September 2010, and in a drastic action designed to underline his seriousness, upon taking office fired the entire twelve-hundred-man police force of the city. By April 2011, he had been appointed the police chief of Chetumal, the capital of the state of Quintana Roo, the state of which the tourist hub of Cancún is a part and where Los Zetas were particularly strong. He was welcomed by a dismembered body and a warning saying "you're next" dumped in the tourist mecca. He summed up his philosophy by telling *La Jornada* that "when I catch a Zeta . . . I kill him. Why interrogate him?" and later "I don't want advisers, I want people on the street. . . . What I want is 'go out and bust some heads,'" declaring 60 percent of his police force "useless . . . fat bellies, diabetes, flat feet."

The state of affairs in Tamaulipas, meanwhile, appeared to be getting even worse. The month the second batch of graves was discovered in San Fernando, I chatted with a young student from Matamoros on the Texas side of the border. Brownsville was bustling, seemingly safe and busy, with the shoppers on East Elizabeth Street going about their business as usual, and people sitting and chatting as they enjoyed a bowl of menudo—the savory Mexican soup made out of beef stomach and chili pepper—in the unpretentious restaurants near the bridge. But across the river, a war was going on. The student's family went back several generations in Matamoros, and even in her own young life she had seen the dramatic change in the city.

"A child can't be in the streets now like when I was young," she told me. "Nowhere is safe. There are gun battles in different neighborhoods, but they never appear in the paper or on the radio."

She was only nineteen.

The following day, I sat in the living room of a local businessman in Reynosa after having driven through streets where buildings would appear at regular intervals pockmarked with bullets or torched and abandoned. Another journalist and I sat in the man's front room—the curtains drawn—on a busy main street as sirens blared outside and the now ubiquitous masked military patrols rumbled past.

"The situation is very delicate right now," the man said, with admirable understatement. "There is a real state of confusion here. The majority of people prefer to have the military patrolling the streets, but there are a lot of families in Tamaulipas calling for their loved ones who have been disappeared for three months, four months. Many people have abandoned ranches in the countryside. What we would like is peace."

CHAPTER TWELVE

Casino Royale

In early May 2011, the poet Javier Sicilia, still in mourning for his murdered son, led thousands of protesters on a march from Cuernavaca, where his son had met his end, to Mexico City in what he proclaimed was a *Movimiento por la Paz con Justicia y Dignidad* (March for Peace with Justice and Dignity), ending with a rally in the Zócalo. Among those who had joined the movement was the Sonora street vendor, Nepomuceno Moreno Nuñez, whose own son had disappeared the previous summer, Pedro Leiva Domínguez, a land reform activist from an indigenous Nahua community in Michoacán that had been besieged by drug traffickers, and Esther Hernández-Palacios, the poet and essayist whose daughter had been murdered in Xalapa in June 2010.

At the Zócalo, Sicilia spoke to a raucous throng, demanding the resignation of Genaro García Luna and saying that "we still believe that it is possible for the country to be reborn and rise from ruin and show the agents of death that the sons and daughters of this country are standing up." He then went on to ask "where were the political parties, the mayors, the governors, the federal authorities, the army, the navy, the church, the lawmakers, the businessmen—where were we all—when the highways of Tamaulipas turned into death traps for defenseless men and women?" It was a cri de coeur from the anguished breast of this battered nation, but the question of precisely how—beyond a handful of gestures—to stop Mexico's seemingly endless dance of bloodshed seemed one that even the poet himself could not answer. In contrast, during a *Cinco de Mayo* ceremony marking the anniversary of Mexico's victory over the French army in 1862, Calderón compared the battle against the cartels to the fight against foreign invaders in years past.

When I went to visit Sicilia later in Cuernavaca, the town's colonial quarter was still radiant, albeit noisy and choked with exhaust, but there was a notable edge in the air of a place so besieged by the drug gangs. Meeting me in a coffee shop with a gurgling fountain owned by an expatriate American from Oregon, Sicilia was much warmer than I had expected from what could be a sometimes prickly public demeanor, and had quite a good sense of humor despite the trauma that he had undergone.

"We are living through a national humanitarian emergency here in Mexico," Sicilia said, smoking Delicado cigarettes as we sat near the window in a back room, the sounds of the street filtering in among the pleasurable aroma of roasting coffee. "A state that cannot guarantee security or justice to its citizens is a state that doesn't exist. Calderón launched a war against drugs, yes, but what I feel is worse is to deny the victims, to say that the killing is all between them [drug traffickers] is to deny the state of crime in this country."

Underlining his point, at the beginning of May, dozens of workers at a factory of the US toy company Mattel were heading to their job outside of Monterrey when Los Zetas attacked a nearby army convoy, sparking a gun battle that killed one worker and wounded five.

On May 8, Mexican marines stormed an island located on Falcon Lake, the border lake where the American boater David Hartley and his wife were attacked the previous September, and killed twelve suspected Zetas while losing one of their own. Nearly two dozen guns, including several assault rifles, were seized. Attackers believed to be Los Zetas assailed an army convoy outside of Monterrey with automatic weapons fire and grenades, wounding five soldiers and leaving one attacker dead. The government announced it was sending hundreds of additional soldiers to the Comarca Lagunera region between Coahuila and Durango, to Monterrey's west.

Though it went all but unnoticed amid the horrors taking place in Tamaulipas, by mid-May 2011 at least 218 bodies had been found in mass graves throughout Durango State, where the Sinaloa Cartel, Los Zetas, and the remnants of the Beltrán-Leyva Cartel had been fighting one another for several years. As security forces combed through more narcofosas—the number of dead would eventually reach 236—police discovered the naked headless bodies of eight men outside of Durango's state capital, including the corpse of the deputy director of the city prison, who had been kidnapped days earlier.

In what would become an ever more frequent phenomenon, the Purépecha people—the local indigenous inhabitants of the Michoacán town of Cherán and a group the Aztecs had never managed to conquer— began setting up roadblocks manned by masked men wielding rifles and machetes in an attempt to ward off narco-backed illegal logging of the area. Many believed the loggers, who were often accompanied by armed men, were affiliated with La Familia. The Purépecha plainly said that their conflict was also with the local police, who were in league with the drug traffickers. It was a testimony to what Mexico had become, a place where civilians had to mask themselves to enforce the law and officialdom in league with criminals could freely show their faces.

In and around Los Cocos in the Petén region of Guatemala, twenty-nine people were slaughtered in mid May, almost all decapitated. The killings occurred almost simultaneously with the murder in El Petén of Haroldo León, the brother of the Izabal drug trafficker Juancho León whom the Zetas had killed in Zacapa in March 2008. A message, scrawled in blood on the wall of a building on the farm where the bodies were found, said the killers were looking for the farm's owner, Otto René Salguero Morales.

Salguero Morales, as it happened, was the brother of one César Augusto Fajardo Rodríguez, who had served in the Guatemalan congress from 2004 until 2007 as a representative from Izabal of the UNE party of Guatemalan president Álvaro Colom (Fajardo Rodríguez eventually left UNE to join the opposition Partido Patriota). Immediately after the killings, as he had done in Alta Verapaz the year before, Colom declared a state of siege in the Petén. Shortly thereafter Colom proclaimed his belief that Los Zetas were responsible for the killings. A former member of the Kabiles, Hugo Álvaro Gómez Vázquez, was arrested shortly thereafter, with government officials charging he was the leader of a Zetas' cell in El Petén. Gómez claimed that, although he had been in the military, he was "a farmer" and had "never been involved in any gang."

Guatemalan authorities later said that Fajardo Rodríguez had stolen a two-thousand-kilo load of cocaine from Los Zetas and was attempting to extort money from the criminal group for its return. Several narcomantas, signed by Los Zetas, later appeared in several parts of the country making the same claim, with one reading that "this war is not with the civilian population or the government, much less the press. The war is against those who work with the Gulf Cartel." The Guatemalan government would later say that another planned massacre—this one in the village of La Democracia—had been detected and prevented.

At a meeting with Honduran president Porfirio Lobo and Salvadoran president Mauricio Funes in the colonial city of Antigua, Colom called for a "democratic security strategy" in Central America. However, a day after he had been kidnapped by armed men, the dismembered body of Allan Stowlinsky Vidaurre, the prosecutor charged with investigating the Petén killings, was found in plastic bags scattered around the center of Cobán in Alta Verapaz. Fifteen people, including four Mexicans, one of whom—Salvador Arguelles Briones from the Veracruz capital of Xalapa—had a cell phone containing a video of the killing, would later be arrested in Cobán in connection with the murder. Guatemalan officials would later say that they had discovered plans for Los Zetas to kill seven employees of the attorney general's office. By the middle of the next month, thirty-five alleged Zetas would be arrested after 130 raids around the country.

North of Guatemala, in one of Los Zetas' strongholds, violence continued as well. In the city of Cárdenas in Tabasco, just south of Veracruz, an attack on an auto body shop on the evening of May 17 killed nine people, days after the body of a woman had been found in the city with a sign warning residents to stay indoors after midnight. In the Monterrey suburb of Guadalupe, gunmen killed three police officers.

Elsewhere in the north, the Gulf Cartel's plaza boss for Miguel Alemán, Gilberto Barragán Balderas, alias El Tocayo, who had been wanted on a US indictment since 2008, was seized by federal police while celebrating his own birthday at a ranch near Reynosa. The day before, soldiers in Cuernavaca had arrested Víctor Manuel "El Gordo Varilla" Valdez Arteaga, the number two of the Beltrán-Leyva spin-off Cártel del Pacífico Sur, and then snatched up Juan Bosco, the head of the town's metropolitan police, who had allegedly been on Valdez's payroll. "He used to alert us to army and federal police crackdowns," Valdez said of Bosco later.

In late May, sixteen police officers near Mexico City were also charged with providing protection to the Beltrán-Leyva–descended La Mano con Ojos cartel.

On the outskirts of Matamoros on May 18, a seventeen-vehicle army convoy encountered a contingent of Gulf Cartel gunmen in an exchange that left three gunmen dead and three in custody, and resulted in the seizure of eighty-three assault rifles and shotguns, five grenade launchers, several grenades, over eighteen thousand rounds of ammunition, and nearly twenty pistols. Many of the items seized were marked "CDG."

Later that month, the Pacific Coast state of Nayarit became the scene of a raging war between the Sinaloa Cartel and elements of the Beltrán-Leyva holdovers and Los Zetas, with one battle, featuring narcos dressed in fake military uniforms, claiming at least twenty-nine lives on a rural roadway, leaving the highway littered with bullet-riddled corpses and thousands of spent shell casings. At the same time, fighting among factions of La Familia and the Knights Templar forced at least seven hundred people to flee their homes in Michoacán, with a number of families forced to sleep on the grounds of a water park in the town of Buenavista Tomatlan.

In Sinaloa itself, questions were being raised about the federal government's logic in maintaining only a few hundred federal police in the heartland of Mexican drug trafficking when they had flooded other states around the country with federal troops. The governor of Sinaloa since the beginning of the year had been Mario López Valdez, the former PRI senator who had switched over to the PAN before running for governor. The prickly Sinaloa PAN congressman Manuel Clouthier, the son of the PAN leader who died in a mysterious 1989 car accident, said plainly that there was "a pact" between the federal government and the Sinaloa Cartel and that Sinaloa "has been a safe state for organized crime to live there and work there and develop with total tranquility." Many wondered aloud whether or not the Calderón government was pursuing a strategy similar to that of the Colombian government in the early 1990s, which collaborated with elements of the Cali Cartel in order to track down and finally eliminate the rather more violent Pablo Escobar.

The war in Mexico continued to spread beyond the country's borders. By May 2011, Guatemalan authorities had recorded over five hundred violent incidents with Los Zetas in the country since the group's first incursion some four years earlier. At least eighty suspected Zetas members were in prison there. El Salvador's minister of defense, David Munguía Payés, speaking to that nation's Canal 33 television station, said that Mexico's cartels had established "a rear guard" for themselves throughout Central America. The statement came a day after a junior officer in El Salvador's army, who had deserted the force several months earlier, was arrested trying to sell assault rifles and uniforms to civilians who he believed were acting as purchasers for Los Zetas. Munguía's comments were echoed the following month by El Salvador's president Mauricio Funes during a meeting in Mexico City with Calderón, during which Funes called the flow of guns through Central America "shocking."

As his former hirelings continued to wreak havoc, the Gulf Cartel's former supreme leader, Osiel Cárdenas, was transferred from a federal penitentiary in Florida to the United States Penitentiary, Administrative Maximum Facility in Florence, Colorado. Flo Max, as it was known, was where the United States housed what it viewed to be its most dangerous inmates in federal custody in isolated conditions virtually devoid of human contact. Among his fellow prisoners would be several leaders of the Aryan Brotherhood prison gang, the "Unabomber" Ted Kaczynski, the Al-Qaeda terrorist Zacarias Moussaoui, and, Cárdenas's own predecessor, former Gulf Cartel leader Juan García Ábrego.

In late May 2011, federal police arrested thirty-six suspected members of La Familia and ten suspected Zetas along with "over 70 rifles, 20,000 weapon cartridges, three grenades and 14 handguns." It was believed the arrested La Familia members were from a faction belonging to Jesús "El Chango" Méndez. Carrying on with La Familia's bizarre, schismatic Christian imagery, Méndez was said to be guarded by a group of gunmen called *Los Doce Apóstoles* (the Twelve Apostles).

A few days later, police said they had nabbed fifteen more suspected Zetas and ten lookouts in Hidalgo. In early June, Víctor Manuel Pérez, aka *El Siete Latas* (The Seven Lids), a Zetas boss in Quintana Roo, was also scooped up. A raid on a Zetas-affiliated metalworking shop in the Tamaulipas town of Camargo yielded two armored cargo trucks, while marines in Coahuila seized eighty automatic rifles, twenty handguns, three grenade launchers, and more than fifty thousand bullets.

In early June 2011, a *narcomensaje* (narco message) written on a blanket put up in the Chihuahua city of Hidalgo del Parral announced an alleged merger between Los Zetas and the enforcers of the Juárez Cartel, stating:

Congratulations to the 42nd Military Zone for fighting Chapo's people. In less than 15 days Parral will be ours.
Sincerely, La Línea and Los Zetas.

In early June 2011, the home of Jorge Hank Rhon, the flamboyant businessman who made his fortune with offtrack betting parlors and had served as Tijuana's PRI mayor from 2004 until 2007, was raided by federal troops who found forty rifles and forty-eight handguns, and promptly detained him. Despite his popularity with some sectors of society, many had never forgotten the allegations that Rhon was in some way involved with the 1988 slaying of journalist Héctor Félix Miranda, who had frequently criticized Rhon in print for his supposed links to the drug trade. Prosecutors said that at least two of the guns seized had links to homicides. Rhon was released a few days later when a federal judge dismissed the weapons charges, but he was immediately re-detained for possible involvement in the murder of twenty-four-year-old Angélica María Muñoz, the former girlfriend of his son, Sergio.

That same month, a group calling itself the Global Commission on Drug Policy released a twenty-four-page document of analysis and recommendations regarding the approach to narcotics worldwide, building on the February 2009 report of the Latin American Commission on Drugs and Democracy. The former presidents Ernesto Zedillo, César Gaviria, and Fernando Henrique Cardoso were now joined by the likes of former United Nations secretary general Kofi Annan, former chairman of the United States Federal Reserve Paul Volcker, and the British entrepreneur and founder of the Virgin Group Richard Branson. The report began with the stark words "The global war on drugs has failed, with devastating consequences for individuals and societies around the world," before going on to call on nations to

> *end the criminalization, marginalization and stigmatization of people who use drugs but who do no harm to others. . . . Encourage experimentation by governments with models of legal regulation of drugs to undermine the power of organized crime and safeguard the health and security of their citizens . . . [and] replace drug policies and strategies driven by ideology and political convenience with fiscally responsible policies and strategies grounded in science, health, security and human rights—and adopt appropriate criteria for their evaluation.*

Few seemed to be listening in Washington yet again, but the Global Commission's report, like that of the Latin American Commission on Drugs and Democracy, was a sign that the once seemingly unyielding facade of strict drug prohibition was beginning to crack, an impression that would only be reinforced in the coming months.

It would be too late for so many in Mexico, however.

On June 7, gunmen attacked a drug rehabilitation center in Torreón, killing eleven people. Hours later, twenty-one bodies, some showing signs of torture and their faces covered with tape, were found strewn outside of Morelia along with a note denouncing "those who continue to rob houses, kidnappers and rapists," the kind of language frequently employed by La Familia.

When Javier Sicilia's peace convoy arrived in Ciudad Juárez to the welcome of mariachi players and several hundred supporters a few days later, Sicilia told the AFP that he was seeking "justice for the victims and a change in the national security model, so it will not only be based on violence."

The same day a report by three US Democratic senators—Dianne Feinstein of California, Charles Schumer of New York, and Sheldon

Whitehouse of Rhode Island—cited Government Accountability Office figures that found that between fiscal years 2004 and 2008 approximately 70 percent of the firearms tracked in Mexico through eTrace (which at the time only the Mexican attorney general's office had access to) came from the United States, with 39 percent coming from Texas, 20 percent from California, and 10 percent from Arizona. The report recommended that access to eTrace be expanded to Mexico's federal police and that Congress renew the 1994–2004 assault weapons ban.

Speaking in San Jose, California, after the report's release, Calderón minced no words, referring directly to the lapse of the assault weapons ban and saying "I accuse the US weapons industry of [responsibility for] the deaths of thousands of people that are occurring in Mexico. . . . You can clearly see how the violence began to grow in 2005, and of course it has gone on an upward spiral in the last six years."

Hours later, a group of gunmen killed five members of a single family, including two children aged three and four, in the Chihuahua municipality of Guadalupe y Calvo.

In the space of a single week near Monterrey in mid-June 2011, a flailing, screaming teenager with a gunshot wound was pulled back to safety after being hung over a city bridge next to a corpse and above another one that had fallen to the roadway below, while a few days later two dead men hanging by their hands were found in Monterrey and in the nearby town of Guadalupe. In the space of twenty-four hours between June 15 and 16, at least thirty-three people would be killed in Monterrey, including five presumed cartel members killed by the army and ten narcos killed in a shootout with one another. Two bodyguards of Nuevo León's PRI governor, Rodrigo Medina, were also among those slain, found dismembered in Guadalupe along with a message that accused the bodyguards of taking money from Los Zetas and went on to say "To Governor Rodrigo Medina, here are two of your bodyguards. . . . Let's see where the hell you can hide." Medina said that "threats" would not keep him from doing his job.

On June 17, eleven people would die when gunmen attacked a military checkpoint on the Xalapa-Veracruz highway. A little over a week later, police found human remains in eleven separate pits and what appeared to be a torture center in the municipality of Juárez, Nuevo León, on the eastern fringes of Monterrey's metro area. As the bodies were being found, nearly twenty people would die in violence in Guerrero and Jalisco, including a fourteen-year-old Guatemalan boy.

A report that Los Zetas leader Heriberto Lazcano was killed in a gun battle on the streets of Matamoros proved false. The government had better luck when La Familia's erstwhile leader José "El Chango" Méndez was captured by federal police in Aguascalientes, with Alejandro Poiré saying the arrest marked the effective end of La Familia as a criminal organization. The government later said that Méndez had been trying to hammer out an alliance with Los Zetas before his arrest. Police had recently found nine bodies, including three dumped in front of the state public security agency in the port city of Lázaro Cárdenas in Michoacán. The day before El Chango's arrest, Miguel Ángel López Velasco, a columnist under the pen name *Milo Vela* for the Veracruz daily *Notiver* and also the editor of the newspaper's police section, was slain along with his wife, Agustina Solano de López, and their twenty-one-year-old son, Misael López Solana, who worked as a photographer for the paper, after gunmen stormed his home early that morning.

At a meeting in the Guatemalan city of Antigua on June 22, US secretary of state Hillary Clinton announced that the Obama administration would be spending nearly $300 million to fight the expansion of organized crime in Central America. It sounded like a great deal of money until one realized that since 2010 Los Zetas had reportedly earned $350 million annually by importing cocaine into the United States alone, but had to spend practically all of that money trying to fight off the Gulf Cartel. During the last week of June 2011, a Catholic priest from Oaxaca, Alejandro Solalinde, raised the alarm about what he said was the kidnapping of at least eighty Central American migrants by armed men who stormed a train heading through the state toward Veracruz. The state government would later say that they had no evidence that anyone had been kidnapped at all. Given the fact that hundreds—if not thousands—of migrants were seized from trains passing north through Mexico every year, often with the complicity of law enforcement and immigration officials, the denials rang suspiciously hollow.

As June 2011 drew to a close, Calderón told an interviewer from Milenio Television that there was "a misunderstanding" regarding his government's war with the cartels, and that he believed that a majority of Mexicans supported his armed strategy though "perhaps silently." As July began, a marine patrol killed fifteen alleged Zetas in the Zacatecas town of San José de Lourdes and detained another seventeen. The next day, more than forty gunmen with automatic weapons and grenades in a convoy of ten vehicles attacked a federal police station in the city of La Piedad in Michoacán, sparking a gun battle in which three assailants died. In a crime that shocked the Catholic community on both sides of the border, Father Marco Antonio Duran Romero, a popular local priest and television host, was shot and killed as he drove through the Colonia Obrera district of Matamoros when he was caught amid a raging gun battle between narco gunmen and the Mexican military. It was believed that the gunmen were from Los Zetas attempting to enter Matamoros.

At the beginning of July, another of the original Zetas, Jesús Enrique "El Mamito" Rejón Aguilar or Z-7, the alleged boss of the cartel cell that killed ICE agent Jaime Zapata earlier in the year, was arrested near Mexico City "without firing a shot." In a video released by the Policía Federal, Rejón, looking sweaty and terrified, answers questions from an unseen interrogator, giving a detailed account of the Zetas war against the Gulf Cartel, the Sinaloa Cartel, La Familia, and the Knights Templar and at one point says "all the guns come from the United States." After expressing regret that he hasn't seen his mother "in seventeen years," he concludes by saying "it's hard, it's cruel, but oh well . . ." Rejón was eventually extradited to the United States where he would plead guilty to conspiracy to import marijuana and cocaine.

A living reminder to Mexico of a time when those with guns fought for more than filthy criminal lucre, on July 3, Isabel Ayala Nava, the widow of the Guerrero rebel leader Lucio Cabañas Barrientos, fell victim to the country's criminal insurgency. She was slain in front of a church in the town of Xaltianguis along with her sister. She had been calling for justice on behalf of their murdered brother. The same week, assault weapon–wielding assailants attacked the Sabino Gordo bar in Monterrey, a known drug spot, killing at least twenty people in an attack believed to be linked to the Zetas–Gulf Cartel war. It was the largest mass killing that anyone could remember ever taking place in the city. Earlier in the day, eleven bodies were found dead of gunshot wounds piled on top of one another outside of Mexico City where the Zetas were fighting the Knights Templar. In Torreón, where the Zetas were fighting the Sinaloa Cartel, ten bodies were found mutilated in an SUV. The government announced that it was sending another eighteen hundred federal police to Michoacán.

It was around this same time that a group of Zetas held a huge fiesta near the municipality of Ixcán in the Guatemalan department of El Quiché. With such Zetas as Comandante W and David "El Chombo" Solórzano Ortiz in attendance, the party was joined by Horst Walter Overdick, known as El Tigre, the Cobán-based narco who had helped the Zetas kill Juancho León three years previously. Video of the event shows all in attendance laughing and joking, watching horse races and singing songs, and the fact that they were able to do so in full view of local villagers showed just how powerful the Zetas tonic of fear had become in Guatemala. As a Guatemalan friend of mine had told me succinctly, "the Mexican drug lords see Guatemala as their rear guard where they can come and hide."

On July 15, twelve state police officers en route to Los Mochis and a bystander were slain at a fake roadblock set up by narcos outside of the Sinaloa city of Guasave. The SEDENA launched *Operación Lince Norte* (Operation Northern Lynx) that month, designed to target Los Zetas and the Gulf Cartel in Coahuila, Nuevo León, Tamaulipas, and San Luis Potosí. The operation would last nearly a month, involving over four thousand soldiers, and result in the arrests of over two hundred people. Over thirty suspected narcos would be killed, including Jorge Luis de la Peña Brizuela, aka *El Pompín,* Los Zetas' plaza boss in the city of Nuevo Laredo.

In the Jalisco town of Ayotlán, six suspected Zetas were killed when soldiers investigating a report of armed men at the Los Arcos hotel were fired upon. The same day, two human heads were found on an Acapulco bridge, jauntily wrapped in colored plastic, while at the Guadalajara airport a Panama-bound man was arrested trying to smuggle $290,000 in

US currency through customs. A few hours later, nine suspected narco gunmen died in a shootout with police and soldiers in Guerrero. Earlier, Ernesto Cornejo, the PAN politician who had survived the June 2009 attack on his car that killed two other people, had been slain in the Sonora town of Villa Juárez by a group of gunmen who shot him many times.

At the end of the month, José Antonio Acosta Hernández, aka *El Diego*, the main boss of the Juárez Cartel's enforcers in La Línea, was arrested in the city of Chihuahua in the state of the same name. Acosta Hernández would eventually admit that he had directed or participated in more than fifteen hundred murders since 2008, including the January 2010 killing of sixteen people in the Villas de Salvárcar barrio. He would plead guilty to racketeering, narcotics trafficking, and money laundering charges, as well as seven counts of murder, including the March 2010 triple homicide of three people connected to the US consulate in Juárez. Extradited to the United States, he would later be sentenced to life in prison.

In late July 2011, a report looking into Operation Fast and Furious by two Republican members of the US Congress, chairman of the United States House of Representatives Committee on Oversight and Government Reform Representative Darrell E. Issa and ranking member of the United States Senate Committee on the Judiciary Senator Charles E. Grassley, was released. Despite the report's often rantingly partisan tone (a hallmark of Issa, animated by an almost pathological dislike of President Barack Obama), it nevertheless brought some interesting information to the public eye for the first time, including the links of the gun-walking program to the weapons seizures in Naco and Mexicali nearly two years before. Ironically, by early August 2011, the United States had trained nearly forty-five hundred new federal police agents in Mexico.

The same week as the Fast and Furious report's release, shepherds in the Nuevo León hinterlands stumbled upon a pair of decomposing bodies and police investigating eventually found another thirteen. In Ciudad Juárez, a prison riot left seventeen dead. Video footage showed that the riot took place during an illegal party conducted with the collusion of prison officials, who were caught on film chatting with hooded, armed inmates before the violence erupted. By July's end, Mexico's *Instituto Nacional de Estadística y Geografía* had released figures showing the number of homicides in the country rose by almost a quarter in 2010 when compared with 2009, from 19,803 in 2009 to 24,374 homicides during 2010.

Valdemar "El Adal" Quintanilla Soriano was believed to be the number two in the hierarchy of financial directors for Los Zetas and a close associate of Heriberto Lazcano and Miguel Treviño at the time of his mid August capture in Saltillo by the army. Upon his arrest, the government said that Quintanilla had been traveling "constantly" between Monterrey, Saltillo, and Monclova in recent weeks. Federal police in Acapulco, meanwhile, seized Moisés "El Coreano" Montero Álvarez, one of the leaders of the Cártel Independiente de Acapulco, and three accomplices. Oswaldo "El Compayito" García Montoya, the leader of the La Mano con Ojos mini-cartel based in Toluca near the capital, was arrested by police on the outskirts of Mexico City.

In the one step forward, one step back nature of the war against the cartels, though, the entire police force of the northern Chihuahua city of Ascensión quit following a series of attacks that had killed the police chief and at least five other officers since May. The force itself was a new one, having been replaced from what was charged was the old narco-controlled police force less than a year before. In Michoacán, the bodies of four state police officers and a civilian from neighboring Colima State were found.

Near Cuernavaca on August 10, Ignacio Flores, a former footballer for the Mexico City club Cruz Azul who had played on the country's 1978 World Cup team, was killed when the car he was traveling in was attacked by gunmen. Death also found the journalist Humberto Millán Salazar, who hosted the program *Sin Ambages* (Plain Language) on *Radio Fórmula* in Culiacán and served as the creator and editor of the online news website *A Discusión*. Millán was kidnapped by armed men on August 24 on his way to the station's studios, and his body found in a field the next day, dead of a bullet wound. In between the two killings, eleven people were slain in Acapulco, and four Mexican navy personnel were kidnapped in Veracruz. In Monterrey, gunmen hung a man from a busy overpass in sight of passing motorists and shot him to death as he tried to claw his way toward escape in front of them.

It was a typical sweltering late Thursday afternoon—the beginning of rush hour—in Monterrey on August 25, and the Casino Royale was filled with patrons attempting to forget their country's troubles by availing themselves of the various games of chance at the gaudy pleasure palace. As they did so, at least eight gunmen arrived in four separate cars. Descending in front of the casino and carrying large bottles containing gasoline, several marched in the casino's main entrance, blazing away with their weapons, as others guarded the getaway cars. Dozens of people ran screaming into the street as the men soaked the carpet, the slot machines, the tables, and the walls with gasoline and then ignited it. The casino was immediately transformed into an inferno, sending thick black smoke billowing into the sky above crackling, infernal orange flames. The attack lasted mere minutes, but when it was over fifty-three people—casino patrons, employees, civilians—were dead.

Many bodies were found inside the casino's bathrooms, where customers had fled in terror from the initial assault. Police took backhoes from a nearby construction site in an attempt to batter down the casino's walls and rescue those trapped inside. It was a shocking act of terrorism that represented the nadir for the city that many thought once symbolized Mexico's bright future.

Following the attack, Felipe Calderón declared three days of mourning in the country and said that Mexico was "not confronting common criminals" but rather was "facing true terrorists who have gone beyond all limits." Calderón went on to lash out at the United States, declaring that if the Americans "are resigned to consuming drugs, then they need to find alternatives . . . and establish clear points of access different from the border with Mexico, but this situation can't keep going on like this." He announced that a $2.4 million reward would be offered for information leading to the capture of the culprits.

Unsurprisingly, the trail for the bloodshed led back to Los Zetas, with the attorney general's office eventually naming four known

Zetas—Francisco "El Quemado" Medina Mejía (a close associate of Miguel Treviño), Baltasar "El Mataperros" Saucedo Estrada, Roberto Carlos "El Toruño" López Castro, and José Alberto Loera Rodríguez, a former professional wrestler whose nom de combat, *El Voltaje* (Voltage), had followed him into the narco life—as being among those behind the attack. Nuevo León officials said that the casino's owners had refused to pay the 130,000 pesos a week demanded by the cartel as protection money. Police would eventually arrest dozens of people, including a number of teenagers, for participation in the crime.

The fallout would spread beyond the narco world and the immediate victims of the attack to also engulf Monterrey's PAN mayor, the Oaxaca-born Fernando Larrazábal Bretón, who had been in office since 2009. Considered a rising star in the party, Larrazábal's ascent was undermined by the arrest of his brother, Jonás, himself a casino magnate, shortly after the attack on charges that he attempted to blackmail the owners of a rival casino. (His accusers subsequently dropped the charges without explanation.) Videos of Jonás visiting casinos and receiving wads of cash were played over and over on television.

Bearing signs of torture, the bodies of two female journalists, Marcela Yarce Viveros and Rocío González, were found in a park near the San Nicolás Tolentino cemetery in Mexico City a week after the casino attack. At the time of her death, Yarce Viveros had been working as the public relations manager for the investigative magazine *Contralínea*, which she had cofounded, though she had not worked as a reporter there for several years, while González was a freelancer who had contributed to *Contralínea* and worked in the past for Televisa, Mexico's main television broadcaster. A Mexico City prosecutor later claimed that robbery was the motive for the killings.

The bullet-riddled body of Samuel "El Metro 3" Flores Borrego, the Gulf Cartel soldier whose murder of Víctor Peña Mendoza had been the spark that set off the Gulf-Zetas war a year and a half earlier, was found in a car on the Reynosa-Monterrey highway on September 2 along with the corpse of Eloy Lerma García, a policeman from the Tamaulipas town of Gustavo Díaz Ordaz. Both men had been stripped to their underwear and tortured before being killed. Juan Reyes "El R1" Mejía González and his Rojos faction of the Gulf Cartel had appeared to have triumphed over their rivals in Los Metros, but it was only a temporary victory.

Following the killing of El Metro 3, the cartel fractured even further, with one faction led by Mario "El Pelón" Ramirez and Héctor "El Metro 4" Delgado Santiago aligning with Rafael "El Junior" Cárdenas in Matamoros, and El Coss forming another based in Reynosa and Tampico. In Hidalgo in early September 2011, police arrested thirty-one suspected Zetas, including sixteen police officers. That same month the navy dismantled a Zetas communications system that had been set up in Veracruz.

The PRI congressmen Moisés Villanueva de la Luz was kidnapped in the Guerrero municipality of Tlapa de Comonfort on September 4 and his body, along with that of his driver, found near the city of Huamuxtitlan two weeks later. Independence Day festivities for 2011 had to be canceled in the Michoacán town of Queréndaro when at least forty armed men appeared and demanded that the crowd disperse before the traditional *grito*, or cry, could be uttered. Between September 14 and 15, at least fifteen people were slain in the Monterrey metropolitan area, including three family members of a policeman who helped identify the Zetas who took part in the casino raid, recalling the deaths of the family of Melquisedet Angulo Córdova, the navy officer killed in the Arturo Beltrán Leyva raid two years before.

Chapter Thirteen

Veracruz

All throughout that terrible summer of 2011, Los Zetas had battered the Gulf Cartel from left to right, while at the same time terrorizing officials and ordinary citizens alike. They appeared to have mastered the art of brazen public terror to such a degree that it seemed as if they were insusceptible to pressure, official or otherwise.

Then, one Tuesday afternoon in late September, in the Veracruz suburb of Boca del Rio, a convoy of vehicles carrying dozens of masked gunmen began blocking traffic and hauling out dozens of bound, tortured, and semi-nude bodies—including those of twelve women—that they dragged from two trucks and dumped in piles in front of terrified drivers. When they were done, thirty-five corpses—many of them daubed with a "Z"—littered the street and banners from the *Cártel de Jalisco Nueva Generación* (CJNG), the Sinaloa Cartel spin-off that operated in the Pacific Coast state of the same name, were unfurled, threatening Los Zetas.

"This will happen to all the Zetas . . . that stay in Veracruz," read one. "The plaza has a new owner."

Several days later, a video appeared online in which five masked men, dressed in black and sitting at a table, read a statement where they apologized "if our acts offended society [or] the people of Mexico" and went on to say that their "intention was to make the people of Veracruz understand that this scourge of society [Los Zetas] is not invincible." Referring to the group speaking as *Los Matazetas* (The Zeta Killers), one of the men went on to state that "our goal is Los Zetas. We respect the armed forces, we understand that they cannot act outside the law, [but] we condemn the bad public servants who support this scourge of society. . . . We are warriors, faceless, but proudly Mexican."

The Ministry of the Interior responded to the statement by saying that "While it is true that the criminal organization known as the Zetas should be defeated, that must occur by legal means and never by methods outside the law." In response, the government ordered additional federal troops and police to Veracruz.

The reaction of local officialdom was telling, with Veracruz attorney general Reynaldo Escobar Pérez telling *Radio Fórmula* that most of the victims had criminal records and links with organized crime, while the state's PRI governor Javier Duarte de Ochoa wrote on Twitter that "the killing of 35 people is deplorable, but it's even more deplorable the same victims chose to extort, kidnap and kill." Escobar would subsequently resign for mysterious "personal reasons." The massacre happened one day before criminal prosecutors from around the country were to begin a meeting in Veracruz. Subsequently, however, some sources claimed to have found evidence that none of those slain had ties to organized crime and only six had criminal records of minor offenses. Simply put, though more selective in their violence, Los Zetas' enemies could be every bit as ruthless as they could be.

Los Zetas' ability to terrorize civilians, however, remained undiminished. On September 13, on Nuevo Laredo's Bulevar Aeropuerto the tortured, blood-soaked bodies of a young man and young woman were hung from a bridge. Next to the bodies was draped a bright yellow banner referring to three websites popular for their forums where residents discussed the violence afflicting the city.

This will happen to all the Internet snitches (Frontera al Rojo Vivo, Blog Del Narco, or Denuncia Ciudadano). Be warned, we've got our eye on you. Attention, Z.

On September 24, the decapitated body of Maria Elizabeth Macías Castro, who managed the newsroom at Nuevo Laredo's *Primera Hora* newspaper, was found dumped at the thirty-foot-tall monument to Christopher Columbus along a busy thoroughfare that had been inaugurated only the previous year. In addition to her newsroom work, Macías had been a frequent poster on matters related to the drug war on the website Nuevo Laredo en Vivo under the handle *La NenaDLaredo* (The girl from Laredo). Headphones and a keyboard were placed next to her head. A note left with the body read:

Nuevo Laredo en Vivo and social networking sites, I'm The Laredo Girl, and I'm here because of my reports, and yours. For those who don't want to believe, this happened to me because of my actions, for believing in the army and the navy. Thank you for your attention, respectfully, Laredo Girl ... ZZZZ.

The killings brought to the forefront, with shocking clarity, the role that the Internet in northern Mexico—and especially in Tamaulipas where traditional investigative reporting had almost completely ceased to exist—had come to play in the chronicling of Mexico's drug war and the flow of information among people there. One of the websites mentioned, in particular, Blog del Narco, had become a repository for all sorts of user-submitted content relating to gun battles and other public safety issues.

As Veracruz and Monterrey convulsed, at the end of September a twenty-two-year-old Mexican woman—a former beauty queen with US citizenship—gave birth to twin girls at the Antelope Valley Hospital in Lancaster, California. Emma Coronel, whom Chapo Guzmán had married on her eighteenth birthday and who was the daughter of Sinaloa Cartel figure Ines Coronel Barrera, returned directly to Mexico after their birth.

Between late August and late September, a series of banners in Acapulco and in communities near Monterrey had proclaimed threats to attack schools there, leading to several school closures. Police subsequently found five severed heads in a sack with a note threatening drug traffickers near a primary school in Acapulco, but it was never proved if the incident was connected with the threats. Soon after, the Knights Templar hung several banners from overpasses in Zihuatanejo, announcing among other things, that

Citizens of this municipality, you are notified that from this day forward the Knights Templar are present. . . . Our work here is against any and all kidnappers and extortionists. Establishing the people's order and tranquility. Thank you.

As if to prove that the Knights Templar's claim was not mere rhetoric, the bodies of seven men, all dead of gunshot wounds, tied together by the legs and with a message identifying them as "criminals," were soon found along the Zihuatanejo-Ixtapa highway, an area historically controlled by the Beltrán-Leyva Cartel and its remnants. In other regions of the country, twelve people died in several attacks in Acapulco and a pair of heads were found on a busy street near a military barracks in Mexico City along with a note reportedly referring to the Mano con Ojos gang.

Long gone were their days as mere enforcers, and by October 2011 many analysts were saying that, along with the Sinaloa Cartel, Los Zetas was Mexico's dominant drug-trafficking organization, with a presence almost everywhere within its borders.

And as if to underscore how the power of the criminals outweighed that of ordinary Mexican citizens, at the beginning of October, Pedro Leiva Domínguez, the Nahua activist from Michoacán who had taken part in Movimiento por la Paz con Justicia y Dignidad of the poet Javier Sicilia, was slain near Xayakalan in that state.

In mid-October 2011 in Saltillo, the Mexican army arrested Benito "Pichollo" Aguilar-Ozuna, a journeyman criminal who the government rather unbelievably claimed was the third-highest-ranking member of Los Zetas and who was believed to oversee the group's operations in Tamaulipas, Coahuila, and Nuevo León. Aguilar-Ozuna was subsequently extradited to the United States and sentenced to nearly twenty years for conspiracy to traffic cocaine by a federal judge. In early October, the body of the Gulf Cartel's former financial mastermind, César "El Gama" Dávila García, was found by Mexican navy personnel in a home in the Reynosa district of Colinas del Sol. Meanwhile, José Alberto "El Voltaje" Loera Rodríguez, the former professional wrestler who had participated in Los Zetas' attack on the Casino Royale, was arrested by police on the Mexico City–Nuevo Laredo highway.

The government launched *Operación Coordinada Veracruz Seguro* (Operation Safe Veracruz), characterized as a move to combat crime and insecurity in the state, on October 4, 2011. Two days later, as if in response, the Mata Zetas (CJNG) dumped thirty-two more corpses around Veracruz city, the majority of them in the Jardines de Mocambo district. Though Mexican navy spokesman José Luis Vergara stressed at a news conference that the CJNG was "just another organized crime gang . . . fighting for control of illicit income and criminal activities," some wondered of the possible collusion of security forces.

As he met a group of victims of violent crime in the capital, Calderón charged that "Veracruz was left in the hands of Los Zetas, I don't know if it was involuntary, probably, I hope so. If we hadn't taken on organized crime, they would have taken over the country." His comments were seen by many as a not-so-subtle reference to the former PRI governor of Veracruz, Fidel Herrera Beltrán, whose links with the Gulf Cartel and Los Zetas were long rumored but never proven and who had been replaced by Javier Duarte de Ochoa, another PRI politician. The PAN candidate whom Duarte had defeated—Miguel Ángel Yunes—had charged that Herrera "handed over the police and police command to these criminal groups, and everyone in Veracruz knows it." By the end of the year, Calderón had fired all eight hundred police officers in the Veracruz-Boca del Rio area and turned over law enforcement duties to the marines and the navy while new officers were trained.

It was a late summer night in Xalapa, the evening drizzly with cold rain, when an acquaintance, a local media worker, and I sat together and dined on local Veracruz dishes at a simple restaurant made out of a converted stable for horses. Outside on the cobblestone streets of the city's old central core, students getting ready to party on Friday night walked up and down, unmindful of the chill. In one corner, a string band—guitars and violin—played the *jarocho* music native to the Huesteca region.

"Him, right there," my companion said, covering his mouth with his hand and indicating almost imperceptibly a rather shambolic, somewhat druggy-looking man in his mid-thirties who was making the rounds to talk with people at various tables. "He's a spy for the cartel."

I looked at the man. Totally unthreatening, ragged, eminently forgettable like a thousand hustlers in tourist and university towns around the world, unlikely to be noticed as he hovered around gathering information. A perfect listening device really.

Later, as we walked through a beautiful old square that still held the cisterns to what had been a colonial laundry, my contact mused on the difficulty of working in such a milieu.

"Here journalists become journalists for the money, not for the love of journalism. Here, journalism exists in the shadow of the government."

The next day, on one of those clear mountain mornings during which Latin American hill towns gradually bestir themselves from sleep to greet the day, I sat chatting with another friend at an organic coffee shop. We sat in a back room of the otherwise empty establishment, and when I asked how things had changed since Javier Duarte de Ochoa had taken over the governor's office from Fidel Herrera Beltrán, the reply startled me.

"He is their slave," my contact, someone with intimate knowledge of the state government, said, employing in our Spanish conversation a vernacular Mexican Nahuatl word—*achichiucle*—that I had never heard before.

"The disappearances of young girls have been going on for a long time," the friend told me, addressing a question I had brought up seeing the many handmade flyers that were festooned to various surfaces around the city, most asking for information about females but some asking for help locating missing children, both male and female, as well. "The majority are from lower class or very poor backgrounds, the most defenseless girls whose families have no information or resources."

My friend estimated that since 2010, at least 250 girls had been kidnapped in and around Xalapa.

"Many people don't report it because of fear," my friend told me. "It's probably many more."

By mid October, Veracruz police chief Arturo Bermúdez Zurita was saying that nearly one thousand state police officers of the force of six thousand had been fired after failing lie detector tests as well as other tests. A few days after his announcement, security forces arrested Carlos "El Bam Bam" Pitalua, the alleged leader of Los Zetas in Veracruz, as well as five other suspected cartel members. The same day, Adrián "El Hongo" Ramírez Soria, leader of the Beltrán-Leyva spin-off Cártel del Centro, was taken into custody. In Piedras Negras, the army freed sixty-one men being held captive by Los Zetas. A week after that, eight bodies were found dumped in a swamp near Veracruz.

In the north, the dominance of the cartels continued to seem total. Four police officers were arrested in early October 2011 in the Monterrey suburb of Juárez when it was revealed that they were allowing Los Zetas to hold kidnap victims in the local jail.

On the morning of October 15, a riot broke out at a prison in Matamoros that lasted for more than two hours, leaving twenty inmates dead. During five days of raids in Tamaulipas around this time, eleven alleged cartel members were killed, thirty-six others arrested, and more than four tons of marijuana seized. In the fighting between Los Rojos and Los Metros, the Metros forces of El Coss had nearly won, and the Cárdenas clan was largely confined to the Matamoros area. The Rojos suffered another serious blow when one of its leaders, Rafael "El Junior" Cárdenas, was arrested in Port Isabel, Texas, on October 20, 2011. Mario "El Gordo" Cárdenas then became the de facto leader of what remained of the Cárdenas family's faction.

Not that things in the west of Mexico were going much better. In a grisly redefinition of "date night," police in Acapulco stopped a car carrying a twenty-one-year-old man and a nineteen-year-old woman near a shopping mall and found within it an ice chest stuffed with a human head and other body parts. The couple had apparently been working as sicarios for La Barredora, which had been warring against the Cártel Independiente de Acapulco. One of La Barredora's leading figures, Christian Arturo Hernández Tarin, had been arrested only days earlier.

At the beginning of October, a video was posted on the Internet claiming to be from the Veracruz branch of the hacker collective Anonymous and in which a male figure in a Guy Fawkes mask with a computer-generated, Spanish-accented voice strode toward the camera and stated:

A member has been kidnapped. . . . We demand his release. We want the army and the navy to know we are fed up with the criminal group Zetas, who have concentrated on kidnapping, stealing and blackmailing in different ways. . . . We are fed up with taxi drivers and police Zetas. . . . [They] are chickens and they have made themselves the most loyal servants of these assholes. For the time being we will not post photos or the names of the taxi drivers, journalists or the newspapers nor the police officers. But if needed, we will publish them including their addresses to see if the government will arrest them. . . . We all knew who they are and where they are. You made a huge mistake by taking one of us.

The group appeared to be making good on its promise when, several weeks later, a website promoting Gustavo Rosario Torres, the PRI politician and former Tabasco state prosecutor whom the anticrime group CCSPJP had accused of working for drug traffickers three years earlier, was defaced with grinning Halloween pumpkins and the words "Gustavo Rosario is a Zeta." Rosario had been working for some time as an adviser for Tabasco's PRI governor, Andrés Granier Melo.

Across the country, on the Pacific Coast, things were no better, and during the course of a few days in late October and early November 2011, ten people were slain in a battle between the army and suspected narcos in Michoacán, while in Sinaloa six more perished in a shootout and gunmen killed five members of the same family riding in a pickup truck near the town of El Rosario, the victims including a seven-year-old boy. Ricardo Guzmán Romero, the PAN mayor of the Michoacán town of La Piedad, was slain in a drive-by shooting as he handed out campaign material just days before state elections for governor, mayors, and loyal deputies. The town's police chief had also been previously killed.

Ovidio Limón Sánchez, believed to be one of Chapo Guzmán's chief deputies, was captured on November 9 by the Mexican army in Culiacán. Limón was on the DEA's Ten Most Wanted list of Mexico's drug traffickers and had been the subject of a provisional extradition request since 2007.

The same day as Limón's arrest, the decapitated body of a man was dumped in front of the same statue of Christopher Columbus in Nuevo Laredo where the journalist Maria Elizabeth Macías Castro's body had been deposited more than a month before. Next to the corpse written on a blanket with black ink was a narcomensaje that read "Hi I'm 'Rascatripas' and this happened to me because I didn't understand I shouldn't post things on social networks." The staff of at least one website—Nuevo Laredo en Vivo—however subsequently said that "Rascatripas" was not affiliated with them and expressed doubts that he had been killed for his online activity.

In the run-up to Guatemala's November 2011 presidential elections—which in the final round pitted the retired general Otto Pérez Molina against a congressman from El Petén of equally dubious reputation named Manuel Baldizón—the newspapers of Mexico's southern neighbor were full of glum lamentation about the spillover of Mexico's violence to a country already wrestling with plenty of its own demons. *Los Zetas: The next president's headache* read *El Periódico* one day. *An election in the time of the Zetas* it read a few days later. The latter article all but accused both men of at least partially financing their campaign with money from drug trafficking and said that Los Zetas had become "the dominant criminal group in Guatemala." When Pérez Molina won the election, he announced that his government would have "a strategic plan to combat drug trafficking . . . in coordination with authorities in the United States and Mexico."

The Calderón government's war on the cartels suffered another bitter blow when on the morning of November 11, a helicopter carrying Minister of the Interior Francisco Blake Mora crashed in dense fog just south of Mexico City, killing Blake as well as seven others, most of them ministry officials (unlike the United States and many other countries, in Mexico no protocol prevented multiple officials from traveling on the same plane). Blake Mora's final Twitter message, on the anniversary of the crash that killed his predecessor almost exactly three years earlier, read:

> *Hoy recordamos a Juan Camilo Mouriño a tres años de su partida, un ser humano que trabajo en la construcción de un México mejor.*

> *(Today we remember Juan Camilo Mouriño three years after his passing, a human being who worked to construct a better Mexico.)*

The death presented eerie echoes of not only the crash that killed Mouriño, but also of the one that killed Guatemala's minister of the interior Vinicio

Gómez in June 2008, a fact that was not lost on those in Mexico. Manuel Clouthier, the PAN congressman from Sinaloa who had denounced the government's alleged alliance with his state's eponymous cartel and who had lost his own father in mysterious circumstances, told reporters that "there are many coincidences because now we have two interior ministers (lost) in one presidential term. . . . Who knows if we'll ever really know what happened." After his death, Blake Mora was temporarily replaced in his post by Calderón government official Juan Marcos Gutiérrez.

In the midterm November elections, the PRI mayor of Morelia, Fausto Vallejo, defeated Calderón's sister, Luisa María Calderón, for the governorship of Michoacán, a state where the left-wing PRD had succeeded in ousting the PRI from the statehouse nearly a decade before. In the Michoacán results, some saw a precursor of the nationwide general election scheduled for the following summer.

Juan Marcos Gutiérrez, who had served as interim interior minister during the period of the elections before being replaced by Calderón's spokesman on security issues Alejandro Poiré Romero, said that a drug cartel had conducted "boldfaced interference" in the electoral process, an obvious reference to the Knights Templar.

In another example of the long and often fatal overlapping of drug trafficking and Mexico's music industry into a *narcocultura,* norteño singer Diego Rivas and two others were slain in Sinaloa on November 13 when gunmen attacked him as he was partying with his friend outside of his home in Culiacán. At the same time, Sinaloa's governor, the former PRI member-turned-independent Mario López Valdez, admitted that he had sent his three children abroad because police had overheard cartel members discussing plans to kidnap his family over the radio.

If the politicians felt fear at exposing themselves, the narcos did not, and the boss of Los Zetas in San Luis Potosí, Alfredo "Comandante Alemán" Narváez, a close confidante of both Miguel Treviño and Iván "El Talibán" Velázquez Caballero, was taken into custody following an army raid in Fresnillo during a horse race he had organized on November 15. A few days later, the army said the Zetas' radio communications network—valued at $350,000—had been seized in Coahuila. In late

November 2011, Tony Tormenta's twenty-three-year-old son Ezequiel Cárdenas Rivera, who had followed in his father's footsteps in the Gulf Cartel, was arrested by the Mexican navy in Matamoros. Three police officers from the border town of Ciudad Acuña in Coahuila were found dead on November 21 after being kidnapped earlier that day. Around the same time, Guatemalan police arrested two Zetas on a football field in the eastern state of Zacapa, and a group of suspected Zetas engaged in a gun battle with police in Suchitepéquez during which three gunmen were wounded and arrested.

Two days before the Guadalajara International Book Fair was set to begin and a day after seventeen bodies were found in burned pickup trucks in Sinaloa, twenty-six bodies, their hands bound and gags stuffed in their mouths, were dumped in a pickup truck and two vans at the city's modernist *Arcos del Milenio*. All the victims were men, and all had died of asphyxia. Authorities later concluded that the massacre was the work of Los Zetas and the Milenio Cartel and was directed against the CJNG, though there was considerable confusion as to whether or not all those killed had any relation to illegal activity. A narcomanta left at the same time as the killings accused Jalisco governor Emilio González Márquez and Sinaloa governor Mario López Valdez of working for the Sinaloa Cartel. The attorney general of Jalisco subsequently arrested three accused Milenio Cartel members for the crime, who allegedly confessed that all the victims had been hanged because "that's how you kill" CJNG members.

In another blow to Mexico's civil society desperately searching for a way out of the violence, Nepomuceno Moreno Nuñez, the Sonora vendor who had been searching for his missing son for over a year and who had become one of the most visible public faces of the poet Javier Sicilia's Movimiento por la Paz con Justicia y Dignidad, was shot to death as he crossed a street in Hermosillo on November 28. Sicilia reacted furiously to the slaying, lashing out at Sonora's PAN governor, Guillermo Padrés Elías, and saying "I blame the governor for the death of this man," and noting that Moreno had been pleading for protection that Padrés never provided. Commenting on the murder, Sonora's state attorney general instead said that Moreno had previously been imprisoned for firearms offenses, implying that this might have played a role in his death. The statement provoked a response from the Interior Ministry that urged public officials not to act in a way that "criminalized victims of violence by emphasizing their criminal records." A Sinaloa cartel lieutenant, Jesús Alfredo Salazar Ramírez, aka *El Muñeco,* was subsequently arrested for Moreno's murder.

Another killing, nearly lost in the river of blood at the time, would have unexpectedly far-reaching consequences. The body of Alfonso Peña, a Tamaulipas businessman, was dumped in a busy part of Nuevo Laredo on November 29 with a message accusing his brother, Antonio Peña, of stealing money from Los Zetas. Antonio Peña, as it happened, was a chief aide to former Tamaulipas governor Tomás Yarrington, and the banner claimed that the stolen money had been meant as a payoff to the governor himself. By the end of the year, the Tamaulipas town of Ciudad Mier, which fighting between the Gulf Cartel and Los Zetas had largely depopulated by late 2010, boasted a battalion of 653 soldiers but an estimated third of its population still had not returned.

In mid December, in Valle Hermoso, just west of Matamoros, an army patrol engaged in a gun battle that left eleven suspect narcos dead and led to the recovery of seventy-three rifles. That same day, Raúl Lucio "El Lucky" Hernández Lechuga (Z-16), the Zetas boss in charge of operations in Veracruz as well as Puebla and Oaxaca, was arrested in the Veracruz city of Córdoba with an arsenal that included 133 rifles, five grenade launchers, nearly thirty grenades, and over thirty handguns. El Lucky's arrest appeared to have little effect on the violence in Veracruz, though, and little more than a week later, in apparent response to his capture, sixteen were killed in a single day around the state, almost all apparently civilians targeted while traveling by public buses or loading vegetables at their places of work.

By December 2011, former Coahuila governor Humberto Moreira would be forced from his position as the PRI's national president amid allegations that during his tenure as governor the state had incurred $3 billion worth of debts connected to loans that were allegedly used for public works projects but which, in fact, largely vanished into the ether.

Deciding that the allegations did not meet the burden of proof, Mexico's attorney general would later opt not to pursue the most serious charges. Moreira was eventually replaced in his role at the head of the PRI by former Quintana Roo governor Pedro Joaquín Coldwell.

By the end of 2011, in the words of one news report, Calderón had "managed to build a large, vetted federal police force" in place of the old corrupt AFI. But the government's one-dimensional approach to the problem of drug trafficking—solely relying on the anvil hammer of the federal police and the army—had turned even once-tranquil corners of the country into war zones as cartels fought the government and one another in an ever more lethal environment. The violence in Mexico seemed to be spreading to sectors of society beyond the drug trade. When protesting university students hijacked buses in Guerrero and used them to block the highway between Acapulco and Mexico City, police opened fire, killing two. In nearby Guadalajara, police later found three dead bodies inside a student group's headquarters. On Christmas Day 2011, soldiers found thirteen bodies stuffed into a truck in Tamaulipas just across the border from Veracruz and a banner referring to the Gulf-Zetas war. A few days later, police in Nuevo León found seven sets of human remains in graves that state officials said were linked to Los Zetas.

At the end of 2011, only seven months before his death at the age of eighty-three, the author Carlos Fuentes, still irascible and hale despite his advancing age, was interviewed by the Canadian Broadcasting Corporation for his take on the drug war. Fuentes had clearly done some thinking about the subject, and his most recent book, *La voluntad y la fortuna* (translated into English as *Destiny and Desire*) had been narrated by a decapitated head washed up on Mexico's Pacific Coast. He didn't pull any punches.

"We've had revolutionary wars," Fuentes told the interviewer. "These were political figures fighting for political causes. The drug lords in Mexico don't bother about this. They say 'We are here to fuck you, we're here to be nasty. We're here to be criminals. Do not make a mistake.' So this is a challenge to the society, a challenge to the government, and a challenge to each Mexican citizen."

Chapter Fourteen

Messages

Messages, interpretations of signs, images. The currency of Mexico's drug war was bodies, to be sure, but it would be incorrect to assume that, however butchered, the savageness had no meaning. Dead bodies were the way the cartels talked to one another, and so were the narcomantas that appeared with dull regularity along the roadways of the cities and elsewhere. If they had been politicians, the narcos would have called it staying on message. But as the coming months would prove, the importance of visual and rhetorical chicanery could be used as adeptly in the political arena as in the drug war's killing fields.

According to Mexico's SSP, between 2006 and 2012, more than sixty-five thousand people had lost their lives as a result of drug cartel violence and security operations. More than twenty-six thousand people had gone missing. The toll of souls removed from the life of Mexico thus made the drug war there arguably the most deadly conflict in the modern era in Latin America save for Guatemala's 1960–1996 war, which left over two hundred thousand dead.

As 2012 began, thirty-one inmates at the Centro de Ejecución de Sanciones in the city of Altamira in southern Tamaulipas died when prisoners from the Gulf Cartel and Zetas factions brawled with homemade knives, clubs, and stones. A few days later, police in Piedras Negras discovered five human heads deposited at various points around the town. A few days after that, two more heads, along with a note signed by the Mano con Ojos gang, were found at the entrance to the Santa Fe shopping mall in Mexico City. The situation in Tijuana, at least, had calmed considerably, with the city's murder rate having fallen from 820 in 2010 to 478 in 2011, with the Sinaloa Cartel, which had been expanding its influence throughout Baja California, and what was left of the Arellano Félix organization overseeing "about a dozen semi-independent trafficking groups in the city."

On January 11 Luis Jesús "Pepito Sarabia" Sarabia Ramón, who had been implicated in the February 2011 slaying of ICE agent Jaime Zapata in San Luis Potosí and who had been an important element of Los Zetas' war against the Gulf Cartel in Nuevo León and Tamaulipas, was arrested by the military on the border of Nuevo León and Coahuila. Mid-January 2012 was marked by multi-casualty gun battles, with police killing seven people in Cuernavaca, and thirteen people dying in Guerrero, including eight slain at a funeral that was attacked by masked men in the city of Atoyac de Álvarez.

In a significant and, for many, perhaps disturbing development, Luis Alberto "El Arqui" Cabrera Sarabia, one of Chapo Guzmán's chief deputies, was killed in Durango near the city of Canatlán on January 21 in the first known instance of a person believed to have been tracked and killed with the assistance of the US drones that had been operating on Mexican soil since at least March 2011.

After hearing him drunkenly ranting "to the four winds" (as one account put it) in the city of Salinas Victoria in Nuevo León about his involvement in the San Fernando massacres and other crimes, some brave soul stole away and dropped a dime on Los Zetas sicario Enrique Aurelio "The Raven" Elizondo Flores. Security forces rushed in and arrested him in late January. He subsequently admitted to having killed at least seventy-five people. When arrested, Elizondo's cell phone contained a video of him dancing to reggae music as he sliced off the fingers of Zetas captives. In other violence likely linked to the cartel, in the early morning hours of January 26, eight men and a woman were slain within minutes of one another near the center of Monterrey.

In advance of a scheduled visit to Mexico by Pope Benedict XVI, the bishop of León, José Guadalupe Martín Rábago, issued a plea "to those who do evil" that "we are living times of grace and peace, and . . . they should help by allowing all these people to come to an event that is totally respectable, and not to take advantage to do anything that could lead to an experience of mourning and death." However, shortly thereafter, gunmen in Ixtapaluca near Mexico City gunned down five municipal police officers.

The government began sending the first of four thousand additional soldiers to Michoacán in early February 2012. At the same time, a month ahead of Pope Benedict's scheduled visit, eleven banners, several signed by the Knights Templar, appeared in Guanajuato, announcing the cartel's intention to participate in the truce as proposed by the bishop. On a more menacing note, the banners advised the CJNG not to *Think about moving in and much less causing violence, precisely at this time when His Holiness Benedict XVI is coming.*

After security forces in Veracruz arrested Zetas operative Juan Francisco "El Pollo H" Alvarado Martagón in early February, he led them to a pair of ranches in rural Veracruz where they found fifteen sets of human remains.

A week later, troops in Jalisco seized fifteen tons of pure methamphetamine, a shocking amount at the time as the total meth seizures worldwide had been thirty-one metric tons for the entire year of 2009. Meth was becoming ever more lucrative for the Mexican cartels, who were expert at product placement and creating a customer base. Between 2007 and 2011, the purity of meth from Mexico increased from 39 percent to 88 percent, while the price fell from $290 per pure gram to under $90.

In mid-February 2012, Guatemala's new president, the former general Otto Pérez Molina, surprised many when, following a meeting with El Salvador's president Mauricio Funes, he said that he would be bringing up the possibility of drug decriminalization at a meeting of Central American leaders the following month. Writing in England's *Guardian* newspaper, Pérez Molina would posit that:

> *Knowing that drugs are bad for human beings is not a compelling reason for advocating their prohibition. . . . The prohibition paradigm that inspires mainstream global drug policy today is based on a false*

premise: that the global drug markets can be eradicated. . . . Drug consumption, production and trafficking should be subject to global regulations, which means that consumption and production should be legalised but within certain limits and conditions. And legalisation therefore does not mean liberalisation without controls.

Pérez Molina would score several notable successes against Los Zetas early in his term, with the arrests of Álvaro "El Sapo" Gómez Sánchez (an associate of the Guatemalan drug trafficker Horst Walter Overdick), the capture of a Zetas operative in the Petén named Gustavo Adolfo Colindres Arreaga, and finally with the arrest of Overdick himself, seized at an apartment complex off the Ruta Interamericana in San Lucas Sacatepéquez. Overdick was subsequently extradited to the United States to face drug-trafficking charges.

The terror sown by Los Zetas hardly disappeared, however, and amid the government's actions, narcomantas in the Petén believed to be from Los Zetas declared "we will begin to kill, we will throw grenades into discos and malls," as well as at the scenes of two murders, where the messages directly threatened Pérez Molina's former rival for the presidency, Manuel Baldizón, with one stating that Los Zetas would "kill even the dog in your home and everyone."

But things were often murkier than they appeared, as was demonstrated when Pérez Molina's personal pilot, Haward Gilbert Suhr, the founder of the Aeroservicios Centroamericanos, S.A. group (which Pérez Molina was a shareholder in) was arrested along with a dozen others in San Pedro Sula, Honduras, and charged with trafficking drug shipments on behalf of the Sinaloa Cartel.

The worst prison violence in Mexico's history broke out in the Centro de Readaptación Social prison in the Nuevo León city of Apodaca on February 19, when Los Zetas inmates slaughtered forty-four inmates linked to the Gulf Cartel and then managed to free over thirty of their own. It was later revealed that the prison administration, the state government, and the federal government had been warned months in advance that the Apodaca facility was "a time bomb" waiting to go off, and there was substantial evidence that prison officials and guards had been bribed. Among those who escaped was Los Zetas' former leader in Monterrey, Óscar Manuel "La Araña" Bernal Soriano. An inmate who was later recaptured referred to the jail as a "sewer" of criminality where prison officials would regularly meet with imprisoned Zetas leaders to collect bribes in exchange for free movement around the facility and facilitate the movement of drugs and alcohol in and out of the prison.

In early March 2012, residents of the Morelos region were horrified when the dismembered bodies of four young people, all students ages fourteen to twenty-one, were found in plastic bags outside of the Barba Azul (Bluebeard) nightclub in Cuernavaca. The victims had been kidnapped the previous day, and a threatening note signed by the heretofore unknown "El Chuky" was left with the bodies. As policemen in Guerrero searched for the bodies that had once been attached to twelve heads dumped outside of a Teloloapan slaughterhouse, gunmen opened fire on them, killing six state and six federal officers and wounding another eleven. A note threatening La Familia had been left along with the heads. At around the same time, two men working for a Mexican company affiliated with the Houston-based Halliburton disappeared outside Piedras Negras.

By February 2012, Antonio Peña, the chief aide to former Tamaulipas governor Tomás Yarrington whose brother, businessman Alfonso Peña, had been murdered and dumped in Nuevo Laredo the previous November, was indicted and arrested by federal agents in the United States on charges of laundering millions of dollars for the Gulf Cartel and Los Zetas. In the indictment Yarrington was also mentioned as having received massive sums from the cartels, with Peña acting as the conduit. Yarrington's successor as Tamaulipas governor Eugenio Hernández Flores, who had seen fit to entrust his personal security to Gulf Cartel hitman Ismael Marino Ortega Galicia during his 2005–2011 tenure, soon fled to Spain. The attorney general's office would later seize ten properties belonging to Hernández in Quintana Roo.

By the end of March 2012, the US Congress had appropriated $1.6 billion since the Mérida Initiative was initiated during fiscal year 2008, money "to strengthen Mexican law enforcement institutions through training for Accredited State Police units in Mexico's three priority states of Chihuahua, Tamaulipas, and Nuevo León." Though funds had also been spent to protect journalists and human rights defenders, and to link more than three hundred Mexican addiction resource centers via an information technology platform, given events in each of the three states mentioned over the preceding four years, any Mexican could fairly ask if it had been money well spent.

The CJNG saw the capture of two of its chief leaders during that month, with Erick "El 85" Valencia Salazar, believed to be the overall head of the organization, captured during an army raid in the Jalisco city of Zapopan, which resulted in the cartel erecting burning barricades throughout the state for the next several days. One of Valencia's chief lieutenants, José Guadalupe Serna Padilla, alias *El Zopilote* (The Vulture), was captured days later.

In the small impoverished Sonora town of Nacozari de García about eighty miles south of the Arizona border, that March authorities uncovered what was believed to have been the first reported instance of human sacrifice connected to Santa Muerte, involving a poor family living on the fringes of the copper mining town clinging to the Sierre Madre who had sacrificed at least three people—two ten-year-old boys and a fifty-five-year-old woman—on the dirt floor of their home. Though it did not involve a foreigner either as perpetrator or victim, the killings reminded some of the cult slayings of American Mark Kilroy and others in Matamoros over two decades earlier. Except this time, rather than the work of a handful of people in a rebel cult, the killings took place as the extension of an actual belief system, even if they were, as adherents charged, aberrant to that system's values.

Nearby, in early April 2012, Francisco "El Quemado" Medina Mejía, one of the members of Los Zetas directly implicated in the August 2011 attack on the Casino Royale in Monterrey, was killed along with three others near Piedras Negras in Coahuila. Around the same time, Mario Arturo Acosta Chaparro, the army general who had been arrested and then released for allegedly protecting the Juárez Cartel in the 1990s, was gunned down in a Mexico City auto body repair shop.

For years it had seemed that Nuevo Laredo was Los Zetas' impregnable fortress. But in late March 2012, the mutilated bodies of dead Zetas began to be found dumped around the city, and narcomantas announcing the presence of the Sinaloa Cartel began to appear, among them one read:

This is how you do away with dumb fucking people, cutting them to pieces, all of those rats that rob and dedicate themselves to kidnapping and killing innocent people, I'm going to show you how I manage my cartel that is 30 years old, not like you people who were shoe-shiners and car-washers and got to where you are through betrayal. Attention El Chapo.

Los Zetas responded in kind, and on the morning of March 28, the dismembered bodies of five men were found in Culiacán, heads and limbs flung down next to torsos and a narcomanta from Los Zetas that read:

Look fucking filthy Chapo if you can't even control your own state, how are you gonna be able to control another state, fucking informant of the DEA traitor that has turned in hundreds of your own stinking people, You ain't shit Attention: Z 40.

Upping the ante, on the morning of April 17, someone parked a 1996 Voyager minivan with no license plates in front of Nuevo Laredo's City Hall. Within the vehicle, stuffed inside ten garbage bags, were the remains of ten men. The Tamaulipas attorney general's office initially told reporters the men were Zetas killed by the CJNG, but after a subsequent investigation the office changed its story, saying that it had determined the identity of ten of the fourteen men killed and that they were "innocent civilians" who had no connection to Los Zetas. After the bodies were discovered, a photo of twenty-two heavily armed gunmen—masked and in full combat gear—was circulated online, the men standing in front of a narcomanta (a similar banner had been unfurled with the corpses) that referred directly to Miguel Treviño and Héctor Beltrán Leyva (whose organizing was likely contracted for the Culiacán murders) and which read:

We have begun to clear Nuevo Laredo of Zetas because we want a free city and so you can live in peace. We are drug traffickers and we don't mess with honest working or business people. I'm going to teach these scum to work Sinaloa style—without kidnapping, without payoffs, without extortion. As for you, 40, I tell you that you don't scare me. I know you sent H to toss heads here in my turf, because you don't have the balls nor the people to do it yourself. Attention, El Chapo. Don't forget that I'm your true father.

Seven days later a car bomb exploded outside the Tamaulipas State Police building near Manuel Avila Camacho Avenue at around 8:00 a.m., a blast that was heard miles away though, remarkably, no one was killed. Police streaming to the scene were then fired upon. It was believed the bomb was the work of the Sinaloa Cartel.

As Nuevo Laredo was erupting, the press in Veracruz were being cut down like flies. On the morning of April 28, *Proceso* reporter Regina Martínez Pérez, who had written about the links between organized crime and elected officials in the state, was beaten to death in her home in the state capital of Xalapa. Though state authorities eventually fingered two low-level criminals as having killed Martínez during the course of a robbery, no one beyond the officialdom that the journalist had worked to expose bought that explanation.

On May 3, the bodies of *Veracruz News* photographer Guillermo Luna Varela, Luna's girlfriend Irasema Becerra, freelance photographer Gabriel Huge Córdova, and former cameraman Esteban Rodríguez were dragged from a canal behind a sewage plant in Veracruz city. Both Luna and Huge had previously worked for the local newspaper *Notiver,* and the three men had previously fled the state after hearing their names were on a hit list, only to return a short time later. The four had been dismembered, and their remains stuffed into plastic bags before being tossed in the canal.

Following the murder of Regina Martínez Pérez, *Proceso* wrote that the killing of journalists was "the result of a broken country, a situation of everyday violence in which extreme acts are not the exception but the daily rule."

Helping to enable those acts, in Washington, by late April 2012, ATF data was concluding that at least sixty-eight thousand guns from the United States had been seized in Mexico during the previous five years, many in the aftermath of cartel gun battles.

After the killing of the journalists in Veracruz, I found myself sitting on the veranda of a fashionable hotel in the city, just off its zócalo and in the shadow of its gleaming white cathedral, a Moorish tiled dome at its top giving the structure a markedly Islamic feel. A few blocks from the leafy square where I sat, with its cafes and artisans selling bracelets and necklaces, the city jutted out into the Gulf of Mexico in a long, meandering *malecón*, where the odor of the raw sea floated over from the old Veracruz Shipyard (its sign written in English). Monuments to Spanish and German immigrants to the city competed with tributes to Mexico's fighting men—especially its navy—gazing severely out to sea as if still ready to defend the nation in battle. This was the city that had been occupied by the Americans from April to November 1914 after the fierce Battle of Veracruz. Today, however, Veracruz was under a different kind of assault.

I chatted with my two dining companions, locals who had witnessed the city's situation firsthand, at a table set back from the street, our conversation largely drowned out by the roar of taxis and near-empty tour buses passing by. During the course of our conversation, the waiter came back to our table on pointless missions to do things like rearrange silverware and straighten napkins, leaning close the whole time and, so it seemed to me, listening.

My companions frankly admitted to the fear that had gripped Veracruz since the killings, and how there was a fear that anyone might fall into the crosshairs of the narcos.

"In this war, your enemy is not a visible enemy."

One felt that, though the narcos' influence in the state government was real, it was hardly unique.

"This is not just a phenomenon in Veracruz," it was said. "You see it in Guerrero, Michoacán, Nuevo León, wherever there is a lot of poverty and misery."

As we spoke, a convoy of masked, heavily armed navy commandos rolled by. That the armed forces were also implicated in abuses seemed rather obvious to my interlocutors, despite the city's long history with the Mexican navy.

"There is an identification with the navy here in Veracruz, a great prestige," one said.

"Peoples' uncles, cousins, and so on are marines, but there have been a lot of human rights violations."

My contact went on to tell me about a furious battle that had gone on in the Rio Medio (Central River) area of the city, a district so violent that locals had taken to punningly calling it *Rio Miedo* (Fear River).

"I asked a general 'What is the protocol for this kind of situation going forward?' And his response was 'The protocol is that there is no protocol.'"

After our conversation, I left the hotel and strolled through the zócalo again toward the sea, down the malecón, passed the memorials to Mexico's war dead and those commemorating the 1914 US invasion. It was humid, tropical, distinctly Caribbean with palm-lined side streets and low-slung residential buildings. In some ways one could see how Veracruz could have once been one of the most bracing and seductive cities in all of Mexico—before the bodies began piling up.

I thought of the lines of one of the best songs by one of my favorite singers, Warren Zevon, who had passed away a decade earlier, where he sang about Woodrow Wilson's guns and a crying maiden before concluding, "Veracruz was dying."

And so it must have seemed to the people of Veracruz.

The tit for tat killing went on in Nuevo Laredo for the next two weeks after the April 24 car bomb until, on the afternoon of May 4, nine blood-soaked bodies—five men and four women—were found hanging from a city bridge. Later that evening, near 9:00 p.m., police found a van containing fourteen decapitated bodes. The heads were found in ice chests near City Hall three hours later. A narcomanta left near the bodies found on the bridge—purportedly from Miguel Treviño—accused the dead of responsibility for the April 24 car bomb and, with reference to Gulf

Cartel deputies Miguel "El Gringo" Villarreal and Héctor "El Metro 4" Delgado Santiago, went on:

Fucking Gulf whores, this is how I am going to end every fucker you send to heat the plaza. . . . We are going to fuck up El Gringo that keeps setting off car bombs. . . . El Metro 4 who asked Comandante Lazcano for mercy when he was kicking the shit out of him; and now El R1 in Reynosa and you. But it's okay, here are your guys. The rest went away but I'll get them. Sooner or later. See you around fuckers.

As Nuevo Laredo was convulsing it appeared almost certain that the PRI, after a decade outside of the presidential palace in Los Pinos, was poised to return in the person of their candidate, former Mexico State governor Enrique Peña Nieto. Despite coming under withering attack by the PRD's Andrés Manuel López Obrador during a presidential debate that also included the PAN's candidate, former national deputy Josefina Vázquez Mota, Peña Nieto appeared resilient, with polls showing him maintaining a double-digit lead over Vázquez Mota and López Obrador trailing in third place. Peña Nieto promised "a new PRI" that "competed democratically and understood change."

But during Peña Nieto's six-year administration as Mexico State governor, the *Observatorio Ciudadano Nacional del Feminicidio* had documented more than one thousand killings of women in the state, and Judge Jose Alvarado ordered that a consortium of thirty-four state agencies reconsider its refusal to declare a "state of alert" for the state. Such a move would have required greater coordination between the agencies involved and, supporters of the move said, force authorities to act. Twenty of the thirty-four agencies had voted against such a move the previous year and, Peña Nieto supporters pointed out with glacial indifference, killings in the state of Mexico were more or less on par with those in Mexico as a whole.

At the *Universidad Iberoamericana* in Mexico City on May 11, at least, many were not convinced. As Peña Nieto, slick in a dark suit and tie, arrived, he was showered with boos by hundreds of students, some wearing masks of former president Carlos Salinas, some waving T-shirts stained with fake blood, and others carrying banners and chanting about the police riot that had victimized so many women and others at Atenco six years before. One student stood up waving a homemade sign reading *Te Odio* (I hate you) and *Ni un aplauso para este asesino* (No applause for this murderer). When the crowd questioned Peña Nieto about the Atenco attacks, his reply was that the violent police response was "a determined action that I personally undertook to restore peace and order. . . . The Mexican state has the right to use public force. But I should also mention, that our action was validated by the Supreme Court."

That response—the Supreme Court portion of which was a total lie—prompted hundreds of students to begin chanting "Get out!" and essentially chase Peña Nieto out of the auditorium through a back door and into a bathroom, calling him a "coward" and saying "Iberoa doesn't want you!" and "Atenco is not forgotten!" before Peña Nieto's security finally extricated him and he drove away.

The following day, though, a number of papers, many with links to the PRI, ran headlines about how Peña Nieto had "succeeded" despite "a boycott" against his speech. Enraged further, students who had been at the protest began posting their videos and commentary about what had happened that day online along with their student IDs. The videos were then spliced together—131 of them—into a montage that took off across the Internet with the hashtag #YoSoy132 (I Am 132), meaning support for the 131 students who had made their voices heard in opposition to the media working on behalf of the Peña Nieto campaign. A week later, thousands of students from a variety of universities marched on two Televisa stations in the capital. Several large protests would continue in the run-up to the presidential vote. The balance of power might still be in the hands of the country's political elites, but the citizens were not as voiceless as they had been in the past.

In bloody Tamaulipas, on May 7 gunmen strafed the offices of the *Hora Cero* newspaper in Reynosa with gunfire. Two days later, police in Ciudad Victoria found the dismembered bodies of three men in various plastic bags strewn about an abandoned Chevrolet pickup at the Soriana Tamatan Shopping Center. The same day in Jalisco, near the scenic Lago de Chapala that had long been popular with US retirees, the decapitated, decaying bodies of eighteen people were found in two cars along with a note from Los Zetas-Milenio alliance claiming responsibility for the crime, believed to be directed against the CJNG. Only six of the victims appeared to have any affiliation with organized crime, Jalisco officials later said.

In the early morning hours of May 13, police found forty-nine bodies—or more accurately pieces of bodies—scattered along the so-called Carretera Interoceánica (Mexican Federal Highway 40) at the municipality of Cadereyta Jiménez just outside Monterrey. A spokesman for Nuevo León state security theorized that the dead might have been killed as much as forty-eight hours earlier, perhaps in Tamaulipas, and dumped where they were found. Nuevo León's state attorney general, Adrián de la Garza, said that some of the bodies had borne Santa Muerte tattoos. A note saying that Los Zetas were responsible for the crime was also left at the scene. Though the killings bore all the hallmarks of Los Zetas, narcomantas placed around Monterrey, allegedly by the cartel, denied responsibility for the killings (while at the same time taking credit for nine bodies hung in Nuevo Laredo earlier in the month), ordering army commander Javier del Real, governor Jorge Domene, and attorney general Adrián de la Garza by name to "do your job as it should be done." Even two months later, Mexican authorities had still not managed to conclusively ID a single victim.

In Sonora, the strangled, tortured body of Marco Antonio Ávila Garcia, who reported on crime for the dailies *El Regional de Sonora* and *El Diario de Sonora* was found outside the city of Guaymas on May 18. He had been abducted from a car wash in Ciudad Obregón the previous day. A message was left with the body, but police would not reveal its contents.

In Nuevo Laredo, someone tossed Molotov cocktails into the Maranhao disco in the very early hours of May 24, setting it aflame. Then, at around 5:30 a.m., another car bomb—loud enough to be heard across the border in Texas—went off in front of Nuevo Laredo's Hotel Santa Cecilia, where elements of the state police stayed. At least ten were injured, eight of them police officers. Mexican officials anonymously told the Associated Press they believed the bomb to be the work of Los Zetas.

At the end of May 2012, narcomantas appeared in several areas of Reynosa denouncing Antonio Peña, the former aide to Tomás Yarrington whose brother had been slain in Nuevo Laredo the previous fall, as well as the former PAN mayor of Reynosa Francisco García Cabeza de Vaca and Manuel Bribiesca Sahagún, the son by a previous marriage of Vicente Fox's second wife, Marta Sahagún, sneeringly referring to the lot as *hampones* (mobsters). The former president's stepson would later plead guilty to fraud in a California courtroom for his role in a complicated natural gas scheme.

On June 12, this time in the Veracruz town of Álamo Temapache, a white Nissan pickup truck with Tamaulipas plates was found to contain fourteen dismembered bodies. A message left at the scene alluded to infighting between Zetas factions. Despite what seemed to be an endless parade of public atrocities, the Calderón government pointed out that, by its figures, the murder rate in Mexico had in fact fallen, with killing during the first quarter of 2012 down 7 percent from the same time period the previous year.

As was evidenced by the May 11 demonstration, the youth were restless, and they had a point. Had the PRI—the party among the major three that had the longest-standing links with organized crime in the country in general and with the Gulf Cartel in particular at the state level—really changed? Despite the telegenic presence of Peña Nieto, one indication of the party's current philosophy of politics may have been contained in documents that a former employee of Televisa passed to the *Guardian* newspaper in early June 2012. Detailed in these documents, which came in the form of several dozen computer files, were plans designed by the *Radar Servicios Especializados* marketing company (controlled by Televisa vice president Alejandro Quintero) that detailed descriptions of how much money the station would charge to raise Peña Nieto's profile nationwide while he was still Mexico State governor and coordinated strategies to attack Andrés Manuel López Obrador and conceal campaign advertising spending by Vicente Fox during Fox's tenure as president. There was also discussion about promoting Tomás Yarrington.

For its part, Peña Nieto's campaign said that "no contract existed of *that* kind" (emphasis added by the author) during his term as governor. The paper also later reported that a body known as "Team Handcock"—a pseudonym for Peña Nieto's political machine—had allied with Televisa itself to produce videos lauding the then-governor (at the time up for re-election) and trashing the PRI's rivals during 2009 legislative elections. Televisa, for its part, denied any wrongdoing. Strangely, there was very little discussion of the drug war during the election itself. All three candidates, it appeared, had little idea of what they could or would do differently.

In June, Calderón signed *La Ley para la Protección de Personas Defensoras de los Derechos Humanos y Periodistas*, which made crimes against journalists and human rights workers federal crimes able to be investigated and prosecuted at the federal level. The law was seen as a reaction to the situation in the Mexican body politic at the state level where many state apparatuses had been in the hands of organized crime for many years. No doubt passengers at Terminal 2 of Mexico City's international airport felt they could also use protection when a wild shootout erupted on June 25 when three federal policemen attempted to arrest several other security agents suspected of cocaine trafficking in a food court area, the gunfire leaving three agents dead and leading the city to replace all of the 348 agents assigned to airport security. Four days after being kidnapped from her home by gunmen, the body of Marisol Mora Cuevas, the PAN mayor of the Veracruz city of Tlacojalpan, was found in Oaxaca. She had been strangled. The following day, yet another car bomb rocked Nuevo Laredo, this one placed directly outside of City Hall, where the PRI mayor Benjamín Galván Gómez had his offices. At least half a dozen people were injured.

On June 27, a three-minute-long video posted to the mundonarco .com website depicted the interrogation and decapitation of three alleged Zetas by the Gulf Cartel. The website said the video was shot in Río Bravo, Mexico. Forced to their knees and surrounded by masked, machete-wielding Gulf Cartel members, five shirtless men with the letter "Z" painted on their chests are forced to recount their names and the fact that they work for "Z-40" before the men surrounding them go to work hacking off the heads of three, which are then held up to the camera as an off-camera voice—believed to be that of Mario "El Pelón" Ramírez—exclaims, "This is how all your filthy people are going to end," before praising the killers with "very good, very good."

Chapter Fifteen

The Executioner's Song

When Andrés Manuel López Obrador held his final preelection rally in Mexico City's Zócalo in the summer of 2012 before an estimated one hundred thousand people, he declared that he would "govern for rich and poor, for the people in the cities and the people in the farms," adding that "we don't want vengeance, we want justice." But, as in 2006, it was not to be.

Undermined by PRI's dirty tricks and his own mercurial personality, López Obrador and the PRD were defeated by Peña Nieto in the July vote, with Peña Nieto claiming victory after an official quick count showed him with 38 percent of the vote, seven points ahead of López Obrador. The PAN's Josefina Vázquez Mota came in third, with around 25.5 percent of the ballot, a stinging refutation of the policies of the previous six years. Beyond the PRI's payoffs, the vote had been even more tainted in Tamaulipas, where voters received anonymous calls claiming to be from the Gulf Cartel ordering them to cast their ballots for the PRI under penalty of death for failing to do so. Interestingly enough, though, such threats did not discourage voters in Matamoros, who elected the PAN candidate for mayor, Leticia Salazar, thus breaking the PRI's long domination of the city.

Though, in his victory speech, Peña Nieto proclaimed that "Mexico won," within a week, tens of thousands of students, unionists, and others were marching through the capital charging the PRI with gaining its electoral victory through vote-buying, citing, among other issues, the fact that the PRI had disbursed gift cards that could be redeemed at grocery stores to its supporters. Eventually, López Obrador would file a lawsuit against Peña Nieto charging that—though he had lost by more than three million votes—"the minority that dominates the country decided a long time ago to impose Enrique Peña Nieto as president of Mexico in order to maintain the corrupt regime that benefits them." The lawsuit would eventually be dismissed, and by the end of August, Peña Nieto was officially declared Mexico's president-elect. López Obrador would eventually quit the PRD entirely.

All of the outrage, though, could not change the fact that after more than a decade in the wilderness, the PRI fox was back in the henhouse of Mexico's federal government. As disastrous in many aspects as the PAN's headlong rush to confront the drug cartels had been, and as bellicose and self-important as López Obrador could be, it was hard to think of a more disastrous outcome for Mexico as a whole.

The political maneuvering of far away Mexico City had little effect on the situation elsewhere in the country, however. A car bomb went off outside the home of Tamaulipas public safety secretary Rafael Lomelí Martínez in Ciudad Victoria just after he arrived home, killing two policemen and injuring seven others, though Lomelí Martínez himself was unharmed. In Nuevo Laredo, the offices of the newspaper *El Mañana* were attacked with grenades and gunfire for the second time in as many months, leading the publication—in an act reminiscent of the plea of Ciudad Juárez's *El Diario* two years earlier—to announce that it would "refrain, for as long as needed, from publishing any information related to the violent disputes our city and other regions of the country are suffering."

After a shootout between suspected narcos and soldiers near a university in San Luis Potosí killed three people on August 9, police found an SUV containing fourteen bodies. They were believed to be men loyal to Iván "El Talibán" Velásquez Caballero, who was attempting to challenge Miguel Treviño for leadership of his faction of Los Zetas. The same day, two men were hung from a Monterrey bridge by their hands and then shot to death. In Fresnillo, police found eight badly decomposed bodies in an abandoned car near a water park.

Two faint bright spots were Ciudad Juárez, where, according to the army general Emilio Zárate Landero, homicides had fallen 42 percent in the first six months of the year—a drop that many locals attributed to the Sinaloa Cartel having "won" the battle for the city's drug routes—and Mexico's 2–1 victory over Brazil to claim the gold medal for football in London's Olympics.

In a clear provocation to the Cárdenas wing of the Gulf Cartel, banners marking the birthday of slain Gulf Cartel Metros leader Samuel "El Metro 3" Flores Borrego appeared around Matamoros in early August. For several days afterward, Matamoros was rocked by gun battles believed to be between Gulf Cartel factions. Over the next two weeks, gun battles in the Tamaulipas towns of Hidalgo and Padilla and a shootout in Reynosa would claim the lives of at least sixteen people, including at least one marine. At the same time Tamaulipas was exploding with Gulf Cartel infighting, more and more Mexicans deported from the United States were being shoved across its bridges, victims—the only word to use—of a US program designed to dump undocumented immigrants as far from their point of origin in the United States as possible, thus making it harder for them to return. The deportees made easy prey for the criminal gangs in the border cities.

The situation for migrants heading north along Mexico's southern border was worse yet, as the discovery of a mass grave in the Chiapas town of Tapachula, near the Guatemalan border, brought home. Contained within it were the bodies of dozens of Central American migrants believed to have been killed by Los Zetas. Mexico's CNDH human rights body would later conclude that between April and September 2010 alone, at least 11,333 immigrants, the vast majority Central American, had been kidnapped in the country.

In the political realm, Édgar Morales Pérez, the PRI mayor-elect of the San Luis Potosí city of Matehuala, and his campaign manager were ambushed in the early morning hours of August 12, 2012, in an attack attributed to Los Zetas. During the same period in Zetas-plagued Veracruz State, four died in gun battles between narcos and security forces, while seven members of a single family, including four children, were slain in another attack. On August 13, gunmen attacked a strip club in Monterrey, gunning down eight men.

Los Zetas' enemies were not resting either, however. In late August, a video appeared of Knights Templar leader Servando Gómez Martínez. Speaking seated at a desk in front of two large framed pictures of the Argentina-born Cuban Communist revolutionary Che Guevara, another one of Pancho Villa, a large sword mounted on the wall, and various other paraphernalia, Gómez began in an avuncular manner, wishing a "good afternoon" to the "citizens, of our city, our state, and our beautiful Mexico" before going on to say that the Knights Templar wanted "to let you know who we really are, what our group stands for, and what our intentions are." He then went on to outline the group's "rules" found in their booklets of conduct, which prohibited "theft, kidnapping, murder for hire, rape and all those crimes that hurt [and] cause so much harm to our society," saying that the group's "role is to help the people, preserve our state, and keep our country free of people who are causing terror." He then continued with a call for an alliance against Los Zetas:

> We also appeal to all the groups . . . to come together and make a common front to fight against Los Zetas, especially against Z-40, Miguel Ángel Treviño Morales, as this person with his boundless ambition has caused so much terror and social confusion in our country, in our Mexico. He is the primary cause of all that is happening in Mexico: Robberies, kidnappings, extortion, and anything that may lead to such actions. We recognize that sometimes our guys are wrong, but there are rules and they will have to pay for their mistakes. . . . We are inviting all groups whether they are those of the Gulf, Sinaloa, Jalisco, or wherever they exist, including many groups that exist in Guerrero . . . to make a common front to attack Z-40, attack Miguel Ángel and kill him. This is an open invitation to perform this.

Gómez then went on to ask Calderón, Genaro García Luna, the PAN, and the congress to "act responsibly . . . take responsibility and act according to the truth, not to take sides in criminal groups" before stating flatly that the Knights Templar "is no cartel, and not an organized crime group, we are a brotherhood." After paying his "respects" to the Mexican armed forces, Gómez then stood up and walked off camera.

It was a strange performance, full of omissions, misrepresentations, and outright lies about the true history of the Michoacán-based criminal organization, but one that showed how Los Zetas' savagery and excesses had provided some handy public relations material to their rivals. To drive the point home, the broken bodies of eleven men, believed to be victims of the Knights Templar, were found on August 26 along a coastal road leading north out of Acapulco. Two weeks later, also in Guerrero State, sixteen bodies were found inside a truck near the town of Coyuca de Catalán toward the border with Michoacán. Several weeks after that, seventeen more bodies were found by villagers celebrating the nation's independence on a highway near the Jalisco town of Tizapan El Alto, also near the border with Michoacán.

In a rural area near always-tense Cuernavaca, federal police officers fired on a US Embassy vehicle on August 24, wounding two active duty CIA agents in what US officials would later say they believed was an attack coordinated by the Beltrán-Leyva Cartel. The police said the shooting had been a case of mistaken identity, with the police believing the car contained kidnappers despite its diplomatic license plates. Eventually, fourteen federal officers would be charged with trying to kill the agents. In other security-related matters, according to government figures that would soon be announced, between 2007 and 2012, over forty-six thousand soldiers and sailors deserted Mexico's armed forces.

Back in Tamaulipas, in late August, Attorney General Marisela Morales confirmed that an arrest warrant had been issued for former Tamaulipas governor Tomás Yarrington for suspicion of aiding the Gulf Cartel. After being suspended from the PRI in May, however, Yarrington had slipped into the shadows, and his whereabouts were unknown. A close Yarrington associate, former Miguel Alemán mayor (and former Tamaulipas state policeman) Raúl Antonio "El Chupón" Rodríguez Barrera would shortly thereafter be gunned down in front of his home in murky circumstances. Eventually, the US government would seize a $640,000 luxury condo that Yarrington had bought on the fourteenth floor of South Padre Island's Bridgepoint Oceanfront Condominiums—allegedly with drug profits— and sell it at auction.

Those familiar with his situation told me that Yarrington could expect little help from the PRI at large, with one friend from the Rio Grande Valley who had followed the governor for years telling me "if they catch him, he's going to get hung out to dry." Eventually, Yarrington was indicted in a Texas court on a host of US federal charges, money laundering and racketeering among them.

One of the remaining Cárdenas brothers, Mario "El Gordo" Cárdenas Guillén, was arrested by the Mexican navy in the Tamaulipas town of Altamira on September 3. Any rejoicing in the rival Metros camp was short-lived, however, as El Coss himself was arrested in Tampico a little over a week later. The scowling El Coss, in a blue shirt and bulletproof vest, was dragged before the media along with ten bodyguards. His arrest left much of what remained of the organization to Mario "El Pelón" Ramírez, the former Reynosa plaza boss who had sided with El Coss during the Gulf split, and Miguel "El Gringo" Villarreal, who promptly set to warring against one another for control of cartel territory. El Pelón, in particular, was a man whose reflexive reliance on extreme violence was believed to rival even that of Los Zetas' own.

The same day Mario "El Gordo" Cárdenas Guillén was arrested, Felipe Calderón gave his final state of the nation speech to the country he had ruled over the previous six years, its streets awash with blood. He managed to be magnanimous in congratulating Enrique Peña Nieto on the latter's electoral victory before defending the decision of his government to wage war against the cartels.

"We made a momentous decision for Mexico," Calderón asserted. "To decisively face criminals, and with this decision Mexico began its long path to a life of liberty and security. With the action of the federal forces and the brave support of our communities, we have prevented criminals from taking control of Mexico."

During his tenure as Mexico's president the *Seguro Popular* programs, which provided health insurance to people unaffiliated with any other program, grew from fifteen million to fifty million. Over 12,600 miles of new roads and bridges were built. International reserves climbed and oil production, long in decline, stabilized. But who would remember any of that?

Calderón's home state of Michoacán was more overrun with drug traffickers than ever before, with the Knights Templar making so much money that it could afford to pay to have military bases, highways, and village squares around the state watched virtually around the clock. The valleys of Jalisco were crawling with gunmen from Los Zetas, the Gulf Cartel, and the Sinaloa Cartel. In Veracruz, the Zetas continued to battle the CJNG. The body of former PAN deputy and businessman Hernán Belden Elizondo was found in the hamlet of La Huasteca, within the Monterrey metro area, on September 12. Belden had been kidnapped days before and his seizure announced to the public by Mauricio Fernández Garza, the eccentric mayor of San Pedro Garza García. It was a move that was widely criticized by those who said it had put Belden's life at further risk. Fernández said he had been merely trying to help.

And the war for Nuevo Laredo was not over. On September 14 the tortured, lifeless bodies of nine men were hung from a bridge in the city. Over the next few days, at least eleven other people would die there. Unlike in previous months, it was believed that many of these deaths were the result of an internal Zetas war between Miguel Treviño and Iván "El Talibán" Velásquez. In all, by mid-month seventy-four people had been killed in the city. Banners hung around Nuevo Laredo announced an alliance between El Talibán's men and those of the Gulf Cartel and the Knights Templar against the Zetas. When a woman attempted to remove the banners, she was shot in the leg. By this point, many people believed that Treviño, not Heriberto Lazcano, had become the dominant force in his wing of Los Zetas, in large part due to his confrontational personality and willingness to go into battle with the troops, while Lazcano stayed largely in the shadows.

Never one to take a perceived slight laying down, in a series of narcomantas displayed in Zacatecas, Fresnillo, and Villanueva, Treviño attacked his rivals in profane and nearly subliterate language, stating in part:

To all Knights Templar and dumb asses that have left with the stupid fag and mediocre El Taliban, you can all suck my dick. You are a bunch of fags that run in packs because one on one you all have sucked my dick and will continue to do so. You are a bunch of thieves, extortionists, and half dead hungry fucks that don't know how to confront me. . . . You are traitors and remember he who betrays once, will betray twice, and all the times that are necessary. Till this day I have never turned in any of my partners. Whoever is doing wrong I'd rather fuck him up, so we are not traitors. I am loyal to the Letter and to Comandante Lazcano pussies. I'd rather die before being a traitor. Who was CDG are locked up. CDG is done. . . . The ones that remain in CDG are thieves, snitches, and pussies that are always doing stupid shit. And they're going to fuck each other up amongst themselves. . . . The Knights Templar are a bunch of crystal meth addicts that are always charging avocado farmers quotas and even schools. So they don't have room to say shit, much less talk about betrayals and shit like that. . . .

And so on.

The war in Tamaulipas went on, with three senior employees of the Tamaulipas State Public Safety Office found slain in their bullet-riddled car in Nuevo Laredo on September 19. The following day, three federal police officers were slain as they went to a bank in the Durango city of Gómez Palacio. Banners—purportedly from Los Zetas—appeared in Zacatecas alluding to the death of Gulf Cartel lieutenant Juan Reyes "El R1" Mejía González. Throughout early October, Reynosa was the scene of repeated gun battles between narcos and law enforcement personnel, with at least five killed in shootouts around the city. Finally, on September 26, Iván "El Talibán" Velázquez Caballero was captured by the Special Forces of the Mexican navy in San Luis Potosí, thereby eliminating one of Miguel Treviño's chief rivals. The Zetas splinter group that he helped create, however, would continue on under the name *Sangre Zeta,* and attempt to challenge Z-40's power in Coahuila and Nuevo León. El Talibán would subsequently be extradited to the United States where he would face trial for conspiracy to possess with the intent to distribute drugs and launder money.

Miguel Treviño's nephew, Alejandro Treviño Chavez, was killed in a shootout with police in Coahuila on October 2. Banners ominously reading *Family for family* appeared around the state after the younger Treviño's death. Their meaning was made clear the next day when José Eduardo Moreira, the twenty-five-year-old eldest son of former Coahuila governor and PRI president Humberto Moreira, was kidnapped and killed, his body found dumped near Ciudad Acuña, just across the Rio Grande from Texas.

Though Moreira's reputation was not good and rumors of his links to Los Zetas long-standing, it was hard not to wince seeing a heartbroken father weeping over the casket of his dead son, and to recoil at the sadism at work behind the mind of Z-40 who, enraged at the death of his cousin, was said to have ordered the hit on the younger Moreira, a hypothesis the former governor himself publicly supported. As the elder Moreira carried his slain son's casket, he told reporters, "I've had to put up with a lot of things, but I can't bear this."

Moreira would later give a series of interviews in which he accused the mining sector in Coahuila of collaborating with Los Zetas, never explaining why, during his term as governor, he apparently never made much of an effort to disrupt such links. Other observers I spoke to talked frankly about how in Coahuila, Los Zetas made use of slave labor to mine coal, which they would then sell to a registered vendor who would in turn sell it to the *Comisión Federal de Electricidad,* Mexico's state-owned electric utility.

Less than a week after the Moreira killing, the navy succeeded in capturing Los Zetas' Tamaulipas boss Salvador Alfonso Martínez Escobedo, aka La Ardilla (The Squirrel), after tracking him to Nuevo Laredo. Thought to be intimately linked to the immigrant massacre in San Fernando and the killing of the American David Hartley, Martínez cut a bizarre figure when trotted out before reporters. He was pint-sized, with a jagged amateurish haircut and incongruously grinning and flashing the "thumbs up" sign as if he had just won some sort of tournament.

La Ardilla's arrest would have been a major story in any normal context, but only hours later it was overshadowed by a far more far-reaching event. Heriberto Lazcano, who had commanded Los Zetas for a decade, was killed on October 7. According to the Mexican navy, a marine patrol stumbled upon Lazcano and a lone companion leaving a Sunday baseball game near the Coahuila town of Progreso, a community about one hundred miles south of the US border with no police force and so isolated that one resident later called it "abandoned, in all the senses of the word."

As security forces approached, the men hopped into a pickup and sped off, shooting rocket-propelled grenades as they went. Allegedly the driver was killed first and then Lazcano, still firing, was shot down around three hundred yards from the vehicle. Why the leader of Mexico's most violent cartel was alone and poorly defended was never explained, but to some it smelled of betrayal.

The body was taken to a funeral home—rather than a government morgue as was standard practice—in the nearby town of Salinas, where fingerprints were taken. A short time later, the corpse was stolen by armed masked men who arrived at the parlor early on Monday morning. Mexican officials would later say that fingerprint matches had identified that body as Lazcano's. Without explaining how, US officials also said they had confirmed Lazcano's identity before the body was stolen. The statement of US officials contradicted an earlier claim by the navy that security forces had "no idea" whom they had killed on that lonely country road in Coahuila. Photos of the corpse, which did indeed bear a strong resemblance to the Zetas chieftain, were distributed by the government and soon proliferated over the Internet. With Lazcano's apparent demise, control of Los Zetas passed on to the dreaded Miguel Treviño, Z-40.

And surrounding Lazcano's death, there was yet another mystery. In November 2004, a sixteen-year-old girl named Silvia Stephanie Sánchez Viesca Ortiz, known to her family as Fanny, was kidnapped off the streets of Torreón in Coahuila, a crime for which La Ardilla later allegedly claimed credit. After Lazcano met his fate, a picture began to circulate on the Internet, allegedly extracted from the drug lord's person after his death, that appeared to show him seated at what resembled a banquet table, unsmiling, dressed in black and appearing every inch the dead-eyed Angel of Death. At his side was a beaming young woman with dark hair, clad in an evening dress. There was some speculation, including from the vanished girl's family, that it might in fact be the long-lost Fanny. It was said that the drug lord had married the young girl, and that she had even had a child with him, a child that was born on the US side of the border but, like so much surrounding the man and the milieu, this was never confirmed. It was another secret that Lazcano would take with him as he breathed his last breath, full of Mexican navy lead, in the dust of the Coahuila countryside.

CHAPTER SIXTEEN

Day of the Dead

It was Day of the Dead in Mexico City. In the cemeteries and along the boulevards of the capital, the colors of devotion, as if in both recognition and defiance of the passage over that final border, were everywhere. I was staying with friends in the Condesa neighborhood, a beautiful district of old, European-style apartment buildings, tree-lined parks, and chic restaurants that nevertheless managed to retain its authenticity. In the panderia across the street from their building—and indeed, almost everywhere—there were the traditional *calaveras de azúcar*, sugar skulls, delicate confections on the bakery shelves that enabled one to taste a sugary sweet bite of mortality. Nearby, in the Panteón Civil de Dolores cemetery, elaborate offerings of fruit and flowers were being left at the tombs, including those of the renowned Mexican singer Agustín Lara, who had sung a beautiful ode to Veracruz years before. Across town, we wandered into the crowded Zócalo and were greeted by a mural featuring the images of *los que se fueron*—those who had departed—during the year, including Carlos Fuentes and the singer Chavela Vargas, all lined up, many grinning, next to a picture of a giant skull, with commentary by those who had passed over the final threshold about the nature of death. In the middle of the Zócalo were brightly colored, truck-sized *alebrijes*, fantastic mythical creatures made out of papier-mâché and popularized by the Mexico City artist Pedro Linares in the 1930s.

Across town in Coyoacán, in the main park where a famous statue of mythical coyotes stands, the inevitable depiction of a skeletal society lady shared space with delicate portraits etched in colored flour on the ground depicting Frida Kahlo, Diego Rivera, Emiliano Zapata,

Pancho Villa, and other figures from Mexico's history. In one corner of the square, a brimming display of remembrances of the dead featured a black and white photo of a nameless beautiful girl in her mid-twenties with dark eyes, gazing silently out on the living. Years ago, in her house in the neighborhood, the Casa Azul, Kahlo had written the words "Often I feel more sympathy for carpenters, shoe repairmen, etc., than for all that herd of fools who think they are civilized, loquacious, so-called scholarly people."

Later that night, my friend and I shared a smoky mezcal he had brought back from a reporting trip to Michoacán at his apartment in Condesa, and we gazed off his balcony into the black night sky, trying to puzzle out where the country might be heading. We felt that we had no answers. Another friend of mine, the journalist Franc Contreras, who knows Mexico probably as well as any other foreign reporter after having lived in the country for twenty years, took me out under a drizzling rain to eat tacos at *El Vilsito,* an auto body repair shop by day that transformed itself into a succulent food stand at night in the Colonia Benito Juárez. Despite the rain, the city churned on with the relentless energy of a world metropolis. Given the terror that existed elsewhere, along Mexico's darkened roads, its river valleys, its coasts, its jagged deserts, we could have been on another planet.

The previous month had witnessed the usual bloodshed. Two soldiers and nine narcos died in a gun battle in Matamoros following the appearance of roadblocks around the city where gunmen dragged drivers and passengers from their vehicles. A week later, ten suspected cartel gunmen were killed while battling soldiers and police in Nuevo Laredo. Migrants were still being kidnapped off Tamaulipas highways, with fourteen kidnapped Central Americans discovered in a shack in Altamira in late October. As November began, it was Reynosa's turn again with cartel gunmen throwing up roadblocks around the city and engaging security forces in shootouts that left at least nine dead.

The end of 2012 appeared to see a settling of accounts of a grimmest sort, but it started with a baby's newborn cries. In October, Alejandrina Gisselle Guzmán Salazar, the pregnant thirty-one-year-old daughter of

Chapo Guzmán, attempted to enter the United States at San Diego's San Ysidro border crossing, telling border inspectors that she wanted to give birth to her child in Los Angeles. Two months later—before the child was born—she was deported back to Mexico after having confessed to trying to enter the United States on a visa belonging to someone else. In early November 2012, Luis Fernando "El Coyote" León Aldana, the nephew of the murdered Guatemalan drug lord Juancho León, met the same fate as his uncle when he was gunned down outside of his home, reportedly over a dispute about a drug shipment he had stolen. A few weeks later, Guatemala's minister of the interior, Mauricio López Bonilla, said that he believed Los Zetas were responsible for a day-long prison riot at the *Fraijanes* 2 penitentiary.

On the morning of November 12, one struggle would come to an end. María Santos Gorrostieta, the former mayor of the Michoacán town of Tiquicheo who had survived three previous assassination attempts, was taking her young daughter to school in Morelia. She never made it. Forced out of her car by armed men, she begged them not to also abduct her daughter. They left the child behind and took the mother. Four days later, some campesinos in San Juan Tararameo came across the brutally pummeled corpse of a woman. It was Santos. She had been severely beaten and died from "severe head trauma," her pretty face nearly unrecognizable. It was said she had been planning to separate from her bodyguard-turned-husband Nereo Patiño Delgado, but it seemed almost impossible to believe that her death was not linked to those who had tried to kill her in the past. In *El País,* the newspaper in which Santos had once spoken of her "responsibility" to the people of Michoacán and her desire to "teach by example," the columnist Salvador Camarena wrote that there were "two governments" in Michoacán, one chaired by PRI governor Fausto Vallejo—whose election was tainted by allegations of narco vote rigging—and the "real" government that

> *for at least seven years has levied taxes and decided who lives and who dies. The latter, which takes names such as La Familia Michoacána or the Knights Templar has just struck again. . . . With their language, of bullets and cowardice, they made Santos Gorrostieta pay for her*

defiance. The other government, the formal one, said exactly what was expected of them, that the state authority will work to solve the murder. Let's see who believes them, because everyone knows that today in Michoacán, justice is a matter for the afterlife. And then maybe.

A few days later, death even found a perhaps more deserving target, when Sergio Barraza, who had confessed to killing Marisela Escobedo and was strongly suspected of killing her mother, Marisela Escobedo Ortiz, in front of the Chihuahua governor's office the previous year, was killed by the Mexican army between the towns of Tabasco and Joaquín Amaro in Zacatecas. He was, they said, part of a group that had opened fire on an army patrol. Nobody bothered to ask too many questions.

In the Sinaloa town of Guamúchil, the beauty queen María Susana Flores Gámez—who had won the *Mujer de Sinaloa* (Woman of Sinaloa) crown the previous February—was shot dead by soldiers who said she was traveling with Sinaloa Cartel member Orso Iván "El Cholo" Gastélum and that they had chased her—and a convoy of gunmen—over nine miles. The army said they fled the vehicle and that the beauty queen had a gun in her hands when she was killed. Local residents said she was shot as she begged for her life. El Cholo and his accomplices somehow managed to get away. What exactly happened—and whether or not Flores Gámez was being used as a human shield—was never determined.

Stewing in jail since his 2010 arrest, Edgar "La Barbie" Valdéz Villareal brought himself back into the headlines in late November 2012 by sending a letter to the newspaper *Reforma* in which he claimed that Calderón's secretary of public security Genaro García Luna had "received money from me, from drug-trafficking groups and organized crime." Federal police spokesman José Ramón Salinas said that the letter was Valdéz's response to failed demands at "blackmail" in order to receive preferential treatment while in custody. In the letter, Valdéz said that Calderón had tried to organize a "truce" among drug traffickers in the country, and that he himself had been arrested for refusing to take part in the pact. The latter point was a claim that, though the government dismissed it, was echoed by other, less compromised, observers, as well.

On December 2—a Sunday—Enrique Peña Nieto was sworn in as Mexico's fifty-seventh president. He announced that he had a thirteen-point plan for the battered nation and spoke of wanting to focus on issues such as education, pensions, and transportation. As with Calderón's inauguration six years before, protests erupted inside and outside of the congressional chambers where the ceremony was held, with some PRD members of the chamber unfurling banners that read *Mexico mourns*. Peña Nieto would quickly prove himself willing to rattle some cages, almost immediately picking a fight with Elba Esther Gordillo Morales, the powerful leader of the 1.4-million-member *Sindicato Nacional de Trabajadores de la Educación* teachers' union, as he pushed for broad education reform that, in theory, at least, would make teachers more accountable and establish federal standards for education to weed out corruption and nepotism.

Gordillo, whose fondness for designer labels and cosmetic surgery was well known, pushed back, and within a few months found herself under arrest for embezzling tens of millions of dollars in union funds for personal use. A short time earlier, Mexico's senate had also approved a labor bill that made it easier to hire and fire workers, but at the same time increased the minimum wage from an hourly rate to a daily one.

The day Peña Nieto was inaugurated, police in Coahuila at an abandoned ranch outside of Torreón found "seven trunks of the masculine sex and different body parts, such as hands, arms, legs and feet, as well as heads . . . in six black plastic bags." A few days later, in Saltillo, the tortured bodies of four men were suspended from a highway overpass. In Tamaulipas, the hacked-up bodies of three men and two women were found in an abandoned delivery truck in the town of El Mante, along with a message signed by the Gulf Cartel, while police in the riverfront town of Soto la Marina found eight bodies along with a note saying that they had been killed precisely because they were Gulf Cartel members. A study by Mexico's *Instituto Nacional de Estadística y Geografía* (INEGI) published in late 2012 showed that 80 percent of the businesses in Tamaulipas had been victims of crime, with firearms used in nearly 40 percent of those instances. That was in comparison to a national rate of 37.4 percent for businesses being victimized by crime.

Peña Nieto's new minister of the interior, former Hidalgo governor Miguel Ángel Osorio Chong, whose time in office there had been marked by allegations of links to Los Zetas, began his tenure by pointing out that, with the splintering of the drug cartels, Mexico had become more dangerous. Peña Nieto's attorney general, Jesús Murillo Karam, another former Hidalgo governor, would soon tell MVS Radio that he believed up to eighty small- and medium-size cartels were operating in Mexico, and criticized the Calderón government's strategy as having "led to the seconds-in-command, generally the most violent, the most capable of killing . . . starting to be empowered and generating their own groups, generating another type of crime, spawning kidnapping, extortion and protection rackets."

One of Peña Nieto's first moves was to dissolve the SSP, which had been a linchpin of the Calderón battle against the cartels. Peña Nieto announced that, in its place, he would be creating a gendarmerie reporting to Osorio Chong, almost certainly setting the stage for an adversarial relationship between the new law enforcement body and the federal police, which the creation of the gendarmerie seemed all but designed to undercut. Peña Nieto also announced that he would be abandoning the Calderón government's policy of parading captured narcos before reporters, using most wanted lists and nicknames, or granting the media access to law enforcement actions. Peña Nieto also announced that contact between US law enforcement agencies would henceforth see an end to sharing information on an agency-to-agency basis and would rather go through "a single window," Osorio Chong's Interior Ministry.

There appeared to be little immediate effect to the change of government. During the first week of December, thirteen bodies were found in two vehicles in Tamaulipas, one in El Mante, one in Soto la Marina, the latter with a note saying the dead were members of the Gulf Cartel. On Christmas Eve, gunmen wearing camouflage and bearing AK-47s attacked the Sinaloa mountain town of El Platanar de los Ontiveros, killing nine men. Residents speculated that the men belonged to Los Zetas. In a macabre holiday spectacle the following day, the beheaded and incinerated remains of five men—four of them policemen—were found on the Jalisco border with Michoacán. A few hours later, a trio of armed men burst into the *Hospital General de Ciudad Victoria* in the Tamaulipas capital and executed a woman with gunfire.

Shortly after Peña Nieto took office, though, strange things began to happen. Noé Ramírez, the former Calderón drug czar who had been jailed since 2008 for allegedly accepting money from the Sinaloa and Beltrán-Leyva cartels, was acquitted in April 2013 by a federal judge and ordered released, with the judge saying the state's main witness had lied and the police had fabricated evidence. A few months later, former Guadalajara Cartel grandee Rafael Caro Quintero, jailed since April 1985 for his role in the murder of DEA agent Enrique "Kiki" Camarena, walked out of Puente Grande prison a free man after a judicial panel released him on the grounds that his trial should have been conducted in a state rather than a federal court. Peña Nieto, Osorio Chong, and Attorney General Karam all claimed they knew nothing of the hearing or the order to release him. The drug lord—who had also been implicated in the murders of Americans John Walker and Albert Radelat and a host of other crimes—quickly disappeared. As of the writing of this book, he has not been seen in public again.

EPILOGUE

Every December, thousands of people from both sides of the US-Mexico border and from all over the Rio Grande Valley gather in Brownsville to honor the Virgin of Guadalupe, the most revered religious icon in Mexico. As I strolled through Brownsville in the slight chill of winter, I came upon the procession beginning at twilight in front of the Catholic diocese of Brownsville. Several thousand worshippers, including hundreds of children, walked without fear through the streets of the Texas town that looked across the Rio Grande toward Matamoros. Walking alongside them were conchero dancers, in indigenous headdresses evocative of Mexico's pre-Hispanic history yet at the same time wittily combining traditions by sporting ponchos with an image of the virgin herself on them. A dozen horsemen, tough, flinty Spanish-speaking vaqueros from the valley, trotted with their mounts along for the ride. I had walked across the bridge to Matamoros earlier in the day, where, at the Museo de Arte Contemporáneo de Tamaulipas, there was a beautiful exhibition of modern art with gold epaulets hung down from the ceiling on string as if it were showering gold, and sculptures made of tenderly arranged wood and leafs. Back in Brownsville, I had gone into my favorite coffee shop, El Hueso de Fraile (The Friar's Bone), where I drank a glass of wine and listened to the son of the Mexican-American owner playing a lilting version of Mississippi John Hurt's "My Creole Belle." Walking through a back alley in Brownsville, the old buildings casting long shadows in the setting sun, I came upon a mural depicting the Virgin of Guadalupe rising in benediction over a childlike angel. *Que Dios los Bendiga*, the writing above the image read. May God bless you.

How many honest, decent, courageous people have to die before the United States looks itself in the mirror and admits the failure of its policies?

In Colombia there was the presidential candidate Luis Carlos Galán, Minister of Justice Rodrigo Lara Bonilla, and the passengers of Avianca

Airlines Flight 203. There were the peasants slain by the left-wing drug traffickers of the FARC and ELN rebel groups, and those slain by the right-wing drug-trafficking paramilitary groups.

In Guatemala there were the twenty-nine peasants killed in the Petén region and Allan Stowlinsky Vidaurre, the prosecutor tasked with investigating the crime.

In Mexico there has been María Santos Gorrostieta, the young mayor of the Michoacán town of Tiquicheo, the Sonora vendor Nepomuceno Moreno Nuñez, asking justice for his son, and Josefina Reyes and her family in Ciudad Juárez. And there have been journalists like Héctor Félix Miranda in Tijuana, José Armando "El Choco" Rodríguez Carreón in Ciudad Juárez, and Regina Martínez Pérez in Xalapa.

The names go on and on. Perhaps one day, instead of building a border fence, a wall modeled on the Vietnam War Memorial in Washington, DC, could be built along the Rio Grande, the names of those killed in the drug war stenciled delicately into it. It could stretch on for miles.

The war that Felipe Calderón launched against Mexico's drug cartels in 2006 was one the United States all but demanded that he undertake and which it actively supported, an extension of its own war on drugs. As I write these lines, eight years later, what has been the impact of that war, both there and here in the United States?

When I began work on this book, I was living in the lilac- and honeysuckle-scented streets of the Irish Channel in New Orleans, but the flowers and the Creole cottages began to smell of human decay soon enough, with the relentless drumbeat of murders—almost all drug-related—in neighborhoods with names like Pigeon Town, Gert Town, and Central City. When I moved to Miami, where this book was finished, I drove across the causeways spanning Biscayne Bay and gazed at a skyline built with money from cocaine, a skyline that cost the lives of thousands of people to build, like the pyramids.

In early 2013, Chapo Guzmán earned the dubious title of Public Enemy Number One of the American city of Chicago for his role in supplying drugs to warring local street gangs in the city. The previous year Chicago had seen 506 murders, largely the result of battles for drug turf between groups such as the Vice Lords and the P. Stone Nation that nevertheless often struck—and continue to strike—down uninvolved civilians unfortunate enough to be caught in their midst.

From Richard Nixon's famous first speech announcing the war on drugs in 1971 until 2012, the United States had spent more than $1 trillion fighting it, a war to which plainly there can be no end. During 2011, of the 197,050 sentenced prisoners under federal jurisdiction in the United States, 94,600 were serving time for drug offenses. Of the arrests made nationwide in the United States in 2012, by far the highest number of them (an estimated 1,552,432) were for drug abuse violations, and of those 82.2 percent were for possession. The United States has 5 percent of the world's population and 25 percent of the world's prisoners, with African Americans sent to prison for drug offenses at ten times the rate of Caucasians.

It is reasonable to conclude from their own statements that all US presidents going back to 1993 used illegal drugs at one point in their lives, and yet they continue to support laws that criminalize those for the very same transgressions and create the ideal market conditions for the cartels that are shredding Mexico today. The United States helped create the maquiladora economy that sucks Mexicans north toward the border and then leaves them at the mercy of the vagaries of the US economy and the influence of the cartels. Since the election of Barack Obama in 2008 and the advent of the Tea Party wing of the Republican Party—an obscurantist, highly ideological current with little grasp of the meaning of either democracy or governance—the political environment in Washington, DC, has been one of manufactured chaos and often deliberate obstruction. Like the narcos, American politicians from the presidency on down don't much factor in the deaths of thousands of poor nobodies into their political plans.

How will they be made to pay for prolonging policies that cause these deaths? How many people who will see these words—including the author—have smoked a joint, done a line of cocaine, or worse, and never thought that much about it? But how many would do it if they knew it came at the cost of a life? How many of those lives are worth that transitory high?

The drug policies of the major drug-consuming countries can and must change. The arguments against exploring decriminalization and a non-military approach to the problem of drug addiction have now been thoroughly exposed for what they are, cynical lies put forth by politicians panhandling for votes through fear, and government agencies and private industries seeking funding. They all know the fallacy of their argument.

In November 2000, the government of Portugal—acting on the recommendations of a committee of specialists such as doctors, lawyers, psychologists, sociologists, and others—passed Law 30/2000, which decriminalized "personal" drug possession and use up to amounts generally thought of to be able to be consumed by one person over a ten-day period, including for drugs such as cocaine and heroin. With an emphasis on dissuasion and prevention of drug addiction as well as treatment, in the thirteen years since the law was passed in Portugal it did "not result in significant increases in drug use or dependencies" among the population there. Rather drug consumption *decreased* among fifteen- to nineteen-year-olds, a particularly at-risk group. According to the Open Policy Institute, now Portuguese police, rather than "running after drug users, wasting time and money interrogating and detaining them, and taking their fingerprints and photos . . . are freed up to focus on combating organized crime and drug dealing. . . . The police are making fewer arrests but are seizing larger quantities of drugs."

In the Netherlands, another illustrative example, the legal sale and consumption of cannabis has, not surprisingly, led to far fewer arrests for minor drug offenses, nineteen per one hundred thousand for marijuana possession in 2005, to cite one example, as opposed to 206 per one hundred thousand in the United Kingdom, 225 per one hundred thousand in France, and 269 per one hundred thousand in the United States that same year. Some 25.7 percent of Dutch citizens admit to having tried marijuana at least once, in line with the European average, as opposed to 30.2 in the United Kingdom and 41.9 percent in the United States.

Following this example and indeed, exceeding it, in December 2013 the South American nation of Uruguay legalized the production and sale of cannabis for personal use.

In the United States, it is the states themselves, rather than the federal government, that have begun to lead the way toward a more intelligent policy. Since 1996, twenty-two states—including California, Massachusetts, Illinois, Maryland, and, ironically, the District of Columbia—have passed laws allowing marijuana to be used for medical purposes. In the 2012 elections that returned Barack Obama to office, 55 percent of Colorado voters approved via Amendment 64 the legalization of adult personal use of cannabis, with private possession of up to one ounce and private cultivation of up to six marijuana plants bearing no penalty.

During the same electoral period, 56 percent of voters in Washington State approved Initiative 502, a slightly more nuanced measure that permits adults to possess up to one ounce of cannabis (and/or up to sixteen ounces of marijuana-infused product in solid form, and seventy-two ounces of marijuana-infused product in liquid form) for their own personal use in private, with the public consumption of marijuana still subject to a civil violation and fine.

These steps may seem like small advances given the river of blood that has flowed through Mexico over the last decade, but they move in the right direction, and they set the stage, at a local level, for Americans—whose drug use has been so instrumental to the misery and violence afflicting so many people in the developing world for so long—to finally, at long last, begin to explore a commonsense approach to their own culpability.

For too many years, the citizens of the United States and Mexico have gazed at one another across a great gulf of mutual incomprehension despite their intertwined histories and cultures, despite the familial links binding them, sunk deeper in the soil than any mere fence could ever hope to dig beneath. The often destructive and shortsighted policies of the more powerful of the two have often negatively—grievously, really—affected the weaker of the two. The political fallout, whether it be the relentless bloodletting of the cartels or the desperate river and desert crossings of undocumented immigrants seeking work, continues to be used as political currency by the very same people who call for their expansion. Between the two neighbors, under the steel shadow of the border fence on one side and the watchful eyes of the cartels on the other, the Rio Grande, little

more than a creek, continues to meander its way to the Gulf, forever joining the two.

And in Mexico itself?

A late 2012 report from the civil society group *Propuesta Cívica* concluded that, in addition to the more than seventy thousand killed since
2006, some 20,851 people had disappeared in Mexico, running the gamut
from security personnel to laborers to housewives to children. The Mexican and American governments succeeded in weakening the Gulf Cartel
but what replaced them—Los Zetas—was even worse. Despite the often
overly credulous coverage of Enrique Peña Nieto and the supposed "new"
PRI, many in Mexico were not convinced.

"There has only been a change in the discourse, but the strategy is
the same or worse," Javier Sicilia told me in Cuernavaca after Peña Nieto's election. "There is no justice, neither in the epoch of Calderón or
the government under Peña Nieto. It is just a rhetorical change." Sicilia
spoke with great factual certitude. Mexico's *Sistema Nacional de Seguridad
Pública* would show that during Peña Nieto's first year in office, more
people had died violently in the country than during Calderón's first year.

By early 2013, dozens of "self-defense" groups—numbering hundreds
of individuals—had sprung up in Guerrero and Michoacán, a response,
they said, to the failure of the Mexican state to address the abuses of the
narcos. The leader of one such group, Hipólito Mora Chávez, who headed
a paramilitary assemblage in the Michoacán town of La Ruana, told film-
makers from Rompeviento Televisión that "all of Michoacán should do
what we are doing, all of Michoacán and, I believe, many other cities in
Mexico. I think that the cities are going to do what we are doing, fighting,
rising up for their freedom. Because that's what it's all about, freedom,
that we no longer had here."

Another group, in the municipality of Tepalcatepec, was led by a
patrician, white-haired physician named José Manuel Mireles who had
lived in California for a decade and returned to Mexico in 2007, just as
the drug war was beginning to spiral out of control. Mireles told one
interviewer that he "wanted the heads" of the leaders of the Knights Templar. Ironically, Mireles said that it was his experience in California, a

state with a poor record of governance, which convinced him that good government could be possible in Mexico as well.

From 2012 to 2013, the murder rate in Tamaulipas increased by 90 percent, and in mid-January 2013, Gulf Cartel commander Héctor "El Metro 4" Delgado Santiago was killed in Reynosa. The exact circumstances of his death remain unclear even now, with some attributing it to Los Zetas and others to Gulf Cartel infighting. As with his predecessors, a chilling fate also awaited Nuevo Laredo's new police chief, Roberto Alejandro Balmori Garza, who disappeared in February 2013 at the same time that two of his brothers (one of whom was a federal prosecutor) were found dead in the trunk of a car in Nuevo León. At the time of this book's writing, he has not been seen since. A February 2013 report that Chapo Guzmán had been killed in a gun battle in the Petén, however, was said by the Guatemalan government to be false, though what exactly took place near the village of San Valentín (the government denied there had been any clash at all) remained obscure.

A gun battle in Reynosa on the evening of March 10 went on for three hours and featured convoys of trucks blazing away at one another with heavy weapons and grenades as Gulf Cartel factions loyal to Miguel "El Gringo" Villarreal battled those loyal to Mario "El Pelón" Ramírez. Though it was never confirmed, it was believed that El Gringo's corpse was among those hauled away by gunmen in "four trucks filled with bodies." At least four corpses were left, bloodied and bullet-riddled, in an SUV near the attorney general's office. At least three dozen people had allegedly been killed during the exchanges. El Pelón had finally realized his goal of becoming supreme leader of the Gulf Cartel, and he reportedly was hard at work forming another group of shock troops, dubbed *Los Deltas,* to take on his rivals. In Tamaulipas in June 2013, the Mexican army freed 165 migrants believed to have been kidnapped by Los Zetas.

Still threatened by Santa Muerte, in May 2013, Hugo Valdemar, the director of communications for the Archdiocese of Mexico, lashed out at the saint as "blasphemous, evil . . . destructive . . . Mafia, organized crime and drug trafficking are not religions." Not to be outdone, the same month, the Vatican declared Santa Muerte "blasphemous" and a "degeneration of religion."

And the icy fingers of death reached all the way into the Mexican capital as well. On a sunny Sunday afternoon in June 2013, twelve youths—eight men and four women—were taken out of the Heaven nightclub off Avenida Reforma in Mexico City and put into four vehicles. They disappeared until two months later, when federal authorities found their bodies buried at a ranch near Tlalmanalco outside the capital. Many of those slain were from Tepito, at least two from families with links to organized crime, and it was believed that they were attempting to take over the turf of a rival drug gang, who kidnapped and killed them.

The reigns of the drug lords tended to be short-lived, and they seem to be getting shorter. As he drove in a pickup with two gunmen down a country highway outside of Nuevo Laredo less than twenty miles from the Texas border on July 15, Miguel Treviño was greeted by a swooping military helicopter and a raid that, the Mexican government said, succeeded in capturing the dreaded Z-40 and his two henchmen without a shot being fired. Treviño's face, bloated and bruised, was quickly splashed across all media venues, with some wondering aloud if the arrest of arguably the most feared man in the world of Mexican drug trafficking meant that Mexico's long nightmare of violence might soon in fact be over. Control of Los Zetas was believed to pass to Z-40's brother, Omar Treviño or Z-42, far less battle-tested than his sibling.

When Z-40 was found, he had in his possession an AK-47 variant that was traced to a disreputable gun seller in a San Antonio suburb, who had been selling firearms at gun shows claiming they were from his "personal" collection, thus relieving him of the need to be licensed by the state and to conduct background checks on people purchasing firearms from him.

In May 2013, a federal appeals court in Washington, DC, had upheld a law introduced by the Obama administration requiring gun dealers in states along the Mexican border to inform federal officials when semi-automatic rifles were purchased multiple times by a single individual during any five-day period. The NRA had attempted to block even that. After his arrest, Treviño reportedly confirmed to the attorney general that Heriberto Lazcano had indeed been killed by security forces in Coahuila in October 2012 and that it was he himself—Z-40—who had given the order that his predecessor's body be seized from the funeral home. A few weeks after Z-40 was arrested, his brother, José Treviño Morales, was convicted by a San Antonio court of using his quarter horse racing business to launder money for Los Zetas. He was sentenced to twenty years in a US federal prison. Surprisingly, one of the witnesses to testify against him was the once-feared Zeta Jesús Enrique "El Mamito" Rejón Aguilar. Only months after Z-40's capture, Francisco Rafael Arellano Félix, of the once powerful Tijuana Cartel, was slain in a Baja California beach resort by a killer who "wore a clown costume complete with a wig and a round red nose."

As his bitter rival Z-40 had been, Mario "El Pelón" Ramírez was captured without a shot being fired, in his case in Reynosa in August 2013, in a multiagency operation that combined military and police forces that also scooped up two of the drug lord's bodyguards and at least $38,000 in cash. It is believed that after El Pelón's capture another of Osiel Cárdenas's brothers, Homero "El Majadero" Cárdenas Guillén, was poised to become a dominant force in what was left of one wing of the organization, while the former Z-9, Galdino "El Mellado" Cruz, controlled the other.

In truth, though, even if some sense of order was present—however tenuous—in Matamoros, elsewhere in Tamaulipas, and especially in Reynosa, control could vary neighborhood to neighborhood and even block to block among various wannabe chieftains. By this point, the magazine *Proceso* was even concluding that the once-mighty Gulf Cartel, whose leaders once controlled a swath of Mexico from the beaches of Cancún to the border with Texas, had degenerated into little more than "a federation of fiefdoms."

But what to make, then, of video that surfaced online in late September 2013 purportedly showing Gulf Cartel members delivering aid to victims of Hurricane Ingrid in the Tamaulipas municipality of Aldama? Despite the passage of so many years and all the losses and fractures the organization had suffered, were they still in fact the "real" government in Tamaulipas? Watching the video it certainly seemed so.

And what to make of my own experience while driving through the Colonia Ferrocarril neighborhood of Reynosa in late 2013? A contact and I had just finished interviewing migrants deported from the United States who were staying at a local shelter and were taking some of the potholed back roads out of the neighborhood to our next interview in another part of the city. As we turned a corner down a narrow lane hemmed in by cement-block houses on either side, there they were: about half a dozen men surrounding two white SUVs bearing assault rifles and staring hard at the passing cars, letting some pass, stopping others. The armed men were in their late twenties and early thirties, dressed in civilian clothes—black T-shirts, baseball caps—and had the look of policemen about them. They were from the Gulf Cartel, my contact later told me, recruiting young men from the neighborhood, though to my eyes they looked as if they were looking for someone in particular in the passing cars. Decades after its birth, the Gulf Cartel, fractured as it was, was still able to set up a heavily armed waylay in the heart of a major city only minutes from the US border on a sunny Saturday afternoon. As we drove gingerly away, a White Yukon with a Santa Muerte insignia plastered to its rear window raced past us.

A few weeks after Miguel Treviño's capture, narcomantas appeared in several locations in Zacatecas, including one displayed in a hotel room, perhaps a cartel first. The banners read in part:

> *Friends and enemies, Señor 40 is still alive, this won't be over until it's over. All this is well structured and managed, nothing happens here and we don't rearrange anything, Señor 40 is still the leader of his group, solid and well managed and united. . . . From now on we are going to show our presence so you know that we are here. . . . Sincerely, The last letter—Señor 40.*

Postscript

After thirteen years on the run, the Sinaloa Cartel's Joaquin "El Chapo" Guzmán was captured at a house in Mazatlán, Sinaloa, in February 2014, at the conclusion of an operation that involved the Mexican marines, US DEA agents, and US federal marshals. It was believed that Ismael "El Mayo" Zambada Garcia and Juan José "El Azul" Esparragoza Moreno, each of whom had been involved in the drug trade for decades, would continue running the cartel.

NOTES

Prologue
xv. *try to identify the dead.*: "Border Region Lives in Fear Amid Mexico Cartel War," Agence France-Presse, May 11, 2011.

xv. *they would have 193 bodies.*: "Hallan 7 nuevas narcofosas en San Fernando Tamaulipas suman 193 cadáveres," *Milenio Noticias,* June 30, 2011.

xvi. *3.5 million trucks crossing annually.*: International Trade, Laredo Development Foundation, www.ldfonline.org/?i=28&/International-Trade, accessed June 4, 2013.

xvi. *fell into the cartel's clutches.*: "Los horrores de San Fernando," *El Informador,* April 30, 2011.

xvii. *active-duty Tamaulipas state police officers.*: Author interviews, May 2011–December 2012.

xviii. *assault that took down Tony Tormenta.*: "Reputed Drug Kingpin Killed in Mexico Shootout," Associated Press, November 6, 2010.

xviii. *at closer to fifty.*: Author interviews, Matamoros, May 2011.

xviii. *new beliefs are taking hold.*: Author interviews, Brownsville, May 2011.

xix. *people of more humble means.*: Quinones, Sam. *True Tales from Another Mexico: The Lynch Mob, the Popsicle Kings, Chalino and the Bronx.* Albuquerque: University of New Mexico Press, 2001, 233–36.

xx. *by a group of Zetas.*: Author interviews, Guatemala City, August 2008.

xx. *bodies of two Mexican nationals.*: "Drugs vs. Democracy in Guatemala," *World Policy Journal,* Winter 2008/09.

xx. *bodyguards for Osiel Cárdenas.*: "The Ghost of the Zetas," *Plaza Pública,* December 8, 2011.

xx. *executive committee of the party.*: Author interview with Comisión Internacional contra la Impunidad en Guatemala (CICIG) investigator, July 2010.

xx. *war officially ended in 1996.*: "La historia de un mito del narcotráfico," *El Periódico,* March 31, 2008.

Chapter One
1. *where people pray a lot.*: "Historia," *Gobierno del Estado de Tamaulipas,* http://tamaulipas.gob.mx/tamaulipas/historia/, accessed August 24, 2013.

3. *border in the mid 1800s.*: Information on Juan Cortina is drawn mainly from these two sources: Thompson, Jerry. *Cortina: Defending the Mexican Name in Texas.* College Station: Texas A&M University Press, 2007; Thompson, Jerry D. (editor). *Juan Cortina and the Texas-Mexico Frontier 1859–1887.* El Paso: Texas Western Press, 1994.

4. *being of Mexican origin.*: Thompson, *Juan Cortina and the Texas-Mexico Frontier,* 14–18.

4. *came to protect his enemies.*: Ibid., 19.

4. *Had been laid to waste.*: Thompson, *Cortina: Defending the Mexican Name,* 77.

4. *US Army and restore order.*: Ibid., 86.

5. completely illiberal politically.": Krauze, Enrique. *Mexico: Biography of Power.* New York: Harper Perennial, 1998, 207–16.

5. of it within Tamaulipas itself.: Hart, John Mason. *Revolutionary Mexico.* Berkeley: University of California Press, 1987, 260.

6. Tamaulipas and several other states.: Ibid., 10.

6. traditional society were especially strong.": Ibid., 7.

6. where it had originally stood.: Quinones, Sam. *True Tales from Another Mexico: The Lynch Mob, the Popsicle Kings, Chalino and the Bronx.* Albuquerque: University of New Mexico Press, 2001, 227–30.

7. people, and also in Querétaro.: Chesnut, R. Andrew. *Devoted to Death: Santa Muerte, the Skeleton Saint.* New York: Oxford University Press, 2012, 27–33.

7. "a cult of crisis".: "El culto a la Santa Muerte," *El Universal,* April 11, 2009.

7. 350,000 acres in the state.: Hart, *Revolutionary Mexico,* 49.

7. hundred Mexicans and four Americans.: Ibid., 63–67.

7. as such at the time.: "Mexicans Resent Invasion," *New York Times,* October 12, 1906.

8. in history by scheming politicans.: For a thorough history of Zapata's life and times, consult John Womack's definitive *Zapata and the Mexican Revolution* (New York: Vintage, 1970).

8. in Chihuahua in July 1923.: For the definitive account of Villa's life, consult Friedrich Katz's *The Life and Times of Pancho Villa* (Stanford: Stanford University Press, 1998). For some interesting contemporary reportage on Villa's rise, read John Reed's *Insurgent Mexico* (New York: International Publishers, 1999 edition, originally published in 1914). Carlos Fuentes's 1995 novel *Gringo Viejo* (The Old Gringo) provides a fascinating fictionalization of Ambrose Bierce's time in Mexico.

9. Blaylock and La Palma colonies.: Hart, *Revolutionary Mexico,* 259.

9. now unhappily obtaining in Mexico.": "President Wilson's Address to Congress, 20 April 1914," www.firstworldwar.com/source/tampicoincident.htm, accessed September 18, 2013.

9. would die in the conflict.: Krauze, *Mexico: Biography of Power,* 419–24.

11. for the first time ever.: For a thorough history of Prohibition in the United States, read Daniel Okrent's *Last Call: The Rise and Fall of Prohibition* (New York: Scribner, 2010) and view the miniseries *Prohibition,* directed by Ken Burns and Lynn Novick, which originally aired on the Public Broadcasting Service in the United States in October 2011.

12. the thread of domination"; successors of the Aztec rulers.": Paz, Octavio. *The Labyrinth of Solitude.* New York: Grove Press, 1985 edition, 298.

12. the United States and Mexico.: "Matamoros Journal: Canaries Sing in Mexico, but Uncle Juan Will Not," *New York Times,* February 9, 1996.

12. a bribe to return it).: "Un hijo de Pancho Villa, muerto a trios," *ABC,* April 27, 1960.

12. its economy grow and diversify.: Krauze, *Mexico: Biography of Power,* 680–85.

13. the Middle East or Vietnam.: Ibid., 717–26.

13. may have been much higher.: "The Dead of Tlatelolco: Using the Archives to Exhume the Past," National Security Archive Electronic Briefing Book No. 201, October 1, 2006.

13. leaders from the 1968 protests).: Krauze, *Mexico: Biography of Power,* 744–52.

13. *were killed in the assault.*: "The Corpus Christi Massacre: Mexico's Attack on Its Student Movement," National Security Archive, June 10, 2003.

13. *state and federal police forces*": "La negra historia de Nazar Haro," *Proceso,* September 9, 2013.

13. *security agencies during this period.*: "Confronting A Nightmare: Disappearances in Mexico," Amnesty International, June 2013.

13. *in at least 143 disappearances.*: "Vinculado a hechos oscuros, dejó múltiples pendientes con la justicia," *Proceso,* April 20, 2012.

14. *"patriotic fraud.":* Oppenheimer, Andres. *Bordering on Chaos: Guerrillas, Stockbrokers, Politicians, and Mexico's Road to Prosperity.* New York: Little Brown & Company, 1996, 192–93.

14. *the PRI and the media.*: Ibid., 83–87.

15. *levels of the Federal Government.":* "Special Message to the Congress on Drug Abuse Prevention and Control," June 17, 1971, www.presidency.ucsb.edu/ws/?pid=3048, accessed August 25, 2013.

15. *cultivated in abundance for decades.*: "The Drug Lord Who Got Away," *Wall Street Journal,* June 13, 2009.

15. *other states before resuming business.*: "Drug Trafficking in Mexico: a First General Assessment, Discussion Paper No. 36," UNESCO, 1999.

15. *remain little more than hamlets.*: "La Operación Cóndor trajo miedo y éxodo en la sierra de Sinaloa," *La Jornada,* May 24, 2009.

16. *long predated their bloody business.*: Quinones, *True Tales from Another Mexico,* 230.

16. *was killed in April 1987.*: For a full account of Pablo Acosta Villarreal's career, consult Terrence Poppa's *Drug Lord: The Life and Death of a Mexican Kingpin* (Cinco Puntos Press, 2010).

16. *formally started operating around 1982.*: Blancornelas, Jesús. *El Cártel: Los Arellano Felix, La Mafia Más Poderosa en la Historia de América Latina.* Mexico City: Debolsillo, 2002, 32.

16. *oust the leftist Sandinista government.):* "A Camarena lo ejecutó la CIA, no Caro Quintero," *Proceso,* October 12, 2013.

16. *between law enforcement and political enforcers.*: "Drug Trafficking Organizations and Counter-Drug Strategies in the US-Mexican Context: A Working Paper by Luis Astorga and David A. Shirk," Woodrow Wilson Center for International Scholars; Trans-Border Institute and University of San Diego, April 2010.

16. *the drug-trafficking organizations deepened significantly.*: Ibid.

17. *we're running up a battle flag.":* "Remarks on Signing Executive Order 12368, Concerning Federal Drug Abuse Policy Functions," www.reagan.utexas.edu/archives/speeches/1982/62482b.htm, June 24, 1982, accessed August 25, 2013.

17. *the world the previous year.*: "CAN MIAMI SAVE ITSELF; A City Beset by Drugs and Violence," *New York Times,* July 19, 1987.

17. *jettisoned over fifteen years previously.*: "Undo This Legacy of Len Bias's Death," *Washington Post,* June 24, 2006.

17. *sentenced to prison for drug offenses.*: "ACLU Releases Crack Cocaine Report, Anti-Drug Abuse Act of 1986 Deepened Racial Inequity in Sentencing," American Civil Liberties Union, October 26, 2006.

17. *presence upon their old home there.:* "United States of America, Plaintiff-Appellee, v. Juan Garcia Abrego, Defendant-Appellant," No. 97-20130, May 6, 1998.
18. *hospital a short time later.:* "El Profe welcomes Garcia Ábrego's downfall," *Brownsville Herald,* January 24, 1996.
18. *is a government-run issue.":* "González Calderóni, hilo de la maraña narcopolítica," *Proceso,* February 5, 2003.
18. *in McAllen, Texas, in 1993.:* "Matan en EU a Guillermo González Calderóni," *La Jornada,* February 6, 2003.
18. *be on the cartel's payroll.:* "González Calderóni, hilo de la maraña narcopolítica," *Proceso,* February 5, 2003.
18. *general from 1988 to 1990.:* "Bribes and Publicity Mark Fall of Mexican Drug Lord," *New York Times,* May 12, 1996.
19. *Salinas had been fraudulently elected.:* "Ex-President in Mexico Casts New Light on Rigged 1988 Election," *New York Times,* March 9, 2009.
19. *Ovando and Román Gil Heraldez.:* "Matan en EU a Guillermo González Calderóni," *La Jornada,* February 6, 2003.
19. *put agents' lives at risk.:* Drugs, Law Enforcement and Foreign Policy: A Report Prepared by the Subcommittee on Terrorism, Narcotics and International Operations of the Committee on Foreign Relations of the United States Senate, December 1988.
20. *"for protection".:* "Drugs, Death and the Occult Meet In Grisly Inquiry at Mexico Border," *New York Times,* April 13, 1989.
20. *as many as forty people.:* "20th Anniversary Of Mark Kilroy Death & Cult Killings," KVEO, March 19, 2009.
20. *on the ranch, and imprisoned.:* "Leader in Cult Slayings Ordered Own Death, Two Companions Say," Associated Press, May 8, 1989.
20. *full use of his left hand.:* "Destiny Made Juan N. Guerra Rich, Powerful," *Brownsville Herald,* January 26, 2013.

Chapter Two

21. *Hernández at the Piedras Negras.:* "Matamoros Journal: Canaries Sing in Mexico, but Uncle Juan Will Not," *New York Times,* February 9, 1996.
21. *DEA Agent Enrique "Kiki" Camarena.:* "Border Search for Clues Ended: Mexico Arrests Suspect in Kidnapping of US Agent," *Los Angeles Times,* February 26, 1985.
22. *more than one hundred people.:* For the definitive account of the Medellín Cartel, consult Guy Gugliotta and Jeff Leen's book, *Kings of Cocaine Inside the Medellin Cartel—An Astonishing True Story of Murder Money and International Corruption* (New York: Simon & Schuster, 1989).
22. *into the United States annually.:* "Drug Trafficking Organizations and Counter-Drug Strategies in the US-Mexican Context: A Working Paper by Luis Astorga and David A. Shirk," Woodrow Wilson Center for International Scholars; Trans-Border Institute and University of San Diego, April 2010.
23. *in Los Angeles and New York.:* "United States of America, Plaintiff-Appelle, v. Juan Garcia Abrego, Defendant-Appellant," No. 97-20130, May 6, 1998.
23. *in connection with the crime.:* "Tijuana Journal; 'The Cat' Clawed Many; Is One His Murderer?" *New York Times,* July 1, 1988.

24. *power within the police force.:* "Leaders of Arellano-Felix Criminal Organization Plead Guilty," US Attorney's Office, October 21, 2009.

24. *murdered in a Venezuela prison.:* "The Drug Lord Who Got Away," *Wall Street Journal,* July 31, 2009.

25. *Ignacio Coronel Villareal, aka Nacho Coronel.:* "Top Mexican Drug Lord Killed in Clash with Army," Associated Press, July 29, 2010.

25. *when his conviction was overturned).:* "Mexican General Once Tied to Cartels Shot Dead," Associated Press, April 20, 2012.

25. *by several stints in prison.:* Rotella, Sebastian. *Twilight on the Line: Underworlds and Politics at the Mexican Border.* New York: W. W. Norton & Company, 1998, 130–72.

25. *perished in the ensuing shootout.:* Ibid., 140.

25. *time, on the same day.:* For one account of the event consult Jesús Blancornelas's *El Cártel: Los Arellano Felix, La Mafia Más Poderosa en la Historia de América Latina* (Debolsillo, 2002). Another good resource is Rotella, *Twilight on the Line.*

26. *firearms and the drug trade.:* "New York Killings Set a Record, While Other Crimes Fell in 1990," *New York Times,* April 23, 1991.

26. *record up to that time.:* "Philadelphia's Killing Spree," *Crime Report,* March 29, 2012.

26. *record 849 murders during 1990.:* "849 Homicides Place 1990: In A Sad Record," *Chicago Tribune,* January 2, 1991.

26. *and became a two-week siege.:* "El Profe Welcomes Garcia Ábrego's Downfall," *Brownsville Herald,* January 24, 1996.

26. *and bribes for some time.:* "Mexican Drug Lord Ends 2-Week Siege of Prison," *New York Times,* May 31, 1991.

26. *his boldness with his life.:* "United States of America v. Juan Garcia Ábrego," May 6, 1998.

26. *US history at that time.:* "Bribes and Publicity Mark Fall of Mexican Drug Lord," *New York Times,* May 12, 1996.

26. *his drug empire in Mexico.:* Ibid.

27. *and sometimes every few days.:* "United States of America v. Juan Garcia Ábrego," May 6, 1998.

27. *at his ranch, El Tlahuachal.:* "Destiny Made Juan N. Guerra Rich, Powerful," *Brownsville Herald,* January 26, 2013.

27. *jail on tax evasion charges.:* "Matamoros Journal: Canaries Sing in Mexico, but Uncle Juan Will Not," *New York Times,* February 9, 1996.

27. *murders of numerous individuals.":* "Bribes and Publicity Mark Fall of Mexican Drug Lord," *New York Times,* May 12, 1996.

27. *$2.5 billion in NAFTA's first year.:* "NAFTA: Free Trade Bought and Oversold," *Washington Post,* September 30, 1996.

27. *"virtually all manufactured goods":* "Mexican Employment, Productivity and Income a Decade after NAFTA," Carnegie Endowment for Peace, February 25, 2004.

27. *country, but for the PRI.:* Oppenheimer, Andres. *Bordering on Chaos: Guerrillas, Stockbrokers, Politicians, and Mexico's Road to Prosperity.* New York: Little Brown & Company, 1996, 83–87.

28. *such as Oaxaca and Guerrero.:* INTERNATIONAL TRADE: Mexico's Maquiladora Decline Affects US-Mexico Border Communities and Trade; Recovery Depends in Part on Mexico's Actions, United States General Accounting Office, July 2003.

28. *the industrial activity in Tamaulipas.:* Ibid.

28. *before joining the revolutionary left.:* Oppenheimer, *Bordering on Chaos,* 236–62.

28. *for the state congress there.:* "Dip. Mercedes del Carmen Guillén Vicente," Cámara de Diputados, http://sitl.diputados.gob.mx/LXI_leg/curricula.php?dipt=369, accessed September 12, 2013.

29. *head of the Gulf Cartel,"; I failed.":* "Probe of PRI Official's Assassination Suggests Possible Drug Cartel Link." *Los Angeles Times,* October 1, 1994.

29. *a time, his mother said.:* "Shame, Disbelief in Suspect's Pueblo," *Los Angeles Times,* October 2, 1994.

29. *family to ensure his silence.:* "Confessed Mexican Killer Implicates Ex-President," Reuters, January 29, 1999.

30. *of involvement in the crime.:* "El diputado Rocha vincula al 'cartel del Golfo' con la trama del asesinato del secretario del PRI," *El País,* October 5, 1994.

30. *"polluted.":* "Caso abierto, desaparición de Manuel Muñoz Rocha," *Milenio,* March 13, 2008.

30. *one long pro-Zedillo campaign advertisement.:* Oppenheimer, *Bordering on Chaos,* 131–33.

30. *masterminding the Ruiz Massieu assassination,:* "Who Killed Ruiz Massieu?" *Washington Post,* January 24, 1999.

30. *conviction that was later overturned.:* "Mexico Frees Ex-Leader's Brother," BBC News, June 10, 2005.

30. *Mexican peso against the dollar.:* Oppenheimer, *Bordering on Chaos,* 216. *building a short time later.:* Ibid., 298–300.

31. *the slaying had been "an accident.":* "Report on Massacre Provokes a Political Storm in Mexico," *New York Times,* February 29, 1996.

31. *Oxford University in the United Kingdom.:* "The Bill Clinton we knew at Oxford," *Independent,* October 11, 1992.

31. *out of one hundred thousand.:* "Incarceration Nation," *Time,* April 2, 2012.

31. *information leading to his capture.:* "Bribes and Publicity Mark Fall of Mexican Drug Lord," *New York Times,* May 12, 1996.

31. *vast sums of money on.:* "Mexico Deports Alleged Drug Cartel Chief to U.S.," *Los Angeles Times,* January 16, 1996.

31. *a cat into a bag":* Guillermoprieto, Alma. *Looking for History: Dispatches from Latin America.* New York: Vintage Books, 2001, 255.

32. *drug cartels even more fraught.:* "Grisly murder points to drugs, powerful figures in Mexico," CNN, December 6, 1996.

32. *ages eighteen, nine, and eight.:* "La ejecutan a ella y a toda su familia," *El Norte,* December 6, 1996.

32. *"sexual slaves.":* "Details Emerge in Slaying of Mexico Family," *Los Angeles Times,* December 25, 1996.

32. *"drink and I don't sing,":* "Matamoros Journal: Canaries Sing in Mexico, but Uncle Juan Will Not," *New York Times,* February 9, 1996.

32. *jail or in the cemetery.":* "Hombres como Garcia Ábrego terminan en la cárcel o en el cementerio," *Proceso,* January 20, 1996.

32. *of the provisions of NAFTA.:* "Destiny made Juan N. Guerra rich, powerful," *Brownsville Herald,* January 26, 1996.

Chapter Three

33. *Matamoros by his early twenties,:* Ravelo, Ricardo. *Osiel: Vida y Tragedia de un Capo.* Mexico City: Grijalbo, 2009, 38–48.

34. *and later had risen through the ranks of the PJF:* "'El Lazca' desafía al poder que le dio vida: el Ejército," *Proceso,* May 16, 2010.

34. *as the Gulf Cartel's head.:* "Historia y estructura del Cártel del Golfo," *Terra,* November 5, 2010.

34. *bricks short of a load.":* Author interview, May 2011.

34. *hubs of Houston and Atlanta.:* "Las operaciones secretas del cártel del Golfo," *Revista Contralínea,* August 30, 2009.

34. *criminal empire from behind bars.:* "Capturaron a Mario Cárdenas Guillén, uno de los jefes del cártel del Golfo," Univision, September 4, 2012.

34. *rise rapidly within its ranks.:* "Cayó 'El Coss,'" *El Mañana,* September 12, 2012.

34. *(Crazy Meme) Vázquez Mireles.:* "Jefe del cártel del Golfo, peligroso rival de Los Zetas," *El Universal,* July 18, 2013.

34. *me nor of the cartel.":* Ravelo, Ricardo. *Osiel: Vida y Tragedia de un Capo.* Mexico City: Grijalbo, 2009, 146.

35. *off from the Sinaloa cartel.:* "Cártel de los Valencia," *El Economista,* August 30, 2011.

35. *drug czar Barry R. McCaffrey.:* "General Gutierrez to Head Up Mexico's War Against Drugs," *Los Angeles Times,* December 6, 1996.

35. *more than one thousand military personnel.:* "Police Reform in Mexico: Advances and Persistent Obstacles," Working Paper Series on US-Mexico Security Collaboration, Woodrow Wilson International Center for Scholars Mexico Institute, May 2010.

35. *in the commission of crimes.:* The Impact of the 1994 Federal Assault Weapons Ban, Brady Center to Prevent Gun Violence, March 2004.

35. *require more than easy optics.:* "Former Mexican Drug Czar Sentenced," Associated Press, March 3, 1998.

36. *explosives, counterespionage, and guerrilla warfare.:* Osorno, Diego Enrique. *La guerra de Los Zetas: Viaje por la frontera de la necropolítica.* Mexico City: Grijalbo, 2012, 323.

36. *jungle warfare tactics, into Los Zetas.:* Ibid., 328.

36. *one of Osiel Cárdenas's bodyguards.:* "'El Hummer' podría ser el asesino de Valentín," *El Debate,* November 8, 2008.

37. *at least one in Texas.:* "The True Story of Los Zetas, the Power Unparalleled in Mexico," *Borderland Beat,* April 15, 2012.

37. *early years as a cartel.:* Mexico's Drug Cartels, A Report for Congress from Congressional Research Service, Foreign Affairs, Defense, and Trade Division, October 16, 2007.

37. *"a ritual people":* Paz, Octavio. *The Labyrinth of Solitude.* New York: Grove Press, 1985 edition, 47.

38. *relationships between Mexico and Texas.":* "Governor Yarrington Availability," Speech delivered by Texas Governor Rick Perry, February 22, 2001, http://governor.state.tx.us/news/speech/9323/, November 19, 2013.

38. *wooden chest as a gift.:* "Rick Perry, the Gifts," *Houston Chronicle,* July 26, 2009.

39. *control of the Gulf Cartel.:* Ravelo, *Osiel,* 136–38.

39. *he had three young children.:* Ibid., 192.

39. *he worked for—strained credulity.:* "Texas Investigators Missed Cartel Boss in 1998," *San Antonio Express-News,* May 29, 2013.

39. *are going to die here.":* "DEA Agent Describes Engaging in Armed Standoff with Drug Kingpin in '99," Associated Press, March 16, 2010.

40. *Don't ever come back.":* "DEA Agent Tells Details of Now-Infamous 1999 Confrontation with Mexican Drug Kingpin," *Houston Chronicle,* March 14, 2010.

40. *a posh disco in Cancún.:* Ravelo, *Osiel,* 188.

40. *against organized crime in Mexico,":* "Opposition Wins Mexican Elections," ABC News, July 3, 2000.

40. *drug-compromised PJF federal police force.:* "Mexico Dissolves Equivalent of FBI," Agence France-Presse, July 26, 2012.

40. *Zedillo government several years before.:* "Police Reform in Mexico: Advances and Persistent Obstacles," Working Paper Series on US-Mexico Security Collaboration, Woodrow Wilson International Center for Scholars Mexico Institute, May 2010.

41. *of great luxury and privilege:* Hernández, Anabel. *Narco Land: The Mexican Drug Lords and Their Godfathers.* New York: Verso, 2013, 101–35.

41. *"erased.":* "The Drug Lord Who Got Away," *Wall Street Journal,* June 13, 2009.

41. *state and municipal authorities"; "criminal megastructure":* "Hidalgo: Los Zetas en el poder," *Progreso,* May 1, 2010.

41. *for the cartel as well.:* "Gulf Cartel, and Its Enforcers, Began Control of Northern Mexico in 2001," *San Antonio Express-News,* April 20, 2013.

41. *unfairly, with the drug trade.:* "Santa Muerte de Tepito cumple seis años," *EFE,* 1 November 1, 2007.

42. *"Dark Saint":* Lewis, Oscar. *The Children of Sanchez: Autobiography of a Mexican Family.* New York: Vintage, 1961, 141.

42. *to Nuevo Laredo in 1998.:* "US Student Became Mexican Drug Kingpin," *New York Times,* September 8, 2010.

43. *known as El Charro (The Cowboy).:* "An American Drug Lord in Acapulco," *Rolling Stone,* August 25, 2011.

43. *in a hail of gunfire.:* "Rival Drug Gangs Turn the Streets of Nuevo Laredo into a War Zone," *New York Times,* December 4, 2005.

43. *on both sides gravely wounded.:* "Drug Boss Captured in Mexico," BBC, March 15, 2003.

43. *had formed the original Zetas.:* Ravelo, *Osiel,* 215–16.

43. *El Meme Loco was arrested.:* "Tiene un narco en prisión nueve años sin sentencia," *El Siglo de Torreón,* September 18, 2012.

43. *Valencia founder Armando Valencia Cornelio.:* "Cártel de los Valencia," *El Economista,* August 30, 2011.

44. *$220,000 by the US government.:* "Timeline: An ICE Informant Run Amok—Or Mishandled?" National Public Radio, February 11, 2010.

44. *to twenty-five years in prison.:* "Cárcel para narco mexicano en EU," *Terra,* April 10, 2007.

44. *the United States, a free man.:* "ICE Informant Linked to Juárez 'House of Death' Freed: Board Grants Informant Asylum Fearing Retaliation From Cartel," KVIA, July 12, 2012.

44. *of the bloodshed they unleash.:* "Mexican Deserters Start Drug Turf War," Associated Press, October 10, 2003.

44. *people including two police officers.:* "Mexico Hit by Wave of Drug Gang Killings," Reuters, January 26, 2004.

44. *been tortured before their confessions.:* "Mexican Man Sentenced to 16 Years for Journalist's Murder," Committee to Protect Journalists, July 23, 2009.

44. *Texas governor the previous year.:* "Former Mexico Officials with Ties to Texas Under Investigation," *San Antonio Express-News,* February 18, 2012.

45. *Apatzingán prison in far-off Michoacán.:* "Mexico's Drug War Pits Government Against Former Elite Commandos," Knight Ridder Newspapers, February 11, 2005.

45. *on a murder-for-hire basis.:* "Mexican Army Deserters Kill for Pay along Border," Associated Press, July 24, 2004.

45. *announcing their presence, terrifying people.:* Corchado, Alfredo. *Midnight in Mexico: A Reporter's Journey Through a Country's Descent into Darkness.* New York: Penguin, 2013, 147.

45. *him until his heart stopped.:* "Journalists Under Fire in Mexico Border Drug War," Reuters, February 13, 2005.

45. *the city of Nuevo Laredo.":* "Rival Drug Gangs Turn the Streets of Nuevo Laredo into a War Zone," *New York Times,* December 4, 2005.

46. *tasked as leading the charge.:* "Los Secretos de El Azul," *El Orbe,* April 17, 2012.

46. *culpability was never conclusively proven.:* "La muerte de Rodolfo Carrillo," *Periódico Noroeste,* September 11, 2008.

46. *hurled grenades at oncoming officers.:* "Mexico Arrests Man Suspected of Leading Drug Cartel's Assassins," *New York Times,* October 30, 2004.

46. *to work for the cartel.:* "'El Lazca' desafía al poder que le dio vida: el Ejército," *Proceso,* May 16, 2010.

46. *time, had orchestrated the hit.:* "Mitos y realidades sobre El Chapo Guzmán," CNN Mexico, April 30, 2013.

46. *77 percent the year before.:* "Mexican Drug Lords Increasingly Powerful," Associated Press, November 7, 2005.

46. *running from a Mexican prison.:* "Mexican Official Says Tijuana, Gulf Cartels Have United," *Los Angeles Times,* January 14, 2005.

46. *federal maximum-security prison in Matamoros.:* "Mexico's Drug War Pits Government Against Former Elite Commandos," Knight Ridder Newspapers, February 11, 2005.

47. *of Núñez, deepened and expanded.:* "Hidalgo: Los Zetas en el poder," *Proceso,* May 1, 2010.

47. *She died eleven days later.:* "Dolores Guadalupe García Escamilla," Committee to Protect Journalists, April 16, 2005.

47. *while driving in his car.:* "Spate of Attacks Targets Journalists in Mexico," *Washington Post,* April 12, 2005.

47. *"owe anybody anything"; those who have been compromised":* "Mexican Border City Police Chief Killed," Associated Press, June 9, 2005.

47. *to hesitate for one minute.":* "In a Lawless Town, the Top Lawman Avoids Trouble," *New York Times,* August 20, 2005.

47. *by the time you read this.":* National Public Radio broadcast, *All Things Considered,* September 22, 2005.

47. *between local police and Los Zetas.:* "Mexican Forces Rescue Dozens Apparently Held by Kidnappers," *New York Times,* June 28, 2005.

47. *toll was far higher.:* "Fight for Control Nuevo Laredo Now Sees Quiet," *Laredo Morning Times,* May 10, 2008.

48. *albeit slightly worse for wear.:* "Texas Town Is Unnerved by Violence in Mexico," *New York Times,* August 11, 2005.

48. *seventeen released, and twenty-three missing.* Ibid.

48. *did not attend her funeral.:* "In a Lawless Town, the Top Lawman Avoids Trouble," *New York Times,* August 20, 2005.

48. *everything turned out well,"; "for mental health reasons.":* "Violence Forces Nuevo Laredo Chief to Quit," *San Antonio Express-News,* March 24, 2006.

48. *has not been seen since.:* "Unorthodox Nuevo Laredo Police Chief's 2006 Disappearance Just Now Comes to Light," *Dallas Morning News,* February 23, 2013.

48. *to Houston, Chicago, and Atlanta.:* "DEA Announces Gulf Cartel/Los Zetas Most-Wanted List," Press release, July 23, 2009.

48. *rights record in Guatemala itself.:* "Official: Mexican Cartels Hiring Common Criminals," Associated Press, April 7, 2011.

48. *leader were among those arrested.:* "Mexico Fears Its Drug Traffickers Get Help From Guatemalans," *New York Times,* September 30, 2005.

48. *intelligence alert also mentioned the suspected presence of Kabiles within the Zetas.:* "Guatemala troops tied to border drug war," *San Antonio Express-News,* August 18, 2005.

49. *Alberto Briceño, aka El Beto.:* "Matan a reo ligado a narcos en Nuevo Laredo; le imputaban ocho homicidios," *La Jornada,* November 21, 2005.

49. *walking openly armed throughout town.:* "Mexican Drug Lords Increasingly Powerful," Associated Press, November 7, 2005.

49. *drugs into the United States.:* "Convicted of bribery, Starr lawman became cop despite prior felony plea," *Monitor,* April 12, 2013.

49. *Zetas and the Gulf Cartel.:* Corchado, Alfredo. *Midnight in Mexico: A Reporter's Journey Through a Country's Descent into Darkness.* New York: Penguin, 2013, 159–60.

49. *allegedly belonged to La Barbie.:* "An American Drug Lord in Acapulco," *Rolling Stone,* August 25, 2011.

49. *corrupt PJF had been retained.:* "Drug Gangs Corrupt Mexico's Elite FBI," Reuters, December 6, 2005.

50. *immediately grew in its place.:* Ravelo, Ricardo. *Narcomex: Historia e historias de una guerra.* Mexico City: Vintage Español, 2012, 28–29.

50. *Texas side of the border.:* "Border Face-Off Involved Men in Mexican Army Uniforms," Associated Press, January 24, 2006.

50. *to big-time cartel operations.:* "Earlier ATF Gun Operation 'Wide Receiver' Used Same Tactics as Fast and Furious," *Washington Post,* October 6, 2011.

50. *stopped by police opened fire.:* "7 Die in Acapulco Shootout," Reuters, January 27, 2006.

50. *pickup to drive to work.:* "Matan a periodista de radio en Nuevo Laredo," *El Universal,* March 10, 2006.

50. *let out for the day.:* "Plainclothes Officers Shot in Mexico," Associated Press, March 16, 2006.

50. *that you learn to respect.":* "US Offers Its Help as Drug Violence Rages," *Washington Post,* April 30, 2006.

51. *saying they were from Cárdenas.:* "Mexico Denies Drug Suspect Paid for Party," Associated Press, April 30, 2006.

51. *Rio Grande for Laredo.:* "Cartels Grip a Border City," *Dallas Morning News,* February 24, 2007.

51. *of drug dealers and murderers.":* "$5M Bounty on Drug Don," Associated Press, June 20, 2006.

51. *Jaime "El Hummer" González Durán.:* "Cartel Leader Believed Slain in Reynosa Violence," *Monitor,* February 17, 2009.

51. *Fox himself in January 2004.:* "Mexico Passes Law Making Possession of Some Drugs Legal," *New York Times,* April 29, 2006.

51. *mending fences and building roads.:* "National Guard Deployment on US-Mexico Border Has Unclear Results," *Washington Post,* December 5, 2011.

51. *actually fallen by 37 percent.:* Corchado, *Midnight in Mexico,* 194.

52. *as a "coward.":* "Candidate Skips Debate; Did He Make a Mistake?" Associated Press, April 26, 2006.

52. *on advertisements against López Obrador.:* "Long History of Vote Fraud Lingers in the Mexican Psyche," *New York Times,* September 6, 2006.

53. *response was even more brutal.:* "Women of Atenco," Amnesty International.

53. *been involved in criminal behavior.:* "Presidents Obama and Peña Nieto's Summit Golden Opportunity to Tackle Human Rights Issues," Amnesty International, April 30, 2013.

53. *López Obrador 35.7 percent.:* "Rivals Declare Victory in Mexican Election," Associated Press, July 3, 2006.

53. *process or affect the results.":* "Tensions Grow Over Mexico Vote as Opposition Plans Rally Saturday," *New York Times,* July 8, 2006.

53. *"there will be instability":* "Leftist Predicts Unrest without Complete Recount of Mexican Election," *New York Times,* July 9, 2006.

53. *demand for a complete recount.:* "Mexico Tribunal Rejects Demand for Vote Recount," *New York Times,* August 5, 2006.

53. *police outside of Mexico's Congress.:* "Protesters Clash with Mexican Police," Associated Press, August 14, 2006.

53. *challenges to the electoral result,:* "Calderón Near Win as Mexican Court Backs Vote," Reuters, August 28, 2006.

53. *out of forty-one million cast.:* "Felipe Calderón: A Politician at Birth," *New York Times,* September 6, 2006.

54. *once preeminent, fell to third.:* "Mexico Leftist to Create Parallel Gov't," Associated Press, August 29, 2006.

54. *make a lunge for power.:* "As Infamous Mexican Cartel Totters, Violence Grows," Associated Press, April 29, 2009.

54. *drug trafficking and money laundering.:* "Former FBI Chief for EP Found Guilty of 2 Charges," *El Paso Times,* August 17, 2006.

54. *[the Lebanese Shiite militia] Hezbollah"*: "House Approves US-Mexican Border Fence," Associated Press, September 14, 2006.

54. *in favor of the act.*: "US-Mexico Fence Building Continues Despite Obama's Promise to Review Effects," *Greenwire*, April 16, 2009.

55. *both federal and state courts."*: "Sec. 102 of H.R. 418, Waiver of Laws Necessary for Improvement of Barriers at Borders," Congressional Research Service, February 9, 2005.

55. *not suspected of unlawful behavior."*: "Reform the Patriot Act," American Civil Liberties Union, May 26, 2011.

55. *51-foot ladder at the border."*: "Arizona Officials, Fed Up with US Efforts, Seek Donations to Build Border Fence," *New York Times*, July 19, 2011.

55. *Electoral Tribunal on September 5.* "Calderón Named Mexico's President-Elect," Associated Press, September 5, 2006.

55. *"to hell with their institutions!"*: "Leftist Vows to Create Separate Gov't," Associated Press, September 5, 2006.

56. *vowed to block Calderón's inauguration.*: "Poll Finds Most Mexicans Oppose Protest," Associated Press, November 27, 2006.

56. *the ceremonial presidential sash.*: Upon leaving office, Fox's personal wealth became the subject of some debate. See "Mexico's Former President Rebukes Critics of His Wealth," *Los Angeles Times*, October 9, 2007.

56. *our nation above our differences."*: "Mexico's New Leader Takes Charge," BBC News, December 1, 2006.

56. *PRD section of the house.*: "Fracas Mars Mexico Inauguration," BBC News, December 2, 2006.

56. *human heads into their midst.*: "Mexican Gunmen Roll Human Heads onto Bar Floor," Associated Press, September 7, 2006.

56. *something you see every day."*: "With Beheadings and Attacks, Drug Gangs Terrorize Mexico," *New York Times*, October 26, 2006.

Chapter Four

57. *"a means of communication"; of the ceremony is destroyed."*: Hubert, Henry and Mauss, Marcel. *Sacrifice: Its Nature and Functions.* Chicago: University of Chicago Press, 1964, 97.

57. *our very way of life."*: "US Officials Laud Transfer of Mexican Drug Suspects," *Washington Post*, January 21, 2007.

57. *"highly secretive hearing"*: "Mexican Drug Kingpin Sentenced to 25 Years in Secret Hearing," *New York Times*, February 25, 2010.

57. Titanic, *perhaps curiously unfortunate symbolism."*: "Decomisan a 'El Coss' relojes hechos con restos del *Titanic*," *El Universal*, September 12, 2012.

58. *way to the United States.*: "Heriberto Lazcano desplazó a sucesores naturales de Osiel Cárdenas, revelan Desertor del Ejército, nuevo líder del cártel del Golfo: informes castrenses," *La Jornada*, February 3, 2008.

58. *and assassins for the cartel.*: "Las panteras, entrenadas para matar," *La Jornada*, April 15, 2009.

58. *general Mauro Enrique Tello Quiñones.*: "Cae célula de Los Zetas que ejecutó al general," *Milenio*, December 2, 2009.

59. *from $1,550 to $3,876 monthly.:* "Cartel Boss: Everyone from Cops to Strippers Worked for Me," *San Antonio Express News,* September 22, 2012.

59. *Tamaulipas, Sinaloa, Guerrero, and Michoacán.:* "Mexican President-Elect Decries Violence," Associated Press, September 27, 2006.

59. *had taken place in Michoacán.:* "The Tough Get Going," *Economist,* January 25, 2007.

59. *Mexico had increased 58 percent.:* "Marching as to War," *Economist,* January 31, 2008.

59. *from Los Zetas' El Hummer.:* "'El Hummer' podría ser el asesino de Valentín," *El Debate,* November 8, 2008.

59. *be arrested for the crime.:* "Detienen a presunto asesino de Valentín Elizalde," *El Siglo de Torreón,* March 22, 2008.

59. *"La santisima muerte" (about La Flaca herself).:* Osorno, Diego Enrique. *La guerra de Los Zetas: Viaje por la frontera de la necropolítica.* Mexico City: Grijalbo, 2012, 53.

59. *he followed suit in Tijuana.:* "Calderón cracks down," January 8, 2007, *The Economist Intelligence Unit ViewsWire.*

60. *: of the methamphetamine precursor ephedrine.:* "Mexico Orders Army Offensive Against Drug Gangs," Reuters, December 11, 2006.

60. *much as a follow-up meeting.* Corchado, Alfredo. *Midnight in Mexico: A Reporter's Journey Through a Country's Descent into Darkness.* New York: Penguin, 2013, 176–77.

60. *just outside of Mexico City.:* "Mexican First Lady's Cousin Found Shot to Death," Associated Press, December 14, 2006.

60. *in running the Gulf Cartel.:* "Capturaron a Mario Cárdenas Guillén, uno de los jefes del cártel del Golfo," Univision, September 4, 2012.

60. *"fighting without pause"; "win the war on crime.".:* "Calderón Vows War on Organized Crime," Associated Press, January 22, 2007.

60. *his life in the struggle.:* Corchado, *Midnight in Mexico,* 174.

60. *tasked with fighting organized crime.:* "Perfil: Noé Ramírez Mandujano," *El Universal,* November 21, 2009.

61. *a finger to do anything":* Author interview, December 2012.

61. *a family allegedly selling drugs.:* "Rodolfo Rincón Taracena," Committee to Protect Journalists, March 1, 2010.

61. *"no truce and no quarter":* "Calderón Vows No Yield in War on Drug Cartels," Associated Press, February 11, 2007.

61. *headed to the city's airport.:* "Cartels Grip a Border City," *Dallas Morning News,* February 24, 2007.

61. *known as the Mérida Initiative.:* The Mérida Initiative: Guns, Drugs and Friends, A Report to Members of the Committee on Foreign Relations of the United States Senate, December 21, 2007.

61. *build strong and resilient communities.":* Mérida Initiative Fact Sheet, US Department of State, www.state.gov/j/inl/merida/, accessed October 2, 2013.

61. *the Dominican Republic, and Haiti.:* "Merida Initiative: Myth vs. Fact," Bureau of International Narcotics and Law Enforcement Affairs, US Department of State, June 23, 2009.

62. *used marijuana in the past,.:* "Bush Hinted at Use of Marijuana," BBC, February 21, 2005.

62. *to factor into this decision.:* "Bush Dodges Cocaine Claims as Campaign Hots Up," *Independent,* August 12, 1999.

62. *the state police in Tabasco.:* "Mexican Drug War Getting Bloodier," McClatchy News Service, March 21, 2007.

62. *kill a Zeta!"; "Lazcano, you're next!".:* "Web Video Shows Mexico Man's Beheading," Associated Press, April 1, 2007.

62. *ritualistic* esprit de corps.*:* "Confirman la muerte de Z-14, fundador de Los Zetas," *La Jornada,* September 4, 2007.

62. *slayings in Mexico that year.:* "Police Find 17 Bodies Across Mexico," Associated Press, April 16, 2007.

62. *according to the DEA.:* "Mexican Drug Cartels Expand Abroad," Associated Press, July 21, 2009.

63. *three more burned in Culiacán.:* "Police Find 17 Bodies Across Mexico," Associated Press, April 16, 2007.

63. *in the city's colonial center.:* "Capturan a presunto líder de célula del cártel del Golfo," *El Universal,* April 17, 2007.

63. *service of the Gulf Cartel.".:* "Capturan a El Chelelo, operador del cártel del Golfo," *El Universal,* April 23, 2007.

63. *dead and two policemen wounded.:* "Capturan en Campeche al fundador de Los Zetas," *La Jornada,* April 18, 2007.

63. *from partying the night before.:* "Es detenido Luis Reyes Enríquez/Bulletin 290/07," Procuradura General de la República (Mexico), June 25, 2007.

63. *and Jesús Enrique "El Mamito" Rejón.:* "Gulf Cartel, and Its Enforcers, Began Control of Northern Mexico in 2001," *San Antonio Express-News,* April 20, 2013.

63. *and one cartel gunman dead.:* "Five Dead in Mexico Drug Cartel Shootout," Associated Press, May 5, 2007.

63. *reported in Mexico: 23.5* tonnes.*:* "Marching as to War," *Economist,* January 31, 2008.

63. *was already at twelve hundred.:* "State of Siege," *Economist,* June 14, 2007.

64. *dismantling of the trafficking operation.".:* PROJECT GUNRUNNER: A Cartel Focused Strategy, US Department of Justice memorandum, Bureau of Alcohol, Tobacco, Firearms and Explosives, Office of Field Operations, September 2010.

64. *study it some more.:* "Some Texans Fear Border Fence Will Sever Routine of Daily Life," *New York Times,* June 20, 2007.

64. *satellite technology and vehicle barriers.".:* "Work on Texas Border Wall to Begin Soon: Chertoff," Reuters, July 19, 2007.

64. *been paid to the company.:* "Chertoff Won't Pay Boeing until It Fixes Virtual Fence," Associated Press, September 21. 2007.

64. *degrade the environment"; bottles and other artifacts.".:* "Chertoff Border-Fence Statement Is Nonsense," *Miami Herald,* October 8, 2007.

65. *"a huge error".:* "Building a Wall Around US a 'Huge Error': Mexican President-Elect," Agence France-Presse, October 26, 2006.

65. *to discuss a possible truce.:* "Las confesiones de 'La Barbie' Edgar Valdez Villareal," http://youtu.be/G21xolHm9lc, ejeCentral TV, accessed September 29, 2013.

65. *his brother, Armando Valdez Villareal.:* "Aquí se ofrecían 30 mdp por su cabeza," *La Prensa,* August 31, 2010.

65. *for less than a year.:* Corchado, *Midnight in Mexico,* 6–10.

65. *atole the church provided.:* "Santa Muerte de Tepito cumple seis años," *EFE,* November 1, 2007.

65. *for the public prosecutor's office,:* "Singer Shot in Mexico ER New Victim of Drug War," *Houston Chronicle,* December 3, 2007.

65. *Morelio bearing sings of torture.:* "Comando armado secuestra y asesina a Sergio Gómez, vocalista de K-Paz," *La Jornada,* December 4, 2007.

65. *of a Río Bravo restaurant.:* "3 Americans Arrested in Gang Battle with Mexican Police," *New York Times,* January 9, 2008.

66. *pay more than market price.":* "Chertoff Warns Landowners Against Blocking Border Fence," *Los Angeles Times,* December 8, 2007.

66. *three federal police officers wounded.:* "3 Killed in Mexican Border Town Shootout," Associated Press, January 7, 2008.

66. *two dozen automatic pistols.:* "3 Americans Arrested in Gang Battle with Mexican Police," *New York Times,* January 9, 2008.

66. *that reported to Heriberto Lazcano.:* "Mexico Takes Fight to Zeta Drug Gang," *Dallas Morning News,* January 10, 2008.

66. *suspected Zetas in Reynosa.:* "3 Killed in Central Mexican Shooting," Associated Press, January 11, 2008.

66. *who is against you.":* "The Long War of Genaro García Luna," *New York Times,* July 13, 2008.

66. *there during the coming year.:* Vulliamy, Ed. *Amexica: War Along the Borderline.* New York: Picador, 2010, 34.

67. *cache of heavy weapons.:* "Mexican Intelligence Helps Nab High-Ranking Official, 3 Bodyguards," *Dallas Morning News,* January 22, 2008.

67. *at two Mexico City mansions.:* "Mexico Captures 11 Alleged Hit Men," Associated Press, January 22, 2008.

67. *bring down entire buildings.:* "Drug Trade Tyranny on the Border," *Washington Post,* March 16, 2008.

67. *cocaine into the United States.:* "Ex jefe de policía de Tamaulipas admite nexos con el CDG," *El Nuevo Herald,* March 5, 2013.

67. *in 2012 and plead guilty.):* "Mexican Police Commander Took the Cartel's Offer He Couldn't Refuse, He Confesses in US Court," *Houston Chronicle,* March 4, 2013.

67. *during a raid in Tijuana.:* "Mexico Seizes Arsenal, Drugs in Tijuana," Associated Press, March 7, 2008.

67. *place still awash in violence.:* "The Long War of Genaro García Luna," *New York Times,* July 13, 2008.

67. *both sides of the border.":* "ATF: New Accord with Mexico Will Boost Gun Traces," Associated Press, October 6, 2010.

68. *man had fired a gun.:* Uniform Impunity: Mexico's Misuse of Military Justice to Prosecute Abuses in Counternarcotics and Public Security Operations, Human Rights Watch, April 2009.

68. *Los Zetas in Guatemala.:* "Los Zetas: el dolor de cabeza del próximo Presidente," *El Periódico,* October 2, 2011.

68. *deputy to Guatemala's congress.:* Hidden Powers in Post-Conflict Guatemala, Washington Office on Latin America, 2003.

69. *guys are Ortega Menaldo's guys.":* Author interview, Guatemala City, August 2008.

69. *attributed to bad weather.:* "Drugs vs. Democracy in Guatemala," *World Policy Journal,* Winter 2008/09.

69. *Guatemala's long border with Mexico.:* Author interview, Guatemala City, August 2008.

69. *behest of organized crime.:* "Absuelven a Quintanilla de espionaje presidencial," *Presna Libre,* October 14, 2010.

69. *that organized crime had torn":* "Anuncian Operativo Conjunto Chihuahua," *Notimex,* March 27, 2008.

69. *who ran afoul of him.:* "Juicio civil a general de Ojinaga: Los crímenes del general Manuel de Jesús Moreno Aviña," *El Heraldo de Chihuahua,* September 5, 2012.

70. *supremacy in the region.:* "Mexican General, 29 Soldiers on Trial for Homicide," Associated Press, January 31, 2012.

70. *trial has yet taken place.:* "Mexico Moves Away from Secret Military Tribunals," *Washington Post,* November 12, 2012.

70. *PFP inspector, was slain.:* "Golpea a la SSP Cártel de Sinaloa," *Diario Cambio,* May 9, 2008.

70. *hospital a few hours later.:* "Gunmen Kill Chief of Mexico's Police," *New York Times,* May 9, 2008.

70. *health of the Mexican people.":* "Ranking Security Official Slain in Mexico," *Los Angeles Times,* May 9, 2008.

70. *Beltrán Leyva the previous January.:* "Sentencian a 60 años de prisión al asesino de mando de la Policía Federal," *La Jornada,* June 12, 2011.

70. *were damaged in the assault.:* "Sinaloa, en jaque por la violencia tras ser asesinado hijo del Chapo," *La Jornada,* May 10, 2008.

70. *SSP head Genaro García Luna.:* "Cercano a García Luna, mando de la PFP ejecutado en la capital," *La Jornada,* June 27, 2008.

71. *mistreatment and don't go hungry.":* "Mexican Cartel Recruiting Hitmen," Associated Press, April 14, 2008.

71. *Territory of the Gulf Cartel.":* "Mexican Drug Cartels Making Audacious Pitch for Recruits," *Washington Post,* May 7, 2008.

71. *on the Gulf Cartel's payroll.:* "Mexico Agents Arrest Border Police Chief," Associated Press, April 17, 2008.

71. *endless debate or protracted litigation,":* "Power to Build Border Fence Is Above US Law," *New York Times,* April 8, 2008.

71. *father of the drug war.:* "Michael Chertoff's Insult," *New York Times,* April 3, 2008.

71. *construction of the border fence.:* "Texas Officials Sue US over Border Fence," *Tucson Citizen,* May 16, 2008.

72. *repair shop on July 10, 2008,:* "10 Dead in Northern Mexico Shootings," Reuters, July 10, 2008.

72. *police were deployed to Sinaloa.:* "Mexico Under Siege," *Los Angeles Times,* July 16, 2008.

72. *by more than 15 percent.:* "Progress in Mexico Drug War Is Drenched in Blood," Associated Press, March 11, 2009.

72. *"obligated to confront crime"; "a pact":* "The Long War of Genaro García Luna," *New York Times,* July 13, 2008.

72. *"coward"; the country's peace and tranquillity.":* "Grenade Attack in Mexico Breaks from Deadly Script," *New York Times,* September 25, 2008.

73. *"grotesque montage":* "Former Mexican State Official Accused," *Los Angeles Times,* August 16, 2008.

73. *bloody hatchet was also found.:* "Mexican Police Suspect That Heads Burned in Ritual," Associated Press, September 1, 2008.

73. *by the Beltrán-Leyva Cartel.:* "Encuentran a 24 ejecutados en La Marquesa," *Milenio,* September 13, 2008.

73. *try to root out corruption.:* "Mexican Border City Desperate to Recruit Police," Associated Press, October 18, 2008.

73. *from Mexico through the county.:* "On the Borderline of Good and Evil," *Los Angeles Times,* April 3, 2009.

73. *accountant for the Gulf Cartel.:* "Zetas' Power Began as Enforcers for Gulf Cartel," *San Antonio Express-News,* April 20, 2013.

73. *names of informants against them.:* "On the Borderline of Good and Evil," *Los Angeles Times,* April 3, 2009.

73. *sentence that he had faced.:* "Ex-Texas Sheriff Gets 5 Years for Helping Drug Cartel," *San Antonio Express-News,* August 27, 2009.

73. *sitting unclaimed for a week.:* "Mexico: Human Heads Sent to Police in Ice Chest," Associated Press, October 2, 2008.

74. *a message threatening La Familia.:* "2 Human Heads with Drug Messages Found in Mexico," Associated Press, October 24, 2008.

74. *was hurt in the incident.:* "US consulate in Mexico Attacked with Gun, Grenade," Reuters, October 13, 2008.

74. *in which we all believe.":* "Ofrece Calderón condolencias a familia de Mouriño," *El Universal,* November 4, 2008.

74. *but were successfully fought off.:* "Es 'El Hummer' probable ejecutor de Valentín Elizalde," *El Universal,* November 8, 2008.

74. *fourteen sticks of dynamite.:* "Largest Cartel Weapons Cache Found in Mexico," Associated Press, November 8, 2008.

74. *comrade might have been betrayed.:* "Cartel Leader Believed Slain in Reynosa Violence," *Monitor,* February 17, 2009.

75. *were dumped in a field.:* "Tijuana's Bloody Weekend Ends with Discovery of Nine Headless Corpses," *Guardian,* December 2, 2008.

75. *was killed by the state,":* "To Kill a Journalist: The Unsolved Murder of Armando Rodriguez," *Texas Observer,* January 24, 2013.

75. *Sinaloa and Beltrán-Leyva cartels.:* "Mexico Traffickers Bribed Former Anti-Drug Chief, Officials Say," *Los Angeles Times,* November 22, 2008.

75. *not been heard from since.:* "American Anti-Kidnap Expert Vanishes," Associated Press, December 16, 2008.

75. *police station killed ten people.:* "Gunbattle Kills 10 in Northern Mexico State," Associated Press, December 11, 2008.

75. *student charges would be kidnapped.:* "Mexican Schools Close as Children Are Threatened," Associated Press, December 10, 2008.

75. kill, I will kill 10.*":* "Mexico Honors Soldiers Beheaded by Drug Cartels," Associated Press, December 22, 2008.

75. *different parts of her body.:* "Women Play a Bigger Role in Mexico's Drug War," *Los Angeles Times,* November 10, 2009.

76. *Mexico since the previous year.:* "Mexico Says Gang Killings Up 117 Percent to 5,376," Associated Press, December 9, 2008.

76. *were 443 murders in Tijuana.:* "As Infamous Mexican Cartel Totters, Violence Grows," Associated Press, April 26, 2009.

76. *narco demands for protection money.:* "Mexico Cartels Go from Drugs to Full-Scale Mafias," Associated Press, August 17, 2009.

76. *830 million, consumed $34 billion.:* "US Must Act to Curb Violence in Mexico," *Miami Herald,* December 22, 2010.

76. *proportions to the United States.":* "Joint Operating Environment 2008," United States Joint Forces Command, November 25, 2008.

Chapter Five

77. *cooperation between the two countries.:* "Dealing with Drugs," *Economist,* May 5, 2009.

78. *with cost overruns and missed deadlines.":* "Janet Napolitano Halts Funding for Virtual Border Fence," *Christian Science Monitor,* March 17, 2010.

78. *mile between 2007 and 2008.:* "Secure Border Initiative Fence Construction Costs," United States Government Accountability Office, January 29, 2009.

78. *illegally built on Mexican territory.:* "Border Fence Built in Mexico By Mistake," Associated Press, February 11, 2009.

79. *from one hundred yards away.:* Author interview, Brownsville, November 2013.

79. *to 1,338,970 by October 2000.":* Charter Evolution in Maquiladoras: A Case Study of Reynosa, Tamaulipas, The University of Texas–Pan American Working Paper #2003-16, January 2003.

79. *vehicles produced by GM Canada.:* "Canada Spends Big to Save GM, So Why Not Mexico?" *Time,* July 3, 2009.

80. *contracted by almost 30 percent.:* INTERNATIONAL TRADE: Mexico's Maquiladora Decline Affects US-Mexico Border Communities and Trade; Recovery Depends in Part on Mexico's Actions, United States General Accounting Office, July 2003.

80. *about 240 pesos (USD 18) per day.":* "Tamaulipas, el pilar industrial," *El Economista,* June 30, 2010.

80. *second-highest category at 55.84 pesos.":* "Mexico to Raise Minimum Wage 4.85 Percent on Average in 2010," Bloomberg, December 17, 2009.

80. *country's chemical and petrochemical production.:* "Tamaulipas, el pilar industrial," *El Economista,* June 30, 2010.

80. *electronics, auto parts, and communications.:* INTERNATIONAL TRADE: Mexico's Maquiladora Decline Affects US-Mexico Border Communities and Trade; Recovery Depends in Part on Mexico's Actions, United States General Accounting Office, July 2003.

80. *to go to the States.":* Author interview, Matamoros, November 2013.

81. *wholesale collapse other countries faced.:* "After Six Years, Mexico's President Felipe Calderon Fell Short of Goals," Fox News Latino, November 30, 2012.

81. *allotted to the whole country.:* Subsidizing Inequality: Mexican Corn Policy Since NAFTA, Woodrow Wilson International Center for Scholars, 2010.

81. *to be paid the difference.:* "Mexican Farmers Affected By Agricultural Subsidies from NAFTA, Other International Agreements," *Huffington Post,* January 11, 2013.

81. *lost in Nuevo León alone.:* "A One-Two Punch," *Economist,* May 27, 2010.

81. *than three dollars per day.:* "On 200th Birthday, Mexico Battered but Not Broken," Associated Press, September 12, 2010.

82. *corrupt and murderous country.:* Ibid.

82. *during the course of 2008.:* Corchado, Alfredo. *Midnight in Mexico: A Reporter's Journey Through a Country's Descent into Darkness.* New York: Penguin, 2013, 194.

82. *Monterrey along the US-Mexico border.:* "22 Killed in Surging Wave of Violence in Mexico," Agence France-Presse, January 29, 2009.

82. *have to teach by example.":* "Torturada y asesinada una exalcaldesa mexicana," *El País,* November 19, 2012.

82. *weapons seized since December 2005.:* "Mexico Says Gulf Cartel Is Most Violent Gang," Associated Press, January 29, 2009.

82. *for protecting them from arrest.:* "Police: Drug Turf Battles Near Mexico's Capital," Associated Press, February 12, 2009.

82. *southwestern part of the city.:* "Cartel Leader Believed Slain in Reynosa Violence," *Monitor,* February 17, 2009.

83. *now he's with the crew"; "leads from the front"; send you straight to hell.":* "Underground Reynosa Rappers Sing About Narco Life," *Monitor,* July 6, 2013.

83. *name "Comandante Veneno" (Commander Venom).:* "Some Cartel Bosses Are Born in the US, but Work in Mexico," *Monitor,* June 22, 2013.

83. *Comales area of Tamaulipas.:* "Convicted of Bribery, Starr Lawman Became Cop Despite Prior Felony Plea," *Monitor,* April 12, 2013.

83. *the Gulf Cartel and Los Zetas"; transport of drugs into Texas.":* Texas Gang Threat Assessment 2010: A State Intelligence Estimate, Produced by the Texas Fusion Center (Intelligence & Counterterrorism Division) for the Texas Department of Public Safety, September 2010.

83. *US consulate in Monterrey.:* "Cartels' Youth Recruitment Worries Authorities," *San Antonio Express-News,* December 6, 2009.

84. *viewed as products, not people.":* Author interview, Matamoros, November 2013.

85. *devotion that I go on.":* Author interview, Reynosa, November 2013.

85. *part of a national network.":* "Mexico Governor: Cartels Behind Northern Protests," Associated Press, February 13, 2009.

85. *be an affiliate of Los Zetas.:* "Detienen en Monterrey a 'El Queco,'" *La Vanguardia,* February 12, 2009.

85. *any single part—of Mexican territory.*": "Mexico Prez Hopes to Quell Drug Violence by 2012," Associated Press, February 27, 2009.

86. *in Mexico, at a minimum.*": "Holder Revives Talk of an Assault Weapons Ban," CBS News, February 26, 2009.

86. *percent—supporting such a ban.*: "Poll: Majority Support Assault Weapons Ban," *Hill,* December 20, 2012.

86. *problem turned into a war"; than the war among cartels.*": "Rights Activist Cites Mexican Army Abuses," *El Paso Times,* February 27, 2009.

87. *unrelenting fight against organized crime.*": "Drugs and Democracy: Toward a Paradigm Shift," Latin American Commission on Drugs and Democracy, February 2009.

88. *neighborhood of $10 billion.*: "Progress in Mexico Drug War Is Drenched in Blood," Associated Press, March 11, 2009.

88. *intelligence work on Mexican cartels.*: "White House Steps Up Anti-Cartel Fight on Border," Associated Press, March 24, 2009.

88. *after he had been kidnapped.*: "Hallan muerto a funcionario de Tancítaro, Michoacán, levantado ayer," *El Porvenir,* March 7, 2009.

88. *homicide, drug-trafficking, and kidnapping indictments.*: "Mexican Army Announces Drug Cartel Arrests," Associated Press, March 23, 2009.

88. *of bullets were also seized.*: "Mexican Drug Cartels Expand Abroad," Associated Press, July 21, 2009.

88. *with federal police in Zacatecas.*: "Mexico: Guatemalan Ex-Soldier in Cartel Pay Killed," Associated Press, April 9, 2009.

88. *been destined for the Zetas.*: "Mexico Drug Cartel's Grenades from Guatemalan Army," Associated Press, June 4, 2009.

89. *far beyond its narco adherents.*: "Mexico's Death Cult Protests Shrine Destruction," Associated Press, April 5, 2009.

89. *I'm not a narco"; "holy war":* "Declaran 'guerra santa' en México," BBC Mundo, April 6, 2009.

89. *candidates, in the forthcoming elections.*: Chesnut, R. Andrew. *Devoted to Death: Santa Muerte, the Skeleton Saint.* New York: Oxford University Press, 2012, 114.

89. *with Calderón in the capital.*: "15 Gunmen, 1 Soldier Killed in Mexican Shootout," Associated Press, April 16, 2009.

89. *murder of a Puebla businessman.*: "Houston Man Sentenced for Smuggling Guns Friday," Associated Press, April 17, 2009.

89. *that left seven people dead.*: "US Stymied as Guns Flow to Mexican Cartels," *New York Times,* April 15, 2009.

89. *to record the buyer's name.*: Ibid.

89. *by quantity or time period.*: "A Review of ATF's Operation Fast and Furious and Related Matters," US Department of Justice Office of the Inspector General. November 2012.

90. *connection with a firearms purchase.*: US Code Title 18, via United States Government Printing Office, www.gpo.gov/fdsys/browse/collectionUScode. action?collectionCode=USCODE, accessed May 29, 2013.

90. *including the authorities knows this."; "an almost chaotic psychosis":* "El Chapo vive en Durango: Arzobispo," *El Universal,* April 18, 2009.

90. *to a certain degree, irresponsible.":* "Mexican Priests: We're Targets of Drug Violence," Associated Press, April 20, 2009.

90. *assault rifles and hand grenades.:* "Detenidos en un bautizo 44 miembros de un cartel," *El País,* April 20, 2009.

90. *drinking and maintain family unity.":* "Cartel Tells Smugglers to Live 'Clean' Life," Reuters, April 20, 2009.

90. *around Acapulco on April 24.:* "9 Found Dead in and around Mexican Resort," Associated Press, April 24, 2009.

90. *an hour of one another.:* "Attacks Kill 7 Mexican Police in Tijuana," Associated Press, April 28, 2009.

91. *the end of the month.:* "Mexico Arrests Drug Gang Boss," BBC, April 30, 2009.

91. *being accomplices to the jailbreak.:* "Suspected Drug Gang Frees 53 from Mexico Prison," Reuters, May 17, 2009.

91. *members of the Beltrán-Leyva Cartel.:* "Shootout Kills 16 in Mexico's Acapulco Resort," Associated Press, June 7, 2009.

91. *police officers in the city.:* "Acapulco, Long Dotted with Tourists, Is Now Home to Drug War," *New York Times,* June 9, 2009.

91. *more independent than ever before.:* "In Mexican City, Drug War Ills Slip into Shadows," *New York Times,* June 13, 2009.

91. *agreement would in fact work.:* "Tamaulipas Police Team Up with FBI, DEA," *Valley Central,* June 30, 2009.

91. *but missing their intended target.:* "12 Killed in Shootout in Central Mexico," Associated Press, June 26, 2009.

92. *maker of methamphetamine in Mexico.:* "Taking on the Unholy Family," *Economist,* July 23, 2009.

92. *five federal agents and two soldiers.:* "Gunmen Attack Federal Forces in Mexico," Associated Press, July 11, 2009.

92. *to be heard from again.:* "Police Find 12 Tortured Bodies in Mexico," Associated Press, July 14, 2009.

92. *be those of federal agents.:* "Mexico Identifies 12 Slain as Federal Agents," Associated Press, July 15, 2009.

92. *Federal Ministerial (PFM) and the Policía Federal (PF).:* "Police Reform in Mexico: Advances and Persistent Obstacles," Working Paper Series on US-Mexico Security Collaboration, Woodrow Wilson International Center for Scholars Mexico Institute, May 2010.

92. *lost five high-profile gubernatorial races.:* "Opposition Wins Majority in Mexican Vote," *New York Times,* July 5, 2009.

92. *agenda, and we have ours.":* "Mexico's Embattled President," *Economist,* September 10, 2009.

92. *several cars in flames.:* "La venganza golpea en Veracruz," *El País,* July 31, 2009.

93. *Jiménez González, only days earlier.:* Ibid.

93. *cocaine from Colombia to Mexico.":* "Assessment of 'Los Zetas' Evolution and Expansion (2001–2009)," Cable from US Drug Enforcement Administration (DEA) Houston office to DEA headquarters in Washington, DC, circa July 2009.

93. *Miguel Treviño, and Alejandro Treviño.:* "DEA Announces Gulf Cartel/Los Zetas Most-Wanted List," Press release, July 23, 2009.

93. *planning to assassinate the president.:* "Cae sicario que planeaba ataque contra el Presidente," *El Universal,* August 10, 2009.

93. *bullet to the head.:* "Las cinco muertes de Raquenel Villanueva," *El Mundo,* August 10, 2009.

94. *assassin of various military personnel.:* "Arraigan a presunto autor de atentado contra Consulado de EU," *El Universal,* August 10, 2009.

94. *other reporters having gone missing.:* "Report: 52 Mexican Reporters Killed in Last Decade," Associated Press, August 19, 2009.

94. *some sort of received gospel.:* "Narcotráfico: Políticos y empresarios, detrás de La Familia que ha capitalizado estrategia anticrimen fallida," *El Universal,* July 22, 2009.

94. *municipality of Coyuca de Catalán.:* "Mexican State Lawmaker Killed," Associated Press, August 20, 2009.

95. *she blamed on the army.:* "Matan a defensora de la zona agrícola en Ciudad Juárez," *El Universal,* January 5, 2010.

95. *gunned down seventeen people.:* "Gunmen Kill 17 People at a Drug Rehab in Mexico," Associated Press, September 4, 2009.

95. *one of Morelia's busiest thoroughfares.:* "Alto funcionario asesinado en Michoacán," Univision, September 3, 2009.

95. *"obsession":* "Tabasco: menor de 16 años planeó el crimen," *Milenio,* September 7, 2009.

95. *during his tenure in office.:* "Calderón Criticized for Naming Controversial Ex-Prosecutor as Attorney General," *Washington Post Foreign,* September 9, 2009.

95. *totally unexpected and politically inexplicable"; number of women in Ciudad Juárez.".:* Cable from US Embassy in Mexico to US Department of State, VZCZCXRO5911, September 15, 2009 (http://wikileaks.jornada.com.mx/cables/gobierno-felipe-Calderón/controvertida-nominacion-de-arturo-chavez-chavez-como-procurador-general-cable-09mexico2701).

96. *Rio Grande to El Paso.:* "Mexico: Human Rights Lawyer Threatened: Gustavo de la Rosa Hickerson," Amnesty International, October 5, 2009.

96. *Mexican army and police.:* Vulliamy, Ed. *Amexica: War Along the Borderline.* New York: Picador, 2010, 151–54.

96. *helping them track down snitches.:* "Former US Anti-Drug Official's Arrest 'a Complete Shock'," *Los Angeles Times,* September 17, 2009.

96. *federal judge in Miami.:* "Ex-ICE Agent Sentenced for Helping Smugglers," *Arizona Republic,* February 19, 2010.

96. *killed in the same bar.:* "5 Men Killed in Shooting in Mexico Border Bar," Associated Press, October 5, 2009.

96. *each year of his life.:* "Sedena presenta a sicario de La Línea," *El Universal,* October 6, 2009.

96. *found in a burned-out pickup.:* "Mayor Slain in Mexican Border Town," Associated Press, October 9, 2009.

96. *licenses, hanging from a bridge.:* "Era funcionario el hombre colgado de puente en Tijuana," *El Universal,* October 9, 2009.

Chapter Six

97. *things and fight for them.":* "Woman Mayor Shows Her Horrific Scars after Surviving Two Assassination Attempts by Mexican Gangs," *Daily Mail,* January 25, 2011.

97. *hundred arrests in nineteen states.:* "Crackdown on La Familia Cartel Leads to More Than 300 Arrests Across US," *Guardian,* October 23, 2009.

97. *of methamphetamine in eight hours.:* "La Familia Cartel Targeted, Police Arrest More Than 300 Across US," Associated Press, October 23, 2009.

98. *1937 land distribution measure.:* "Ejecutan en Sonora a Margarito Montes, líder de la UGOCP, y a 14 personas más," *La Jornada,* October 3, 2009.

98. *reference to Arturo Beltrán Leyva.:* "Mexican Mayor Announces Death of Drug Boss Hours Before Body Found," *Guardian,* November 5, 2009.

98. *they will pay for it.":* "Mexico Mayor Announces Death Before Body Is Found," Associated Press, November 3, 2009.

98. *"tough group"; "complicated things.":* "El comando 'rudo' de Mauricio Fernández," *Milenio,* November 3, 2009.

98. *"white knights or death squads.":* "Ojo por ojo: ¿Comandos blancos o escuadrones de la muerte?" *El Universal,* November 4, 2009.

98. *to take advantage of that.":* "Mexican Mayor Announces Death of Drug Boss Hours Before Body Found," *Guardian,* November 5, 2009.

98. *"vocation"; "kill those bastards":* "El Alcalde," A Film by Carlos F. Rossini, Emiliano Altuna and Diego Enrique Osorno, http://vimeo.com/18768132.

99. *for involvement in the killing.:* "Mexican Officers Accused of Role in Police Commander's Death," *Houston Chronicle,* November 9, 2009.

99. *aka El Araña (The Spider).:* "Zetas Leader Arrested in Monterrey," Action 4 News, October 22, 2010.

99. *Soledad de Doblado in Veracruz.:* "Pasillos del Poder: 'El Gonzo,' Solo en la Morgue," *El Piñero de la Cuenca,* November 5, 2009.

99. *for disappointing the letter Z).:* "Ejecutan a mando de la SSP," *Diario Liberal del Sur,* November 7, 2009.

99. *administration dubbed Operation Wide Receiver.:* "Documents Reveal Reactions to Disputed A.T.F. Investigations in Arizona," *New York Times,* October 31, 2011.

99. *administration for years to come.:* "A Review of ATF's Operation Fast and Furious and Related Matters," US Department of Justice Office of the Inspector General, November 2012.

100. *under Operation Fast and Furious.:* "The Department of Justice's Operation Fast and Furious: Fueling Cartel Violence," Joint Staff Report Prepared for Rep. Darrell E. Issa, Chairman of the United States House of Representatives Committee on Oversight and Government Reform, and Senator Charles E. Grassley, Ranking Member of the United States Senate Committee on the Judiciary, July 26, 2011.

100. *over Mexico before we acted.":* "Mexican President: Gangs Were 'Taking Over' Mexico," Associated Press, November 26, 2009.

100. *deaths of five people.:* "Matan a los líderes zetas en Nuevo León," *Milenio,* December 5, 2009.

100. *police officers in the process.:* "Shootouts in Northern Mexico Kill 13 After Raid," Associated Press, December 5, 2009.

100. *alluding to the Beltrán-Leyva Cartel.:* "8 Killed in Separate Attacks in Mexican State," Associated Press, December 11, 2009.

100. *woman and her three-year-old daughter.:* "Drug-Related Violence, Bombings Kill 50 in Mexico," Agence France-Presse, December 15, 2009.

101. *nearby town of Tepoztlán.:* "Mexican Drug Lord Is Killed in a Raid," *New York Times,* December 18, 2009.

101. *killed three alleged cartel members.:* "Mexican Kingpin's Death Could Spark More Bloodshed,"Associated Press, December 17, 2009.

101. *special forces of the Mexican navy.:* "US Law Enforcement Role in Mexico Drug War Surges," Associated Press, March 19, 2011.

101. *Another sister was injured.:* "Revenge in Drug War Chills Mexico," *New York Times,* December 23, 2009.

101. *killers were from Los Zetas.:* "Mexico Says Cartel Killed Hero Marine's Family," Associated Press, December 23, 2009.

101. *later be arrested in Culiacán.:* "Mexican Agents Arrest Brother of Beltran Leyva, Drug Lord Killed in Raid," *Washington Post,* January 4, 2010.

101. *were killed in the city.:* "Drug-Related Violence, Bombings Kill 50 in Mexico," Agence France-Presse, December 15, 2009.

101. *at least thirteen people died.:* "Drug Violence Leaves 23 Dead in Northern Mexico," Agence France-Presse, December 21, 2009.

101. *deploy a peacekeeping force there.:* "Mexico Border City Groups Call for UN Peace-keepers," Associated Press, November 12, 2009.

101. *Azteca) involvement in twenty-four.:* PROJECT GUNRUNNER: A Cartel Focused Strategy, US Department of Justice memorandum, Bureau of Alcohol, Tobacco, Fire-arms and Explosives, Office of Field Operations, September 2010.

102. *companies maintained operations in Mexico.:* "US Businesses Reluctant to Open in Mexico," Associated Press, May 15, 2011.

102. *Bank Secrecy Act in US history.:* "Wachovia's Drug Habit," *Bloomberg Markets Magazine,* July 7, 2010.

102. *in New Mexico and Oklahoma.:* "FBI Says Zetas Laundering Scheme Used BofA Accounts," *Wall Street Journal,* July 9, 2010.

102. *in Brownsville, Chicago, and Atlanta.:* "Wachovia's Drug Habit," *Bloomberg Markets Magazine,* July 7, 2010.

103. *brought against the bank itself.:* "HSBC Pays $1.9 billion to Settle US Probe," CNN Money, December 11, 2012, http://money.cnn.com/2012/12/10/news/companies/hsbc-money-laundering/, accessed June 12, 2013.

103. *cash at a single time.:* "Outrageous HSBC Settlement Proves the Drug War Is a Joke," *Rolling Stone,* December 13, 2013.

103. *to fight the drug war.:* "Bailout Recipients," ProPublica, http://projects.propublica.org/bailout/list, June 3, 2013, accessed June 12, 2013.

103. *in prison for drug-related offenses):* "Incarceration Nation," *Time,* April 2, 2012.

103. *facilitating the cartels' bloody business.:* "How a Big US Bank Laundered Billions from Mexico's Murderous Drug Gangs," *Observer,* April 3, 2011.

103. *is sufficient to influence policy.:* Author interview, June 2013.

104. *trade and other illegal activities.:* "Drug Money Saved Banks in Global Crisis, Claims UN Advisor," *Observer,* December 12, 2009.

104. *by an astonishing 1,600 percent.:* "Presumed Guilty: How Prisons Profit Off the War on Drugs," MSNBC, August 14, 2013.

104. *States at any given time.:* Banking on Bondage: Private Prisons and Mass Incarceration, American Civil Liberties Union, November 2, 2011.

104. *over $2.9 billion by 2010.* Gaming the System: How the Political Strategies of Private Prison Companies Promote Ineffective Incarceration Policies, Justice Policy Institute, June 2011.

104. *year on federal lobbying.* Ibid.

104. *neighborhood of $18 million.:* Banking on Bondage: Private Prisons and Mass Incarceration, The American Civil Liberties Union, November 2, 2011.

104. *contributed well over $6 million.:* Gaming the System: How the Political Strategies of Private Prison Companies Promote Ineffective Incarceration Policies, Justice Policy Institute, June 2011.

104. *promotion of prison privatization.:* Banking on Bondage: Private Prisons and Mass Incarceration, The American Civil Liberties Union, November 2, 2011.

105. *correctional facilities to house them.":* Corrections Corporation of America, Securities and Exchange Commission Form 10-K, at 19-20 (2010).

105. *could materially adversely impact us.":* The GEO Group, Securities and Exchange Commission Form 10-K for Fiscal Year Ending January 2, 2011.

105. *before making seizures or arrests.":* "D.E.A. Launders Mexican Profits of Drug Cartels," *New York Times,* December 3, 2011.

105. *Ecuador to Dallas to Madrid,":* "US Agents Aided Mexican Drug Trafficker to Infiltrate His Criminal Ring," *New York Times,* January 9, 2012.

106. *Mexico City in November 2010.):* "Tenía capo colombiano sus lujos en Reclusorio Oriente," *Reforma,* February 25, 2012.

Chapter Seven

107. *you're not doing your job.:* Corchado, Alfredo. *Midnight in Mexico: A Reporter's Journey Through a Country's Descent into Darkness.* New York: Penguin, 2013, 252.

107. *comply there will be war.":* Grayson, George W. and Logan, Samuel. *The Executioner's Men: Los Zetas, Rogue Soldiers, Criminal Entrepreneurs, and the Shadow State They Created.* Piscataway: Transaction Publishers, 2012, 198.

108. *in and around Ciudad Juárez.:* "Mexico's Drug Wars Take Death Toll to Record High," *Guardian,* January 11, 2010.

108. *who then ambled casually away.:* "Mexico Urged to Protect Activists After Campaigner Shot Dead," Amnesty International, January 6, 2010.

108. *pluralistic and decentralized [contemporary political situation],":* Drug Violence in Mexico: Data and Analysis from 2001–2009, Trans-Border Institute at University of San Diego, January 2010.

109. *making inroads against organized crime.:* "Scenesetter for the Opening of the Defense Bilateral Working," Cable from US Embassy in Mexico, January 29, 2010.

109. *others just beginning their lives.:* "Juárez Massacre: Football Players, Honor Student Among 16 Victims," *El Paso Times,* February 2, 2010.

109. *were somehow involved in organized crime.:* "Matanza, asunto de pandillas: Calderón," *El Ágora,* February 3, 2010.

109. *jeered by an angry crowd.*: "Mexican Bishops Criticize Gov't Drug War Strategy," Associated Press, February 16, 2010.

109. *celebration of a neighbor's birthday.*: Author interviews, Ciudad Juárez, September 2010.

110. *drug trade in Guatemala.*": "Los Zetas controlan el narcotráfico en Guatemala," *El Periódico,* January 12, 2010.

110. *latter's uncle four years earlier.*: "Alleged Chief of Violent Mexican Cartel Captured," Associated Press, January 12, 2010.

110. *for working with the gang.*: "Arrested Tijuana Cops Were Hailed as Models,"Associated Press, February 10, 2010.

111. *to the state capital Morelia.*: "Sufre emboscada alcaldesa Michoacána," *La Jornada,* January 23, 2010.

111. *attempts against her life.*: "La exalcaldesa de Tiquicheo murió por un golpe 'severo' en la cabeza," CNNMéxico, November 17, 2012.

111. *bed fighting for her life.*: "Exalcaldesa de Tiquicheo: cuando la muerte ronda," *Proceso,* November 19, 2012.

111. *PRD's ticket, and lose.*: "María Santos Gorrostieta," *Economist,* December 8, 2012.

111. *Michoacán, had assigned to her.*: "Exalcaldesa de Tiquicheo: cuando la muerte ronda," *Proceso,* November 19, 2012.

111. *"beautiful mariachi notes,"*: "Cercanos familiares y amigos celebraron el enlace," *El Sol de Morelia,* September 23, 2011.

111. *obligation to respect human rights.*": "Mexican Bishops Criticize Gov't Drug War Strategy,"Associated Press, February 16, 2010.

111. *personally threatened by criminal violence.*: "Anger in Ciudad Juárez as Mexico Loses Drug War," *Time,* February 22, 2010.

111. *Sinaloa cartel in that state.*: "José Vázquez Villagrana 'El Jabalí' operador de 'El Chapo' fue capturado en México," Univision, February 22, 2010.

111. *of protecting the Sinaloa Cartel.*: "Mexico Captures Sinaloa Cartel Cocaine Trafficker," Associated Press, February 22, 2010.

111. *headquarters and kidnapped six officers.*: "Gunmen Kill 13 People in Southern Mexican Town," Associated Press, February 24, 2010.

112. *Zetas in the pivotal town.*: "Detienen a El Tocayo, líder del cártel del Golfo," *La Jornada,* May 21, 2011.

112. *more than two dozen grenades.*: "New Border Violence Erupts with Mexico Cartel Rift," Associated Press, March 13, 2010.

112. *several of the state's policemen:* "Gunmen Kill 13 People in Southern Mexican Town," Associated Press, February 24, 2010.

112. *fracturing of the Gulf-Zetas alliance.*: "Mexico's Drug Wars Rage Out of Control," *Guardian,* March 24, 2010.

112. *ordered to forfeit $50 million.*: "Gunmen Kill 13 People in Southern Mexican Town," Associated Press, February 24, 2010.

112. *hitman who had been arrested.*: "Mexican Police Say Drug Hit Men Killed Journalist," Associated Press, March 1, 2010.

112. *tests proved inconclusive—were threatened.*: "Rodolfo Rincón Taracena," Committee to Protect Journalists, March 1, 2010.

112. *and David Silva—went missing.:* "Silence or Death in Mexico's Press," Committee to Protect Journalists, September 8, 2010.

113. *alive, and five still missing.:* "New Border Violence Erupts with Mexico Cartel Rift," Associated Press, March 13, 2010.

113. *cartels united against the 'Z'.":* Ibid.

113. *three men with bullet wounds.:* "8 Youths Die in Attack on Party in Western Mexico," Associated Press, March 13, 2010.

113. *lying on the ground nearby.:* "Mexico's Drug War Takes Growing Toll on Americans," Associated Press, March 21, 2010.

113. *of police officers, killing him.:* "24 Killed in Western Mexico; 11 in One Shootout," Associated Press, March 13, 2010.

114. *seven, were wounded but survived.:* "Investigators Seek Motive in 3 Slayings in Mexico," Associated Press, March 15, 2010.

114. *were found along a roadside.:* Ibid.

114. *on Televisa several weeks later.:* "Video of Massacre in Creel," *Borderland Beat,* April 12, 2010.

114. *had its roots in US prisons.:* "Barrio Azteca Gang Member Extradited from Mexico to the United States to Face Charges Related to US Consulate Murders in Juárez, Mexico," US Department of Justice, August 26, 2011.

114. *assailants on the ground.:* "Army, Drug Gangs Battle in Mexico Amid Blockades," Associated Press, March 19, 2010.

114. *and MEX 322,000 (USD 26,000).* "Cayó operador de los Beltrán Leyva en Monterrey," Univision, March 19, 2010.

114. *that he suspected of corruption.:* "Grisly Find in Mexico: Dismembered Police Officers," Associated Press, March 22, 2010.

115. *supporters of the Beltrán-Leyva Cartel.:* Ibid.

115. *San Pedro Garza García's security forces.:* "Keeping His Spies Close, and Maybe a Cartel Closer," *New York Times,* April 20, 2010.

115. *for control of the territory.:* "Mexican Families Flee Homes in Fear of Reprisals After Druglord's Killing," *Guardian,* November 12, 2010.

115. *area belongs to the Zetas.":* "Continuing Violence in Northern Mexico Between the Gulf Cartel and Los Zetas," US Department of Homeland Security memo, March 25, 2010.

115. *letters "C.D.G." scrawled in blood.:* "Police Chief Decapitated in Northern Mexico Town," Associated Press, March 27, 2010.

116. *note threatening La Barbie:* "Mexican Suspect: Killing Targeted US Guard's Car," Associated Press, 30 March 30, 2010.

116. *of compromised local security forces.":* US Embassy in Mexico cable, April 16, 2010.

116. *Mexico majoring in computer security.":* "Narco-Blogger Beats Mexico Drug War News Blackout," Associated Press, August 13, 2010.

116. *letter "Z" had been carved.:* "5 Gunmen Killed in Shootout with Mexican Soldiers," Associated Press, April 2, 2010.

116. *"euphoria"; "nothing"; replacements are already out there.":* "Proceso en la guarida de 'El Mayo' Zambada," *Proceso,* April 3, 2010.

116. *bloody two-year war of attrition.:* "AP Exclusive: Sinaloa Cartel Takes Ciudad Juárez," Associated Press, April 9, 2010.

117. *time in over a year.:* "Police Take Over from Army in Mexico Border City," Associated Press, April 8, 2010.

117. *happened to be passing by.:* "6 Mexican Police Officers Killed in Ciudad Juárez," Associated Press, April 23, 2010.

117. *justice for her slain daughter.:* "Man Seeks Asylum, Justice for Murders in His Family," *El Paso Times,* June 9, 2011; "Mexico Shock Verdict Puts Legal Reform on Trial," Associated Press, January 21, 2011.

117. *providing intelligence to Los Zetas.:* "Guatemala Says Drug Investigator Tipped Off Cartel," Associated Press, April 13, 2010.

117. *"prevailing environment of impunity"; "northern and eastern rural areas":* "Ranchers and Drug Barons Threaten Rain Forest," *New York Times,* July 17, 2010.

117. *were linked to Los Zetas,:* "6 Former Guatemala Soldiers Linked to Mexican Cartel," Agence France-Presse, September 6, 2010.

117. *the country's border with Mexico.:* "Zetas 'están por todas partes' en la frontera de Guatemala con México," *Prensa Libre,* September 6, 2010.

118. *soldiers in Nuevo Laredo.:* "2 Children Killed in Mexico Border State Shootout," Associated Press, April 5, 2010.

118. *eight of them partially burned.:* "Mexico: 12 Found Dead in Pacific Coast State," Associated Press, April 7, 2010.

118. *him a short time later.:* "Inminente la muerte del hijo de Nacho Coronel," *El Occidental,* April 15, 2010.

118. *fourteen people around the state.:* "La cacería: 'Nacho' Coronel," *Noroeste,* August 1, 2010.

118. *men hanging from a bridge.:* "At Least 80 Gunmen Terrorize Mexican Town, Kill 4," Associated Press, April 9, 2010.

118. *rapists, child killers and traitors.":* "Mexico: Cartels Team Up to Destroy Hit Men Gang," Associated Press, April 12, 2010.

118. *along a roadside in Cuernavaca.:* "Mexico: Drug Violence Has Killed 22,700 Since 2006," Associated Press, April 13, 2010.

118. *convoy an easy target.:* "Mexican State Security Minister Can't Trust Her Own Police," *Los Angeles Times,* June 27, 2010.

119. *assessment to be dramatically premature.:* "US Intelligence Says Sinaloa Cartel Has Won Battle for Ciudad Juárez Drug Routes," Associated Press, April 9, 2010.

119. *to storm the prison there.:* "Shootings Kill 16 People in Mexican Border City," Associated Press, April 28, 2010.

119. *in Mexico since December 2006.:* "6 Mexican Police Officers Killed in Ciudad Juárez," Associated Press, April 23, 2010.

119. *an upscale Mexico City suburb.:* "Major Drug Cartel Leader Captured in Mexico," *Houston Chronicle,* April 23, 2010.

119. *or dumped by the roadside.:* "Getaway for Mexican Elite Now Cartel Battleground," Associated Press, April 28, 2008.

119. *pitch near Acapulco in May.:* "5 Killed While Playing Soccer in Southern Mexico," Associated Press, May 3, 2010.

119. *move drug shipments through it.:* "Drug Cartels Disrupt Basic Services in Mexico," Associated Press, November 6, 2010.

120. El gobernador Zeta *(Governor Zeta).:* "Los desaparecidos no célebres," *Proceso,* May 27, 2010.

120. *"was like quicksand,":* "Mass Grave in Taxco, Mexico, Is Largest Discovered in Violent Drug Wars," *Washington Post,* June 24, 2010.

120. *cartels operating in the area.:* "Mexican Candidate Killed in Drug-Plagued Region,"Associated Press, May 13, 2010.

120. *of the cartels in Tamaulipas.":* "José Mario Guajardo fue asesinado por el narco: César Nava," *Notimex,* 13 May 13, 2010.

120. *was freed for $30 million.:* "Mexican Pol Negotiated $30 mn Ransom with Captors," *EFE,* December 22, 2010.

120. *narcos] are from the PRI.":* "Candidates Threatened in Local Mexico Elections," Associated Press, May 15, 2010.

120. *Sinaloa cartel's El Mayo Zambada.:* "Jesús Vizcarra buscará gubernatura de Sinaloa," *El Economista,* February 15, 2010.

121. *Beltrán-Leyva Cartel and Los Zetas.:* "Cancún Mayor Charged with Ties to Drug Cartels," Associated Press, June 1, 2010.

121. *dollars of cocaine trafficking proceeds.:* "Mexican Ex-Governor Tells US Judge He Laundered Drug Money," Reuters, August 2, 2012.

121. *chief justice Aurelio Hernández Palacios.:* "Asesinan a joven empresario de Xalapa y a su esposa," *Milenio,* June 9, 2010.

121. *under control of Los Zetas.:* Author interviews, Xalapa, August 2013.

121. *obtain justice for her daughter.:* Hernandez-Palacios, Esther. *Diario de una madre mutilada.* Mexico City: Premio Bellas Artes de Testimonio Carlos Montemayor, 2010.

121. *direct threat to his power.:* "¿Qué le hicieron a mi niña?," *Proceso,* February 7, 2003.

121. *"total agreement"; "totally protected.":* Author interview, Xalapa, August 2013.

122. *Herrera denied that too.:* "Witness: Bribes Paid Off Mexican Gubernatorial Candidate," *Austin American-Statesman,* April 18, 2013.

122. *Tamaulipas municipality of Ciudad Madero.:* "19 Slain at Mexico Rehab Clinic, 20 in Second City," Associated Press, June 11, 2010.

122. *Several assailants were also killed.:* "Gunmen Ambush Mexican Police, Killing 10 Officers," Associated Press, June 14, 2010.

122. *won't let its guard down.":* "Calderón Asks for Mexicans' Support as Toll Rises," Associated Press, June 16, 2010.

122. *that he had been murdered.:* "Mexican Singer Shot Dead Just Hours After Denying Reports He Had Been Murdered," *Daily Mail,* June 28, 2010.

123. *that have been beheaded."; out into a parking lot.:* "Gov. Jan Brewer Talks of Beheadings in the Arizona Desert," *Politifact,* June 25, 2010.

123. *were often seen as being.:* "Leading Politician Rodolfo Torre Cantú Murdered in Mexico," *Guardian,* June 29, 2010.

Chapter Eight

124. *be around only 40 percent.:* "Mexican President's Allies Lead in Key Elections,"Associated Press, July 5, 2010.

124. *that left twenty-one people dead.:* "Mexico Drug Gangs in Deadly Border Gunfight," Associated Press, July 2, 2010.

124. *demanding justice for his son.:* "Asesinan a Nepomuceno Moreno por buscar a su hijo," *El Informador,* November 29, 2011.

125. *was dismissed in June 2009.:* "Matan a Obdulio Solórzano y a un guardaespaldas," *El Periódico,* July 9, 2010.

125. *to launder illicit drug profits.:* Author interview with investigator, Miami, July 2010.

125. *former general Otto Pérez Molina,:* "El tenebroso cartel de los Durmientes," *El Periódico,* July 12, 2011.

125. *having links to organized crime.:* "Hidden Powers in Post-Conflict Guatemala," Washington Office on Latin America, September 4, 2003.

125. *member of La Línea.:* "Mayor: Car Bomb Used in Attack on Mexican Police," Associated Press, July 16, 2010.

125. *wounded at least twenty-one people.:* "Car Bomb Signals New Dimension to Mexican Drug War," Associated Press, July 17, 2010.

126. *state, including thirteen policemen.:* "La Resistencia y los Zetas se disputan la plaza de Jalisco," *La Jornada,* July 26, 2010.

126. *Río Bravo at the time.:* "Details of Drug Smuggling through Valley Emerge at Gulf Cartel Trial," *Monitor,* September 27, 2012.

126. *more than 120 bullet casings.:* "Officials Say Gunmen Kill 17 at Party in Mexico," Associated Press, July 18, 2010.

126. *Durango to commit the killings.:* "Mexico's Drugs War: in the City of Death," *Guardian,* September 16, 2010.

126. *reportedly left several gunmen dead.:* "Gunbattles Paralyze Mexican City Across from Texas," Associated Press, July 22, 2010.

126. *in Ciudad Mier in Tamaulipas.:* "8 Suspects Killed in Clash with Mexican Soldiers," Associated Press, July 22, 2010.

126. *would eventually yield thirty-eight bodies.:* "38 Bodies Found at Northern Mexico Dumping Ground," Associated Press, July 24, 2010.

127. *letter "Z" painted on them.:* "Death of a Mexican Drug Lord May Not Make People Feel Safer," *New York Times,* July 30, 2010.

127. *government's crackdown in 2006.:* "Mexico Ready to Debate Legalisation as War on Drugs Claims 28,000 Lives," Associated Press, August 4, 2010.

127. *business is dominating other people.":* "Mexico: Cartels Move Beyond Drugs, Seek Domination," Associated Press, August 4, 2010.

127. *past twelve months alone.:* "ATF: New Accord with Mexico Will Boost Gun Traces," Associated Press, October 6, 2010.

127. *thieves, we're not all corrupt.":* "Mutiny, Firings Roil Mexico's Federal Police," National Public Radio, September 10, 2010.

127. *kidnapping and extortion ring.:* "Cayeron otros dos expolicías federales por extorsionadores," *El Regional,* August 21, 2011.

128. *being a Gulf Cartel sicario.:* "La PGR arraiga al escolta del gobernador de Tamaulipas acusado de narco," CNNMéxico, July 6, 2010.

128. *"northeastern triangle of violence":* "Governor: Violence Paralyzes Mexico Border Areas," Associated Press, August 12, 2010.

128. *increases their areas of power.".* "Ex-Mexico President Calls for Legalizing Drugs," Associated Press, August 8, 2010.

128. *had been shot to death.:* "Mexican Mayor Found Dead 3 Days After Kidnapping," Associated Press, August 18, 2010.

128. *secretly working for the cartel.:* "Mexico: Zetas Gang Ordered Killing of Mayor," Associated Press, August 24, 2010.

128. *intellectual author of the crime.:* "Jefe de los Zetas mató a Cavazos," *El Universal,* September 28, 2010.

128. *killed one of his bodyguards.:* "Police Arrested in Northern Mexico Mayor's Killing," Associated Press, August 20, 2010.

128. *traitor Edgar Valdéz Villareal.".* "4 Decapitated Bodies Hung from Bridge in Mexico," Associated Press, August 22, 2010.

Chapter Nine

129. *fourteen women had been slain.:* "Drug Cartel Suspected in Massacre of 72 Migrants," Associated Press, August 25, 2010.

129. *that followed the soldier's arrival.:* "The Mexican Massacre That Shook All of Latin America," *Time,* August 26, 2010.

129. *to pregnant women and young girls.:* Ibid.

129. *to a hospital in Matamoros.:* "Mexican Massacre Investigator Found Dead," *Guardian,* August 27, 2010.

129. *had also survived the massacre.:* "Mexico Confirms 2nd Migrant Survived Massacre," Associated Press, September 1, 2010.

129. *these matters was well known.:* This terrifying journey is described from the migrant's point of view in the masterful book *The Beast: Riding the Rails and Dodging Narcos on the Migrant Trail,* written by Oscar Martínez, a journalist for El Salvador's El Faro.

130. *passed right through Zetas territory.:* Martínez, Oscar. *The Beast: Riding the Rails and Dodging Narcos on the Migrant Trail.* New York: Random House, 2013, 93.

130. *keep from coming to light.:* "Zetas Massacre 72 Migrants in Tamaulipas," Cable sent from United States Consulate in Matamoros to United States Secretary of State, August 26, 2010.

130. *shortly after he was kidnapped.:* "Mexican Massacre Investigator Found Dead," *Guardian,* August 27, 2010.

130. *grenade explosions had rocked Reynosa.:* "Mexican Drug Traffickers Blamed in Killing of Second Mayor," *Los Angeles Times,* August 30, 2010.

130. *people were reported seriously wounded.:* "Mayor in Violent Mexican Border State Killed," Associated Press, August 29, 2010.

130. *found along a Tamaulipas roadside.:* "3 Suspects in Mexico Migrant Massacre Found Dead," Associated Press, September 9, 2006.

130. *failing to pass anticorruption tests.:* "Mexico Says Drug Lord 'the Barbie' Captured," Associated Press, August 31, 2010.

131. *visit Osiel in Matamoros.";* *high, we got along ok.";* *their mothers don't love them.".* "Las confesiones de 'La Barbie' Edgar Valdez Villareal," http://youtu.be/G21xolHm9lc, ejeCentral TV, accessed September 29, 2013.

131. *cost of achieving it today.*": "Calderón: Violence Price Worth Paying in Drug War," Associated Press, September 3, 2010.

131. *forty-two hundred rounds of ammunition.*: "Mexico: Soldiers Kill 25 in Gunbattle Near Border," Associated Press, September 2, 2010.

131. *drug gangs since December 2006.*: "Mexican Mayor Found Dead 3 Days After Kidnapping," Associated Press, August 18, 2010.

132. *abuses are virtually inevitable.*": Abused and Afraid in Ciudad Juárez: An Analysis of Human Rights Violations by the Military in Mexico, Report by Washington Office on Latin America (WOLA) and the Centro de Derechos Humanos Miguel Agustín Pro Juárez A.C. (Centro Prodh), September 2010.

132. *rights and rule of law,*": "US Withholds Millions in Mexico Antidrug Aid," *New York Times*, September 3, 2010.

132. *certain parts of the country*"; *more indices of insurgency.*": "Hillary Clinton: Mexican Drug Gangs Are 'Morphing into Insurgency'," *Telegraph*, September 9, 2010.

132. *suffer from US drug consumption.*": "25 Slain in Mexican City; 85 Escape Border Prison," Associated Press, September 10, 2010.

132. *his office during a meeting.*: "El alcalde del municipio de El Naranjo es asesinado en su oficina," CNNMéxico, September 8, 2010.

132. *their task by prison guards.*: "25 Slain in Mexican City; 85 Escape Border Prison," Associated Press, September 10, 2010.

133. *orders of La Barbie before his arrest.*: "Mexican Police Neutralize Car Bomb in Border City," Associated Press, September 11, 2010.

133. *black San Antonio Spurs T-shirt.*: "Mexico Arrests Key Suspect in Beltran Leyva Cartel," *Los Angeles Times*, September 14, 2010.

133. *an editor at the paper.*: "Luis Carlos Santiago," Committee to Protect Journalists, September 16, 2010.

133. *for the warmth of home,*": "Murdered El Diaro Intern May Not Have Been Intended Target," *El Paso Times*, September 17, 2010.

133. *to kill three police officers.*: "La Linea Claims Responsibility for El Diario Killing," *Borderland Beat*, September 18, 2010.

133. *to publish or stop publishing.*": "Mexico Newspaper Pleads Druglords for Truce," Agence France-Presse, September 19, 2010.

133. *public, kidnapping, extorting and killing.*": "Mexico Makes Veiled Criticism of Border Newspaper," Associated Press, September 20, 2010.

133. *fifty-five grenades, and military uniforms.*: "22 Gunmen Killed in Battle with Mexican Soldiers," Associated Press, September 10, 2010.

134. *responsibility in these tragic events.*": "In Mexico, a War Every Century," *New York Times*, September 14, 2010.

134. *same bar in two months.*: "Gunmen Kill 7 in Bar in Mexican Border City," Associated Press, September 17, 2010.

134. *later dismembered in a ravine.*: "6 Abducted Police Found Slain in Mexican State," Associated Press, September 19, 2010.

135. *SUV with Texas license plates.*: "Gunmen Kidnap 9 Mexican State Lawmen, 2 Found Dead," Associated Press, September 18, 2010.

135. *month that killed eight people.:* "Ejército captura a líder zeta en QR," *El Universal,* September 27, 2010.

135. *Public Safety for unspecified reasons.:* "Asesinaron a pedradas al alcalde de Tancítaro, Gustavo Sánchez Cervantes," *La Jornada Michoacán,* September 28, 2010.

135. *gunmen and a marine died.:* "Small-Town Mayor Stoned to Death in Western Mexico," Associated Press, September 27, 2010.

135. *his ranch near the town.:* "Ejecutan a alcalde de NL; es el segundo en 35 días," *Milenio,* September 23, 2010.

135. *in Matamoros injured three people.:* "30 Gulf Cartel Suspects Captured in North Mexico," Associated Press, September 29, 2010.

135. *to recuperate from his wounds.:* Author interview, McAllen, November 2013.

135. *building and into custody.:* "Denuncian secuestro de presuntos marinos," *El Universal,* September 29, 2010.

135. *Tormenta was already a dead man.:* Author interview, McAllen, November 2013.

136. *double from the year before.:* "Ultralight Aircraft Now Ferrying Drugs Across US-Mexico Border," *Los Angeles Times,* May 19, 2011.

136. *Michoacán were kidnapped in Acapulco.:* "Mexico Probing Acapulco Tourist Kidnapping Report," Reuters, October 2, 2010.

136. *they killed are buried here.":* "18 Bodies Found in Mexico Mass Grave Near Acapulco," Associated Press, November 3, 2010.

136. *six grenades, and two handguns.:* "20 Kidnapped in Acapulco Had No Criminal Records," Associated Press, October 5, 2010.

136. *subsequently discovered near Miguel Alemán:* "Mexican Investigator Probing Lake Shooting Slain," Associated Press, October 10, 2010.

136. *citing their corruption and inefficiency.:* "Mexican Leader Sends Bill to Disband Local Police," Associated Press, October 6, 2010.

137. *center of the program.:* "ATF: New Accord with Mexico Will Boost Gun Traces," Associated Press. October 6, 2010.

137. *to show its true side.":* "Tijuana Gains Some Bounce Amid Mexico's Drug War," Associated Press, October 7, 2010.

137. *others hung from bridges.:* "Beheadings, Hangings Plague Tijuana Amid Festival," Associated Press, October 10, 2010.

137. *fighting, there's a tremendous bloodbath.":* "Calderón Sees a Drug War Success," Associated Press, October 8, 2010.

137. *while returning from his farm.:* "Mayor-Elect Shot as Hits on Mexico Politicos Climb," Associated Press, October 9, 2010.

137. *you are going to win"; date from the previous year.:* "Mexico: Alleged Chat Between Lawmaker, Capo Leaked," Associated Press, October 14, 2010.

137. *life of a fugitive.:* "Politics Enables Mexican Fugitive to Defang a Law," *New York Times,* December 14, 2010.

138. *western reaches of Monterrey.:* "Mexican Marine, 3 Gunmen Killed in Shootout," Associated Press, October 15, 2010.

138. *to be from Los Zetas.:* "Gunmen Kill Local Official, Son in Ciudad Juárez," Associated Press, October 17, 2010.

138. *fighting with everything they have.*; *at a military barracks there.*: "Gunbattles Stir Panic in 2 Mexican Border Cities," Associated Press, October 20, 2010.

138. *Monterrey suburb of García.*: "Zetas Leader Arrested in Monterrey," Action 4 News, October 22, 2010.

138. *scorched-earth war against one another.*: "Student Becomes New Police Chief in Mexican Town," *Guardian,* October 21, 2010.

138. *front of the police station.*: "The Last Police Chief Was Beheaded. Now a 20-Year-Old Student Is Stepping Up," *Guardian,* October 21, 2010.

138. *several killings in Ciudad Juárez:* "Ex-Prosecutor's Kidnapped Brother Shown on Video," Associated Press, October 25, 2010.

138. *played in the background.*: "Third Video of Prosecutor's Brother Depicts Torture," *Borderland Beat,* February 12, 2011.

138. *collusion with Chihuahua state police.*: "Ejecutores de Mario González debían cometer más asesinato," *La Jornada,* November 6, 2010.

Chapter Ten

141. *terrified inhabitants in its wake.*: "Enfrentamientos entre narcotraficantes y fuerzas de seguridad genera caos en aldeas de Petén." *El Periódico,* October 7, 2010.

141. *or there will be blood.*: "Cinco muertos deja balacera en Petén," *Prensa Libre,* October 7, 2010.

142. *its headquarters in South Carolina,*: "Mexican Agents Trained in US to Fight Drug Gangs," Reuters, October 22, 2010.

142. *whom was a thirteen-year-old girl.*: "Death Toll in Juárez Attack Rises to 14," *New York Times,* October 24, 2010.

142. *Horizontes del Sur killings.*: "Mexico Official: 2 Dead Men May Be Massacre Gunmen," Associated Press, October 26, 2010.

142. *message of the city's resurgence.*: "Massacre in Tijuana Recalls Worst Era," *New York Times,* October 25, 2010.

142. *Coahuila capital of Saltillo.*: "Gunbattle in Northern Mexico Kills 3 Bystanders," Associated Press, October 24, 2010.

142. *Nayarit, just south of Sinaloa.*: "15 People Killed in Mexican Car Wash Massacre," Associated Press, October 27, 2010.

142. *grenades and automatic weapons fire.*: "Terrified Mexican Police Force Resigns," *Financial Times,* October 27, 2010.

142. *influence of alcohol and drugs.*: "A Mexico Massacre in Unfamiliar Place: the Capital," Associated Press, October 29, 2010.

142. *various parts of the city.*: "US, Mexico Probe Americans' Deaths in Border City," Associated Press, November 2, 2010.

142. *city the following Tuesday.*: "Six US Citizens Killed in Past Week in Ciudad Juárez," Agence France-Presse, November 4, 2010.

142. *offensive, and nothing justifies it.*: "Mass Held in Mexico Chapel Built by Drug Lord," Associated Press, November 2, 2010.

143. *three helicopters, and seventeen vehicles.*: "Top Mexican Drugs Lord Killed in Fierce Gunbattle with Military," *Observer,* November 7, 2010.

143. *a soldier were killed,:* "Reputed Drug Kingpin Killed in Mexico Shootout," Associated Press, November 6, 2010.

143. *day at closer to fifty.:* Author interviews, Matamoros, May 2011.

143. *brains all over the place.":* Author interview, May 2011.

143. *who would be Guajardo's replacement.:* "Dead Line," *Texas Monthly,* April 2011.

144. *signed "Sincerely, Los Zetas Unit.":* "Drug Lord's Death Could Empower Zetas," *Borderland Beat,* November 11, 2010.

144. *message signed by Los Zetas.:* "20 Killed Over Weekend in Mexican Border City," Associated Press, November 7, 2010.

144. *government pressure did not cease.:* "Caught in the Crossfire," *Miami Herald,* January 18, 2011.

145. *deal had been hammered out.:* Author interview, Guatemala City, November 2010.

145. *state with force and decision.":* "Letter: Mexican Cartel Offers to Dissolve Itself," Associated Press, November 10, 2010.

145. *was falling on hard times.:* "Detainee Says Mexico's La Familia Gang in Decline," Associated Press, November 17, 2010.

145. *of interest in the offer.:* "Mexico: Mayor with Drug Cartel Links Goes Missing," Associated Press, November 25, 2010.

145. *characterization the victim's widow disputed.:* "Más incógnitas que respuestas, a dos años del asesinato de Silverio Cavazos," *Proceso,* November 21, 2012.

145. *gun battles lasting for hours.:* "Mexican Families Flee Homes in Fear of Reprisals After Druglord's Killing," *Guardian,* November 12, 2010.

145. *useless, by the roadside.:* "Refugees: No Return to Town Hit by Mexico Drug War," Associated Press, November 22, 2010.

145. *war's first displaced-person's camp.:* "The Drug War's First Displaced-Persons Camp," *Economist,* November 15, 2010.

145. *in Tamaulipas by 48 percent.:* "Presume Poiré operación Noreste; bajan crímenes en Tamaulipas," *Milenio,* November 30, 2010.

145. *more than a month later.:* "Residents Return to Cartel-Ravaged Town in Mexico," Associated Press, December 1, 2010.

146. *PRI's Enrique Peña Nieto:* "Carlos Montemayor González: El narcocharro," *La Vanguardia,* November 27, 2010.

146. *home state suffered another blow.:* "Mexico Arrests La Familia Drug Gang Figure," *Los Angeles Times,* November 30, 2010.

146. *less than two months before.:* "Matan a directora de Seguridad en Chihuahua," *El Universal,* November 29, 2010.

146. *Palomas, near the Texas border.:* "Mexican Troops Find 18 Bodies Near US Border," Reuters, November 29, 2010.

146. *in the last fifteen months,":* "Mexican Drug Gang Leader Confesses to Killings," *New York Times,* November 28, 2010.

146. *trial for the consulate slayings.:* "Barrio Azteca Leader Extradited from Mexico to United States to Face Charges Related to the US Consulate Murders in Juárez, Mexico," Department of Justice Office of Public Affairs press release, June 29, 2012.

146. *officers, innocent people and children.":* "Interrogation Veronica Treviño Molina, Zeta," YouTube, http://youtu.be/Y3-Zy7Btt9Y, accessed April 22, 2013.

146. *role in the drug business.:* "Mexico's Drugs Cartels Increasingly Recruiting Women, Study Finds," *Guardian,* December 5, 2010.

147. *cartel of the same name.:* "La historia de 'El Ponchis', el 'niño sicario' capturado en México," *Semana,* December 3, 2010.

147. *sentence allowed for a minor.:* "Boy, 14, Jailed for Murder in Mexico," Associated Press, July 27, 2011.

147. *return to the United States.):* "Mexico: Teen hit man freed, sent to U.S.," CNN, November 30, 2013.

147. *army patrol on December 7.:* "Mexico: Soldiers Kill 6 Gunmen in Northern Mexico," Associated Press, December 7, 2010.

147. *in his hometown of Arteaga,:* "Mexican Drug Lord Appears on Teachers' Payroll," Associated Press, December 8, 2010.

147. *including an eight-month-old baby.:* "Eccentric La Familia Cartel Chief Killed in Mexico," Associated Press, December 10, 2010.

147. *"long live La Familia Michoacána."* "Mexicans March in Support of 'Craziest' Kingpin." Associated Press, December 12, 2010.

147. *heavily armed group of gunmen.:* "Border Patrol Agent Dies in Rio Rico Gunbattle," *Tucson Sentinel,* December 15, 2010.

147. *the United States from Mexico.:* Officer Down Memorial Page, www.odmp.org/officer/20596-border-patrol-agent-brian-a-terry, accessed May 29, 2013.

147. *scene of the killing.:* "A Review of ATF's Operation Fast and Furious and Related Matters," US Department of Justice Office of the Inspector General, November 2012.

148. *later be arrested in Sinaloa.:* "Cae implicado en homicidio de agente fronterizo," *El Economista,* September 14, 2013.

148. *in the head and killed her.:* "Mexico Mom Killed Demanding Justice for Slain Teen," Associated Press, December 17, 2010; "Mexico Shock Verdict Puts Legal Reform on Trial," Associated Press, January 21, 2011.

148. *place curbs on the press.:* "Guatemalan Military Seizes Drug-Plagued Province," Associated Press, December 19, 2010.

148. *arrested ten alleged Zetas members.:* "Detienen a diez y recuperan pista aérea en Alta Verapaz," *Prensa Libre,* December 21, 2010.

148. *netted 220 assault rifles.:* "Decomisan arsenal, aeronaves y dinero, y encuentran dos cadáveres," *El Periodico,* December 22, 2010.

148. *transferred out of the department.:* "Guatemala Transfers 335 Cops out of Embattled Province," *EFE,* December 23, 2010.

148. *believed to be Zetas.:* "Trasladan a otros 10 reos capturados en San Marcos," *El Periódico,* December 11, 2010.

148. *during his successful campaign for president.:* "Supuestos 'Zetas' amenazan con ataques y hablan de corrupción," *El Periódico,* December 29, 2010.

148. *siege for another thirty days.:* "Colom prorroga 30 días más el Estado de Sitio en Alta Verapaz," *El Periódico,* January 19, 2011.

149. *violence in Mexico since 2006.:* "30,000 Killed in Mexico's Drug Violence Since 2006," Associated Press, December 16, 2010.

148. *3,111 in Ciudad Juárez alone.:* "Mexico Border City Has Record Drug Killings in '10," Associated Press, January 1, 2010.

149. *previous day was also found.:* "Erika Gándara sigue desaparecida, era la única policía de su municipio," *La Vanguardia,* December 30, 2010.

149. *were killed in coordinated attacks,:* "Police Officers, Doctor Killed in Mexico Shootings," Associated Press, December 30, 2010.

149. *from an underpass, partially clothed.:* "Woman Hanged from Overpass in Northern Mexico," Associated Press, December 31, 2010.

149. *don't have balls to grab"; And a prosperous New Year!":* Kidnapper Rescued from Custody in Monterrey, *Borderland Beat,* December 29, 2010.

Chapter Eleven

150. *accusing them of being informers.:* "Teenagers Shoot It Out with Mexican Police," Associated Press, January 5, 2011.

150. *while driving home from Saltillo.:* "Missing Mexican Mayor Found Slain," *EFE,* January 8, 2011.

150. *shot it out with police.:* "Teenagers Shoot It Out with Mexican Police," Associated Press, January 5, 2011.

150. *found dangling from a bridge.:* "Mexican Police Arrest 2 in Tijuana Beheading," Associated Press, January 6, 2011.

150. *few days of the year.:* "¿Qué le hicieron a mi niña?," *Proceso,* February 7, 2003.

150. *Zetas treatment of impostors.:* "Mexico Arrests Leader of 'Saint Death' Cult," Reuters, January 4, 2011.

150. *tortured while in police custody.:* "Mexican Police Detain Head of Death Saint Church," Associated Press, January 4, 2011.

150. *beginning of January 2011.:* "Mexican Cartel Announces 1-Month Truce," Associated Press, January 2, 2011.

151. *killed by the Sinaloa Cartel.:* "Man Slain on Acapulco Highway; 31 Dead in 4 Days," Associated Press, January 10, 2011.

151. *stormed a cartel safe house.:* "12 Suspects, 2 Soldiers Die in Mexico Gunbattle," Associated Press, January 14, 2011.

151. *evening of January 17.:* "Mexico Says Zetas Drug Gang Figure Arrested," *Los Angeles Times,* January 19, 2011.

151. *El Gran Patio shopping mall.:* "Abaten en Poza Rica a El Pachis, líder de Los Zetas en Veracruz," *La Jornada,* January 20, 2011.

151. *Monterrey suburb of Guadalupe.:* "Suspected Mexican Cartel Operative Dies," Associated Press, January 20, 2011.

151. *of the group's original founders.:* "Mexico Navy Catches a Founder of Zetas Drug Cartel," Associated Press, December 12, 2011.

151. *"a monopoly on authority":* "Cuando tomé el gobierno, Coahuila estaba casi en manos del narco: Rubén Moreira," *Proceso,* November 27, 2013.

151. *laundering, bank fraud, and wire fraud.:* "2 Former Mexican Officials Indicted in US," Associated Press, November 27, 2013.

152. *was linked to Los Zetas.:* "Soldiers Kill 10 Gunmen in Northern Mexico Clash," Associated Press, January 22, 2011.

152. *soccer match in Ciudad Juárez,:* "Gunmen Kill Seven at Mexico Soccer Match," Agence France-Presse, January 24, 2011.

152. *"completely dissolved,":* "Mexican Government: La Familia Cartel in Retreat," Associated Press, January 25, 2011.

152. *of two of their colleagues.:* "Mexican Town's Cops Quit After Colleagues Beheaded," Associated Press, January 27, 2011.

152. *"state government enforcement efforts"; Zetas and switch sides.":* "Nuevo Laredo Police Chief Slain by Gunmen," *Houston Chronicle,* February 4, 2011.

152. *at McAllen, where she died.:* "Husband, Slain Missionary Defied Cartels to Share Their Faith," *San Antonio Express-News,* January 28, 2011.

152. *not even determine their gender.:* "Authorities Find 6 Burned Bodies in Mexico's North," Associated Press, January 30, 2011.

152. *dollars from the Beltrán-Leyva Cartel.:* "Nada contra Añorve; pero la PGR lo investigó por narcotráfico," *Excélsior,* January 28, 2011.

153. *double its staff in 2004.:* "Homeland Security Chief Cancels Costly Virtual Border Fence," CNN, January 14, 2011.

153. *gunmen were killed by marines.:* "Gang Gunbattles, Street Blockades in Mexico," Associated Press, February 2, 2011.

153. *come out and fight.":* "Narco-Banners Addressed to 'El Lazca' Appear in 4 States," *Borderland Beat,* February 4, 2011.

154. *local official Raul Rivera Molina.:* "MPGR indaga crimen de general en Tamaulipas," *El Universal,* February 4, 2011.

154. *work of Los Zetas.:* "Nuevo Laredo Police Chief Slain by Gunmen," *Houston Chronicle,* February 4, 2011.

154. *in power, then imagine us.":* "N.L. Residents and Local Officials React to Manuel Farfan's Killing," Pro 8 News, February 4, 2011.

154. *their parents were apparently kidnapped.:* "Mexico Kidnaps Apparently Leave 25 Kids on Streets," Associated Press, February 3, 2011.

154. *been held captive in Reynosa.:* "Mexico Army Rescues 44 Kidnapped CentAm Migrants," Associated Press, February 8, 2011.

154. *presence of armed men.":* "9 Killed in Battle Between Mexican Troops, Gunmen," Associated Press, February 10, 2011.

154. *flee crashed into his car.:* "6 Dead, 37 Injured in Attack on Mexican Nightclub," Associated Press, February 12, 2011.

154. *grenades into a bar there.:* "Attack on Mexican Nightclub Kills 6, Wounds 37," Associated Press, February 12, 2011.

154. *with bullets inside a car.:* "18 Killed Cartel-Plagued Northern Mexican Town," Associated Press, February 14, 2011.

154. *in the middle of Monterrey.:* "El titular del Centro de Inteligencia de Nuevo León es asesinado," Notimex, February 14, 2011.

154. *for involvement in the killing.:* "Mexico Arrests 2 Cops in Senior Officer's Killing," Associated Press, February 16, 2011.

154. *outside of San Luis Potosí.:* "Gunmen Shoot Two US Agents in Mexico," Agence France-Presse, February 16, 2011.

154. *penetrate their vehicle's armor plating.:* "Jaime Zapata's Death: One Year Later, Still Many Unanswered Questions," *Washington Post,* February 16, 2012.

155. *partner, Victor Avila, was gravely wounded.:* "Drug Gang Shot US Agents, Mexican Governor Says," NBC News and news services, February 16, 2011.

155. *line of duty in Mexico.:* "American Immigration Agent Killed by Gunmen in Mexico," *New York Times*, February 15, 2011.

155. *traveling in had diplomatic plates.:* "Mexicans Knew They Shot US Agents," *New York Times*, February 16, 2011.

155. *one of the likely perpetrators":* "Mexico Captures Suspect in Killing of US Federal Agent," Agence France-Presse, February 23, 2011.

155. *belonged to a rival cartel.:* "Mexico Army: Suspect Says ICE Agent Slain in Error," Associated Press, February 24, 2011.

155. *be involved in the killing.:* "Authorities: Mexican Drug Lord Tied to Death of ICE Agent Captured," CNN, July 6, 2011.

155. *time, was also arrested.:* "Presentan a 'Pepito Sarabia', líder de Los Zetas en NL y Tamaulipas," *Milenio*, January 13, 2012.

155. *with the soldiers in Acapulco.:* "Soldiers Kill 8 Gunmen in Northern Mexico Clashes," Associated Press, February 18, 2011.

155. *Guerrero state capital of Chilpancingo.:* "4 Thrown to Deaths from Bridge in Southern Mexico," Associated Press, February 18, 2011.

155. *twelve drivers and customers dead.:* "12 Taxi Drivers, Fares Killed in Mexican Resort," Associated Press, February 20, 2011.

155. *kill three of the attackers.:* "Jaime Rodríguez relata ataque en su contra," *Milenio*, February 25, 2011.

156. *would kill a young bodyguard.:* "Mexican Mayor Survives Bullets, Gets His Own Song," Associated Press, April 24, 2011.

156. *a car in the city.:* "3 Young Girls Killed in Mexico Border Attack," Associated Press, February 24, 2011.

156. *unknown assailants the previous August.:* "3 Relatives of Slain Mexican Activist Josefina Reyes Found Dead," Associated Press, February 25, 2011.

156. *But it has a price.":* "Zeta Recalls His Life, Warns Against It," *Brownsville Herald*, February 19, 2011.

156. *been discovered in the state.:* "Mexican Soldiers Find 17 Bodies in Mass Graves," *Guardian*, March 2, 2011.

157. *"practically a massacre":* "Convoy Ambush Kills 7 Mexican Police, 1 Prisoner," Associated Press, March 7, 2011.

157. *revenge for an attempted kidnapping.:* "Acapulco Police Find 3 Human Heads Near Tunnel," Associated Press, March 7, 2011.

157. *receiving threats against her life.:* "Mexican Police Chief Applies for US Asylum While in Hiding," *Guardian*, March 10, 2011.

157. *to return to her job.:* "Mexico Town Fires Young Police Chief Who Left Post," Associated Press, March 7, 2011.

157. *from operating in the state.:* "Signs Announce New Gang in Western Mexico," Associated Press, March 10, 2011.

157. *$1 per kilogram of meat.:* "Mexico Details La Familia Extortion Practices," Associated Press, June 26, 2011.

158. *"fight against materialism,"; lance-and-shield–bearing medieval horsemen.:* "Mexico Cartel Issues Booklets for Proper Conduct," Associated Press, July 20, 2011.

158. *also undermines national sovereignty.":* "Mexican Senate Angry at Reports US Let Guns South," Associated Press, March 10, 2011.

158. *Gutierrez both pleaded guilty.:* "Former Columbus Mayor Sentenced in Gun-Smuggling Case," *Las Cruces Sun News,* June 14, 2012.

158. *left eight suspected narcos dead.:* "Mexican Army Raid Drug Camp, 8 Gunmen Killed," Associated Press, March 11, 2011.

158. *to death in Nuevo Laredo.:* "Soldiers Kill 4 Alleged Kidnappers in Mexico," Associated Press, March 14, 2011.

158. *with Obama in March 2011.:* "US Drones Fight Mexican Drug Trade," *New York Times,* March 19, 2011.

159. *City alone numbered sixty-nine people.:* "US Law Enforcement Role in Mexico Drug War Surges," Associated Press, March 19, 2011.

159. *effectiveness of the armed forces.:* "WikiLeaks Spat Leads to US Diplomat Resigning," *Financial Times,* March 20, 2011.

159. *killed by the Knights Templar.:* "5th Child Victim Killed in Mexico Drug Violence," Associated Press, March 17, 2011.

159. *Acapulco and killed ten men.:* "Gunmen Kill 10 Men in Mexican Resort Town Bar," Agence France-Presse, March 19, 2011.

159. *of abuses against minors.":* "Book of Kids' Drawings Chronicles Mexico Drug War," Associated Press, March 23, 2011.

159. *Ecuador that lasted several weeks.:* "Relative of Fugitive Cartel Chief Captured, Mexico Officials Announce," *Los Angeles Times,* March 24, 2011.

160. *physical, sports and educational activities."; darkness" in Félix Gallardo's captivity.:* "Mexican Drug Lord's Family: He's Suffering in Jail," Associated Press, March 22, 2011.

160. *found next to a freeway.:* "Caen ejecutores de 'La Gata', animador de Televisa Monterrey," *Terra Mexico,* May 22, 2012.

160. *discussed drug traffickers by name.:* "Hallan cuerpo de periodista en fosa clandestina en Chinameca," *Milenio,* June 1, 2011.

160. *that of five police officers.:* "'Cae el 'Dragón'; ejecutó a policías en Coatzacoalcos," *Diario de Xalapa,* May 30, 2011.

160. *in the country's northeastern mountains.:* "Mexican Drug Cartels Move into Central America," Associated Press, March 13, 2011.

161. *three, including a two-year-old.:* "7 Bodies Found in Car Abandoned in Central Mexico," Associated Press, March 29, 2011.

161. *men and a ten-year-old boy.:* "Twenty Killed in Under 24 Hours in Mexican City," Agence France-Presse, April 2, 2011.

161. *silence and my silence, Juanelo.):* Periódico de Poesía, www.periodicodepoesia.unam. mx/index.php?option=com_content&task=view&id=1747&Itemid=98, accessed June 30, 2013, author's translation.

161. *exist in me anymore,"; going to enter hell.":* "Mexico Poet Javier Sicilia Leads Anger at Drug Violence," BBC, April 22, 2011.

162. *under this stupid war any more.":* "Mexico Drug War: Corpses Found in Tamaulipas Mass Grave Identified," *Guardian,* April 8, 2011.

162. *is located, for the killing.:* "Mexico Holds Suspect Over Juan Francisco Sicilia Murder," BBC, May 25, 2011.

162. *attempt to law enforcement officials.:* "Another Arrest Made in Mexico's Sicilia Case," *EFE*, October 18, 2011.

162. *to have the men killed.:* "Las 10 revelaciones más polémicas de La Mano con Ojos," *La Vanguardia*, August 16, 2011.

162. *narcos likened to a fungus.:* "Cayó 'El Hongo', líder del cártel del Centro," *El Sol de Toluca*, October 27, 2011.

163. *Chihuahua, Durango, Coahuila and Veracruz.":* "Report: 230,000 Displaced by Mexico's Drug War," Associated Press, March 26, 2011.

163. *been kidnapped in the country.:* "UN Questions Mexican Army's Role in Drug War," *Christian Science Monitor*, April 1, 2011.

163. *of the city's main boulevards.:* "9 Killed as Gunmen, Authorities Clash in Mexico," Associated Press, April 4, 2011.

163. *people, including men and women.:* "59 Bodies Found in Pits in Mexican Border State," Associated Press, April 6, 2011.

163. *scheduled from San Luis Potosí.:* "Mexican Cops Checking Abductions Find Mass Grave," Associated Press, April 7, 2011.

164. *then it was anyone,"; only raise half the ransom.:* "Sledgehammer Used in Mexico Killings," *Washington Post*, April 25, 2011.

164. *before their bodies were found.:* "Mexican Cops Checking Abductions Find Mass Grave," Associated Press, April 7, 2011.

164. *in raids had been released.:* "Mexico Seeks to ID Victims of Latest Mass Grave Find," Agence France-Presse, April 7, 2011.

164. *desert between two army roadblocks.:* "Mexican Gunmen Tap Bus Passengers in Mass Killing," Associated Press, April 7, 2011.

164. *linked the crime to Los Zetas.:* "PGR acusa a 'Los Zetas' como responsables de las 116 muertes en Tamaulipas," CNNMéxico, April 12, 2011.

164. *"completely destroyed.":* "Los horrores de San Fernando," *El Informador*, April 30, 2011.

165. *"Who wants to live?":* "Testigo de masacre en San Fernando relata pesadilla," *La Policía*, April 18, 2011.

165. *"suicide missions" against rival cartels.:* "Mexican Crook: Gangsters Arrange Fights to Death for Entertainment," *Houston Chronicle*, June 11, 2011.

165. *is not worth anything here.":* "Mexican Mass Grave Toll Rises to 116," *Guardian*, April 16, 2011.

165. *were extracted from the narcofosas.:* "Hallan 7 nuevas narcofosas en San Fernando Tamaulipas suman 193 cadáveres," *Milenio Noticias*, June 30, 2011.

165. *as five hundred additional corpses.:* "En San Fernando hay fosas con 500 muertos más: Wallace," *El Siglo de Torreón*, August 22, 2011.

165. *was "more than six hundred.":* "600 fosas en San Fernando, dice el autor de las matanzas," *La Crónica*, June 18, 2011.

165. *"fragile local institutions"; local security agents in crime":* "Mexico Massacre Question: How Did It Happen Twice?", Associated Press, April 16, 2011.

165. *to the level of violence*: "Holy Week Vacations Marred By Violence; San Fernando Body Count Reaches 196," Cable from the US Consulate in Matamoros to US Secretary of State Hillary Clinton, April 2011.

165. *and [now] widely publicized phenomenon.*: "Tamaulipas Mass Graves," United States Consulate at Matamoros to US Department of State, April 2011.

166. *Zetas cell in San Fernando.*: "Detienen al 'Kilo', responsable de matanza en Tamaulipas," *El Economista*, April 16, 2011.

166. *2009 and dumped in Tijuana.*: "Central Wash. High School Dropout Accused in Mexico Mass Killings," KOMO, May 7, 2011.

166. *society without preying on others.*: "Is Former Tieton Resident Now a Mexican Drug Cartel Leader?", *Yakima Herald-Republic*, April 20, 2011.

166. *Ciudad Victoria's La Peregrina slum.*: "Central Wash. High School Dropout Accused in Mexico Mass Killings," KOMO, May 7, 2011.

166. *of Santa Muerte on it.*: "'Kilo' Photos a Window into Mexico's Future Written," *InSight Crime*, April 27, 2011.

166. *. . . highly psychotic and violent.*: "Psicópata, líder de Los Zetas en San Fernando," *El Economista*, April 19, 2011.

166. *for involvement in the killings.*: "Mexico Nabs Police Accused of Backing Gang Massacre," Reuters, April 13, 2011.

166. *been linked to the case.*: "Una implicada en la matanza de Tamaulipas es entregada por su madre," *Notimex*, April 16, 2011.

166. *be arrested some months later.*: "Enrique Aurelio Elizondo 'El Arabe' confesó sus crímenes en una borrachera," Univision, April 9, 2012.

166. *arrested would climb to seventy-three.*: "Mexico Charges 73 in Tamaulipas Mass Grave Deaths," Associated Press, June 1, 2011.

167. *Quintana Roo city of Benito Juárez.*: "La Policía Federal detiene a un presunto abogado de 'Los Zetas' en Q. Roo," CNNMéxico, April 21, 2011.

167. *during an assault in Veracruz.*: "Mexican Troops Kill 10 Gunmen in Gulf Coast State," Associated Press, April 19, 2011.

167. *some twenty assault rifles seized.*: "Soldier, Gunman Killed During Cartel Gunbattle in Miguel Aleman," KGBT, April 21, 2011.

167. *dealerships and several other businesses.*: "Sledgehammer Used in Mexico Killings," *Washington Post*, April 25, 2011.

167. *near the city's bus terminal.*: "Body Parts Found in Upscale Mexico City District," Associated Press, April 24, 2011.

167. *were found near the capital.*: "5 Decapitated Bodies Found Near Mexican Capital," Associated Press, May 3, 2011.

167. *held by kidnappers in Reynosa.*: "Mexican Military Rescues 52 Hostages in Border City," CNN, April 29, 2011.

167. *INM employees were subsequently arrested.*: "Freed Migrants Accuse Mexican Immigration Agents," Associated Press, May 9, 2011.

167. *mirrors of a home gym.*: "Police Discover Hidden Arsenal in Ciudad Juárez," Associated Press, April 30, 2011.

168. *fat bellies, diabetes, flat feet.*: "Pancho Villa Relative Is Mexico's Newest Tough Cop," Associated Press, May 4, 2011.

Chapter Twelve

170. *for defenseless men and women?":* "Thousands March Against Violence in Mexico City," Associated Press, May 8, 2011.

170. *foreign invaders in years past.:* "Mexico President Compares 1862 Battle to Drug War," Associated Press, May 5, 2011.

171. *of crime in this country.":* Author interview with Javier Sicilia, Cuernavaca, August 2012.

171. *killed one worker and wounded five.:* "US Businesses Reluctant to Open in Mexico," Associated Press, May 15, 2011.

171. *several assault rifles, were seized.:* "13 Killed in Lake Gunbattle in Northern Mexico," Associated Press, May 9, 2011.

171. *Durango, to Monterrey's west.:* "Mexico Sending Troops to North Amid Attacks," Associated Press, May 7, 2011.

171. *one another for several years.:* "Mexican Forces Unearth 17 More Bodies; Toll at 218," Associated Press, May 15, 2011.

171. *number of dead would eventually reach 236.:* "429 Bodies Found So Far in 2 North Mexico States," Associated Press, June 7, 2011.

172. *had been kidnapped days earlier.:* "Mexico's Drugs War Escalates as Eight Headless Bodies Discovered in Durango," *Guardian,* May 12, 2011.

172. *league with the drug traffickers.:* "Mexico Town Stands Up to Drug Gangs with Barricade," Associated Press, May 18, 2011.

172. *in Zacapa in March 2008.:* "Sube a 29 cifra de personas muertas en finca de La Libertad, Petén," *Prensa Libre,* May 15, 2011.

172. *owner, Otto René Salguero Morales:* "Guatemala: Massacre Work of Mexico Drug Gang Zetas," Associated Press, May 16, 2011.

172. *of siege in the Petén:* "Presidente Álvaro Colom decretó estado de Sitio en Petén," *Prensa Libre,* May 17, 2011.

172. *were responsible for the killings.:* "Colom: 'Zetas' podrían ser responsables de masacre," *El Periódico,* May 17, 2011.

172. *Zetas' cell in El Petén:* "Confusa investigación de presunto zeta capturado," *El Periódico,* May 19, 2011.

172. *"a farmer"; involved in any gang.":* "Suspect Arraigned in Massacre at Guatemalan Ranch," Associated Press, May 20, 2011.

173. *criminal group for its return.:* "Ganadero robó droga a grupo de narcotraficantes los Zetas," *Prensa Libre,* May 19, 2011.

173. *country, making the same claim,:* "Zetas dejan mantas advirtiéndole a la prensa limitar su cobertura," *El Periódico,* May 22, 2011.

173. *work with the Gulf Cartel.":* "Guatemalan bishops call for prayer, action after massacre on farm," Catholic News Service, May 24, 2011.

173. *had been detected and prevented.:* "Ministro dice que se evitó masacre por narcotráfico," *El Periódico,* November 20, 2011.

173. *"democratic security strategy":* "Centroamérica define estrategia de seguridad," *Prensa Libre,* May 20, 2011.

173. *of Cobán in Alta Verapaz.:* "Zetas dejan mensaje junto a restos humanos," *El Periódico,* May 24, 2011.

173. *in connection with the murder.:* "Capturan a supuestos responsables de asesinato de fiscal en Cobán," *El Periódico,* June 5, 2011.

173. *of the attorney general's office.:* "Autoridades descubren plan para matar a fiscales," *Prensa Libre,* June 7, 2011.

173. *130 raids around the country.:* "Autoridades accionan contra los Zetas," *Prensa Libre,* June 18, 2011.

173. *gunmen killed three police officers.:* "Gunmen Kill 9 in Mexican Gulf Coast State," Associated Press, May 18, 2011.

173. *at a ranch near Reynosa.:* "Mexican Police Catch Gulf Drug Cartel Leader," Associated Press, March 20, 2011.

173. *allegedly been on Valdez's payroll.:* "Detienen a líder del cártel del Pacífico Sur y mando policial aliado al grupo," *EFE,* May 19, 2011.

174. *army and federal police crackdowns,":* "Mexican Army Arrests Suspected Drug Boss and Police Ally," Reuters, May 19, 2011.

174. *La Mano con Ojos cartel.:* "Mexico Detains 16 Police Who Protected Drug Gang," Associated Press, May 19, 2011.

174. *items seized were marked "CDG.":* "3 Dead, Arms Cache Seized Near Mexican Border City," Associated Press, May 19, 2011.

174. *town of Buenavista Tomatlan.:* "29 Dead, 700 Flee as Gang Battles Hit West Mexico," Associated Press, May 26, 2011.

174. *"a pact"; develop with total tranquility.":* "In Sinaloa, Cartel Operators Hide in Plain Sight," Associated Press, June 4, 2011.

175. *members were in prison there.:* "Se contabilizan 500 hechos de los Zetas en Guatemala," *Prensa Libre,* May 21, 2011.

175. *"a rear guard"; as purchasers for Los Zetas.:* "El Salvador: Mexico Cartels Seeking Army Weapons," Associated Press, June 1, 2011.

175. *"shocking.":* "Funes: Zetas Scouting for El Salvador's Weapons," Associated Press, 21 June 21, 2011.

175. *Cartel leader Juan García Ábrego.:* "Ex-Cartel Boss Is Doing Harder Time Now in Feds' Supermax," *Houston Chronicle,* May 18, 2011.

175. *three grenades and 14 handguns.":* "Mexico Detains Nearly 50 Members of 2 Drug Gangs," Associated Press, May 28, 2011.

175. Los Doce Apóstoles *(the Twelve Apostles).:* "El Chango Méndez estaba rodeado por sus '12 apóstoles'," *Excélsior,* June 22, 2011.

175. *ten lookouts in Hidalgo.:* "Police Nabs 15 Zetas Lookouts, 10 Police in Mexico," Associated Press, May 31, 2011.

176. *Roo, was also scooped up.:* "Capturan a Víctor Manuel Pérez alias El Siete Latas, líder de Los Zetas en Quintana Roo," *La Policiaca,* June 4, 2011.

176. *more than fifty thousand bullets.:* "Mexican Army Seizes Drug Gang's Armored Trucks," Associated Press, June 6, 2011.

176. *Sincerely, La Línea and Los Zetas.":* "Dejan narcomensaje a militares en Parral," *El Ágora,* June 2, 2011.

176. *links to the drug trade.:* "Former Tijuana Mayor Held Over Alleged Gun Cache," Associated Press, June 4, 2011.

176. *seized had links to homicides.:* "2 Guns in Ex-Tijuana Mayor's Home Tied to Murders," Associated Press, June 10, 2011.

176. *girlfriend of his son, Sergio.:* "Ex-Mayor of Tijuana Investigated in Killing," *New York Times,* June 14, 2011.

177. *societies around the world,":* *appropriate criteria for their evaluation.":* War on Drugs: Report of the Global Commission on Drug Policy, Global Commission on Drug Policy, June 2011.

177. *in Torreón, killing eleven people.:* "Gunmen Kill 11 at Drug Rehab Center in Mexico," Associated Press, June 7, 2011.

177. *rob houses, kidnappers and rapists,":* "21 Bodies Found with Warning Notes in Western Mexico," Agence France-Presse, June 9, 2011.

177. *only be based on violence.":* "Mexico Peace Convoy Arrives in Ciudad Juárez," Agence France-Presse, June 10, 2011.

178. *the 1994–2004 assault weapons ban.:* "Halting US Firearms Trafficking to Mexico: A Report by Senators Dianne Feinstein, Charles Schumer and Sheldon Whitehouse to the United States Senate Caucus on International Narcotics Controls," June 2011.

178. *in the last six years.":* "Report: 70 pct of Arms Seized in Mexico from US," Associated Press, June 13, 2011.

178. *municipality of Guadalupe y Calvo.:* "Gunmen Kill 5 Members of Family in Northern Mexico," Associated Press, June 12, 2011.

178. *fallen to the roadway below,* "Teen Survives Being Shot, Dangled from Bridge," Associated Press, June 9, 2011.

178. *nearby town of Guadalupe.:* "2 Men Dangled from Mexico Bridges in a Day," Associated Press, June 14, 2011.

178. *shootout with one another.:* "Gang Warfare Kills 33 in Monterrey, Mexico," BBC, June 16, 2011.

178. *the hell you can hide.";* *"threats":* "Gunmen Kill Mexican Governor's Guards, Leave Threat," Reuters, June 15, 2013.

178. *checkpoint on the Xalapa-Veracruz highway.:* "9 Bodies Discovered in Southern Mexico," Associated Press, June 18, 2011.

179. *including a fourteen-year-old Guatemalan boy.:* "Remains Found in 11 Pits in Northern Mexico," Associated Press, July 25, 2011.

179. *streets of Matamoros proved false.:* "Top Zeta Leader Lazcano Reportedly Killed in Gun Battle Friday in Matamoros," *Brownsville Herald,* June 17, 2011.

179. *Familia as a criminal organization.:* "El Chango Méndez estaba rodeado por sus '12 apóstoles'," *Excélsior,* June 22, 2011.

179. *Los Zetas before his arrest.:* "La Familia Leader Sought Alliance with Ex-Rivals," Associated Press, June 22, 2011.

179. *of Lázaro Cárdenas in Michoacán.:* "9 Bodies Discovered in Southern Mexico," Associated Press, June 18, 2011.

179. *his home early that morning.:* "Miguel Ángel López Velasco," Committee to Protect Journalists, June 20, 2011.

179. *organized crime in Central America.:* "US Pledges More Foreign Aid to Fight Drug Cartels," Associated Press, June 22, 2011.

179. *fight off the Gulf Cartel.:* "Revelan en EU operación de Zetas," *Reforma,* June 3, 2013.

179. *through the state toward Veracruz.:* "Migrants Kidnapped in Mexico," Associated Press, June 28, 2011.

179. *had been kidnapped at all.:* "Mexican Govt: No Evidence Migrants Were Kidnapped," Associated Press, June 29, 2011.

180. *"a misunderstanding"; perhaps silently.":* "Mexico President Feels 'Misunderstood' in Drug War," Associated Press, June 28, 2011.

180. *Lourdes, and detained another seventeen.:* "Mexican Marines Kill 15 Cartel Suspects in Battle," Associated Press, July 1, 2011.

180. *in which three assailants died.:* "3 Gunmen Killed in Mexico After Attacking Police," Associated Press, July 2, 2011.

180. *Zetas attempting to enter Matamoros.:* "Zetas Try to Enter Matamoros; Priest Killed in Crossfire," *Monitor,* July 2, 2011.

180. *"without firing a shot.":* "Mexico Nabs Top Lieutenant of Dreaded Zetas Cartel," Reuters, July 4, 2011.

180. *guns come from the United States.";* *"in seventeen years,";* *cruel, but oh well . . .":* "Entrevista a Jesús Enrique Rejón Aguilar," Policía Federal, (http://youtu.be/YUD5Tcq9NIw) July 2011, accessed September 8, 2013.

180. *to import marijuana and cocaine.:* "Mexico's 'Los Zetas' Cartel Member Pleads Guilty to Drug Conspiracy Charges," *Latin American Herald Tribune,* February 3, 2013.

180. *behalf of their murdered brother.:* "Asesinan a viuda de Lucio Cabañas," *El Imparcial,* July 4, 2011.

181. *hundred federal police to Michoacán.:* "At Least 40 Killed in Mexico in 24-Hour Period," Associated Press, July 9, 2011.

181. *fear had become in Guatemala.:* "Los Zetas: el dolor de cabeza del próximo Presidente," *El Periódico,* October 2, 2011.

181. *they can come and hide.":* Author interview, Guatemala City, July 2010.

181. *Sinaloa city of Guasave.:* "12 Police, Bystander Killed in Mexico Ambush," Associated Press, July 15, 2011.

181. *city of Nuevo Laredo.:* "Nuevo Laredo Zeta Boss Killed," *San Antonio Express-News,* August 4, 2011.

182. *US currency through customs.:* "6 Presumed Cartel Members Killed in Mexico Battle," Associated Press, July 23, 2011.

182. *police and soldiers in Guerrero.:* "11 Killed in Shootings in Southern Mexico," Associated Press, July 25, 2011.

182. *who shot him many times.:* "Ejecutan a delegado del Comité Estatal del PAN en Sonora," *Milenio,* July 21, 2011.

182. *US consulate in Juárez.:* "Juárez Drug Cartel Leader Pleads Guilty to Charges Related to US Consulate Murders and Is Sentenced to Life in Prison," United States Department of Justice, April 5, 2012.

182. *sentenced to life in prison.:* "US Court Jails Mexican Drug Gangster Blamed for 1,500 Hits," Associated Press, April 6, 2012.

182. *Mexicali nearly two years before.:* "The Department of Justice's Operation Fast and Furious: Fueling Cartel Violence," Joint Staff Report Prepared for Rep. Darrell E. Issa, Chairman of the United States House of Representatives Committee on Oversight and

Government Reform, and Senator Charles E. Grassley, Ranking Member of the United States Senate Committee on the Judiciary, July 26, 2011.

182. *federal police agents in Mexico.:* "US Widens Role in Battle Against Mexican Drug Cartels," *New York Times,* August 6, 2011.

182. *investigating eventually found another thirteen.:* "Mexico Police Find 15 Bodies in Clandestine Grave," Associated Press, July 27, 2011.

183. *inmates before the violence erupted.:* "Video Shows Mexico Prison Guards' Involvement in Shooting Bloodbath," Associated Press, July 28, 2011.

183. *to 24,374 homicides during 2010.:* "Study: Mexico Homicides Rose 23 Percent in 2010," Associated Press, July 28, 2011.

183. *"constantly":* "Capturan a operador financiero de 'Los Zetas'," *Proceso,* August 3, 2011.

183. *Acapulco, and three accomplices.:* "Detienen a 'El Coreano', líder de cártel de Acapulco Policía," *Milenio,* August 1, 2011.

183. *outskirts of Mexico City.:* "Mexico Arrests Trafficker Accused of 600 Killings," Associated Press, August 11, 2011.

183. *less than a year before.:* "Mexico Town's Entire Police Force Quits After Officers Gunned Down," Associated Press, August 5, 2011.

183. *neighboring Colima State were found.:* "4 Police Officers Found Slain in Western Mexico," Associated Press, August 9, 2011.

183. *in was attacked by gunmen.:* "Muere en atentado ex campeón del futbol mexicano," *El Sol de Cuernavaca,* August 11, 2011.

183. *dead of a bullet wound.:* "Aparece el cuerpo del periodista Humberto Millán Salazar," *Milenio,* August 25, 2011.

183. *people were slain in Acapulco,:* "Police: 11 People Slain in Acapulco, Mexico," Associated Press, August 15, 2011.

184. *were kidnapped in Veracruz.:* "4 Mexican Navy Personnel Kidnapped by Drug Gangs," Associated Press, August 15, 2011.

184. *escape in front of them.:* "Man Hung from Mexico Bridge, Shot to Death," Associated Press, August 24, 2011.

184. *above crackling, infernal orange flames.:* "Video del grupo armado que atacó a Casino," *El Universal,* August 26, 2011.

184. *rescue those trapped inside.:* "53 Dead in Attack on Casino in Northern Mexico," Associated Press, August 25, 2011.

184. *keep going on like this."; capture of the culprits.:* "Mexican President Declares 3 Days of Mourning," Associated Press, August 26, 2011.

185. *among those behind the attack.:* "Revelan identidad de líderes del ataque al Casino Royale," *Milenio,* September 12, 2011.

185. *cartel as protection money.:* "Terror en el Casino Royale de Monterrey; los Zetas, detrás del atentado," *Excélsior,* August 26, 2011.

185. *over and over on television.:* "Jonás Larrazabal, hermano del alcalde de Monterrey, 'jurídicamente libre'," CNNMéxico, November 14, 2011.

185. *Televisa, Mexico's main television broadcaster.:* "Asesinan a las periodistas Marcela Yarce Viveros y Rocío González," *La Jornada,* September 2, 2011.

185. *motive for the killings.:* "Robbery Motive in Mexican Journalists Killings," Associated Press, October 4, 2011.

185. *town of Gustavo Díaz Ordaz.:* "Abaten a 'El M3' en Tamaulipas," *El Universal,* September 3, 2012.

186. *tortured before being killed.:* "Sources: Fatal Gunshots on McAllen Expressway Point to Gulf Cartel," *Monitor,* September 27, 2011.

186. *based in Reynosa and Tampico.:* "Special Agent Details 2011 Interview with Rincón," *Brownsville Herald,* September 27, 2012.

186. *Zetas, including sixteen police officers.:* "Key Gulf Cartel Figure Killed in Northern Mexico,"Associated Press, September 2, 2011.

186. *been set up in Veracruz.:* "Mexican Navy Dismantles Zeta Communication System," Associated Press, September 9, 2011.

186. *of Huamuxtitlan two weeks later.:* "Hallan cuerpo de diputado federal Moisés Villanueva," *Notimex,* September 17, 2011.

186. *or cry, could be uttered.:* "Gunmen Force Mexico Mayor to Cancel 'El Grito'," Associated Press, September 15, 2011.

186. *Leyva raid two years before.:* "Matan a familia de policía que identificó a 'zetas'," *El Imparcial,* September 15, 2011.

Chapter Thirteen

187. *was unfurled, threatening Los Zetas.:* "Dumping of 35 Bodies Seen as Challenge to Zetas," Associated Press, September 21, 2011.

187. *plaza has a new owner.":* "Bodies of Innocents Used as Props in Mexico's Drug War," *InSight Crime,* June 8, 2012.

187. *[or] the people of Mexico"; [Los Zetas] is not invincible."; warriors, faceless, but proudly Mexican.":* "Comando armado se responsabiliza por cádaveres arrojados en Veracruz," *La Vanguardia,* September 27, 2011.

188. *by methods outside the law.":* "Mexico Rejects Video Call to Exterminate Cartel," Associated Press, September 27, 2011.

188. *troops and police to Veracruz.:* "Mexican Prez Orders Federal Forces to Veracruz," Associated Press, September 28, 2011.

188. *begin a meeting in Veracruz.:* "Dumping of 35 Bodies Seen as Challenge to Zetas," Associated Press, September 21, 2011.

188. *criminal records of minor offenses.:* "Bodies of Innocents Used as Props in Mexico's Drug War," *InSight Crime,* June 8, 2012.

188. *eye on you. Attention, Z.":* "Mexican Cartels Hang, Disembowel 'Internet Snitches'," *Wired,* September 15, 2011.

189. *placed next to her head.:* "Maria Elizabeth Macías Castro," Committee to Protect Journalists, September 24, 2011.

189. *respectfully, Laredo Girl . . . ZZZZ.":* "Woman's Decapitation Linked to Web Posts About Mexican Drug Cartel," Associated Press, September 25, 2011.

189. *to Mexico after their birth.:* "Wife of Mexican Drug Lord Gives Birth in California," Associated Press, September 27, 2011.

189. *leading to several school closures.:* "School Threats Spread to Northern Mexico," Associated Press, September 30, 2011.

189. *was connected with the threats.:* "5 Severed Heads Found in Mexico Resort of Acapulco," Associated Press, September 27, 2011.

189. *order and tranquility. Thank you.*: "Aparecen 3 narcomantas en Zihuatanejo, se las adjudican Los Caballeros templarios," Agencia de Noticias IRZA, September 28, 2011.

190. *Beltrán-Leyva Cartel and its remnants.:* "Zihuatanejo amanece este domingo con 7 ejecuciones," *La Voz de Zihuatanejo,* September 29, 2011.

190. *in several attacks in Acapulco:* "Police Find 7 Bodies Dumped in Pacific Resort," Associated Press, October 2, 2011.

190. *Mano con Ojos gang.:* "2 Severed Heads Found in Mexico City with Message," Associated Press, October 4, 2011.

190. *almost everywhere within its borders.:* "2 Powerful Cartels Dominate in Mexico Drug War," Associated Press, October 1, 2011.

190. *near Xayakalan in that state.:* "Ejecutan en Michoacán a activista del Movimiento por la Paz," *Proceso,* October 7, 2011.

190. *Tamaulipas, Coahuila, and Nuevo León.:* "Mexico Military Reports Capture of Cartel Figure," Associated Press, October 13, 2011.

190. *cocaine by a federal judge.:* "Extradited Mexican with Ties to Zetas Sentenced in Large-Scale Cocaine Trafficking Conspiracy," Department of Justice, April 25, 2013.

190. *district of Colinas del Sol.:* "Hallan ejecutado a César Dávila García, alias 'El Gama' operador financiero del Cártel del Golfo," *La Policiaca,* October 12, 2011.

190. *Mexico City–Nuevo Laredo highway.:* "Capturan a El Voltaje, jefe zeta implicado en ataque al Royale," *Milenio,* October 5, 2011.

191. *Jardines de Mocambo district.:* "Marina reporta el hallazgo de 32 cuerpos en Veracruz," CNNMéxico, October 6, 2011.

191. *illicit income and criminal activities":* "Mexico: 'Zeta Killers' Kill At Least 67 People," Associated Press, October 7, 2011.

191. *have taken over the country.":* "Mexican President: State Was Left to Drug Cartel," Associated Press, October 14, 2011.

191. *everyone in Veracruz knows it.":* Ibid.

191. *while new officers were trained.:* "Mexico Port City Police Infiltrated by Zetas Gang," Associated Press, December 23, 2011.

192. *as well as other tests.:* "Mexico Fires Nearly 1,000 Police in Gulf State," Associated Press, October 19, 2011.

192. *five other suspected cartel members.:* "Carlos Pitalua, supuesto líder 'zeta' en Veracruz, es detenido por marinos," CNNMéxico, October 26, 2011.

192. *Centro, was taken into custody.:* "Mexico Nabs Alleged Zetas Local Chief, 5 Others," Associated Press, October 27, 2011.

192. *being held captive by Los Zetas.:* "Mexico Soldiers Rescue 61 People Held by Drug Gang," Associated Press, October 17, 2011.

192. *in a swamp near Veracruz.:* "8 Bodies Found Dumped in Mangrove Swamp in Mexico," Associated Press, November 1, 2011.

193. *victims in the local jail.:* "Mexican Police 'let drug gang hold kidnap victims in local jail'," Associated Press, October 7, 2011.

193. *hours, leaving twenty inmates dead.:* "Twenty Die in Mexican Prison Fight Near US Border, Associated Press, October 16, 2011.

193. *four tons of marijuana seized.:* "Marines Kill 11, Nab 36, Find 4 Tons of Marijuana," Associated Press, October 11, 2011.

193. *confined to the Matamoros area.:* "Officials: Gulf Cartel Rift Points to Renewed Violence," *Monitor,* August 12, 2012.

193. *of the Cárdenas family's faction.:* "Special Agent Details 2011 Interview with Rincón," *Brownsville Herald,* September 27, 2012.

193. *Cártel Independiente de Acapulco.:* "Detienen a jefa de sicarios de 'La Barredora' con restos humanos en Acapulco," *La Policiaca,* October 25, 2011.

193. *been arrested only days earlier.:* "Mexico Fires Nearly 1,000 Police in Gulf State," Associated Press, October 19, 2011.

194. *by taking one of us.":* "Anonymous Veracruz," YouTube, http://youtu.be/3ZL0E1J 7wOg, uploaded on October 6, 2011.

194. *PRI governor, Andrés Granier Melo.:* "Internet Becomes a New Battleground in Mexico's Drug Wars," *Guardian,* October 31, 2011.

194. *victims including a seven-year-old boy.:* "Gunmen Kill 5 Members of Family in Western Mexico," Associated Press, November 3, 2011.

194. *had also been previously killed.:* "El alcalde de La Piedad, Michoacán, muere por un ataque de un grupo armado," CNNMéxico, November 2, 2011.

194. *provisional extradition request since 2007.:* "Cae operador de 'El Chapo'; era de los 10 más buscados por la DEA," *Proceso,* November 10, 2011.

194. *post things on social networks."; killed for his online activity.:* "Mexican Man Decapitated in Cartel Warning to Social Media," *Wired,* November 10, 2011.

195. *The next president's headache.":* "Los Zetas: el dolor de cabeza del próximo Presidente," *El Periódico,* October 2, 2011.

195. *time of the Zetas":* "Una elección en tiempo de los Zetas," *El Periódico,* October 7, 2011.

195. *United States and Mexico.":* "Partido Patriota prioriza combate frontal de los Zetas," *Prensa Libre,* January 6, 2012.

195. *traveling on the same plane).:* "El paraje frío donde cayó el helicóptero en el que viajaba Blake Mora," CNNMéxico, November 11, 2011.

195. *to construct a better Mexico.)":* "Mexican Official's Last Tweet Recalls Previous Fatal Crash," *Los Angeles Times,* November 11, 2011.

196. *ever really know what happened.":* "Blake Mora: Key Strategist in Mexico's Drug War," Associated Press, November 11, 2011.

196. *scheduled for the following summer.:* "Ex-Ruling Party Wins Violence-Scarred Mexican Race," Associated Press, November 15, 2011.

196. *"boldfaced interference":* "Official: Drug Cartel Tried to Skew Mexico Vote," Associated Press, November 19, 2011.

196. *of his home in Culiacán.:* "Norteño Singer Diego Rivas Gunned Down in Sinaloa," Associated Press, November 14, 2011.

196. *his family over the radio.:* "Gov of Drug-Plagued Mexico State Sends Kids Abroad," Associated Press, November 25, 2011.

196. *had organized on November 15.:* "Cae en Fresnillo jefe de 'Los Zetas' en San Luis Potosí," *Proceso,* November 17, 2011.

196. *had been seized in Coahuila.:* "Official: Drug Cartel Tried to Skew Mexico Vote," Associated Press, November 19, 2011.

197. *Mexican navy in Matamoros.:* "Detienen a Ezequiel Cárdenas Rivera 'El Junior', hijo de 'Tony Tormenta'," Univision.com, November 29, 2011.

197. *being kidnapped earlier that day.:* "3 Police Officers Found Dead in Mexico Border City," Associated Press, November 22, 2011.

197. *eastern state of Zacapa,:* "Los detenidos en Zacapa son miembros de los Zetas," *El Periódico,* November 21, 2011.

197. *gunmen were wounded and arrested.:* "Hombres atacan a agentes de la PNC," *Prensa Libre,* November 11, 2011.

197. *"that's how you kill":* "Matanza en Guadalajara: más datos, más sospechas," *Proceso,* December 22, 2011.

198. *role in his death.:* "Nepomuceno Moreno, activista del Movimiento por la Paz, es asesinado," CNNMéxico, November 28, 2011.

198. *by emphasizing their criminal records.":* "Local Officials Reprimanded in Mexico Slaying Case," Associated Press, December 1, 2011.

198. *subsequently arrested for Moreno's murder.:* "Atrapan a 'El Pelos', asesino del activista Nepomuceno Moreno," *La Prensa,* November 4, 2012.

198. *payoff to the governor himself.:* "Vinculan a Yarrington con el asesinato de Torre Cantú," *El Informador,* February 11, 2012.

198. *population still had not returned.:* "Mexico Tries New Tactic to Restore Border Towns," Associated Press, December 6, 2011.

198. *recovery of seventy-three rifles.:* "Mexican Troops Kill 11 Gunmen Near US Border," Associated Press, December 13, 2011.

198. *grenades, and over thirty handguns.:* "Mexico Says Captured Cartel Leader Had Arsenal," Associated Press, December 14, 2011.

198. *at their places of work.:* "16 Killed in Violence in Mexican State," Associated Press, December 22, 2011.

198. *largely vanished into the ether.:* "Loan Scandal Topples Head of Mexico's PRI Party," *Los Angeles Times,* December 3, 2011.

199. *pursue the most serious charges.:* "Exculpa PGR a Humberto Moreira de deuda ilegal," *Milenio,* November 21, 2012.

199. *large, vetted federal police force":* "Violence Tops Results of Mexico's 5-Yr Drug War," Associated Press, December 10, 2011.

199. *police opened fire, killing two.:* "2 Students Die in Clash with Mexican Police," Associated Press, December 12, 2011.

199. *inside a student group's headquarters.:* "3 Bodies Found at Mexican Student Group Office," Associated Press, December 15, 2011.

199. *referring to the Gulf-Zetas war.:* "13 Bodies Found in Mexican Drug Cartel Battle," Associated Press, December 26, 2011.

199. *were linked to Los Zetas.:* "Police Find 7 Bodies in Northern Mexico," Associated Press, December 28, 2011.

199. *challenge to each Mexican citizen.":* "Carlos Fuentes on Mexico's Drug War," CBC The National, November 28, 2011, http://youtu.be/1SVZIX9q764, accessed June 19, 2013.

Chapter Fourteen

200. *thousand people had gone missing.*: "Confronting a Nightmare: Disappearances in Mexico," Amnesty International, June 2013.

200. *homemade knives, clubs, and stones.*: "31 internos muertos y 13 heridos tras una riña en el reclusorio de Altamira," *La Jornada*, January 5, 2012.

200. *various points around the town.*: "Police Find 5 Severed Heads in Northern Mexico," Associated Press, January 7, 2011.

200. *shopping mall in Mexico City.*: "2 Decapitated Bodies Left at Posh Mexico City Mall," Associated Press, January 11, 2012.

201. *trafficking groups in the city.*": "Tijuana Sees Drop in Drug Violence," *San Diego Union-Tribune*, January 7, 2012.

201. *of Nuevo León and Coahuila.*: "Presentan a 'Pepito Sarabia', líder de Los Zetas en NL y Tamaulipas," *Milenio*, January 13, 2012.

201. *killing seven people in Cuernavaca,*: "Police Kill 7 Gunmen in Central Mexico Gun Battle," Associated Press, January 16, 2012.

201. *city of Atoyac de Álvarez.*: "13 Killed, 8 at Funeral, in Violent Mexico State," Associated Press, January 22, 2012.

201. *since at least March 2011.*: "'El Arqui' cayó donde aviones no tripulados buscan a 'El Chapo'," *Informador*, January 24, 2012.

201. *killed at least seventy-five people.*: "Enrique Aurelio Elizondo 'El Arabe' confesó sus crímenes en una borrachera," Univision, April 9, 2012.

201. *fingers of Zetas captives.*: "Mexican Drug Assassin Videotaped Himself Dancing in the Street to Reggae Music as He Cut Off Fingers of Victims," *Daily Mail*, April 9, 2012.

201. *near the center of Monterrey.*: "9 Killed in Violence-Plagued Northern Mexican City," Associated Press, January 27, 2012.

202. *experience of mourning and death.*": "Drug Gang Banners in Mexico Ahead of Pope Visit," Associated Press, February 7, 2012.

202. *down five municipal police officers.*: "5 Police Shot Dead in Town Outside Mexico City," Associated Press, January 24, 2012.

202. *Michoacán in early February 2012.*: "Official: Mexican Army Sends More Troops to West," Associated Press, February 3, 2012.

202. *by the bishop of León.*: "Dejan 'Caballeros Templarios' 11 narcomantas en Guanajuato," *Reforma*, February 6, 2012.

202. *Holiness Benedict XVI is coming.*": "Drug Gang Banners in Mexico Ahead of Pope Visit," Associated Press, February 7, 2012.

202. *entire year of 2009.*: "Found in Mexico: 15 Tons of Meth, 15 More Bodies," Associated Press, February 9, 2012.

202. *pure gram to under $90.*: "Cartels Flood US with Cheap Meth," Associated Press, October 11, 2012.

202. *American leaders the following month.*: "Guatemala Says It's Weighing Drug Legalization," Associated Press, February 15, 2012.

203. *not mean liberalisation without controls.*": "We Have to Find New Solutions to Latin America's Drugs Nightmare," *Guardian*, April 7, 2012.

203. *Guatemalan drug trafficker Horst Walter Overdick).*: "Álvaro el Sapo Gómez, allana ruta de zetas en el país," *Prensa Libre,* February 24, 2012.

203. *named Gustavo Adolfo Colindres Arreaga,*: "Vinculan a supuesto Zeta con la masacre de Petén," *El Periódico,* March 22, 2012.

203. *Interamericana in San Lucas Sacatepéquez..*: "Cae Horst Walter Overdick Mejia, Presunto Socio de Los Zetas," Secretaria de Comunicación de la Presidencia de Guatemala, April 3, 2012.

203. *grenades into discos and malls,"*: "Los Zetas dejan mantas con amenazas a la población civil en Petén," *El Periódico,* March 12, 2012.

203. *in your home and everyone."*: "Mensajes en crímenes aluden a Baldizón," *El Periódico,* March 23, 2012.

203. *behalf of the Sinaloa Cartel.*: "Presidential Pilot Trial Raises Questions of CentAm Elite Corruption," *InSight Crime,* November 20, 2013.

203. *"a time bomb":* "En el caso Apodaca hubo incompetentes, ciegos y sordos," *La Vanguardia,* February 24, 2012.

204. *out of the prison.*: "Recapturan a reo y destapa 'cloaca' de penal," *Milenio,* March 17, 2012.

204. *been kidnapped the previous day,*: "Hallan en Cuernavaca cuatro estudiantes descuartizados," *La Jornada,* March 9, 2012.

204. *was left with the bodies.*: "En la colonia La Pradera; dos de ellos eran menores de edad," *El Sol de Cuernavaca,* March 9, 2012.

204. *left along with the heads.*: "Mexican Police Killed During Hunt for Headless Bodies," Associated Press, March 20, 2012.

204. *Halliburton disappeared outside Piedras Negras.*: "Zetas Crimping Gas Industry in Northern Mexico," *Houston Chronicle,* September 23, 2012.

204. *Peña acting as the conduit.*: "Former Tamaulipas Governor Named in Texas Money Laundering Case," *Valley Centra,* February 10, 2012.

204. *tenure, soon fled to Spain.*: "Detecta la Siedo que el ex gobernador Eugenio Hernández está en España," *La Jornada,* June 14, 2012.

204. *to Hernández in Quintana Roo.*: "Asegura PGR 10 propiedades a Eugenio Hernández en Quintana Roo," *Proceso,* June 8, 2012.

205. *Chihuahua, Tamaulipas, and Nuevo León."*: "The Merida Initiative: Expanding the US/Mexico Partnership," Bureau of Western Hemisphere Affairs of the US Department of State, March 29, 2012.

205. *for the next several days.*: "Cayó Erick Valencia Salazar, líder del Cártel Jalisco Nueva Generación," *La Jornada Jalisco,* March 10, 2012.

205. *Vulture), was captured days later.*: "Trasladan a 'El Zopilote' a la Ciudad de México," *Informador,* March 20, 2012.

205. *dirt floor of their home.*: "Mexican Agents Probe Family in Santa Muerte Ritual Murders," Associated Press, April 1, 2012.

205. *near Piedras Negras in Coahuila.*: "Un autor del ataque al casino Royale muere en un enfrentamiento," CNNMéxico, April 4, 2012.

205. *City auto body repair shop.*: "Mexican General Once Tied to Cartels Shot Dead," Associated Press, April 20, 2012.

206. *through betrayal. Attention El Chapo.*: "'Narcomantas' Herald Chapo's Incursion into Mexico Border State," *InSight Crime*, March 28, 2012.

206. *You ain't shit Attention: Z 40.*: "Z40 Answers Chapo by Leaving His Own Butchery and Message," *Borderland Beat*, March 28, 2012.

206. *Zetas killed by the CJNG,:* "14 Bodies Found in Minivan Outside Nuevo Laredo City Hall, According to Tamps. Gov't," *Monitor*, April 17, 2012.

206. *"innocent civilians":* "Desligan al 'Chapo Guzmán' de la masacre en Nuevo Laredo, Tamaulipas," *La Policiaca*, April 24, 2012.

207. *that I'm your true father.*: "El Chapo demuestra su poder en Nuevo Laredo, Tamaulipas," Blog del Narco, April 18, 2012.

207. *scene were then fired upon.:* "Car Bomb Explosion Followed by Shootout in Nuevo Laredo," Action 4 News, April 24, 2012.

207. *to expose bought that explanation.:* "Murder of Mexican Reporter in Veracruz Spotlights Official Hostility Toward Press," McClatchy Newspapers, May 16, 2013.

207. *return a short time later.:* "Mexico Journalists Tortured and Killed by Drug Cartels," *Guardian*, May 4, 2012.

207. *being tossed in the canal.:* "Three Journalists Slain in Mexico's Veracruz," Al Jazeera, May 4, 2012.

208. *exception but the daily rule.*: "Proceso ante el crimen de Regina Martínez," *Proceso*, April 29, 2012.

208. *aftermath of cartel gun battles.:* "US: Mexico Seized 68,000 Guns from US Since 2006," Associated Press, April 26, 2012.

209. *City Hall three hours later.:* "Ahora fue Tamaulipas, autoridades hallan 23 muertos," *Excélsior*, May 5, 2012.

210. *See you around fuckers.*: "Ejecutan y cuelgan a nueve personas en Nuevo Laredo," *San Luis Voy*, May 4, 2013.

210. *Obrador trailing in third place.:* "Mexican Front-Runner Fends Off Debate Attacks," Associated Press, May 6, 2012.

210. *"competed democratically and understood change.*: "Are Mexicans About to Vote for the Return of the 'Perfect Dictatorship'?," *Guardian*, June 30, 2012.

210. *in Mexico as a whole.:* "Mexico Judge Orders Probe into Killings of Women," Associated Press, March 6, 2012.

211. *run-up to the presidential vote.:* "YoSoy132: How a Mexican Student Movement Was Born," *Huffington Post*, June 30, 2012.

211. *newspaper in Reynosa with gunfire.:* "Gunmen Open Fire on Reynosa Newspaper," *Monitor*, May 7, 2012.

211. *the Soriana Tamatan Shopping Center.:* "Dismembered Bodies Left at Mall in Tamps. Capital," *Monitor*, May 9, 2012.

212. *be directed against the CJNG.:* "Narcoviolencia vuelve a Jalisco; hallan 18 cuerpos en dos vehículos," *Excélsior*, May 10, 2012.

212. *crime, Jalisco officials later said.:* "Mexico's Drug War Rocks US Expat Stronghold," Reuters, June 18, 2012.

212. *dumped where they were found.:* "Asesinaron en Tamaulipas a los 49 descuartizados hallados en Cadereyta," *Proceso*, May 31, 2012.

212. *also left at the scene.:* "Police Find 49 Bodies by a Highway in Mexico," *New York Times,* May 13, 2012.

212. *as it should be done.":* "Con narcomantas, se deslindan Los Zetas de masacre de 49 en Cadereyta," *Proceso,* May 16, 2012.

212. *conclusively ID a single victim.:* "Unidentified Bodies, Missing Cases Mount in Mexico,"Associated Press, July 23, 2012.

212. *would not reveal its contents.:* "Marco Antonio Ávila García, El Regional de Sonora and El Diario de Sonora," Committee to Protect Journalists, May 18, 2012.

212. *May 24, setting it aflame.:* "Explota coche bomba y se incendia discoteca en Nuevo Laredo," *Notimex,* May 24, 2012.

212. *eight of them police officers.:* "Estalla coche bomba en Nuevo Laredo; al menos 10 heridos," *Excélsior,* May 24, 2012.

212. *work of Los Zetas.:* "Mexico Gang Launches Car Bomb Near US Border," Associated Press, May 24, 2012.

213. *lot as* hampones *(mobsters).:* "En mantas, ligan a Yarrington con Manuel Bribiesca y aspirante panista al Senado," *Proceso,* May 30, 2012.

213. *complicated natural gas scheme.:* "El hijastro de Fox acepta su culpabilidad por fraude," *Proceso,* October 12, 2012.

213. *to contain fourteen dismembered bodies.:* "Abandonan 14 cuerpos desmembrados en Veracruz," *Proceso,* June 12, 2012.

213. *to infighting between Zetas factions.:* "Hallan 14 cadáveres en Veracruz; es un ajuste de cuentas entre zetas, dice la policía," *La Jornada,* June 13, 2012.

213. *time period the previous year.:* "Storm Clouds with Silver Linings," *Economist,* May 19, 2012.

213. *"no contract existed of* that *kind":* "Computer Files Link TV Dirty Tricks to Favourite for Mexico Presidency," *Guardian,* June 7, 2012.

214. *rivals during 2009 legislative elections.:* "Mexican Media Scandal: Secretive Televisa Unit Promoted PRI Candidate," *Guardian,* June 26, 2012.

214. *organized crime for many years.:* "Los delitos contra periodistas serán perseguidos por autoridades federales," CNNMéxico, June 22, 2012.

214. *agents assigned to airport security.:* "Mexico City Replaces Airport Police After June Shooting," BBC, August 19, 2012.

214. *She had been strangled.:* "Alcaldesa veracruzana fue ahorcada con un lazo: Procuraduría," *Proceso,* June 28, 2012.

214. *dozen people were injured.:* "Coche bomba estalla frente a alcaldía de Nuevo Laredo," *Excélsior,* June 29, 2012.

214. *very good, very good.":* "Drug Cartel Rivals Behead Zetas on Camera," ABC News, June 28, 2012.

Chapter Fifteen
215. *people in the farms"; vengeance, we want justice.":* "Mexico Focuses on Man Expected to Lose Election," Associated Press, June 27, 2012.

215. *for failing to do so.:* Author interviews, Matamoros and Reynosa, November 2013.

215. *"Mexico won,":* "Peña Nieto Claims Victory in Mexico Elections," *Guardian,* July 2, 2012.

215. *grocery stores to its supporters.:* "Students March Against Mexico's Election Result," Associated Press, July 8, 2012.

216. *corrupt regime that benefits them.":* "Mexico Presidential Runner-Up Files Lawsuit Against Peña Nieto," *Guardian,* July 13, 2012.

216. *officially declared Mexico's president-elect.:* "Mexico's Enrique Peña Nieto Officially Declared Election Winner," *Los Angeles Times,* August 31, 2012.

216. *Martínez himself was unharmed.:* "Car Bomb in Northern Mexico Kills 2, Wounds 7," Associated Press, July 3, 2012.

216. *of the country are suffering.":* "Mexico Paper Won't Cover Violence After Attack," Associated Press, July 12, 2012.

216. *of his faction of Los Zetas.:* "Even More Brutal Leader Takes Over Mexico's Zetas," Associated Press, August 24, 2012.

216. *then shot to death.:* "Police Find 14 Bodies Stuffed into SUV in Mexico," Associated Press, August 9, 2012.

216. *car near a water park.:* "8 Bodies Found Inside Car in Northern Mexico," Associated Press, August 10, 2012.

216. *for the city's drug routes:* "Mexico Army: Border City Killings Plunge This Year," Associated Press, July 11, 2012.

217. *around Matamoros in early August.:* "Officials: Gulf Cartel Rift Points to Renewed Violence," *Monitor,* August 12, 2012.

217. *be between Gulf Cartel factions.:* "Matamoros Struck by Fierce Firefights," *Monitor,* August 9, 2012.

217. *towns of Hidalgo and Padilla,:* "At Least 12 Killed in Tamaulipas Shootouts," Associated Press, August 22, 2012.

217. *of at least sixteen people,:* "Mexico: 4 Gunmen Killed in Reynosa," *Monitor,* August 15, 2012.

217. *including at least one marine.:* "Amid Regular Firefights, Mexican Border Cities Under Siege," *Monitor,* August 25, 2012.

217. *gangs in the border cities.:* "Deportees to Mexico's Tamaulipas Preyed Upon by Gangs," *Los Angeles Times,* September 8, 2012.

217. *have been killed by Los Zetas.:* "Sifting for Answers in a Mass Grave in Tapachula, Mexico," *Los Angeles Times,* September 12, 2012.

217. *been kidnapped in the country.:* "Mexico Ignores Migrant Kidnappings, Group Says," *EFE,* September 26, 2012.

217. *were slain in another attack.:* "SLP: matan a alcalde electo; arrecia ola de ataques en estados," Excélsior, August 13, 2012.

217. *Monterrey, gunning down eight men.:* "Gunmen Kill Eight in Hail of Bullets at Mexico Strip Bar," Reuters, August 14, 2013.

218. *we are a brotherhood.";* up and walked off camera.: "La Tuta Mensaje íntegro de Los Caballeros Templarios," Blog del Narco YouTube channel, http://youtu.be/N8cDgC-mhl0g, posted August 24, 2012.

219. *leading north out of Acapulco.:* "Mexican Authorities Find 11 Corpses Northwest of Acapulco," Reuters, August 26, 2012.

219. *toward the border with Michoacán.:* "16 Bodies Found in Truck in Southern Mexico State," Associated Press, September 10, 2012.

219. *near the border with Michoacán.:* "17 Mutilated Bodies Found in Central Mexico," Associated Press, September 16, 2012.

219. *despite its diplomatic license plates.:* "US Car Was Targeted in Mexico Ambush," Associated Press, September 2, 2012.

219. *trying to kill the agents.:* "Mexico Charges Cops with Trying to Kill CIA Agents," Associated Press, November 9, 2012.

219. *sailors deserted Mexico's armed forces.:* "En cinco años, más de 46 mil militares desertaron del Ejército y la Armada," *La Jornada,* April 11, 2012.

219. *his whereabouts were unknown.:* "Mexican Judge Orders Arrest of Ex-Governor on Drug Charges," Reuters, August 29, 2012.

219. *of his home in murky circumstances.:* "Ejecutan a 'El Chupón'," *El Mañana,* November 1, 2012.

219. *sell it at auction.:* "At Upscale SPI Tower, $640,000 Bid Buys Condo Linked to Former Mexican Governor," *Monitor,* August 16, 2013.

220. *get hung out to dry.":* Author interview, McAllen, Texas, December 2012.

220. *laundering and racketeering among them.:* "Fugitive Ex-Tamaulipas Governor Indicted on Money Laundering, Drug Charges," *Monitor,* December 2, 2013.

220. *of Altamira on September 3.:* "Detiene Marina a Mario Cárdenas Guillén, líder del cártel del Golfo," *La Jornada,* September 4, 2012.

220. *for control of cartel territory.:* "Gulf Cartel Infighting Reignites with Reynosa Firefights," *Monitor,* March 18, 2013.

220. *that of Los Zetas' own.:* "Jefe del cártel del Golfo, peligroso rival de Los Zetas," *El Universal,* July 18, 2013.

220. *from taking control of Mexico.":* "Mexican President Delivers Last State-of-the-Nation Speech," CCTV, September 4, 2012.

220. *would remember any of that?:* "After Six Years, Mexico's President Felipe Calderon Fell Short of Goals," Fox News Latino, November 30, 2012.

221. *watched virtually around the clock.:* "Gang Rules 6 Years After Start of Mexico Drug War," Associated Press, November 2, 2012.

221. *Gulf Cartel, and the Sinaloa Cartel.:* "Zetas, Chapos y Golfos . . . los dueños de la región Valles de Jalisco," *Proceso,* November 9, 2012.

221. *continued to battle the CJNG.:* "Caen operadores de Los Zetas y del cártel de Jalisco en Coahuila y Veracruz," *Proceso,* November 13, 2012.

221. *metro area, on September 12.:* "Hallan cadáver de Hernán Belden Elizondo, exdiputado del PAN," *El Economista,* September 12, 2012.

221. *been merely trying to help.:* "El alcalde de San Pedro Garza García y su siniestra bola de cristal," *Proceso,* September 15, 2012.

221. *bridge in the city.:* "Nine Corpses Found Hanging from Bridge in Northern Mexico," Reuters, September 14, 2012.

221. *been killed in the city.:* "Violence Continues in Nuevo Laredo with 11 More Dead," *Laredo Morning Times,* September 17, 2012.

221. *was shot in the leg.:* "Banners Claim an Alliance Has Been Formed Against the Zetas," *Laredo Morning Times,* September 18, 2012.

222. *betrayals and shit like that. . . .":* "Z40: Sends Messages to CDG, Taliban and Knights Templar," *Borderland Beat,* September 21, 2012.

222. *Nuevo Laredo on September 19.:* "State Officials Slain in Northern Mexico," *EFE,* September 20, 2012.

222. *Durango city of Gómez Palacio.:* "6 Mexico Police Slain in 2 Attacks," *Los Angeles Times,* September 20, 2012.

222. *Reyes "El R1" Mejía González.:* "Los Zetas colocan narcomantas en Zacatecas," *Mexico Rojo,* September 21, 2012.

222. *in shootouts around the city.:* "Expect More Shootouts in Reynosa, Says Tamps. Law Enforcement Official," *Monitor,* October 4, 2012.

222. *one of Miguel Treviño's chief rivals.:* "Antes de ser capturado, El Talibán declaró la guerra a los máximos líderes de Los Zetas," *La Jornada,* September 28, 2012.

222. *in Coahuila and Nuevo León.:* "Nace Sangre Zeta," *El Diario de Coahuila,* February 27, 2013.

222. *distribute drugs and launder money.:* "Extradited Zetas Boss Appears in Texas Court," Associated Press, November 22, 2013.

222. *"family for family".:* "Mexico's Moves Against Zetas Leaders Heighten Tension Along Border with Texas," *Dallas Morning News,* October 8, 2012.

223. *Rio Grande from Texas.:* "Son of Controversial Mexican Politician Slain in Border Town," *Los Angeles Times,* October 4, 2012.

223. *former governor himself publicly supported.:* "'El Z-40' es el autor intelectual del asesinato de mi hijo: Moreira," *Proceso,* October 26, 2012.

223. *but I can't bear this.":* "Son of Prominent Mexican Politician Shot Dead," Reuters, October 4, 2012.

223. *effort to disrupt such links.:* "Zetas Cartel Occupies Mexico State of Coahuila," *Los Angeles Times,* November 3, 2012.

223. *Mexico's state-owned electric utility.:* Author interview, December 2012.

223. *won some sort of tournament.:* "Mexico Gang Leader Held in Massacre of Migrants," *New York Times,* October 8, 2012.

223. *senses of the word.":* "Mexico Says Drug Lord Taken Down by Accident," Associated Press, October 10, 2012.

224. *hundred yards from the vehicle.:* "Zetas' Next Boss May Be Worse Than the One Just Killed," *San Antonio Express-News,* October 10, 2012.

224. *parlor early on Monday morning.:* Ibid.

224. *identified that body as Lazcano's.:* Ibid.

224. *before the body was stolen.:* "US Knew Dead Zeta Leader's ID Before Body Stolen," Associated Press, October 13, 2012.

224. *"no idea".:* "Mexican Officials Fail to Identify Dead Man as Leader of Zetas Cartel," *Guardian,* October 10, 2012.

224. *milieu, this was never confirmed.:* "La otra incógnita: nadie sabe dónde está supuesta novia de 'El Lazca'," *Proceso,* October 13, 2012.

Chapter Sixteen

226. *passengers from their vehicles.:* "Mexico Shootout Leaves 2 Soldiers, 9 Gunmen Dead," *EFE,* October 13, 2012.

226. *police in Nuevo Laredo.:* "10 Die in Shootouts in Mexican Border City," *EFE,* October 21, 2012.

226. *in Altamira in late October.:* "14 Kidnapped Central American Migrants Found in Mexico," *Los Angeles Times,* October 29, 2012.
226. *left at least nine dead.:* "Shootouts in Mexican Border City Leave 9 Dead," *EFE,* November 4, 2012.
227. *visa belonging to someone else.:* "Alejandrina Gisselle Guzmán Salazar, Reputed Mexican Drug Lord's Daughter, Pleads Guilty," Associated Press, December 19, 2012.
227. *drug shipment he had stolen.:* "Asesinan a familiar de 'Juancho' León," *El Periódico,* November 5, 2012.
227. *riot at the* Fraijanes *2 penitentiary.:* "Gobernación señala a zetas de planificar motín en cárcel," *Prensa Libre,* November 21, 2012.
227. *kill her in the past.:* "Exalcaldesa de Tiquicheo: cuando la muerte ronda," *Proceso,* November 19, 2012.
227–28. *"two governments"; And then maybe.":* "Torturada y asesinada una exalcaldesa mexicana," *El País,* November 19, 2012.
228. *to ask too many questions.:* "Asesino de Ruby Marisol fue abatido por militares en Zacatecas," *Milenio,* November 21, 2012.
228. *hands when she was killed.:* "Soldiers: Mexico Beauty Queen Had Gun in Her Hands," Associated Press, November 27, 2012.
228. *she begged for her life.:* "Crónica del fin de María Susana: Pasarela de la muerte," *Proceso,* December 2, 2012.
228. *take part in the pact.:* "From Mexican Jail, Top Cop Accused," *Wall Street Journal,* November 28, 2012.
228. *less compromised, observers, as well.:* For another take on the "truce" allegation, see the journalist Alfredo Corchado's 2013 book *Midnight in Mexico: A Reporter's Journey Through a Country's Descent into Darkness* (Penguin Press).
229. "Mexico mourns.":* "Enrique Peña Nieto Takes Office as Mexico's President," Associated Press, December 2, 2012.
229. *weed out corruption and nepotism.:* "Mexican Leader Proposes Sweeping Education Reform," Associated Press, December 10, 2012.
229. *union funds for personal use.:* "Mexico Teachers Union Head Arrested," Agence France-Presse, February 27, 2013.
229. *rate to a daily one.:* "Mexico Passes Radical Labour Reforms," Reuters, November 14, 2012.
229. *in six black plastic bags.":* "7 Dismembered Bodies Found in Northern Mexico," *EFE,* December 2, 2012.
229. *suspended from a highway overpass.:* "4 Tortured Bodies Found Hanging from Highway Overpass in Northern Mexico City of Saltillo," Associated Press, December 7, 2012.
229. *they were Gulf Cartel members.:* "13 Bodies Found in Vehicles in Northern Mexico," Associated Press, December 8, 2012.
229. *businesses being victimized by crime.:* "En Tamaulipas, el 80 percent de negocios tiene inseguridad," *Milenio,* December 18, 2012.
230. *kidnapping, extortion and protection rackets.":* "Mexico Says Some 80 Cartels at Work in Country," Associated Press, December 18, 2012.
230. *all but designed to undercut.:* "Is It Worth Creating a Gendarmerie in Mexico?," *InSight Crime,* December 10, 2012.

230. *access to law enforcement actions.:* "The Death of M4 Shrouded in Secrecy," *Borderland Beat,* January 28, 2013.

230. *Osorio Chong's Interior Ministry.:* "Mexico Ends Open Access for US Security Agencies," Associated Press, April 29, 2013.

230. *members of the Gulf Cartel.:* "13 Bodies Found in Vehicles in Northern Mexico," Associated Press, December 8, 2012.

230. *men belonged to Los Zetas.:* "En Concordia, masacres e impunidad," *Proceso,* January 3, 2013.

230. *Jalisco border with Michoacán.:* "Navidad violenta: ahora decapitan y calcinan a 4 policías en Jalisco," *Proceso,* December 25, 2012.

231. *executed a woman with gunfire.:* "Sujetos armados asesinan a mujer en hospital de Tamaulipas," *El Universal,* December 26, 2012.

231. *police had fabricated evidence.:* "Mexico Judge Acquits Ex-Drug Czar Linked to Cartel," Associated Press, April 15, 2013.

231. *order to release him.:* "Freed Mexico Drug Lord Caro Quintero Got a Huge Head Start," *Los Angeles Times,* August 29, 2013.

231. *host of other crimes:* "Mexican Drug Lord's Release Reopens Wounds for Victims' Relatives," *Los Angeles Times,* August 19, 2013.

Epilogue

233. *street gangs in the city.:* "Cartel Kingpin Chicago's New Public Enemy No. 1," Associated Press, February 14, 2013.

234. *be caught in their midst.:* "In a Soaring Homicide Rate, a Divide in Chicago," *New York Times,* January 2, 2013.

234. *there can be no end.:* "Incarceration Nation," *Time,* April 2, 2012.

234. *serving time for drug offenses.:* Prisoners in 2011, United States Department of Justice Bureau of Justice Statistics, December 2012.

234. *82.2 percent were for possession.:* Crime in the United States 2012: FBI Uniform Crime Report, United States Department of Justice, September 2013.

234. *times the rate of Caucasians.:* Criminal Justice Fact Sheet, National Association for the Advancement of Colored People, www.naacp.org/pages/criminal-justice-fact-sheet, accessed October 7, 2013.

235. *seizing larger quantities of drugs.":* "Drug Policy in Portugal: The Benefits of Decriminalizing Drug Use," Open Society Institute, June 2011.

235. *41.9 percent in the United States.:* "Coffee Shops and Compromise: Separated Illicit Drug Markets in the Netherlands," Open Society Foundations Global Drug Policy Program, July 2013.

236. *marijuana plants bearing no penalty.:* "Colorado Legalization," National Organization for the Reform of Marijuana Laws, http://norml.org/legal/item/colorado-legalization?category_id=1582, accessed August 25, 2013.

236. *civil violation and fine.:* "Washington Legalization," National Organization for the Reform of Marijuana Laws, http://norml.org/legal/item/washington-legalization?category_id=1582, accessed August 25, 2013.

237. *laborers to housewives to children.:* "List of 1000s of Missing Raises Doubts in Mexico," Associated Press, December 22, 2012.

237. *the same or worse,"; just a rhetorical change.":* Author interview with Javier Sicilia, Cuernavaca, August 2013.

237. *than during Calderón's first year.:* "En el primer año de Peña, más muertes violentas que con Calderón," *Proceso,* November 29, 2013.

237. *we no longer had here.":* "Michoacán: una lucha a muerte ... por la vida," Rompeviento Televisión YouTube channel, http://youtu.be/R5RafZpdH2E, broadcast November 7, 2013, accessed November 17, 2013.

237. *"wanted the heads":* "Si caen los 7 líderes Templarios, dejamos las armas: autodefensas en MVS," Aristegui Noticias YouTube channel, interview conducted on November 18, 2013, http://youtu.be/lAwMAiCLlJM, accessed November 21, 2013.

238. *possible in Mexico as well.:* "Modesto Doctor Returns to Mexico, Fights Drug Gangs," McClatchy, November 19, 2013.

238. *Tamaulipas increased by 90 percent,:* "Tamaulipas' Murder Rate Up 90 Percent, Kidnappings Double, US State Department Says," *Monitor,* July 13, 2013.

238. *others to Gulf Cartel infighting.:* "Few Details Known About Quiet Fall of Feared Gulf Cartel Kingpin," *Monitor,* January 27, 2013.

238. *has not been seen since.:* "Police Chief of Mexico Border City Missing, Brothers Killed," *San Antonio Express-News,* February 19, 2013.

238. *clash at all) remained obscure.:* "Guatemala: No Evidence of Gunfight or Capo's Death," Associated Press, February 22, 2013.

238. *to Mario "El Pelón" Ramírez.:* "Gulf Cartel Infighting Reignites with Reynosa Firefights," *Monitor,* March 18, 2013.

238. *"four trucks filled with bodies.":* "Four Trucks Filled with Bodies After Reynosa Firefight," *Monitor,* March 11, 2013.

238. *near the attorney general's office.:* "Reynosa Shootout: Dozens Dead, Trucks Filled with Bodies," *Monitor,* March 12, 2013.

238. *to take on his rivals.:* "Jefe del cártel del Golfo, peligroso rival de Los Zetas," *El Universal,* July 18, 2013.

238. *been kidnapped by Los Zetas.:* "Mexico Rescues 165 Kidnapped Migrants Near US Border," BBC, June 6, 2013.

238. *drug trafficking are not religions.":* "Iglesia católica arremete contra la Santa Muerte," *Excélsior,* May 9, 2013.

238. *"blasphemous"; "degeneration of religion.":* "Vatican Declares Mexican Death Saint Blasphemous," BBC, May 9, 2013.

239. *who kidnapped and killed them.:* "Mass Kidnap, Killing Shakes Image of Mexico City," Associated Press, August 24, 2013.

239. *without a shot being fired.:* "Mexico's Most Brutal Drug Lord Has Been Captured, But That Won't Change Anything," *Rolling Stone,* July 24, 2013.

239. *people purchasing firearms from him.:* "Feds: Zetas Leader's Gun Came from San Antonio," *San Antonio Express-News,* September 21, 2013.

239. *attempted to block even that.:* "Blow to NRA as Court Allows US to Track Gun Sales in States on Mexican Border," *Guardian,* May 31, 2013.

239. *seized from the funeral home.*: "Confirma el Z-40 deceso de El Lazca en 2012; él ordenó robar el cuerpo, asegura," *El Diario de Coahuila,* August 18, 2013.

240. *in a US federal prison.*: "Brother of Mexico Drug Cartel Chiefs Gets 20 Years for US Money Laundering," Reuters, September 6, 2013.

240. *Enrique "El Mamito" Rejón Aguilar.*: "Ex-Zetas Co-Founder Testifies in Money Laundering Trial," *Austin-American Statesman,* April 29, 2013.

240. *a round red nose.*": "Eldest Brother of Mexico's Arellano Felix Drug Clan Killed by Gunman in Clown Costume," Associated Press, October 19, 2013.

240. *at least $38,000 in cash.*: "Detalles de la captura del X-20, el líder del Cártel del Golfo," Univision, August 18, 2013.

240. *Cruz, controlled the other.*: Author interviews, Matamoros, Reynosa and McAllen, November 2013.

240. *"a federation of fiefdoms."*: "El Cártel del Golfo se desgarra ..." *Proceso,* August 24, 2013.

240. *Tamaulipas municipality of Aldama?.*: "Cartel Del Golfo Apoyando Aldama, Tamps," http://youtu.be/YaFqh2WebXA, accessed September 23, 2013.

241. *The last letter—Senor 40.*": "Zacatecas: Zeta Mantas Appear Including One in Hotel Room," *Borderland Beat,* July 28, 2013.

BIBLIOGRAPHY

Blancornelas, Jesús. *El Cártel: Los Arellano Felix, La Mafia Más Poderosa en la Historia de América Latina.* Mexico City: Debolsillo, 2002.

Chesnut, R. Andrew. *Devoted to Death: Santa Muerte, the Skeleton Saint.* New York: Oxford University Press, 2012.

Corchado, Alfredo. *Midnight in Mexico: A Reporter's Journey Through a Country's Descent into Darkness.* New York: Penguin, 2013.

Grayson, George W. and Logan, Samuel. *The Executioner's Men: Los Zetas, Rogue Soldiers, Criminal Entrepreneurs, and the Shadow State They Created.* Piscataway: Transaction Publishers, 2012.

Guillermoprieto, Alma. *Looking for History: Dispatches from Latin America.* New York: Vintage Books, 2001.

Gugliotta, Guy and Leen, Jeff. *Kings of Cocaine Inside the Medellin Cartel—An Astonishing True Story of Murder Money and International Corruption.* New York: Simon & Schuster, 1989.

Hart, John Mason. *Revolutionary Mexico.* Berkeley: University of California Press, 1987.

Hernández, Anabel. *Narco Land: The Mexican Drug Lords and Their Godfathers.* New York: Verso, 2013.

Hernandez-Palacios, Esther. *Diario de una madre mutilada.* Mexico City: Premio Bellas Artes de Testimonio Carlos Montemayor, 2010.

Hubert, Henry and Mauss, Marcel. *Sacrifice: Its Nature and Functions.* Chicago: University of Chicago Press, 1964.

Krauze, Enrique. *Mexico: Biography of Power.* New York: Harper Perennial, 1998.

Lewis, Oscar. *The Children of Sanchez: Autobiography of a Mexican Family.* New York: Vintage, 1961.

Martínez, Oscar. *The Beast: Riding the Rails and Dodging Narcos on the Migrant Trail.* New York: Random House, 2013.

Okrent, Daniel. *Last Call: The Rise and Fall of Prohibition.* New York: Scribner, 2010.

Oppenheimer, Andres. *Bordering on Chaos: Guerrillas, Stockbrokers, Politicians, and Mexico's Road to Prosperity.* New York: Little Brown & Company, 1996.

Osorno, Diego Enrique. *La guerra de Los Zetas: Viaje por la frontera de la necropolítica.* Mexico City: Grijalbo, 2012.

Paz, Octavio. *The Labyrinth of Solitude.* New York: Grove Press, 1985 edition.

Poppa, Terrence. *Drug Lord: The Life and Death of a Mexican Kingpin.* El Paso: Cinco Puntos Press, 2010.

Quinones, Sam. *True Tales from Another Mexico: The Lynch Mob, the Popsicle Kings, Chalino and the Bronx.* Albuquerque: University of New Mexico Press, 2001.

Ravelo, Ricardo. *Narcomex: Historia e historias de una guerra.* Mexico City: Vintage Español, 2012.

———. *Osiel: Vida y Tragedia de un Capo.* Mexico City: Grijalbo, 2009.

Reed, John. *Insurgent Mexico.* New York: International Publishers, 1999 edition.

Rotella, Sebastian. *Twilight on the Line: Underworlds and Politics at the Mexican Border.* New York: W. W. Norton & Company, 1998.

Thompson, Jerry. *Cortina: Defending the Mexican Name in Texas.* College Station: Texas A&M University Press, 2007.

Thompson, Jerry D. (editor). *Juan Cortina and the Texas-Mexico Frontier 1859–1887.* El Paso: Texas Western Press, 1994.

Vulliamy, Ed. *Amexica: War Along the Borderline.* New York: Picador, 2010.

Index